HOMESICKNESS

HOMESICKNESS

OF TRAUMA AND THE LONGING FOR PLACE IN A CHANGING ENVIRONMENT

RYAN HEDIGER

UNIVERSITY OF MINNESOTA PRESS
MINNEAPOLIS • LONDON

The University of Minnesota Press gratefully acknowledges the financial assistance provided for the publication of this book by the University Research Council at Kent State University.

Published by the University of Minnesota Press
111 Third Avenue South, Suite 290
Minneapolis, MN 55401-2520
http://www.upress.umn.edu

Printed in the United States of America on acid-free paper

Library of Congress Cataloging-in-Publication Data
Names: Hediger, Ryan, author.
Title: Homesickness : of trauma and the longing for place in a changing environment / Ryan Hediger.
Description: Minneapolis : University of Minnesota Press, [2019] | Includes bibliographical references and index. | Identifiers: LCCN 2018055520 (print) | ISBN 978-1-5179-0653-5 (hc) | ISBN 978-1-5179-0654-2 (pb)
Subjects: LCSH: Social ecology. | Place attachment. | Homesickness.
Classification: LCC HM861 .H43 2019 (print) | DDC 304.2—dc23
LC record available at https://lccn.loc.gov/2018055520

UMP BmB 2019

To my mother and father,

SUSAN *and* DENNIS HEDIGER

Contents

Preface

Climate Change Refugee Nightmares

In Newtok, Alaska, Sabrina Warner has been having unsettling nightmares. She says, "I dream about the water coming in." Warner's dream involves "a huge wave rearing up out of the water and crashing over her home, forcing her to swim for her life with her toddler son," as Susanna Goldenberg summarizes it in *The Guardian*. Goldenberg's rendition continues: "Warner climbs on to the roof of her small house. As the waters rise, she swims for higher ground: the village school, which sits on 20-foot pilings. Even that isn't high enough. By the time Warner wakes, she is clinging to the roof of the school desperate to be saved."[1]

Warner's home village on the west coast of Alaska, "about 400 miles south of the Bering Strait," is slowly being washed away, producing, Goldenberg writes, some of "America's first climate refugees." Goldenberg explains that the Yup'ik Eskimo, who have lived in Newtok "for centuries," will have to move before the town erodes away. The Ninglick River surrounds Newtok on three sides, carrying off as much as one hundred feet of land each year. The place itself is disappearing, putting the culture and people whose identities are tied to this spot at grave risk, haunting them with premonitions. Goldenberg explains that similar crises are being confronted by "more than 180 native communities in Alaska, which are flooding and losing land because of the ice melt that is part of the changing climate." By the time you read these words, Newtok, the place, may already be gone.

Images of flooding, of displacement, and of families and children stranded on roofs amid rising waters have become common in the United States since Hurricane Katrina and the cultural response that ensued. Spike Lee's powerful documentary *When the Levees Broke: A Requiem in Four Acts,* the post-traumatic HBO series *Treme,* and many other texts have made the reality of disaster displacement part of the frightening zeitgeist.[2] In the Anthropocene, our notions of place are becoming radically, violently revised. The massive emissions of carbon dioxide and other greenhouse gases have unleashed geological and climatological forces that remind us of the limits of human control. Global warming displaces the home right under our feet, mobilizes it, sends its climatic regime poleward and wayward ("wayward" because "global weirding," greater unpredictability, is one consequence of climate change). But posthumanism and other recent theoretical movements have shown that we never quite "had a home"; home is a way of organizing a complex set of ideas, including memory, desire, heritage, and so on, and it has always been more complex and less scrutable than we tend to admit. The reality of human mortality, which Timothy Morton calls "weakness" in *Hyperobjects,* reminds us that we have never "had" a place.[3] Anthropogenic global warming greatly intensifies our awareness of this notion.

Recognizing some of these complexities of home and its evanescence, many scholars have instead embraced notions of mobility and cosmopolitanism. However, that solution is not as easy or as satisfying as it might appear. Mobility, I argue in the chapters that follow, needs to be understood with much more complexity, and, doing this, the importance of place becomes clearer. The local and the planetary need to be understood in dialogue, much like nature and culture. *Homesickness* is written from the persuasion that, if we recognize the desire for home *as* a desire, then we become able to use the complex web of associations in life-affirming ways, helping us revise understandings of human life and humanity's place in the biosphere. Indeed, I believe that without a notion of the local and the home, it becomes very difficult to make meaning of human life more broadly.

So I propose that in the notion of "homesickness" we should hear two distinct resonances. First, in a changing world inhabited by mortal, changeable creatures, we never really "have" a home, and so we are always to some extent homesick. Second, our desire for home is shorthand for a set of important hopes worth defending—serious and genuine relationships to places and their biotic regimes and landforms; membership in vital cultures, human and nonhuman; and resistance to capital-infused forms of globalization that flatten differences and turn life and place into mere resources. Our homesickness, then, understood in a complex way, is not something to dismiss as sentimental or old-fashioned or reactionary. It is a structure of feeling to come to terms with and even to cultivate, a sensibility to inhabit, and a hope to pursue.

Those are the more ideal forms of homesickness, the ones to embrace. However, as in the case of Sabrina Warner's nightmares about flooding, contemporary global capitalism continues to generate many terrible forms of homesickness. While I contend that homesickness is a feature of subjectivity across time, that we always understand ourselves in light of the past to some extent, I do not mean to naturalize all forms of homesickness. Warner's experiences and premonitions of flooding, along with the many other forms of traumatic homesickness discussed in this book—violent dislocations in slavery, miseries of childhood abandonment, desperate poverty, and violence in war—are neither inevitable nor natural. A central reason for investigating homesickness in this book is to separate the inevitable forms of weakness and loss from those that are contingent and avoidable. It is also to defend nostalgia as a fundamental and often positive feature of life that sustains our connections to others, human and nonhuman. Homesickness, then, is not just a nightmare but also a strange and illuminating dream, a suspension, and a stay against the sense that we must always move forward and away from what we have known and loved.

Introduction

Homesickness

Philosophy is really homesickness, an urge to be at home everywhere.
—Novalis, quoted in Jacques Derrida, *The Animal That Therefore I Am*

Haunted by Dreams of Home

Consider a common American dream: Phil Cottrell, confronting a series of difficulties growing out of the troubled economy and tough housing market in the United States of 2008, began questioning his lifestyle. "Rootless and striving for fifteen years, and almost forty years old," Peter T. Kilborn writes in his book *Next Stop, Reloville: Life inside America's New Rootless Professional Class,* Cottrell began thinking about moving back to Indiana, where he grew up. Cottrell says, "I would like to buy the old homestead. It was built in the 1830s."[1] But despite this glimmer of homesickness, this desire to inhabit a known place redolent of deeper personal meanings, this haunting from the past, Cottrell would, Kilborn writes, "keep shooting" for the next target in his career procession.

Cottrell, a rising and ambitious manager in the field of sales information, which is oriented around collecting data about shoppers, had already endured one divorce. He and his families had lived in Chicago; Indianapolis; Sussex, New Jersey; Alpharetta, Georgia, outside Atlanta; and Pittsburgh. He lived near Pittsburgh when he spoke to Kilborn, and it was there where his second marriage was about to come undone in large part because of these trying moves. He would soon be turned down for the next promotion at work, lose the job he had, and lose custody of his two girls from his first marriage.[2]

But these were probably temporary setbacks. He would keep striving under the logic he described to Kilborn: "Not moving suppresses your wages and career potential in today's global business environment."[3] Kilborn, a former *New York Times* reporter, notes that the sentence sounds a little robotic.

Cottrell's feelings evoke a common experience in contemporary life, among the relatively privileged managerial and professional classes in developed nations as well as among the less fortunate.[4] For Cottrell, the logic of upward social mobility offers both a promise and a trap, and the feeling of what I am calling "homesickness" in this book is the result. Homesickness, in general terms, is the feeling of dislocation from one's culture, identity, and geography, and the desire to better belong, to be more at home in the world. It is commonly expressed as a wish to return to a known place, but in fact it is generally more complex than that. In *Homesickness,* my treatment of the feeling also emphasizes the "sickness" dimension of the word, recalling as it does mortality, embodiment, and ordinary human weakness and disability. I mean to evoke both the desire to go home, a kind of nostalgia; and the awareness, which registers often as a kind of nausea and weakness, that we are far from home and perhaps always will be.[5] This feeling signals *displacement,* or *dis-location,* exposing the dread that has always haunted mobility, perhaps particularly its more modern forms that developed since the nineteenth century.

In other words, it is useful to distinguish a complex homesickness from something like a simple or sentimental homesickness. This distinction is parallel to the one drawn by Leo Marx between the sentimental pastoral and the complex pastoral, though I have reservations about the use of "sentimental" here because it risks reproducing the default rejection of emotions, pathos, and affect that is part of the problem I seek to criticize in this book.[6] Why call this "homesickness," one might ask? One clear advantage is concreteness; the word evokes material, worldly desires. That advantage deepens in light of posthumanism and much recent theory that foregrounds human embodiment, animality, materiality, and situatedness. Indeed, I want to suggest that homesickness is a particularly posthumanist sensibility that needs to be explored and even cultivated.[7] As psychology professor Clay Routledge points out in his 2016 book, *Nostalgia: A Psychological Resource,* new social science on this understudied emotion reveals that "nostalgia promotes psychological growth," that it can "help people maintain a sense of authenticity," and that, contrary to knee-jerk dismissals of nostalgia as simplistic, it "motivates exploration and creativity."[8] Routledge argues that nostalgia deserves a reappraisal as an important affective resource for enduring change, hardship, and dislocation—for resilience, in short. I am arguing that it is also a way we come to terms with human weakness and mortality. While I use the word "homesickness" predominantly in my argument, drawing on its rich connotations of both "home" and "sickness," I regard the term as basically synonymous with "nostalgia."

Denaturalizing and Historicizing Mobility

The need to move has increasingly been understood as inevitable, even natural. In this age of great mobility, questions of globalism have therefore become central to inquiries into cultural identity, economic development, environmental concerns, and much more. As Ursula K. Heise points out in *Sense of Place and Sense of Planet: The Environmental Imagination of the Global,* the term "globalism" has taken different valences in different contexts, and it is part of a larger discourse that has also begun "to recuperate the term 'cosmopolitanism' as a way of imagining forms of belonging beyond the local and the national."[9] Heise's book reinforces those efforts, arguing ultimately in favor of an "eco-cosmopolitanism" that would embrace a yet broader sense of identity, including the nonhuman. Scholars of cosmopolitanism, the high hope for an enlightened, global perspective, often point to Johann Wolfgang von Goethe, or Immanuel Kant, as the modern impetuses of a global sensibility.[10] Contemporary thinkers like Heise have worked to revise and reinvigorate that cosmopolitan tradition.[11]

While there is much to celebrate and pursue in these hopes, they cannot be well realized until we better understand their blind spots, or deficiencies. *Homesickness* studies those shadier regions of cosmopolitan desires, focusing on the weakness, locality, and mortality that are unavoidably part of all life. My approach has much in common with disability theorist Lennard J. Davis's notion of "dismodernism." Davis underscores that "*all* humans are . . . wounded," that subjectivity should not—cannot—aim for "autonomy and independence but dependence and interdependence."[12] While cosmopolitanism can accent and improve such interdependence, some cosmopolitanisms suggest an autonomous self at home everywhere in the world, which exaggerates human independence. Further, as critics of cosmopolitanism have shown, its tendency toward universalism can also tend to privilege some forms of selfhood over others.[13] In light of such concerns, this book regards cosmopolitanism at best as potentially useful if engaged critically, or at worst as a harmful fantasy, focusing on one of its clearest effects: homesickness. Perhaps homesickness is to cosmopolitanism as dark ecology is to its sunnier straight cousin ecology.[14] In light of such concerns, I advocate for what can be a called a critical cosmopolitanism.

In other words, much hinges on which cosmopolitanism we mean, since there is no single version. Importantly, for instance, cosmopolitanism is itself founded on awareness of limits, alongside its expansive optimism. In Jacques Derrida's short essay "On Cosmopolitanism," he recalls Kant's insistence that we *must* be open to accepting all others—we must be cosmopolitans—because the world is finite; there is not infinite room.[15] Having reiterated this root awareness of limitations, Derrida adds another dimension. He urges that cosmopolitanism is also curtailed by the need to make hospitality realistic. We must avoid the "danger" that hospitality could become "a pious and irresponsible desire, without form and without potency."[16] For Derrida, these are challenging limitations. In this book, I reinforce our sense of these weaknesses by relying on posthumanist criticisms of the Enlightenment and of humanism, criticisms, that is, of the intellectual systems that undergird cosmopolitanism.[17]

In one sense, then, homesickness can be understood to name, in shorthand, the gap between the ideal hopes of cosmopolitanism and the material reality of human limitations. Most idealistically, cosmopolitans set out to become citizens of the world intellectually, geographically, linguistically, and otherwise, and the project always proves more challenging than they might have imagined. More practically, a person decides to move in hopes of a better job or life, not fully appreciating all the losses that attend to displacement. In these scenarios, our limitations come into view, partly caused by, or causing, a longing for familiar places and forms of life. Thus, the more mobility we can experience, the more deeply we can understand both the opportunities and the costs of movement. This paradoxical structure—common to much knowledge and to philosophies of knowledge, as registered, for example, in Genesis—is the defiling and alienating cost of knowing too much.

The "freedom" to move resembles, then, the opportunity to philosophize. Both begin from a seeming position of strength, often only then to expose our weaknesses and limitations. While I just suggested that this is an old problem of knowledge (probably a prehistorical one), it has taken distinctive form in modernity, as knowledge and its processes and machinery have accelerated. In *The Shock of the Anthropocene,* Christophe Bonneuil and Jean-Baptiste Fressoz summarize this dimension of modernity as "a long process of Weberian 'disenchantment,' [a] pre-eminence of 'instrumental rationality' (Adorno and Horkheimer) and negation of the world as given otherness (Arendt), a process that has made the moderns 'men without a world' (Déborah Danowski and Eduardo Viveiros de Castro)."[18] This worldlessness is homesickness in the negative sense.

So homesickness evokes the unnecessary and negative consequences of neoliberal consumer capitalism, in which labor and consumption are the prevailing values, at the expense of all else. Human history has steadily optimized the production of laboring subjectivities, made them mobile, and trained them to perform as cogs in the capitalist machine. Homesickness is partly the dread and melancholy that arise from the traumas of these changes—the separation from family networks and geographical particularities, weather patterns, ecologies, and so on; the resistance to the astonishing amount of time spent laboring, and for what? A newer Cadillac? Homesickness registers the dissonance between, on the one hand, earlier understandings of labor, often connected to a Protestant instrumentalism of life on this planet in favor of hopes for a good place in heaven, and, on the other hand, contemporary understandings of life, even among many Protestants and other Christians, that more powerfully value happiness in this life.

The dislocating traumas of colonialism, war, and anthropogenic global warming bring homesickness into sharp relief. But posthumanism has been at work in revealing the more fundamental and ordinary homesickness or unhomely always already present in human life: the rats in cities, the microorganisms in the soil we depend on, the bacteria covering the surface of the human body. These ordinary truths make our lives and bodies seem strange. Canonical at this point is the idea, reiterated by Donna Haraway,

> that human genomes can be found in only about 10 percent of all the cells that occupy the mundane space I call my body; the other 90 percent of the cells are filled with the genomes of bacteria, fungi, protists, and such, some of which play in a symphony necessary to my being alive at all, and some of which are hitching a ride and doing the rest of me, of us, no harm. I am vastly outnumbered by my tiny companions; better put, I become an adult human being in company with these tiny messmates. To be one is always to *become with* many.[19]

While recent findings suggest the proportion, by number, of human to non-human genome in the human body is more like one to one,[20] Haraway's account of life, accenting multiplicity, cooperation, and inescapable tolerance of difference, has much to recommend it for a postcolonial, posthumanist era. Similarly, Timothy Morton's observation in *Hyperobjects: Philosophy and Ecology after the End of the World* radically reframes our sense of familiar life: what we call oxygen is "bacterial pollution from some Archean cataclysm"; our cells' energy producers, mitochondria, are "anaerobic bacteria hiding in my cells from the Oxygen Catastrophe."[21] One creature's pollution is another creature's lifeblood. Yet somehow both bacteria and the mammals who live on their pollution have managed, so far, to persist.

But posthumanism reveals the uncanny, the "unhomely," or *unheimlich,* in another important way. In *What Is Posthumanism?* Cary Wolfe underscores human reliance on both our technological and biological surroundings, an emphasis that renders strange much of what seems familiar to definitions of our species.[22] The traditional, triumphalist, anthropocentric story takes human tool use as a power, an ability, but posthumanism reveals it also as a dependence, a need. Indeed, even a cursory reading of the history of war, with its perpetual ratcheting up of weaponry and interspecies assemblages of horses, carts, and more, from one side to the opposing one(s), underscores human dependence on and even desperation for technologies.[23] Similarly, in *Dark Ecology: For a Logic of Future Coexistence,* Timothy Morton's critique of the whole history of agriculture leads him to argue that "'civilization' was a long-term collaboration between humans and wheat, humans and rock, humans and soil, not out of grand visions but out of something like desperation."[24] In light of such ideas, Wolfe points out that the theme of "decentering" the human—common in much recent environmental thought—has done too little to recognize how our ideas of thinking and meaning must also change in posthumanism.[25]

Homesickness therefore brings the sense of estrangement found in discourses like postcolonialist criticism, discussed further below, to the "dominant" culture of the United States but relies even more on a posthumanist framework to elaborate it, insisting that displacement is a reality of embodied, material life, experienced by all humans, though to greater and lesser extents and, crucially, to greatly variable effects. What exactly do I mean by "posthumanism"? I borrow Wolfe's conception, presented via its genealogy in *What Is Posthumanism?* Wolfe likens posthumanism to

> Jean-Francois Lyotard's paradoxical rendering of the postmodern: it comes both before and after humanism: before in the sense that it names the embodiment and embeddedness of the human being in not just its biological but also its technological world, the prosthetic coevolution of the human animal with the technicity of tools and external archival mechanisms (such as language and culture).[26]

These dimensions are prior to and undergird humanism, but for Wolfe, the term "posthumanism" also evokes what comes after humanism.

> Posthumanism names a historical moment in which the decentering of the human by its imbrication in technical, medical, informatics, and economic networks is increasingly impossible to ignore, a historical development that points toward the necessity of new theoretical paradigms (but also thrusts them on us), a new mode of thought that comes after the cultural repressions and fantasies, the philosophical protocols and evasions, of humanism as a historically specific phenomenon.[27]

These changes are historical, and to be historical they must be specific: they derive from particular geographical and national programs, despite the common rhetoric of cosmopolitan universalism. Those histories have been contested, often in terms of scale. For instance, Heise compellingly summarizes the work of Fredric Jameson and others to show deep tensions in our attitudes regarding geographical scale, the local versus the global. She writes of a "conflict between a conceptualization of national identity as either an oppressive hegemonic discourse or a tool for resistance to global imperialism, and of local identity as either an essentialist myth or a promising site of struggle against both national and global domination," leading historian Arif Dirlik, Heise reports, "to declare a theoretical stalemate."[28] Heise rightly encourages us "to think of such contradictions as a starting point for reflecting on the kinds of categories and abstractions that are commonly used in cultural theory."[29]

I argue here that we should regard questions of scale rhetorically and circumstantially (hence "site of struggle," not absolute truth); we should be cautious of theoretical approaches that universalize the value of the global at the expense of the local, or that insist on thinking only on long-term scales. Thus it is one thing to recognize human mobility at the scale of 100,000 years and quite another to be a climate refugee newly moved into a place with vastly uneven development and huge economic disparities. These are not equivalent forms of mobility, and naturalizing movement in broad terms as some thinkers do mystifies important differences. Attention to the feeling of homesickness helps bring such nuances into view. Of course, as signaled in this chapter, I also recognize the need to engage big, cosmopolitan ideas.

Homesickness and the desire for place are the results not just of specific historical and geographical forces, however—forces that humble excessive human pride. They also result from what I argue is a widely disavowed temporal structure of subjectivity. To be a subject is precisely to be a culmination of experiences in places with forms of life and nonlife, landscapes, animals, partners, friends.[30] Everything is in play in creating a "subject." But for these realities to become conscious and to amount to an identity, they must always be based on the past. That is, subjectivity is always too late. It never fully arrives at the present moment because that moment, as affect theory teaches us, has not yet been fully registered in the self. In *Politics of Affect*, for example, Brian Massumi describes how the experience of an event registers affectively as "thinking-feeling," exposing the subject to change: "In the heat of the encounter, we are immersed in eventful working-out of affective capacities. We have no luxury of distance from the event from which we can observe and reflect upon it." This "thinking-feeling" is "pre-subjective": "It can only retrospectively be 'owned,' or owned up to, in memory and post facto reflection, as a content of an individualized experience."[31] Subjectivity, in other words, is itself past-oriented in this sense, even as it fancies itself to face the future. The subject, insofar as it is a subject—a relatively coherent and stable identity—*must* be rooted in the past.[32] In *Dark Ecology*, Timothy Morton makes a similar point, arguing that "a loop form" is "basic to the structure of thought."[33]

Hence the strange and mysterious power of homesickness, and the deep dread of it from the perspective of a progressivist, mobile modernity. These are contrasting forms of temporality: recursive, circular, ecological; seasonal temporality versus linear temporality. The intoxicated future obsession of technocratic rationalism generates a long shadow in homesickness, a reality long present in critiques of modernity.[34] In this feeling, we recognize not only the extraordinary force of places to make and inform our lives (hence "home-"); we also feel but commonly disavow the fundamental weakness of subjectivity (hence "-sickness"). By "weakness" I mean that the subject cannot keep up with the movement of time, and that the subject is porous and always already engaged with the big, wonderful—and frightening—world.[35] Weak subjectivity means partly unbound subjectivity. This structure of identity has profound implications for questions of ethics, as has been much discussed by a range of thinkers but also for epistemological and ontological questions. In sum, subjectivity is itself a condition of homesickness. The Anthropocene, with its imperative to reimagine temporality both past and future, underscores even more firmly the individual subject's uncanny relationship to time.

It is important to clarify here an element of this argument that has already begun to appear. There are two distinct meanings of "homesickness" in this book: one is historical; the other is existential. In the existential sense, I show that self-consciousness and subjectivity produce homesickness because they expose the divisions of a self that constantly thinks about and seeks to understand its own reality by referencing the past. The importance of memory and the retrospective processing of experience further accent this homesickness.[36] But additionally, I show in this book that this existential structure of the self takes distinctive forms in each historical, social, and ecological context. The importance of these particularities is only heightened when we recognize the materiality of the self, so that the terms and realities of our homesickness are never the same for different people, never universal. Thus, homesickness is a nearly universal element of selfhood (acknowledging unusual exceptions, such as memory loss or dementia), yet it is also different in every case.

One further clarification about this book's argument: I also propose homesickness as a mode of interpretation more specifically for critics. In that mode, we embrace a nonlinear movement in time, returning to older texts with new concerns in order to revisit them and reframe the present. While such a practice is not new, its stakes and its dynamics are distinct in this study, situated in the Anthropocene. Such homesick modes of recursive interpretation loosen the firmness of the present and facilitate rethinking possibilities of the future. A homesick method recognizes how past historical and social practices have been materialized and institutionalized all around us, not just in homes and housing but in government, road systems, and even ecological regimes, imbricated as they are in cultural systems too. The past is present and helps dictate the future. A homesick method of interpretation acknowledges how the present is oddly displaced into other temporal frames, much as the human self is presented as porous and necessarily, inescapably relational. The self is displaced into its contexts. I am calling this selfhood "weak," with permeable boundaries. Ultimately, since for me homesickness is a fundamental dimension of selfhood, it would thereby be inevitable that interpretations of texts would also partake of this logic.

Ecocriticism and Homesickness

The attitude toward nostalgia and homesickness in ecocriticism is ambiguous. Many ecocritics evince the more general cultural wariness about nostalgia,[37] but the common ecocritical tendency to emphasize ecological losses can be seen as nostalgic. Indeed, as Jennifer K. Ladino shows in *Reclaiming Nostalgia: Longing for Nature in American Literature,* that feeling need not be seen as reactionary.[38] Ladino's case is still an exception, however. Much more recent theorizing in the rapidly growing field of ecocriticism has worked to link environmental discourses with theories of mobility, deterritorialization, urbanization, and so on. Many critics have insisted that distinctively contemporary forms of city life—for instance, urban gardens, bicycle lanes, and rooftop solar arrays—are part of the solution to environmental degradation and global warming. These solutions, and others like them, depend on globalization and its technological innovations and transnational solidarities to a significant degree. They also depend on rethinking the cultures surrounding environmentalism, which has often tended toward a kind of puritanical self-denial and an often tacitly antitechnological bent, especially in the United States.[39]

The globalization of environmental risk requires planetary thinking and solutions, argues Heise in *Sense of Place and Sense of Planet,* leading her to be strikingly dismissive of the local at times.[40] While I agree with Heise on the need to think big, it is harmful to imagine that approach as excluding the local. Instead, under the uncanny dynamics of homesickness, we can recognize the strangeness of the local, pulsating as it does with the nonlocal and, to ordinary rational selfhood, with the mysterious. This is why I find additional guidance in thinking homesickness from new materialist and posthumanist strains of ecocriticism. For instance, Timothy Morton has insistently sought to unsettle the default Enlightenment sense that the self stands outside or apart from the world in a position of rational judgment. Instead, he relentlessly shows how utterly immersed we are in the world. His book *The Ecological Thought* urges that the very term "environment" is part of the problem, since it supposes a gap between humans and the rest of the world that is simply not real. Morton insists that we are inescapably bound in the world, in the "mesh," the term he prefers to "environment."[41] In *Hyperobjects* Morton deepens that logic to suggest that even the notion of "ecology" may be part of the problem. Similarly, Stacy Alaimo's *Bodily Natures* works through the implications of the fact that human bodies and the material environment are enmeshed as Morton insists.[42]

Alaimo's and Morton's work, as part of a larger theoretical movement sometimes called new materialism (or object-oriented ontology), overlaps with ecocriticism and posthumanism. New materialism enriches our sense of just how much materiality, our own and that of the nonhuman "mesh," impacts our thinking and being. Indeed, to a significant extent, we *are* our materiality. With this point, new materialism extends the robust scholarship, across disciplines, investigating the materiality of environmental traumas at personal, community, and national levels. A milestone text in that tradition is Rachel Carson's *Silent Spring*, which emphasizes a kind of agency (if not in so many words) in the chemicals humans have devised.[43] But human tools and material life have long been recognized as central to our environmental sensibility. In *Green Imperialism: Colonial Expansion, Tropical Island Edens and the Origins of Environmentalism, 1600–1860*, Richard H. Grove shows that concerns about human impact on the environment extend well back in time, developing in parallel with colonial expansion. Effectively, I would summarize, the advent of ocean-worthy vessels and cultures of exploration exposed imperialists to new insights about environment. Grove contends that "the crucially pervasive and creative impact of the tropical and colonial experience on European natural science and on the western and scientific mind after the fifteenth century has been almost entirely ignored." Further, he argues that "indigenous, and particularly Indian, environmental philosophy and knowledge" greatly impacted Western thought tracing back to these earliest moments in the fifteenth century.[44]

In *Dark Ecology*, thinking recursively in a homesick style, Morton reaches much further back, to the dawn of agriculture in the Fertile Crescent 12,500 years ago, to note the paradoxes of human understanding of and action toward environment. Citing both Genesis and *The Ramayana of Valmiki*, he underscores the striking fact that these "two ancient texts written within agricultural temporality condemn agriculture." Both texts understand the period prior to agriculture as a time of innocence, as a "Golden Age," in *The Ramayana*'s terms. Is this the original homesickness? Probably not.[45] But it is an important one. Morton argues that these texts suggest "an agricultural *autoimmunity*, an agricultural allergy to itself." That is, right from the dawn of the massive change in human/land relationships that constitute agriculture as such, there developed a grievous sense of its wrongfulness: "Foundational Axial (agricultural) Age stories narrate the origin of religion as the beginning of agricultural time: *an origin in sin.* The texts are almost shockingly explicit, so it's strange we don't think to read them that way. Pretty much out loud, they say that religion as such (was there 'religion' beforehand?) was founded in and as *impiety.*"[46]

Morton's case in *Dark Ecology* radically reworks the familiar triumphalist narratives of human progress, revealing the dogged sense of loss and trauma that have attended drastic changes to the treatment of self, land, and environment. Nonetheless, the Anthropocene means that these changes have become planetary, and a dimension of responding to them must be at that scale. Yet, by admitting humanity's entanglement with the rest of the planet at the most fundamental levels, "thinking global" becomes not only more necessary but also more difficult. Morton attests to the difficulty in particular in *Hyperobjects.*[47] The more we recognize the complexity of life and humanity's place in it, the harder it is to imagine the whole, the planetary. Heise and other writers have also recognized this catch-22 but still insist that we must attempt to do so in a world so embroiled in catastrophic risk. In *Homesickness* I acknowledge this central paradoxical fact, arguing that one consequence of admitting complexity is the need to give the local its due; the global must always appear in the terms of the local. Or, as Laura (Dassow) Walls puts it her introduction to a panel discussion, "The global is local at every point."[48] Thinking global requires *also* thinking local, and vice versa. In other words, "global" and "local" are necessarily poles in a continuum of geographical orientation. Both are important, and neither can be neglected as we labor to understand and improve the place of humans in the biosphere.

As mortal creatures, we are local beings. The body we inhabit moves and changes, yes, but it is itself also a highly particularized location. It is so particularized, in fact, that it escapes final knowledge. In this vein, object-oriented ontologist Graham Harman insists that, viewed as objects, individual humans are "withdrawn." As he claims, "The term 'objects' does not refer to some pampered set of 'natural kinds' at the expense of other realities.

Anything that is real can be regarded as an object."[49] And all objects are utterly local in their withdrawn status. Morton, working in this same intellectual framework, argues likewise in *Dark Ecology.* He notes, "Many have pronounced the death of place since the 1970s." However, he counters, "space has by no means conquered place. That postmodern meme was simply a late symptom of the modern myth of transcending one's material conditions." Instead, "*exactly the opposite has occurred.* From the standpoint of the genuinely post-modern ecological era, what has collapsed is (the fantasy of empty, smooth) space. 'Space' has revealed itself as the convenient fiction of white Western imperialist humans."[50] This does not mean we should revert to cloying conceptions of place, which Morton glosses mockingly as "presence, villages, the organic, slow time, traditions."[51] Instead, the object-oriented ontological concept of place is uncanny and strange. Indeed, the particular is always uncanny because it is not a concept; it is a manifest physical reality that we cannot fully access or know.[52] Further yet, the local, the affective, and the mortal—these are what make life worth living. They *are* life. Excessive emphasis on the nonlocal risks devaluing the particularity of real life.

It is worth pausing here to highlight a tension that traverses much of this literature. On the one hand, Morton and other new materialists insist on human immersion in the mesh of the world, the environment. On the other hand, object-oriented ontology emphasizes the withdrawn status of things, which cannot be fully known. In the first account, we cannot make final distinctions between entities and their environments; in the second account, we cannot collapse entities back into environment. One way out of this problem is to recognize both positions as true. The self, for example, is far less independent than Enlightenment dogmas would suggest, but there is nonetheless a distinction between self and environment. Cary Wolfe addresses this problem in *What Is Posthumanism?,* relying on Niklas Luhmann's description of the relationship between systems and environments. In Luhmann's account, the relationship is complex and even counterintuitive. He notes that systems are distinct from their environments but entirely and intricately in exchange with them. In short, each system reproduces a simplified version of the environment by way of sensing apparatuses. So the environment is entirely present in the system, but a distinction between system and environment remains nonetheless.[53]

The elusive complexity of places makes them difficult to profoundly access. Indeed, crucially for *Homesickness,* as Morton writes in *Hyperobjects,* "my situatedness and the rhetoric of situatedness in this case is not a place of defensive self-certainty but precisely its opposite. That is, situatedness is now a very uncanny place to be."[54] This uncanniness, one of my key words in this book, relates to Morton's key words in *Hyperobjects,* including "hypocrisy" and "weakness,"[55] which underscore the provisionality of human knowledge without offering an escape to the ironic postmodern posture.

Being among real things emphasizes the uncanny particularity of knowledge. Dealing with the realities of anthropogenic climate change, hyperobjects, and a Real more difficult to understand than is commonly recognized impacts language *and* of course all our nonlinguistic encounters.[56] For Morton, we must simultaneously recognize the weakness of human knowledge and language and, nonetheless, put what we know to work in dealing with accelerating problems on a real Earth, with real pollution and real global warming. This is why Morton quotes Graham Harman, addressing our deepening awareness of complexity: "By coming to terms with an increasing range of objects, human beings do not become nihilistic princes of darkness, but actually the most sincere creatures the earth has ever seen."[57] In *Dark Ecology* Morton nuances and clarifies this move, working "to get to the third darkness, the sweet one, through the second darkness, the uncanny one."[58] Both of these lie beyond "the first darkness" of nihilism. The "sweet" perspective allows that, like individual people, Earth is singular and singularly, distinctively vulnerable, and at this stage in history we must work to keep it habitable.

By contrast, Morton suggests of postmodernism, "the ultimate goal of this project, it seems, was to set up a weird transit lounge outside of history in which the characters and technologies and ideas of the ages mill around in a state of mild, semiblissful confusion."[59] This description applies to some forms of cosmopolitanism too. Morton's answer to this concern is to bring us back to Earth, to a real world, but one too Real to fully know. Thus, the ontological gesture of coming back to things themselves is haunted by the awareness of its failure. We are deterritorialized at home, "scooped out from the inside."[60] Morton thus pushes postmodernism so far beyond itself that it deserves another name, such as "the Age of Asymmetry" or "the Anthropocene."[61] This age, I am arguing, makes many of us particularly homesick. While the subject as such, as I claimed above, is always homesick, haunted by the gap between self and thoughts about the self, the particularity of our historical moment also intensifies this experience by facilitating both greater personal movement and greater changes to the planet. It takes work, Morton's writing implies, to arrive at the sweetness of homesickness, work required by the changes of modernity. This is not your parents' nostalgia, not an easy nostalgia. Its potential sweetness is borne of suffering and complex understanding. It is a blues, a terranean homesick blues, perhaps, with all its rich connotations of pleasure in pain and sophistication of comprehension.

One such complexity traces back to the ideology of work connected to the rise of agriculture and its affiliated regime of tools and thoughts, which Morton terms "agrilogistics" in *Dark Ecology*.[62] In the age of the Anthropocene, as we gain new perspective on work machines like the steam engine and the gasoline internal combustion engine by better understanding their massive effects, our notions of labor prove to be an essential part of the problem. This pertains not just to newer technologies. Large-scale systemization (and work) made possible by—and performed in—the first agricultural revolution twelve thousand or so years ago set in motion many of the trends that have led to global warming, trends cast in new light by posthumanism and other discourses. Even often-idealized human systems like law prove blame-worthy, not only in their unjust application to marginalized or disempowered groups but at their foundations. Cary Wolfe reinforces the latter view in his trenchant analysis *Before the Law*, which, for example, exposes the horrors of concentrated animal feeding operations (CAFOs), as aligned with the very intellectual structure of law itself.[63] Human-created systems enable increasingly large-scale actions, and, as Timothy Clark argues in *Ecocriticism on the Edge: The Anthropocene as a Threshold Concept*, it is scale itself that is essential to seemingly benign activities becoming destructive.[64] One person driving a car is globally inconsequential, but a billion-plus driving are another story.

We must think big, but we cannot blindly rush to thinking only at the planetary scale. Open the temporal and geographical scale wide enough, and none of these debates matters one bit, since Earth will have been consumed by the sun. Our debates cannot remain out at that scale. We must use such insights to better revisit "local" life, to remember the weak vulnerability of particular regimes of life and put that locality into dialogue with a very robustly conceived set of planetary ideas. We need the local and the global as tools to think with. We are too weak and too vulnerable to surrender either.

The paradoxical relationship between the local and the global plays out in the human longing for place. The desire for home—homesickness—is crucial to human orientation in practically everything, and it often grows alongside increased mobility. This desire for home actually drives much of our labor; also, much recreation, even exotic and distant travel, hinges on the stability of home and ideas of home.[65] Indeed, no thinking at all is possible without a nostalgic backward movement in interpretation. We need nostalgia, but we cannot simply trust all its forms. Simple nostalgia of many kinds is a risk. And in the age of mass production, our nostalgia may become commodified, focusing on ephemeral consumer objects, as Gary Cross details in his book *Consumed Nostalgia: Memory in the Age of Fast Capitalism.*[66]

Homesickness thus often focuses on the inverse of theories of identity that emphasize mobility as a kind of power or ability; mobility also involves a slippery, uncanny sense of loss and weakness. Many mobility theorists recognize that humans and other forms of life have unequal access to places. Not everyone can travel. This book deepens that point by emphasizing how all relationships with places are clearly determined to some extent by mortal weakness. Some are stuck in place. Others have been dislocated, or had their home places changed. Yet others have been pierced or infected by the recognition that human limitation means that even travel itself is local in a way, since a tourist or traveler carries distinctive biases, blindnesses, and histories along with him- or herself. Travelers are also subjected to the accidental circumstances of a particular trip: strange weather, the motivations or errors of companions or even of a tour guide or company, and all the other local realities of a given moment and place.

This relentlessly local and particular quality of experience means even ostensibly stable places are evasive in "normal" times. As the seventeenth-century Japanese poet Bashō puts it in a haiku, "Even in Kyoto— / hearing the cuckoo's cry— / I long for Kyoto."[67] The place haunts him even as he inhabits it, even in the manifestly *present* song of the cuckoo, as his subjectivity attunes to a "Kyoto" that he can only access by memory. The word "Kyoto," as a word, literally has no meaning otherwise except with reference to the past; that is what language systems do: they embed and calcify past experiences and understandings with reference to the world.

In the abnormal times of the Anthropocene, places get even stranger. Glenn Albrecht evokes some of these issues with his neologism "solastalgia," defined as "the pain experienced when there is recognition that the place where one resides and that one loves is under immediate assault . . . a form of homesickness one gets when one is still at home."[68] That is, contemporary forms of mobility entail dislocation for those who move and dislocation for those who are intruded upon. The historical examples of the latter go back as far as history itself and beyond, and this book argues that such experiences are so fundamental as to require further naming and theorizing.

Further, while homesickness is a sign of the unavoidable weakness of human life, it also indicates distinctiveness and value. As Rosemarie Garland Thomson concludes in *Extraordinary Bodies: Figuring Physical Disability in American Culture and Literature,* the distinctive body—the "disabled" or alter-abled body—can be understood as "extraordinary rather than abnormal."[69] Similarly, the unique particularity of regions and local cultures is perhaps better understood as potentially valuable precisely for its eccentricity. That idea, familiar from American regionalism and postcolonialism, for instance, is often connected to the sentimental, the irrational, and the regressive. Yet, as work in affect theory, new materialism, environmental humanities, and disability studies suggests, distinctiveness is in fact more normal and more "natural" than the constructed notions of homogeneity often reinforced by Enlightenment ideas from science, and in ostensibly progressivist institutions such as mass schooling. To recognize idiosyncrasy is potentially deeply liberating and more radical than much Enlightenment radicalism.

The *Unheimlich*: Unhomely Nation-States

Estranging the familiar and deconstructing the systematic are crucial to Jacques Derrida's intellectual program, and we might gloss their importance this way: genuine thinking is only possible via such defamiliarization, such homesickness. In the epigraph of this introduction, I quote the poet Novalis, whose comment uniting philosophy and homesickness is scrutinized by Derrida in his much-cited book *The Animal That Therefore I Am.* Derrida underscores questions about whether homesickness should be taken seriously, as when Martin Heidegger emphasizes cosmopolitan, urbane challenges to Novalis's view, asking, "Has not contemporary city man, the ape of civilization, long since eradicated homesickness?" Derrida summarizes Heidegger's account this way: "He [the modern city-dweller] laughs when one speaks to him of homesickness."[70] But Heidegger does not think it is so easy to dismiss melancholy, homesickness, nostalgia. For Derrida, this problem pulls Heidegger back into the human animality he wishes to disavow. For my argument in *Homesickness,* it also pulls us back into the local and the particular, whose uncanny presence resists global systemizing.

These ideas of displacement and also homesickness at home, the sense of solastalgia discussed by Glenn Albrecht, have been addressed in postcolonial criticism. For example, in *The Location of Culture,* Homi K. Bhabha discusses such homesickness in terms of the "unhomely."[71] "Unhomely" is a more precise translation of the German word *unheimlich* used by Sigmund Freud and often translated as "uncanny."[72] Freud explains that the uncanny is "related to what is frightening—to what arouses dread and horror."[73] But the particular brand of horror that he defines as uncanny is that "which leads back to what is known of old and long familiar."[74] The *unheimlich* thus names realities that seem familiar but prove strange, unmooring us from the batch of objects and scenes that we commonly use to anchor our sense of self. This idea is central to my meaning in using the synonym "homesickness" throughout this book. Bhabha's treatment of the unhomely is instructive. Like many thinkers on cosmopolitanism, Bhabha turns to Goethe's idea of a world literature, hoping that it might be not about "the 'sovereignty' of national cultures, nor the universalism of human culture," but rather should engage with "transnational histories of migrants, the colonized, or political refugees."[75] Bhabha shows the complex mixtures that actually comprise national identities. In effect, Bhabha asks us to recognize that to live in a global world is to live in a postcolonial world.

In *Homesickness,* I recognize that, to some degree, we are all migrants with hybrid identities, and we are all embroiled in the uneven exercise of power. A focus on homesickness reveals complications in national stories that tend to be smoothed over in condemnations of pathos and the desire for place. To show this, I turn to a range of cultural products, largely literature but also film and other texts, particularly those that highlight marginal identities or identities under the stress of change. My focus on what is mostly a single, ostensibly national literature and culture—that of the United States—therefore complicates that appellation by attending to authors and producers of texts who highlight their marginal condition. The texts studied here demonstrate the slippery, fleeting character of designations like "American" or "U.S." literature, especially when viewed in the frameworks of postnational theorists like Bhabha, of cosmopolitan theorists, and of posthumanist thinkers. What does it mean to connect writing (more generally, marking) with such a vast and varied place as "the United States"? In that sense, *Homesickness* is written in the spirit of Rob Nixon's important question, framed in *Slow Violence and the Environmentalism of the Poor*: "What would it mean to bring environmentalism into a full, productive dialogue with postcolonialism?"[76]

This book's method turns ideas of national literature inside out. Rather than assuming from the first that national literatures make neat, interpretable wholes, I begin with a postcolonial-inspired assumption of political unevenness and national heterogeneity. Perhaps a better way to put this is that this approach exposes the mixture, fluidity, and impurity always present in the lives of human animals and in the texts we produce. Our national designations have always been rhetorical and fleeting. Bhabha cites a marvelous "stammering, drunken" line from Salman Rushdie's *The Satanic Verses* to this effect: "The trouble with the Engenglish is that their hiss hiss history happened overseas, so they dodo don't know what it means."[77] In both content and style, Rushdie complicates here—deconstructs, if you like—the word and the idea of "English," blurring and slurring its articulation. The same can be done to "United States" with regard to contemporary colonialism and imperialism, and with regard to "American" domestic politics. Even much of the *internal* history of the United States happens beyond the comprehension of many Americans, who are focused on more routine elements of life; those who pay rigorous attention still cannot know everything. Thus, as citizens, Americans live unhomely lives, confronting the uncanny political realities of their homeland. This is true of every nation-state, a fact that helps explain persistent problems with ostensibly rational democratic systems.

Bhabha argues that the "'unhomely' is a paradigmatic colonial and postcolonial condition" with "a resonance that can be heard distinctly, if erratically, in fictions that negotiate the powers of cultural difference in a range of transhistorical sites."[78] Such colonial and semicolonial conditions are not just "abroad"; they are visible and present across the social bodies of many developed nations like the United States, in pronounced divisions of social class and ethnicity. These frictions of cultural difference spark into flames in modern wars both internal to and between nation-states, drastically intensifying the estrangement of individuals and populations and presenting some of the clearest examples of homesickness. Warfare turns on power, but it necessarily therefore entails disempowerment, subjugation, and displacement. War reveals weakness. To this point Robert Post, introducing the 2006 collection *Another Cosmopolitanism*, urges that "the conflagration of World War II made manifest the inescapable interdependence of the globe. For the past half century, we have grown ever more tightly interconnected by the expanding international circulation of persons, capital, commerce, pollution, information, labor, goods, viruses, and so on, *ad infinitum*."[79]

A key word in Post's description of contemporary interdependence is "inescapable," underscoring that *open* exchange and *freedom* of movement are only part of this picture; compulsion and need are central too. Post's statement, highlighting circulation of both information and viruses, for instance, reiterates Derrida's claims, mentioned above, that cosmopolitanism grows partly out of limitations and weaknesses. Likewise, more than some treatments of cosmopolitanism, the volume that Post introduces recognizes such problems with globalization, centered on vulnerability: his opening paragraph highlights our "frail, robin's egg planet" as seen in the images from space as key to contemporary life (Figure 1). Those famous, powerful images of Earth reiterate the need to include environment in our considerations of cosmopolitanism—an eco-cosmopolitanism of the sort Heise advocates, as noted above.

Indeed, the paradox involved in these pictures is the clearest and most prominent example of homesickness, in which the opportunity to travel—literally to the moon!—inaugurates a renewed sense of desire for home and recognition of weakness at/as home. If the contemporary sense of planet Earth derives in large measure from those photographs, as Post joins many others in claiming, that sense is one of homesickness, of dislocation and exposure. It is a posthumanist homesickness made possible by astonishing regimes of technology including not only the space program and all its undergirding science but also the photographic sensing apparatuses and the ability to publish and distribute the resulting images.

All that power and travel, then, paradoxically produce a countermovement, a renewed and intensified attention to the more local concerns here on Earth. Like complex homesickness more generally, this scenario is ironic, since the very same technologies and social regimes that make possible this renewed understanding of the planet also put the planet in great peril. That is what we mean by "the Anthropocene." These same paradoxes also appear at more local scales in the forms of "development" that are "uneven," in the realities of science that have required reductive approaches to nonhuman and often human life, and so on. The space program, science, and colonialism—these are all part and parcel of the industrial age and its paradoxical effects. *Homesickness* exposes and investigates these more complex effects, that dark

Figure 1. Homesick for planet Earth. "The Blue Marble" photograph taken of Earth on December 7, 1972, by the Apollo 17 crew after leaving Earth, heading toward the moon. From NASA.

side of mobility and humanist optimism. As environmental justice scholars have long insisted, unhomeliness, or homesickness, partly results from being denied access to familiar places, or from those places undergoing radical changes themselves. Changes to places, of course, affect nonhuman life as well—often, much more profoundly than human life—creating feedback loops of trauma and homesickness that cycle back to humanity and then turn outward again to the nonhuman. As global warming moves whole biomes, unsettles weather patterns, and leads to species extinctions, homesickness of a general kind grows across species. The possibility—though not inevitability—of those changes is latent in the image of Earth seen from afar.

Historicizing Mobility: A Sketch of American Homesickness

Kilborn's book *Next Stop, Reloville,* discussed at the beginning of this introduction, describes a whole category of cases like Phil Cottrell's, examples of extensive mobility in an increasingly globalized world. Kilborn acknowledges the long history of similar professional-class mobility, reminding us of Britain's Hudson's Bay Company and East India Company,[80] for instance, but he also notes that the sheer numbers of people moving and the ease with which they—we—do so today are new things under the sun. Such cosmopolitan mobility, then, is both new and old. Stephen Greenblatt, in his recent collection *Cultural Mobility: A Manifesto,* emphasizes the old to make the larger point that mobility is and has long been the norm in human life.[81] He argues that "vital global cultural discourse . . . is quite ancient; only the increasingly settled and bureaucratized nature of academic institutions in the nineteenth and early twentieth centuries" would make the opposite seem true, that the feeling of "'at-homeness'" is a "necessary condition for a robust cultural identity."[82] Greenblatt criticizes this embrace of the local and the grounded, of "at-homeness," instead reasserting the cosmopolitan dream of mobility and aligning it with the large amount of theoretical work focused on hybridity, postnationalism, transatlanticism, and the many other forms of border crossing prevalent today.

Greenblatt's historicization of the love of home is itself debatable, as is clear in light of historian Susan J. Matt's study *Homesickness: An American History.*[83] She too recognizes our attitude as profoundly period bound but emphasizes shifts moving in the opposite direction of those noted by Greenblatt. "Before the twentieth century," Matt writes, "homesickness was a widely acknowledged and discussed condition."[84] In the nineteenth century, especially before the Civil War, Matt explains, there prevailed "a domestic sentimentalism that regarded the love of home, family, and, in particular, mother as ennobling."[85] Americans had to *learn* "to leave home with ease," and as they did so, attachment to home began to be seen as a sign of backwardness. Matt writes, "The modern attitude toward homesickness" supposes "that movement is natural and unproblematic," that it is "a central and uncontested part of American identity." "Once seen as the mark of a refined and sensitive nature," homesickness has since come to be seen as "inconsequential" and childish, as a sign of "backwardness" and even "prissiness."[86] Matt reports how debates about homesickness also became entangled in the racist views of African Americans and Native Americans, who were often seen as more emotionally involved with their home places. The cluster of issues surrounding this shifting attitude toward homesickness is more nuanced and complex than Greenblatt's manifesto allows. Instead, homesickness is intimately connected to our cultural and economic means of production in a given time and cannot be easily or simply characterized as good or bad.

Matt emphasizes that leaving home is commonly traumatic, even though that trauma appears and functions differently in different periods and places. She shows how Enlightenment ideas in the eighteenth century "celebrated the freely moving individual who maximized happiness and who could be at home anywhere in the world."[87] But clearly this dream is largely a fantasy, an idealized form of a more complex reality. Indeed, Jennifer Rae Greeson has shown how such notions of independent individuality, particularly the possessive individuality of modern capitalism, are triangulated with ideas of slavery. Greeson, working especially with John Locke's writings, claims that "to be owned, the self must first be alienated, entered into the market, 'thingified.'"[88] From that point, the distinction is whether one owns oneself or someone else does. So the cosmopolitan dream happens *after* the self is alienated, just as the hope for religious piety happens after the original sin of agriculture. Alienated selves either must reclaim self-ownership—the Enlightenment dream—or be owned as slaves. Isolating and commodifying the self in this way, Matt argues, led to the neglect of "communal imperatives," and the feeling of homesickness was increasingly repressed and ignored. But, Matt notes, the rejection of and departure from one's home place nonetheless "carried hefty emotional costs," whether admitted or not.[89]

A crucial period in the development of contemporary attitudes toward homesickness, Matt shows, was the Civil War, which required soldiers "to transform . . . love of home into martial spirit." Thus "how to love home and simultaneously leave it" was an essential problem of the era.[90] This difficulty continues to play out in the twenty-first century, as U.S. soldiers serve in Iraq and Afghanistan, driven in part by patriotism and love of home. The extremes of war trauma help us recognize more clearly the negative notions involved in homesickness—the uncanny strangeness of the familiar, even the dread and dislike of what we know, such a common experience for returning soldiers. The dislike of home—sickness at home—is clear in a range of texts, from Ernest Hemingway's story "Soldier's Home," to Bobbie Ann Mason's Vietnam War novel *In Country*, to the recent case of Pat Tillman, as

I show in greater detail in chapter 6. I underscore this dislike of home, the reverse of conventional meanings of the term "homesickness," as prominent in the set of emotions in complex homesickness.

While Greenblatt blames nineteenth- and twentieth-century institutional specialization for the increased value placed on place and home, Matt's more detailed history demonstrates that the picture is much more complicated. As I noted, she shows that during precisely that period—the nineteenth and twentieth centuries—homesickness was becoming less and less valued. Furthermore, Matt recognizes that "between 1607 and 1789, roughly half of the 600,000 Europeans and all 300,000 of the Africans who landed on American shores were not free, arriving either as servants or slaves. . . . Their lack of autonomy influenced how they thought about the places they left and the journeys they made."[91] This issue of autonomy is essential to the dynamics of homesickness and desire for place, and raises questions about what it means to emphasize a "vital global cultural discourse" as Greenblatt does. Much too rarely has that discourse taken account of the full complexity of global movement for all parties involved, including the many who were moved by force. In 2015, for instance, "more than 70 million people" were forced migrants worldwide, reports Mark Tran in *The Guardian*.[92] Similarly, in *The Shock of the Anthropocene*, Bonneuil and Fressoz note, "At the present time, 20 to 30 million people each year migrate in the wake of natural disaster, and the UN envisages 50 million environmental migrants a year by 2030, due in particular to changes linked to climate disturbance."[93]

Matt shows that early immigrants to the Americas did miss home in various ways, although the feeling was subject to scrutiny and debate then, as now, if often for different reasons. Those who came to the Americas to make money, for instance, sometimes "consumed substantial amounts of liquor 'to solace them for losing the comforts of a settled life.'" Such migrants "invested little time or effort in making the colony habitable or pleasant," and that was reflected in the poor construction of their homes and the like,[94] a vicious circle of place behavior exemplifying one trend of modernity. Matt further notes, "Virginia colonists with the lowest social status generally had most cause to long for home and the least ability to act on their longings."[95] Such desires in the case of slaves might translate into a wish not to return to Africa but to return to adopted homes in the New World, homes that slavery denied them.[96] Such homesickness for adopted homes recurs into contemporary times, especially among those subject to frequent mobility, even voluntary mobility, as I show particularly in chapter 3. These feelings demonstrate that mobility involves loss even for those who choose it.

Yet for many settlers, especially those who came to New England for religious reasons, being distant from home was part of their spiritual belief system: "Earth was but a temporary resting stop on the pilgrimage to heaven. Consequently, they should not be overly attached to particular places. Some Puritans saw their ability to withstand separation as proof of their piety."[97] Puritans and many others inhabited, as Matt aptly puts it, "a culture where pain and suffering were seen as *natural* and *inevitable* components of the human condition, and these beliefs shaped the ways they expressed and acted on their yearnings."[98] Greenblatt's move to embrace mobility itself bears traces of this sort of naturalization. He suggests that place desire is the cultural construction while mobility is somehow more general, more universal. I am arguing instead that place desire and mobility must be understood in dialogue.

Matt notes that Enlightenment ideas changed the debate about homesickness in complex and sometimes opposite ways. On the one hand, the Puritan idea of suffering as instructive lost sway, opening space to register genuine, personal feelings of homesickness. That is, the pain of homesickness began to be seen as other-than-inevitable in mortal life, as something worth addressing and correcting. On the other hand, the embrace of rationality in the Enlightenment encouraged people to reject home and the familiar, to be "self-directed and autonomous, pursuing happiness, possessing rights and abilities that went beyond those conferred by their families, their churches, or their towns."[99] This confluence—often, conflict—of ideas helped produce the establishment of a medical category for the desire for home: in 1688, Matt explains, Johannes Hofer, "a Swiss scholar," coined the word "nostalgia" "from two existing Greek words, *nostos,* meaning 'return home,' and *algia,* the word for pain."[100] This neologism medicalized the idea of homesickness, which Matt points out had clearly already been present in European cultures in different form. (The basic plot of *The Odyssey* indicates that a complex desire for home is indeed an old emotion.) The English word "homesickness" would not be coined until the 1750s. The development of this terminology set the stage for further debates about home desire. While one thread led to the cosmopolitan orientation, another developed into the "domestic sentimentalism" noted above that understood "the love for home, family, and, in particular, mother, as ennobling."[101]

Matt's history shows that this tension persisted throughout the period of great American mobility. Between 1800 and 1850, while "a higher percentage of people, almost half the population, crossed state lines to change residences," a figure higher "than in any comparable later period," ambivalence tagged along.[102] Many moved west, only to return after either successful or unsuccessful enterprises. Indeed, as Matt notes, commerce, or capitalism, oriented much of this mobility. It was often colored in idealistic tones of independence, but lack, desire, and poverty were often in fact strong motivations as well. So, Matt writes, "homesickness gradually became a marker of dependence and inadequacy,"[103] but mobility is often a sign of precisely those same traits—dependence and inadequacy.

The forced mobility of slaves, of Native Americans, and of the poor and the destitute recalls key human failures by reiterating the profound potential for violence and irrationality in Enlightenment systems of knowledge. The exaggerated and fetishized notion of self-mastery, still very much in sway, often relies on a disavowed enslavement of many others in a deeply violent social and economic structure; as noted above, the very idea of mastery bears within it the notion of slavery. In this vein, Matt asserts, "The slave auction was perhaps the most obvious and extreme example of the way human affections and emotions came to be shaped by market forces in antebellum America."[104] The misery of broken-up slave families has long been a central focus revealing the evil of the institution. Slavery's horrible effects and the power of the emotions are explored with ferocious intensity in Toni Morrison's *Beloved,* a book that also reveals how homesickness can focus not so much on a particular place left behind but on a cultural-life-as-home that must be reconstituted, as I explore in chapter 4. The protagonist Sethe, her family, and Paul D desire not so much a *particular* place but a decent, humanized social role *somewhere.*

Mobility, Violence, and Universals: War, Trauma, and Homesickness

Beloved, and the more mundane contemporary example of Phil Cottrell, relates to points Greenblatt makes. He acknowledges that in the Jewish experience, mobility has often been exceedingly trying. Greenblatt references mobility in both the literal and figurative senses, recalling not only great human migrations but mobilizations and importations of cultural belief systems, as when Christianity, by way of the concept of *figura,* read the Torah as the Old Testament and understood Jews to presage Christians. Mobilizing a whole religious system in this way is deeply problematic for Greenblatt. He aligns it with "attempted cultural (and, of course, actual) murder."[105] In making this point, Greenblatt raises a problem for all cosmopolitan impulses, which by definition reframe and thereby revise individual cultural traditions. Greenblatt also allows that we cannot divorce, for instance, the growth of world literatures in English from the "international capitalism" that has helped spread the language and the artifacts that make such changes possible.[106] While Greenblatt cites Goethe's dream of a world literature prepared to enrich everyone culturally, he also notes that "its optimism [has been] spectacularly disproved by almost two centuries of fathomless hatred and bloodshed."[107] So, despite his avowed manifesto in favor of mobility, Greenblatt admits mobility's very real pitfalls.[108]

Then again, as Heise argues in *Sense of Place and Sense of Planet,* a focus on rootedness has its own negative examples, most notably in "the National Socialist rhetoric of Germans' natural connectedness to 'blood and soil.'"[109] Heise cites this case as "the most extreme" among many unsettling examples of an insistence on place and dwelling, common today, she notes, in American environmentalist thinking. Heise uses such cases to justify her case for eco-cosmopolitanism, but it is clear from Greenblatt's points that either approach—an exclusive embrace of home or of mobility—is potentially harmful. Further, Bonneuil and Fressoz suggest that it is an "outdated historiography" that connects the return-to-the-soil movement with fascism and Nazism. Instead, they *contrast* such fascist ideologies with the earlier and quite different "back-to-nature socialism" and related movements, which rejected industrial capitalism.[110]

Practically, a placeless mobility theory risks disavowing or denying its tacit political orientations and assumptions, the all-too-familiar problem of ethnocentrism visible in many imperialistic traditions, from Britain to Japan, China to the United States. Recalling the particularity of perspective forces us back into the local and the situated. As David Harvey urges, our hopes for "an emancipatory and liberatory form of global governance" depend on carefully articulating the global with each form of the local, and this is a necessarily ongoing process.[111] We cannot escape it with an embrace of a vague cosmopolitanism that is too readily aligned with a homogenizing form of globalized capitalism. Similarly, Gary Snyder, a target of Heise's critique of the local, notes in *Nobody Home*, "I am suspicious of any easy notions of cosmopolitanism . . . that would use ideas of bigness and one-ness to displace the local, to displace 'home village.'"[112] Snyder's point closely resembles Derrida's caution about an impractical or too idealistic cosmopolitanism. The local is where any idea makes its impact.

In this book, I therefore insist that we should not—indeed cannot—choose between the planetary and the local. It is more productive to think that difference like the nature/culture distinction, which ecocriticism and the dominant trends in poststructuralist theory have pushed hard to problematize, to deconstruct. Despite Heise's superficial criticism of Gary Snyder,[113] Snyder offers a compelling overall framework for thinking this place/mobility dialectic. For example, one of his essays in *A Place in Space*, "The Rediscovery of Turtle Island," describes the urge to become "reinhabitory" this way: "it simply implies an engagement with community and a search for the sustainable sophisticated mix of economic practices that would enable people to live regionally and yet learn from and contribute to a planetary society." Just prior to this definition, Snyder insists, "This doesn't mean some return to a primitive lifestyle or utopian provincialism."[114] Even Snyder's earliest publications have a cosmopolitan flair, attuned to the vast complexity of Earth's many cultures. He also insists on recognition of life's vulnerability, and his work has consistently included the more-than-human world in a "posthumanist" way; he uses this term in "The Rediscovery of Turtle Island,"[115] first given as a talk in 1993, in very much the same sense that Donna Haraway and Cary Wolfe use it.

Snyder gives his cosmopolitanism potency—to use Derrida's word, quoted above—by grounding it rigorously in the local, even as he remains oriented by thinking big. Answering to suggestions that humanity has a "destiny in outer space," for instance, Snyder reminds us that "we are already traveling in space—this is the galaxy, right here."[116] What we think of as geographical stasis, as being in the same place, is always already movement at another scale. Similarly, in *Hyperobjects*, Morton offers a radical defamiliarization of human scales of meaning, exposing the ephemerality of much that seems fixed and stable. These large truths underlie the feeling of homesickness explored in this book, but they also clarify our need to come back to local scales in order to have any hope of doing things, of practicing, say, a real eco-cosmopolitanism. It must be informed with rigorous, planetary knowledge, and attend carefully to each circumstance of application, a kind of functional paradox shuttling between the global and the utterly local.

Embracing paradox in this way, however, is a delicate maneuver. Paradoxes and contradictions often lead to violence, whether of the slower kind explored by Rob Nixon in his book *Slow Violence and the Environmentalism of the Poor*, or of the blindingly obvious, faster sort. Such contradictions haunt cosmopolitan hopes. David Harvey's 2009 book *Cosmopolitanism and the Geographies of Freedom* offers a clear account of some of those difficulties. Harvey does not argue for surrendering the cosmopolitan dreams of global knowledge and justice but rather for tempering them in the awareness that "all universalizing projects, be they liberal, neoliberal, conservative, religious, socialist, cosmopolitan, rights-based, or communist, run into serious problems as they encounter the specific circumstances of their application. Noble phrases and ideals crumble into shoddy excuses, special pleadings, misunderstandings, and, more often than not, violent confrontations and recriminations."[117] He cites a few of the countless historical examples: not only post-9/11 U.S. policy in Iraq and Afghanistan but Britain in India, "the Catholic Church in South America, the Chinese in Tibet," and so on.[118]

These difficulties are intractable in deep ways, as Mary Louise Pratt has also compellingly shown in her article "Harm's Way: Language and the Contemporary Arts of War."[119] War has been a steady companion of cosmopolitanism historically, and it dramatizes with special clarity the challenges of all cross-cultural exchange. Pratt notes that for war and violence to take on meaning, they require language. This fact raises questions about whose perspectives to rely on, and, more basically, in which language? While planning to engage in commerce or travel is a different story, the challenges of language and cultural difference remain. Without shared understanding and shared language, the hopes for a peaceful cosmopolitanism become much more difficult.

Thus, in cases of war, and in cosmopolitanism debates in general, the problem of this tension between the local and the global (or universal) remains firmly entrenched. Indeed, as Routledge notes, the word "nostalgia" derives from a military context. As remarked above, it "was coined in 1688 by the Swiss medical student Johannes Hofer," who understood it "as a medical disease afflicting Swiss soldiers and mercenaries who had travelled from their Alpine homes to the plains of Europe to wage war."[120] War's dislocation produces unrest even for—sometimes especially for—soldiers. For a further example, Harvey cites Seyla Benhabib's important criticisms of cosmopolitanism. Benhabib notes that Kant's actual cosmopolitan formulations or the language of American political ideals—both of which are important models for modern cosmopolitanism in general—are necessarily marked with their own local and historical conditions and therefore limitations. She argues, again as Harvey reports, "that the cosmopolitan principles themselves may have to be modified and even radically reformulated . . . under the impact of the geographical, ecological, and anthropological particularities encountered."[121] Each of these last three terms may be passed over quickly, but of course each opens worlds of complexity.

Indeed, the problem Harvey underscores, of universalizing projects sliding into violence, is redoubled when we define our concerns as eco-cosmopolitan, in a posthumanist way that includes other nonhuman forms of life and matter. In the nonhuman realm, human expansion and globalization have led to massive violence. For one thing, the spread of meat eating that has accompanied globalization is ecologically expensive and systematically violent in terms of the food animals themselves.[122] And more profound is the sixth extinction event happening now, which reaches far beyond even genocide, as whole species disappear in unthinkable numbers.

Deepening this challenge, reports Elizabeth Kolbert in *The Sixth Extinction: An Unnatural History,* is the recognition that during mass extinction events, "the usual rules of survival are suspended. Conditions change so drastically or so suddenly (or so drastically and so suddenly) that evolutionary history counts for little. Indeed, the very traits that have been most useful for dealing with ordinary threats may turn out, under such extraordinary circumstances, to be fatal."[123] Kolbert is writing about species' own challenges to survive, but her point also applies to scientists and others attempting to solve contemporary ecological crises as part of an eco-cosmopolitan effort. The wrong ideas, scaled up to eco-cosmopolitanism, could prove even more harmful. Yet, as Morton notes above discussing postmodernism, despite our awareness of these hazards, we must act. The complex dynamics of mass extinctions thus exemplify the complexities of the Anthropocene, in which familiar modes of thinking and acting prove unhelpful and even destructive, as Clark argues in *Ecocriticism on the Edge.*[124] But we cannot resort to an ironic postmodern stance.

Another way to put this argument is that a singular cosmopolitanism, of the sort evoked with Thomas Freidman's grossly reductive but clever phrase "flat world," is impossible.[125] "Flat world" thinking presumes a mastery that is both violent and finally delusive, glossing over great complexities that cannot be unworked even if everyone agreed that doing so were desirable. The slow violence of colonialist and imperialist histories as described by Nixon, for example, demonstrates the challenges of practical globalism or cosmopolitanism. Signs of this human weakness are everywhere in histories of the modern period, threaded through the work of Foucault, Derrida, Julia Kristeva, and many others. Indeed, postmodernism and the theoretical revolution in literary studies in the twentieth century are both fundamentally informed by a sense that representations and knowledge are particularized, nonuniversal, and fractured. This point is taken up by nearly every scholar cited in this chapter. Instead of a singular cosmopolitanism, we need a complex eco-cosmopolitanism, a critical cosmopolitanism that could also be called an uncanny or a localized cosmopolitanism that constantly moves between scales and between theory and practice. It should be a paradoxical yet dynamic cosmopolitanism, then, that does not simply rest in the tensions—local versus global, theory versus practice, and so on—but continually turns and engages them.

Homesickness as Haunting, as Second-Order Perception

We cannot rest at one scale (say, global) or in one disposition (like cosmopolitanism) because knowing is too particular. Posthumanism's skepticism about knowledge is rooted largely in this particularity, in awareness of how knowledge and perception work, in a more rigorously conceived rationality, as Wolfe argues.[126] Thus, much twentieth- and twenty-first-century theory and philosophy underscore the gap that appears between an object and its representation, or between a thing and its concept.[127] This idea is key to the notion in phenomenology, for example, that all perception is situated and partial. Maurice Merleau-Ponty shows that when we view an object in space, we must infer the object's back side, the nonvisible part. We cannot directly see all sides of a three-dimensional object.[128]

As noted above, new materialist scholars such as Graham Harman, Jane Bennett, and Levi R. Bryant push these ideas about the opacity and depth of objects much further. For instance, in *Vibrant Matter* Bennett recognizes the challenge of putting broad ideas to work in particular scenarios: "If a set of moral principles is actually to be lived out, the right mood or landscape of affect has to be in place."[129] Similarly, in *Guerilla Metaphysics* Harman explores the way nonhuman objects call to and instruct viewers, reversing familiar notions of human agency and knowing. Working with ideas from philosopher Alphonso Lingis, Harman describes how perception involves becoming unhoused from ourselves, noting, for instance, that even at home, when we look around at familiar objects, we find we "are never quite at home with substances, which always tempt us beyond the point where we are now."[130] Harman celebrates Lingis's critique of the widely held anthropocentric idea that "the transcending free human is the source of all significance in the universe."[131] That notion often subtends cosmopolitan thinking too. But for Harman, humans do not transcend in this way. Instead, "we use our bodies to enter the style of any environment," learning from it and adapting to its calls and suggestions.[132] In this account, significance is partly something external that we recognize rather than something purely internal that we create.

Situating knowledge and perception, or putting it back into a complex world, involves stepping behind our habitual, familiar modes of sensing. Such scenarios can be understood structurally in the terms Niklas Luhman presents as foundational to perception and to consciousness. Introducing Luhman's *Theories of Distinction,* William Rasch writes, "The problem of self-consciousness, as the German idealists well knew, is the problem of paradox. How can the self refer to itself without making of itself something other than itself, something that can be referred to, pointed to, as if it were not what was doing the pointing?"[133] This scenario involves perceiving a self that perceives, or seeing the self as a seer. In *What Is Posthumanism?* Wolfe, drawing from Derrida and Luhmann, presents this situation as self-referential autopoiesis.[134] Luhmann writes about such perceptions as "second-order" observations; there is an observation of an observation. Self-consciousness is thus second-order perception. In colloquial terms, our self-consciousness is the ghost of ourselves haunting us.

Self-consciousness introduces a gap between the self and ideas of the self, and I contend that a symptom of that gap is a kind of *unheimlich,* or a homesickness. That is, consciousness itself instantiates a homesickness (as did perhaps, before that, movement, and before that, the enclosure of environment in a cell, as in single-cell organisms). Luhmann's work, described by Wolfe in *What Is Posthumanism?*, shows how every perceptive system is founded on this paradoxical gap. Since the system depends on the gap for its very existence, the difference between reality and the perceiving system can only be seen from *another* vantage point, another perceiving system.[135] A central point of *Homesickness* is that a sense of such realities is often expressed in terms of the loose, vague, and wonderfully powerful nostalgia for ideas of home. Home orients our desires and values in retrospect to a large degree, another foundational paradox. In other words, we look to a past to orient the present and, in doing so, consolidate and order that past. The *desires* of the present create the need for a usable past; we thus make or at least reduce and render legible the past. Homesickness also works prospectively, guiding future plans based on an imagined or rendered past, a reality engaged by speculative fiction, for instance. While this dimension of home is less a focus of this book, many of the claims about how homesickness functions also apply to prospection.

The structure of feeling or perception in homesickness amounts to a second-order observation: that is, while in first-order observations of home we learn the particulars of place by inhabiting it and watching it closely, by leaving a place we become able to observe those first-order observations from a further remove. As noted above, the famous pictures of planet Earth from outer space are probably the clearest example of this structure of perception, in which our more first-order perceptions here on the planet are deeply changed by the second-order perception of Earth from elsewhere. It is telling that second-order observations of home—such as Earth from space—commonly bear an emotional freight of loss alongside their insights. The very existence of a second-order observation of home means one has left, never to be able to reinhabit home in a naïve, innocent way. I contend, then, that all second-order observations of home are partly traumatic woundings. From this perspective, the concept of "haunting" that flits through this book takes additional resonance.

Further, this means that when we feel homesickness, we know both more and less of "our" place. We know more in that we can position "home" in a new frame of reference, a classically cosmopolitan gesture. But we know less in this particularly posthumanist sense that we lose ownership over knowledge itself, since we must recognize that knowledge paradoxically requires distance, and second-order knowledge requires yet further distance. Knowledge, then, like self-consciousness, is a form of estrangement. It is a form of weakness that is something other than purely rational, a haunting.

Homesickness therefore signals human limitations in two profound ways, since it involves estrangement from both knowledge and home. This displacement or decentering makes homesickness instructive and useful, but viewed with cognizance of human limitation and mortality, we should take seriously the pathos of loss in it. The loss is real. Herein lie two central critiques of cosmopolitanism, then: cosmopolitanism, in its association with Enlightenment rationality, often tends to elide or denigrate emotion; cosmopolitanism tends to ignore individual particularity, vulnerability, and trauma, as noted in Harvey's discussion, cited above. Homesickness reveals both pathos and weakness.

Reinhabitation and eco-cosmopolitanism are both marked by this reality. Reinhabitation supposes an initial departure (hence "re-") and implies a trauma. We cannot quite recover the old place—or, that is, our old sense of the place. Cosmopolitanism cannot help but be local, partial, and imperfect. That means each *application* of a cosmopolitanism is local and distinct at every point, and, from the other side, each version of cosmopolitanism being applied is itself local insofar as it *derives* each time from unique circumstances. There is no pure or neutral or unmarked cosmopolitanism. Yet I am advocating for a program of cosmopolitan reinhabitation or of localized eco-cosmopolitanism—they amount to the same thing in my mind. They require a complex awareness of the global/local tension and of the situatedness of all perceptions.[136]

Earth, Stranger: Mobility as a Limited Resource

Posthumanism and an uncanny eco-cosmopolitanism show us that home—as in planet Earth—is in fact more strange to us than we commonly imagine. Can it really be that small sphere hanging in black, as in the photographs? This observation conflicts with the growing sense that humans are effectively domesticating the whole planet. Much environmental thinking has supposed that the human presence is now so dominant in the world that, as activist-scholar Bill McKibben puts it in the title to one of his books, we are facing "the end of nature."[137] But of course that claim depends essentially on how we define nature. In a broad sense, everything is natural, and everything has not and will not "end" any time soon, so far as we are aware. So McKibben and others are talking about the end of a particular idea of nature.[138] In a broader sense, nature is merely changing (even if at a frightening and dangerous rate). This distinction is far from trivial. If we assume that humanity has brought the end to nature, it seems very difficult—impossible, really—to escape humanity and human solipsism. But that is circular logic. Humans are everywhere; therefore, we cannot escape humans.

Posthumanism and other such trends in environmental thought recognize that, yes, human beings have a huge and dangerous influence on "nature," or the world's "mesh." But posthumanism emphasizes that alterity, or otherness, is and has always been rampant in human life. Posthumanism, then, takes us in the opposite direction; it insists that there is and has always been very much more "nature" right inside humanity than we commonly notice. This point complicates the often-harmful human/nonhuman distinction rigidly deployed in arguments like McKibben's.

Instead, we ought to regard the human/nonhuman distinction as rhetorical: that is, as an absolute, logical distinction, it is clearly false. There is no clear or final distinction. However, in many cases, the distinction is useful and necessary—when understood as provisional and situational—that is, as rhetorical. For instance, to address global warming, we need the distinction at times so that we can distinguish genuine causes of warming from the denialist posture asserting that global temperature is "natural." This rhetorical approach to meaning sometimes sets off alarm bells in thinkers accustomed to the purity of logical thought, but human language is weaker than that. All our creations of meaning are circumstantial. (Even a single word—say, "great"—can mean opposite things in different circumstances, for instance.) Thinking human/nonhuman differences in a more supple fashion allows us to imagine responses to environmental trauma as co-creations with the rest of life, involving humans as something other than an inherently sullying or corrupting force.

Human life has always and must always depend on other forms of life, from the plants whose fruits and seeds we eat, whose respiration we require; to the animals many raise, kill, and consume; to the geological systems that produce and reproduce landforms that make the other forms of life possible. Life depends now, as ever, on intricate relationships among the living and the nonliving, as Derrida underscores.[139] We can recognize ourselves as hybrid, natural beings, kin to other animals and made up at fundamental cellular and genetic levels of long-established processes. This view significantly shifts our notions of the human and of human undertakings. In that framework, *Homesickness* offers a rereading of mobility, mobility that is driven not by an utterly independent, cerebral self but by a composite, embodied, communal being with a glimmer of self-consciousness. From that perspective, human movement looks itself like a natural event, to some extent. But here again we need a *rhetorical* deployment of the natural/unnatural distinction. Certainly all human activity, including the burning of fossil fuels, is, in a way, natural. Indeed, extinction is natural, even at the massive scales happening now. But so then is the human (and nonhuman) activity of cultural change, of debate, inquiry, and revision of traditions, which can include more complex attitudes toward mobility and homesickness.

There is a further step: in a rapprochement between humans and nature,[140] mobility should be seen not simply as a human phenomenon but as a reality of materiality itself. When Greenblatt urges that the "apparent fixity and stability of cultures is, in [Michel de] Montaigne's words, 'nothing but a more languid motion,'"[141] a posthumanist can recognize there an adequate description of mountains, landscapes, and even planets and stars. If we widen the frame enough, we know that the most fixed points of reference, like the sun, are swinging through a fathomless outer space faster than we can imagine, as Snyder noted above. So mobility is a condition of reality, but that fact raises more questions than it solves. When is mobility desirable? When is it, as it can seem for Phil Cottrell, obligatory, seemingly harmful and bewildering? These questions have bearing on all life—human and nonhuman—today. How much mobility, and of what kinds, can mortal human creatures take? Arctic terns may be made of such stuff as to endure tens of thousands of migratory miles every year, flying some three hundred miles a day,[142] but what can humans stand, and under which conditions?

Furthermore, on a planet increasingly affected by the scale of human action and enterprise, what human mobility can this version of the world, with its regimes of flora and fauna, stand? As ecologist David S. Wilcove shows in his 2008 book *No Way Home: The Decline of the World's Great Animal Migrations,* ironically, human mobility and expansion are increasingly curtailing other animals' opportunities to be mobile. He describes the decline of migratory songbirds and butterflies; the threats to great mammal migrations of wildebeests, zebras, and more in Africa; and the serious threat to the North Atlantic right whales, among many other examples. These are migrations impeded on land, by sea, and in the air, Wilcove insists. Such changes are astonishingly massive, and it seems shameful to brush over them as I have just done in the space of two sentences. Such is the character of life in the present moment.

Mobility, it turns out then, is a limited resource, at least when viewed in the particular circumstances where it actually occurs. Contemporary human mobility is expensive in multiple senses—economic, social, environmental/ecological, and political. Again, just at the level of the ecological, Kolbert writes in *The Sixth Extinction* about the massive, probably unprecedented collapse of amphibian populations: amphibians are "the world's most endangered class of animals."[143] This collapse is being caused by a fungus (*Batrachochytrium dendrobatidis*, or Bd) almost certainly spread around the globe by humans, particularly human mobility that deliberately included frogs, unknown to be either infected or a threat. Kolbert points out, "Without being loaded by someone onto a boat or a plane, it would have been impossible for a frog carrying Bd to get from Africa to Australia or from North America to Europe. This sort of intercontinental reshuffling, which nowadays we find totally unremarkable, is probably unprecedented in the three-and-a-half-billion-year history of life."[144]

In light of such information, hastily naturalizing mobility as an absolute condition sounds like another humanist fantasy, an illusory dream. It risks blinding us to the many forms of dislocation, entrapment, or death experienced by humans and nonhumans alike, whether because traditional migratory patterns have been interrupted or because people cannot afford (or, often, cannot imagine how) to move. Instead of simply naturalizing movement, we need to interpret and practice it more carefully, with more rigor, and more pathos. We need to see mobility in the context of the historical development of transportation technologies, enabled by the massive, silent power of fossil fuels, which has forced human beings to become better at judging what kinds of mobility we should accept and facilitate.

To advocate an eco-cosmopolitanism responsibly, to encourage a persistently critical and reflective attitude, we might recognize the term as a kind of oxymoron. After all, "eco" traces back to the Greek word for "house," while "cosmopolitanism" suggests being an inhabitant of the cosmos, of no-place, or of everywhere, as per the epigraph of this chapter. Perhaps this double-bind should encourage us, like Friedrich Nietzsche, to imagine ourselves less as philosophers and more as story-tellers, thinkers, and poets. Posthumanism and related discourses suggest that the highest aims of philosophy are unattainable for humans, mortal creatures. Instead, our concepts must be relentlessly situated and recalibrated. Literary forms of meaning, in their insistent particularity, are especially well suited to these forms of understanding, so they, and more generally the humanities (or posthumanities), should be important tools for the Anthropocene and its challenges.

I mentioned above Gary Snyder's work as one model for these tasks. His engagement with the philosophy and practice of Asian Buddhism and affiliated intellectual traditions involves accenting how thinking about home moves in two directions in this way. Home often orients our moral desires, our ethics of care, and our compassion. In these passions of morality, though, we leave the homes of ourselves and our buildings; we disown them and share them and so become homeless, in a sense. This recognition of homelessness is a condition of our mutual vulnerability and of the openness of our selves. Home, rigorously understood, tends to work this way. It implies both a grounding for concern and an inescapable openness to a wider world. In his essay "The World and the Home," Homi K. Bhabha makes a similar point: "The unhomely is the shock of recognition of the world-in-the-home, the home-in-the-world."[145]

Summary of Chapters

Despite contemporary highbrow derision of homesickness, this book demonstrates that the feeling remains powerful and is visible everywhere in culture. Exploring this abjected terrain, I analyze the desire for place in a range of texts mostly published since World War II, largely literature but also film and, briefly, television. The chapters focus on the dynamics of identity and home in a place, or among the placed, and investigate the meaning of home for travelers and dislocated persons, or the displaced. Seizing on several recurrent tropes—including home on fire, home as an animal body, and home as absent—the chapters explore the sense of home as temporary, entrapping, or destructive, in addition to considering it as a figure for the reliable, the enabling, or the constructive. The point is not to reassert the value of a simple homesickness but rather to demonstrate its complex density of meaning, to recognize the strange, often nonhuman tenor of a robustly conceived homesickness. The argument casts ownership of both self and property into doubt in light of the recursive action of a selfhood that is always too late, always in pursuit of itself. This approach also turns the ostensibly national literature of the United States inside out, underscoring its status as varied and heterogeneous, as posthumanist. I emphasize the intimate alterity of the nonhuman, which haunts us with both its radical proximity—it is us—and its evasive otherness. In this uncanny realization of our deep imbrication in the nonhuman mesh of the world, I emphasize human weakness—to know, to be—that is also a compelling, valuable, and ineluctable openness to the world, an openness that we should actively cultivate in the Anthropocene.

The chapters move in sequence from the local to the planetary. I begin with a focus on the body in chapter 1, consider house and home in chapter 2, compare free and forced mobility in chapters 3 and 4, investigate shopping and homelessness in chapter 5, and address war in chapter 6. Despite this steadily widening scope, each chapter puts the local into active dialogue with the planetary. More specifically, chapter 1 first treats E. Annie Proulx's short story "The Half-Skinned Steer" as a haunting icon of the Anthropocene and then addresses the strange homecoming of her novel *The Shipping News.* Chapter 2 studies Marilynne Robinson's first novel, *Housekeeping,* and Peter Hedges's novel *What's Eating Gilbert Grape,* as well as the film made from the latter book, emphasizing the stories' resistance to entrapment-in-place. That resistance culminates in an effort to burn down the family homes, which I characterize as a dramatic rejection of prevailing ontologies and modes of life in the Anthropocene. Chapter 3 investigates not entrapment but the opposite danger: cosmopolitan mobility, overindulgence, and desire in relation to Hemingway. I first explore Hemingway's own mobility in life and its impact on his writing, then address his exploration of intimacy, language, and animality in *The Garden of Eden.*

Chapter 4 investigates the violent, forced mobility treated in Toni Morrison's *Beloved,* leading to Sethe's unspeakably horrible decision to kill her children in order to save them from slavery. Maternal care thereby becomes uncanny and unhomely; the novel's haunting motif emphasizes both the trauma of slavery and the problem of justice as an uncanny relation to the deceased and the not-yet-born. Chapter 5 investigates the contemporary practice of shopping, focusing especially on Walmart as an *unheimlich* home of the modern self. I read Novalee, the picaresque protagonist of Billie Letts's sentimental novel *Where the Heart Is,* camped illegitimately in a Walmart store, as a representation of this version of (dis)placed subjectivity, all the more so because of the pulpish character of the novel. I show that the novel demonstrates how the capitalist subject of choice is subtended by a subject of interests or, better, a subject who suffers. Chapter 6 investigates war as one of the most dramatic forces of dislocation, producing homesickness both for soldiers and for citizens who remain home, even those who play no direct role in conflict. Treating war writing by Ernest Hemingway, Tim O'Brien, Bobbie Ann Mason, and Annie Proulx, the chapter shows how the supercharged form of agency in war throws an equally long and dark shadow; after such agency, humans have difficulty recalibrating their sense of self. In this way, war creates a distinctively agrilogistical or anthropocenic homesickness.

1

Suffering in Our Animal Skins

Uncanny Embodiment, Wildness, and Mortal Place in Annie Proulx

> And all that distance Tin Head can see the raw meat of the head and the shoulder muscles and the empty mouth without no tongue open wide and its red eyes glaring at him, pure teetotal hate like arrows coming at him.
>
> —Annie Proulx, "The Half-Skinned Steer"

The house is one kind of home, to paraphrase Gary Snyder.[1] The body is another, and the two are interwoven. Much as Donna Haraway shows human life to be enfolded with the lives of other species and with our tools in *When Species Meet,* and as Cary Wolfe shows the importance of recognizing language as "the most fundamental prostheticity of all," our (prosthetic) homes are interwoven with our bodies.[2] Particular forms of embodiment impact the structures of homes—more obviously, children, the alter-abled, and the elderly all require coordination between their physical persons and their physical homes. But so do we all; physical structures reflect and inform everyone's embodiment. Homes also engage and impact the physical realities of climate, local ecology, global ecology, as well as cultural values, not least those about embodiment. A grassy suburban American backyard, with its tacit assumptions about how bodies should occupy space, is not only unequally available but unequally desirable. Further, much as an individual's body image is a near-ghost to the physical body,[3] our more general cultural images and meanings of the body haunt the actual body. The body is therefore another terrain of homesickness, on the one hand something we long to inhabit well, with familiarity, and on the other hand something always threatened by estrangement, sickness, and death.

The body in the discourse of cosmopolitanism is often either obscured entirely or generalized, understood as mobile, flexible, and transnational.[4] Yet I am insisting in this book that embodiment is the site of particularity and mortality.[5] Indeed, embodiment troubles the very metaphor of "site," which tends to render entities into abstractions, thereby effacing their particularity. Bodies *matter.* Without an embodied "naturecultural" practice of cosmopolitanism, the discursive effort means little; what we body forth is the test of our cultural ideas. Homes and bodies are fleshed-out knots of natureculture, to borrow Haraway's terminology,[6] and these knots are perishable and impermanent. In chapter 2, for instance, I explore how even the home itself, an icon of stability, can be subject to radical revisions, to transformation and destruction. Indeed, the stability of the home and the social position it signals is often precisely the problem: inhabitants are often trapped in place. "Burning Down the House," the title and subject of chapter 2, simultaneously evokes resistance to that entrapment and a traumatic recognition of the truth of entrapment, of weakness and mortality.

Most of Annie Proulx's fiction dramatizes human fallibility and weakness, often rendering them at once tragic and comic. For Proulx, human life is easily reduced to a "finger-snap,"[7] especially in contrast to the much larger time scales visible in landscapes, oceans, and so on. Proulx's stories thus often tell us something about what it is like to live in the age of the Anthropocene, when ostensibly fixed verities of human meaning have begun to waver, wobble, and collapse. In the Anthropocene, the activities of those finger-snaps aggregate hugely, to render the ostensible background—environment—unstable, and that disruption of environment then cycles back to human culture in a destabilizing feedback loop. In the Anthropocene, we are all homesick, more so than usual.

But homesickness is indeed the usual; subjectivity is precisely being haunted by a past that informs the present, a past that *haunts* partly because it remains *other,* even in retrospect, a past bigger than we are, more than we can own or control in our rational and deliberative subjectivity. *That is who we are.* This uncanny recognition, homesickness, is a ghost presence of the past that infiltrates and estranges the present, and in the next few pages, to establish the motif of this chapter, I conjure up a ghostly image or icon of that feeling from Annie Proulx: a castrated bull cow, partly killed and half-skinned, that rises again like a zombie and haunts the humans who have mutilated it.

The Half-Skinned Steer as an Icon of Homesickness

In her stunning Wyoming story "The Half-Skinned Steer," Proulx sketches the life of Mero, who in early adulthood escapes the claustrophobic world of his father's Wyoming ranch, only to be drawn back decades later by the inescapable fact of mortality. Proulx opens this story in her archly knock-down, abrupt, violent style, perfectly suited to her subject: "In the long unfurling of his life, from tight-wound kid hustler in a wool suit riding the train out of Cheyenne to geriatric limper in this spooled-out year, Mero had kicked down thoughts of the place where he began" (21). Like so many other migrants, Mero tries to repress memories of home; as a tough Wyoming cowboy by origin, he has "kicked down" those thoughts. But this machismo is haunted by a disavowed weakness. The kicking violence glosses masculine posturing as a cover for limited agency; the need for such repressive force bespeaks the power of those memories and of forces beyond our control, which we might rage against, like King Lear. In Proulx's story, those thoughts, ghostlike and strange as a half-skinned steer, do not stay down but rise again as a specter of death itself. That is the story's central plot device: Mero's *re-membering,* bit by bit, pieces of his Wyoming youth, all under the sign of a partly *dis-membered* animal. Proulx tells the story of his late-life return to Wyoming, persistently interrupting that narrative with Mero's intrusive and unbidden memories. Though Mero had "never circled back" to see his brother and father (21), in this story he finally returns, too late, to an uncanny home emptied of his deceased family. Mero's brother's funeral is the motivation: "He would see his brother dropped in a red Wyoming hole. That event could jerk him back; the dazzled rope of lightning against the cloud is not the downward bolt, but the compelled upstroke through the heated ether" (23). The figure is apt. The sheer natural reality of lightning is metonymic for another mysterious reality, that of life and death, and of events in general, of what happens to us beyond the relatively small sphere of subjective agency where we seem to master our lives. Lightning, and its capacity to "jerk," evokes the massive alterity of a world and reality we do not control: homesickness.

The story of the half-skinned steer is one part of Mero's memory, a story-within-the-story, told by his father's girlfriend years before. It emphasizes the strange, the uncontrolled, the inept, the bizarre, like a zombie version of story, or a strange ghost of ordinary narrative, of familiar human life and meaning. It is a gothically satirical revelation of human fallibility, this tale about Tin Head, a disabled man who, in his and his family's human animal need to eat, kills and begins skinning a steer. Partway through the job, Tin Head tires and "starts thinking about dinner," leaving the half-skinned steer on the ground after cutting out its tongue, "which is his favorite dish" (32). Not only does he leave the messy job of skinning incomplete, surrendering to his own appetite; it turns out Tin Head has failed to kill the steer. He discovers this fact after he has eaten "half his dinner" and taken a nap. When he returns to complete the skinning job, the steer is gone. All that is left is the tongue he had cut out (35).

In the initial logic of this story, Tin Head is a pathetic figure, embarrassing, slovenly, utterly distinct from Mero. In the girlfriend's words: "Tin Head never finished nothing he started, quit halfway through a job every time. Even his pants was half-buttoned so his wienie hung out. He was a mess with the galvy plate eating at his brain and his ranch and his family was a mess. But, she said. They had to eat, didn't they, just like anybody else?" (26–27). In this framework, by contrast, Proulx produces Mero, a man who rejects all of it—the meat-eating, the harsh Wyoming landscapes, the poverty and solitude that for Proulx are central to the actuality of the mythologized West. Mero escapes to a competent life in the eastern United States, where he had traveled widely, "made money," "got into local politics and out again without scandal," and made a success of himself, dreading the "bankrupt and ruined" status he was sure had seized upon the inhabitants of his original home, his father and brother (21). So he had stayed away.

But over the course of the story, as he is returning home to Wyoming, the very competent and able Mero displays more and more vulnerability, disability, and fallibility, partly due to his old age, a reality that awaits us all if we survive long enough.[8] By the story's end, Mero inhabits the place of Tin Head in a very specific sense: he too is staring at the eye of the half-skinned steer, as is the reader. The others—Tin Head, the steer—come home to us, as us. After dinner, seeing that the steer is gone, Tin Head goes looking for him, finding him tongueless in his trauma with "red eyes glaring at him, pure teetotal hate like arrows coming at him, and he knows he is done for and all his kids and their kids is done for, and that his wife is done for and that every one of her blue dishes has got to break, and the dog that licked the blood is done for, and the house where they lived has to blow away or burn up and every fly or mouse in it" (37). Tin Head imagines his utter vulnerability along this metonymic chain of kids, family, dishes, and houses on fire. The power of this image and this story so inhabits Mero that, by the close of Proulx's larger story, Mero himself is seeing that same "red eye" of the steer.

Despite Mero's understanding of himself as capable and successful, he cannot free himself from the disorienting force of this remote Wyoming ranch and all it represents. He remembers just enough of the ranch to feel confident when he returns but not enough to successfully navigate it, and at the story's end we expect he will die in the extreme weather event of a snowstorm. This *particular* ranch thus signifies his weakness, fallibility, and mortality. Mero and Tin Head share their disability in the face of a tough, mute, and traumatizing world, the Real, imaged by a creature whose gruesome condition is the result (and the representation) of their weakness and their accumulated errors. Disability, initially imaged only in Tin Head, becomes Mero's and, finally, the reader's and humanity's more generally.

This truth comes to Mero in stages over the course of the story. Driving back to Wyoming from Massachusetts, his mind is repeatedly jerked back to the past he wishes to forget. Mero's involuntary recollections seem driven by his physical and geographic position, reiterating the power of place to direct human thinking and action. Further, his memories of home are a sort of trauma, and as Cathy Caruth argues, that trauma cannot be easily controlled, revealing the limits of human agency more generally.[9] In this scenario, Mero gradually recalls this tale of the half-skinned steer told by his father's unnamed girlfriend—"now he couldn't remember her name" (23), in one of Mero's many surprising failures of competence. The girlfriend is "a teller of tales" (24) with a "convincing liar's voice" (26), and Proulx likens her appearance to that of a horse, "with her arched neck and horsy buttocks" (24). She gulps Everclear, bites her fingernails until they bleed, and plays the three men of the house—two brothers and their father—"like a deck of cards" (24). Drawing on and radically estranging the western U.S. cowboy register, Proulx describes Mero's youthful response to the story before Proulx finishes relating it: "Mero had thrashed all that ancient night, dreamed of horse breeding or hoarse breathing, whether the act of sex or bloody, cutthroat gasps he didn't know. The next morning he woke up drenched in stinking sweat, looked at the ceiling and said aloud, it could go on like this for some time" (25).

The girlfriend's provocation of this animalized and bizarre sexual desire—a kind of hyperrealism or surrealism—dramatically rewrites that feeling in the age of Photoshop and artificial beauty. The animalized horse/hoarse rhyme suggests a whole chain of human/animal associations and kindred selfhood, revolving around embodiment: breathing, sex, reproduction, weakness, and violence. Mero admits to himself the deeper truth about why he left the ranch all those years before: "He'd wanted a woman of his own without scrounging the old man's leftovers." Mero has to leave, then, not because he is so capable and cosmopolitan but because he is weak before the forces of ordinary animal desire and loneliness. Further, driving to Wyoming to attend his brother's funeral in the story's present tense, Mero allows that "what he wanted to know now, tires spanking the tar-filled road cracks and potholes, funeral homburg sliding on the backseat, was if Rollo [his brother] had got the girlfriend away from the old man, thrown a saddle on her and ridden off into the sunset" (25).

Like other characters in Proulx's Wyoming stories, this unnamed girlfriend reverses many cowboy stereotypes. Although female, she dominates the men in the house. And like Proulx, she delivers a dark truth of Wyoming life. She distills the isolation that is the reality of much cowboy living; the oddly Oedipal tensions she evokes in the three men are as much a result of Wyoming's wide-open spaces as of anything else. Her horsiness animalizes humans. Her presence haunting Mero's memory in this story is thus a return of the repressed in terms of animality, sexuality, geography, and mortality, all at once. Her compelling and strange liar's tale comes back to Mero in pieces over the course of the story, and the tale ends up braiding itself into Mero's own life story and, to the extent that Proulx's story is a success, into our culture's larger narrative.

In this story, then, human mortality, animality, and imperfection drive the main character away *and* require his return. Mero can be seen to stand in for the histories of modernity and humanism, with their faith in human progress and reason. And his failures cue parallel histories of class inequalities, environmental crisis, animal abuse, and so on, histories central to the Anthropocene and the posthumanist era. In this story, and in the many others investigated in this book, these concerns center around this relationship to home I am calling homesickness. While the Enlightenment has tended to privilege the public over the private, the cosmos over the ecos, and the doing over the witnessing, homesickness unsettles and even sometimes reverses those binaries in underscoring our situated, private, passive mortality.

By implication, the steer at story's end is also stalking and staring at the reader. Like Mero, like Tin Head, we are hard-pressed fully to escape our roots, however hard we work to become cosmopolitan or eco-cosmopolitan. Instead, our dreams of eco-cosmopolitanism are haunted by the home we think we escape. Indeed, we are always already haunted by the lost place, since even before we leave we have rendered it into an idea and an image;[10] we have thus simplified home, mobilized it, and even made it fungible perhaps in order to facilitate a thinking and a decision that permits us to depart. This is what thinking is, in part: a rendering, a reducing, and an orienting that in its very action sets up ghosts. Thinking, decisions, consciousness reiterate the paradoxical gap of self-consciousness that makes a homesickness of selfhood. We ghost our place by thinking about it. It then spooks us into leaving and haunts us once we have gone, making it uncanny and *unheimlich.* In this story's metaphorics, then, the quirky and distinctive locale of Wyoming is synecdoche for each person's limitations and localness, or parochialism. Formally, the broken-up, gradual recall of this tale-within-a-tale over the course of Proulx's story reiterates the difficulty of its content and import. It cannot be faced all at once.

As a kind of rewritten myth of the West, then, this story-within-a-story functions as an example or synecdoche of *unheimlich* realities, of big, unnerving truths. In this and in many of Proulx's Wyoming stories, her aesthetic of strangeness sorts well with posthumanist perspectives. For instance, Timothy Clark suggests in "Nature, Post Nature" that the age of the Anthropocene lends new significance to art and narrative that underscores surprising and "counterintuitive" understandings.[11] He notes, "What seems reasonable, commonsensical, rational self-interest and purposiveness on the scale of an individual life may present the picture, en masse, of humanity as an unprecedented primate superorganism, which acts out ultimately destructive laws of ecology and population dynamics that both result from and in many ways override the myriad seemingly free decisions of people's day-to-day affairs of life within the individual horizon of the 'manifest image.'"[12]

For Clark, as for Timothy Morton in *Hyperobjects,* the Anthropocene requires a radically wider conception of time, something more like, Clark suggests, Gary Snyder's attempt "to encompass a view of human life from the Pleistocene until the late twentieth century" in *Mountains and Rivers without End.* For Clark, working at such scales "serves to highlight the provisional, finite mode of our knowledge."[13] Proulx's "The Half-Skinned Steer" is a particularly vivid treatment of such ideas. Proulx compresses a lifetime into a story about death, drastically reducing the import of our three-score years and ten, even contracting the complex effects of history into her image of a lightning strike. Our lives are like the inhuman effects of the weather. Mero's sweaty, disoriented weakness in the night after hearing his father's girlfriend's story evokes broader human responses to our own uncanny news of the Anthropocene, which is itself a paradoxical sign of human imperfection. Our very ability to impose our sense of order on the world has generated this massive form of disorder; or so it looks to us and to other creatures who rely on the recent version of Earth's climate—from a broader, inhuman, and non-Earthly perspective, climate change really does not matter. Like Mero, we might want to escape to Massachusetts, so to speak, and to a regime of healthful living, but larger forces—as in lightning—are at work on us.

Like Mero, and like Sabrina Warner discussed in my preface, we live in the midst of the powerful story that comes to us fitfully, being too strange and huge to see all of it at once. I argue in this chapter that Proulx's short story, and much of her fiction, demonstrates these disorienting realities of life on Earth, as though this familiar rock in the solar system were all a new wilderness to us, an uncanny home, a place we hardly know at all. We are haunted by this awareness as this chapter, and *Homesickness* as a whole, is haunted by Proulx's story of the half-skinned steer, and by the steer itself, a twice-deformed animal zombie, a victim, and a sign or an icon of posthumanism. Its very existence as "steer" is agrilogistic, reiterating the history of agriculture and human partnerships with, and violence against, other animals. The steer also evokes the strangeness of our own bodies, utterly intimate, the very stuff of ourselves, yet also uncanny partly because they are mortal, the classic sign or proof of our human limitations.[14]

Wildness, the Not-Me, and the Uncanny: Situating Constructionism

Homesickness and the bittersweet appeal of idiosyncratic places are constant themes in Proulx's work. They appear, for instance, in her novel *The*

Shipping News, awarded the Pulitzer Prize and the National Book Award.[15] There, as in many of her Wyoming stories published in a series of books (*Close Range, Bad Dirt,* and *Fine Just the Way It Is*), human weakness—and human value—are revealed in wild places, places that have not been entirely human-dominated or made cosmopolitan.[16] An essay collection edited by Alex Hunt, *The Geographical Imagination of Annie Proulx: Rethinking Regionalism,* centers on this conflict between the global and the local.[17] In his introduction to the book, Hunt argues that Proulx's approach exposes the "ragged edges of the Real," quoting Cornel West for this characterization.[18] Hunt compellingly shows that Proulx interrupts the mythology of western American spaces and so offers a point of resistance to the postmodern, capitalist ethos, very much akin to the argument of *Homesickness.* Further, Hunt's point that regionalism cannot rescue characters from their feeling of homesickness is also key to this chapter, though my reading of questions of home in a posthumanist framework, underscoring human weakness, leads to different emphases. Most especially: I show that Proulx's characters must come to terms with their weak animality. In other words, the at-least-partial geographical determinism often exhibited in Proulx's texts intimately connects to human animality, our inability to escape several realities: our bodies, our basic needs, and the locality and particular histories of our perceptions and perceptive systems. That is homesickness in this book's sense.

At stake in these texts and in many cosmopolitan debates is the general relationship between distinctive regions and globalizing forces. This tension can be framed in various ways in addition to the local and the global: the country versus the city, the "developed" versus the "undeveloped," and so on. But the long-standing discourse opposing wilderness to civilization is particularly appropriate to Proulx's work, since wilderness is an abiding interest of hers (made manifest again in her newest novel, *Barkskins*).[19] But what exactly do I mean by "wilderness," especially in light of the significant and often-compelling criticism the idea has received? Two large collections of essays edited by J. Baird Callicot and Michael P. Nelson offer many examples of that criticism: *The Great New Wilderness Debate* and its follow-up, *The Wilderness Debate Rages On.*[20] Additionally, prominent thinkers, including William Cronon ("The Trouble with Wilderness"), Annette Kolodny (*The Lay of the Land*), and more recently Stephanie Rutherford (*Governing the Wild*), have explored problems with the wilderness idea.[21] These critics rightly decry a series of grave problems that attend the wilderness model:

indigenous peoples' displacement, imperialism, the problematic retrenchment of the nature/culture divide, the naturalization of masculine violence, and much more. A number of wilderness critics recommend other metaphors or figures for naming nonhuman nature. Timothy Morton argues for the term "the mesh" to describe nature.[22] Another common suggestion is that we think of nature as a kind of garden.[23]

However, a case can be made for a revised notion of wilderness that registers criticisms like those mentioned above. Indeed, in this chapter I argue that Proulx's conception of wilderness does exactly that. But why take the effort to preserve the word "wilderness"? Most essentially because the wilderness tradition foregrounds the radical otherness of places and of the nonhuman more generally. The wilderness tradition reminds us that our notions of human subjectivity are limited, and it offers us a route into criticizing those notions,[24] in keeping with the work of posthumanist thinkers like Morton, Wolfe, and so on. Central to these scholars' work and to the wilderness tradition is what we today could call a critique of the excesses of constructionist thinking, which can tend to turn everything into an artifact of human beings. In that sense, the version of "wilderness" I am advocating resembles the one that Cronon defends, when he insists, quoting Gary Snyder, that there is a wildness everywhere, not just in places formally designated "wilderness areas."[25] Similarly, object-oriented ontology and other new materialisms have done much to bring such human and nonhuman wildness into focus, while the Anthropocene clarifies the wildness in the world even in more familiar places, as we recognize the limits of human control over climate and environment. In this sense, "wilderness" simply names reality (Reality?), understood richly, its strangeness, its queerness, if you like.[26]

Although the tradition of American wilderness writing often seems dominated by masculinist individuation and self-assertion, a parallel tradition of wilderness writing—by women and men—emphasizes how wilderness experience exposes the weakness of the individual human, from Mary Rowlandson to John Muir to Marilynne Robinson, and including Proulx. In many cases these two threads—individualism and weakness—are woven together in the same text, and the sense of exposure to a powerful world offers important orientation, corrective, and perspective. Proulx's texts offer a compelling counterpoint to some criticisms of wilderness discourse, including Timothy Morton's recent arguments. Morton and others point out that ideas of American wilderness are constructed and are beholden to a particular and problematic historical moment in modernity. Morton's critique in *The Ecological Thought* is especially cogent: "In the idea of pristine wilderness, we can make out the mirror image of private property: Keep off the grass, Do Not Touch, Not for Sale. Nature was a special kind of private property, without an owner, exhibited in a specially constructed art gallery. The gallery was Nature itself, revealed through visual technology in the eighteenth century as 'picturesque'—looking like a picture."[27] Even more trenchantly, Morton adds, "Wilderness areas are giant, abstract versions of the products hanging in mall windows."[28]

While the wilderness idea is clearly a human construction in a sense, understood through particular historical technologies and habits, the notion of constructionism in Morton's account here, as in Cronon's influential earlier essay "The Trouble with Wilderness," risks effacing the nonhuman, especially in the hands of more full-throated constructionists. There are a number of other approaches in ecocritical writing that adjust against this danger. In *Writing for an Endangered World,* for instance, Lawrence Buell instead advocates a kind of "mutual constructionism with the physical environment (both natural and human-built) shaping in some measure the cultures that in some measure continually refashion it."[29] Similarly, in *When Species Meet,* Haraway advances her notion of companion species, which refigures our ideas of materiality and life, "retying some of the knots of ordinary multispecies living on earth."[30] That book mostly concerns relationships among organisms, what she calls "critters,"[31] but her emphasis on the complex interrelations of companion species resonates with Buell's phrase. For Haraway, "To be one is always to *become with* many."[32] To think of life as a kind of multispecies knot in a complex material world is to revise the social constructionist tradition in a serious way. It is also a figure of speech appropriate to this chapter's treatment of Annie Proulx's novel *The Shipping News,* with its main character, Quoyle, and its metaphorics of knots.

Perhaps even more fittingly, Jane Bennett's new materialist work also engages with and complicates the constructionist tradition. Opening *Vibrant Matter: A Political Ecology of Things,* she notes stages in the social constructionist work that followed upon Michel Foucault's death in 1984: "The initial insight was to reveal how cultural practices produce what is experienced as the 'natural,' but many theorists also insisted on the material recalcitrance of such cultural productions."[33] Her book likewise displays "the negative power or recalcitrance of things," but she adds to that idea their "positive, productive power."[34] For Bennett,

> The idea of thing power bears a family resemblance to . . . what Henry David Thoreau called the Wild or that uncanny presence that met him in the Concord woods and atop Mount Ktaadn and also resided in/as that monster called the railroad and that alien called his Genius. Wildness was a not-quite-human force that addled and altered human and other bodies. It named an irreducibly strange dimension of matter, an *out-side*.[35]

Inquiries into wilderness and wildness, flawed though they sometimes are, engage an outside. These traditions investigate uncanny experiences in places like Ktaadn, but, Bennett underscores, wildness is also a mode of experience available in many places, beyond those commonly seen as "wilderness." In other words, there is a hesitation here over terminology. Thoreau refers to this general notion, as Bennett reports, as the "Wild," and Gary Snyder uses the term in much the same way in *The Practice of the Wild.* He argues that wilderness has shrunk drastically in the United States, for instance, but that "wildness is not limited to the 2 percent formal wilderness areas. Shifting scales, it is everywhere: ineradicable populations of fungi, moss, mold, yeasts, and such that surround and inhabit us. Deer mice on the back porch, deer bounding across the freeway, pigeons in the park, spiders in the corners."[36] He goes on to include "our bodies," language, and many forms of social order as legible in terms of the wild.[37] In light of these ideas, the distinction between the wild and the wilderness begins to blur. From the perspectives of new or vital materialism, with an eye on recognizing the uncanny attributes of the Real in the age of the Anthropocene, everything can look a little like wilderness. For this reason, I find a fissure in Morton's work between the ideas in slightly earlier texts such as *Ecology without Nature* and *The Ecological Thought,* and the object-oriented ontology turn he makes in *Realist Magic, Hyperobjects,* and *Dark Ecology.*[38]

In light of such ideas, unlike Morton, I am reluctant simply to reject the whole tradition of writing about wilderness and the wild. Instead, that tradition can be aligned with ideas of hyperobjects, with uncanny matter, with radical rethinking of human selfhood. To do so requires more attention to, not dismissal of, the way such ideas as wilderness get "constructed."

Posthumanism is one context in which to do so. As noted in the introduction, Cary Wolfe's scholarship (especially *What Is Posthumanism?* and *Critical Environments*), building from Niklas Luhmann's structuralist theory, reminds us that to understand how observation works, we must think structurally, a point insisted on by Morton as well.[39] Luhmann shows that every observational system has a constitutive blind spot, a structuring principle that permits the system to work. He underscores that this blind spot is only visible from the perspective of another system.[40] That account describes how criticisms of wilderness discourse work. Scholars use the framework of another discourse to view wilderness discourse and thereby can produce a critique. But the reverse procedure can also be undertaken. Wilderness discourse, and others like it, permits us to see the blind spots of *constructionist* discourse, blind spots that are less clear to those working within it.

Most particularly, the core assumption of constructionist discourse is that every observation is created; it relies on an observer who is always already immersed in a cultural system that structures what he or she sees. That recognition is crucial. But one of the core assumptions of wilderness discourse, which is also crucial, is that every observation involves an inhuman *not-me*, an observed that is radically different from the observer. Luhmann uses the distinction "system/environment" to name these two domains.[41] Wilderness or wildness discourse reveals the otherness, the alterity of the environment; constructionist discourse helps us recognize that, in being perceived, alterity or environment is always "constructed" by a system. Both approaches offer useful observations, not final truths. That is, Luhmann's systems approach requires that we see each truth claim as an observation by a system, always subject to a new observation from a different observing system that can destabilize it. The debates about wilderness demonstrate how that framework functions, as exchanges among scholars tend to focus more on one dimension or another. One side emphasizes the system (the constructionists); the other side emphasizes the environment (wilderness thinkers, as well as new materialists and others, including Morton—sometimes—with his notion of hyperobjects).

Proulx's fiction, with its relentless exposure and criticism of human vanity, foregrounds the otherness of the not-me. For her, wilderness, or probably more accurately, *wildness,* seems to be a basic condition of the material world, visible everywhere, in towns and in the backcountry, to echo Gary Snyder's account of this term, noted above. In Proulx's hands the confrontation with wild landscapes demonstrates human weakness, humility, and especially mortality, upending conventional accounts of (often masculinist) agency and human identity. The reality of death, itself an unknown and unknowable reality, is exemplary. Indeed, the wild otherness of death resembles the otherness of wilderness, and acknowledging both requires new and comparatively humble conceptions of human agency and selfhood.

Two caveats: First, to be clear, I do not intend here merely a defense of familiar ideas of wilderness. I agree that this concept and its history need to be shaken up and viewed afresh. Thus "homesickness" is another way to name the disorientation that people often experience in "wilderness," a disorientation that is also a reorientation at a much different—often larger—scale. Along this line, Rob Nixon, in his discussion of Abdelrahman Munif's quintet of novels *Cities of Salt,* makes a similar point about a translation problem in rendering those books into English. Munif had titled the series "*al-Tih,*" Arabic for something like "wilderness." That is, in fact, how the phrase is often translated, Nixon writes. But, Nixon goes on to explain, the phrase "refers not merely to wilderness as place, but to wilderness as an existential human condition, the state of being lost in the wilderness."[42] This is a fine summary of much of what I mean to evoke with the word "homesickness."

Second, in many ways Proulx's work is very much consonant with Morton's approach to matters of gender, human ability and agency, and so on, but in Morton's enthusiastic exposure of the particularity of the wilderness idea, its historical imbrications and therefore limitations, he risks the fantasy that by criticizing and exposing historical trends, we can make ourselves entirely free of them. Bennett reminds us that this is not so easy, that "constructed" realities are recalcitrant and even agential. The wilderness is one kind of place, following one notion of value, yes, as Morton notes, but it is an abuse of language (to borrow a phrase from Emmanuel Levinas) to call wilderness an "art gallery," as Morton does.[43] That terminology renders whole regimes of life and whole landscapes into passive clay. They are influenced by, not made by, humanity. In other words, and in contrast to the primary orientation of much of the rest of Morton's work, his account of wilderness areas tends to reify a (masculinist) human agency, rendering humanity as the great romantic artist who molds, say, all of Yellowstone into a work of art. To accept such terminology, we would, at the very least, need a radical, posthumanist, vital materialist reworking of our conception of "art." But still, even to call Yellowstone a co-creation of humans and many lifeforms, and material forms, would grossly underestimate the roles of nonhumans in that place.

Embodied Homesickness in *The Shipping News*

Proulx's writing has the opposite orientation, shrinking the meaning of human life radically. *The Shipping News* presents places that seem to dominate the humans who live in them. Although neither of the book's primary settings is a wilderness as we conventionally understand the term, both are wild insofar as they defy human agency and control. Proulx's protagonist Quoyle is himself an embodiment of humbler ideas about humanity. From the first, Proulx calls attention to his unusual physique. The novel's second sentence describes him as "hive-spangled, gut roaring with gas and cramp" (1). As a child he had been taller and bigger than all his classmates. He is "a great damp loaf of a body" (2). His body seems to dominate his subjectivity, rather than the other way around—something that is truer for everyone than we commonly admit. Quoyle is, then, by his own physical nature, an outcast from the start. Proulx continues, "At the university he took courses he couldn't understand, humped back and forth without speaking to anyone, went home for weekends of excoriation. At last he dropped out of school and looked for a job, kept his hand over his chin" (3).

In the space of two pages, Proulx has rammed through this brutal account of Quoyle's early life, the characteristic brevity of her style, peppered with staccato sentence fragments, reinforcing the harshness of a world that does not care about the likes of a Quoyle. Proulx's strikingly harsh and distinctive linguistic style, used to tell Quoyle's story of transformation, itself evokes his otherness, his strangeness, his withdrawn individual status (in the language of object-oriented ontology). The prickly, "kinked," idiosyncratic craft of literary language renders *unheimlich* this human medium for communication, which, from an Enlightenment perspective, might otherwise have smoothly, fluently revealed an idealized, perfectly proportioned, rational man (yes, man, conventionally, alas).[44] But from a posthumanist perspective, Quoyle's bodily, physical strangeness is also an example of a larger reality for every human being. As Donna Haraway reports, in a touchstone notion for posthumanism, "90 percent of the cells [of the human body] are filled with the genomes of bacteria, fungi, protists, and such, some of which play in a symphony necessary to my being alive at all."[45] As I noted in the introduction, new findings suggest that the proportion is closer to fifty-fifty,[46] but in any case, we are all much stranger in person than we commonly imagine.

Proulx bashes Quoyle into and out of friendships, jobs, and romance—a rapid-fire approach to plotting and temporality that she intensifies in many of her Wyoming stories, as noted above and explored further at the close of this chapter. Quickly she has Quoyle meeting his wife, Petal Bear, whose interest in him lasts the space of *one page* in the book. Petal Bear begins her marital infidelities after a single happy month and is indifferent to Quoyle's persistent love during the marriage's "six kinked years of suffering" (13). Nonetheless, they have the children Bunny and Sunshine, whom Petal, their own mother, literally ceases to recognize, in one of Proulx's signature moments of black comedy. Quoyle thus complicates conventional gender norms by acting as the caretaker of his children, and in being the vulnerable emotional partner in his failed marriage. His seeming "weakness," although partly personal flaw, is also an example of human fallibility. Most any relationship studied closely, with its strange fluctuations and embarrassments, reveals human imperfection.

Quoyle's mess of a life is equated with the mess of a place he and his family at first inhabit, what Proulx calls "bedraggled Mockingburg," New York. Proulx's fictionalized name "Mockingburg" already suggests what her description makes explicit, that this place is a satirical cousin to the many American towns consisting largely of strip malls and asphalt, wrought by the dominance of the automobile and by laissez faire planning. She describes it as

> a place in its third death. Stumbled in two hundred years from forest and woodland tribes, to farms, to a working-class city of machine tool and tire factories. A long recession emptied the downtown, killed the malls. Factories for sale. Slum streets, youths with guns in their pockets. . . . Who knew where the people went? Probably California. (10–11)

This place is as haphazard as Quoyle's marriage. The description of capitalist development from the forest to the present is a kind of slow-motion decimation, a stumbling, a "third death," which demonstrates anything but the optimistic perpetual improvement that is the fantasy of certain visions of economic change (and which reiterates how important a rhetoric of death is to Proulx's work). Proulx's Mockingburg stands in for many such places across the American/Canadian rust belt, from Michigan to Quebec to Upstate New York.

But Proulx quickly springs Quoyle and his daughters from this dystopia to go to a better place, for a better life. This happens for horrible reasons, though, when Quoyle's wife, just before dying in a car crash, sells *her own girls* for $7,000. Then Quoyle's parents in Newfoundland commit suicide. These absurdly dark plot turns reinforce Proulx's harsh take on the course of typical human lives. The children, fortunately, are recovered before they come to the worst of what their purchaser intended for them, and Quoyle finally brings his family to the notably wild, remote, and harsh place of his roots, Killick Claw, Newfoundland, where he starts work as a newspaper reporter. There, in order to make a new life for his family, Quoyle must first confront his unsettling heritage, the sickness at the root of his identity. Proulx explains, making this point early in the book, that "Quoyle hated the thought of an incestuous, fit-prone, seal killing child for a grandfather, but there was no choice" (25).

Going home, oftentimes, is not easy, and this difficult life is epitomized in Proulx's descriptions of Newfoundland as a harsh place. Indeed, the character of the place and people's lives in it are mutually informative. That is, Newfoundland and other such wild places more sharply reveal realities of human life everywhere. A key moment of the book demonstrates how Proulx uses the particularities of this place to reveal wider truths about human life, a cosmopolitan gesture in a sense but also one that undermines the confidence of cosmopolitanism: Quoyle finishes one of his newspaper stories and goes out for a walk. Soon, he works his way out to the water line: "At last the end of the world, a wild place that seemed poised on the lip of the abyss. No human sign, nothing, no ship, no plane, no animal, no bird, no bobbing trap marker nor buoy. As though he stood alone on the planet. The immensity of sky roared at him and instinctively he raised his hands to keep it off" (209). This place wholly resists human frames of interpretation or activity, with a sky that "roars" and the long, negative sentence revealing the place by telling what it lacks. Proulx's sentence fragments reinforce this sense. The writing style is studded with the recalcitrance of the world.

Quoyle's thoughts of this place, on the same page, similarly emphasize the radically inhuman power of the sea and ice, which dwarfs human presence.

> These waters, thought Quoyle, haunted by lost ships, fishermen, explorers gurgled down into sea holes as black as a dog's throat. Bawling into salt broth. Vikings down the cracking winds, steering through fog by the polarized light of sun-stones. The Inuit in skin boats, breathing, breathing, rhythmic suck of frigid air, iced paddles dipping, spray freezing, sleek back rising, jostle, the boat torn, spiraling down. Millennial bergs from the glaciers, morbid, silent except for waves breaking on their flanks, the deceiving sound of shoreline where there was no shore. Foghorns, smothered gun reports along the coast. Ice welding land to sea. Frost smoke. Clouds mottled by reflections of water holes in the plains of ice. The glare of ice erasing dimension, distance, subjecting senses to mirage and illusion. A rare place. (209)

In this account the sea swallows human life in toto—Vikings, Inuit, and modern-day fishermen—a much more drastic compression of time than even Quoyle's personal history early in the novel. This temporal compression intensifies the other disorienting, inhuman effects of a harsh northern landscape on multiple physical senses: the visual confusion of the sea-land boundaries, the muffled sounds, the taste of salt, the intense cold, all of which is underscored by this final fragmentary tag, "a rare place," an ostentatiously bare understatement—as if language could only crudely gesture. Such a water- and landscape is kin to the human characters of Proulx's book, who move similarly through liminal regions of new marriage, deception, loss, and rebirth, surviving (or, perhaps, holding form) haphazardly. The key attributes of being human are interpretable in nonhuman terms, like all are merely material realities going through their changes. It is an exemplary, posthumanist approach to literary meaning and style in the Anthropocene. Proulx culminates her account of the harshness of human life in a harsh world when Quoyle glimpses a dead man floating in a yellow coat in the rough water just below his perch above the sea.

Here again, Quoyle does not inhabit some comfortable observer's remove. This is not ironic postmodernism, not here in the real world. He quickly boards a boat, hurrying to tell someone about the dead man. Proulx writes, "In ten minutes, . . . he knew he'd made a mistake" (210). His boat is quickly capsized, and he finds himself bloodied in rough and frigid water, rising and falling in the waves "like a chip," as Proulx perfectly puts it (211). He is pressed by the current toward the very place he saw the dead man, a journey both literal and metaphoric as Quoyle grows fatally chilled. But just as he slips into the classic final descent to hypothermic fatality, thinking wistfully of sleep, he is snagged from the waters by a local, Jack Buggit, who is said to have an instinct for locating drowning people, having saved many near fatalities. Quoyle is then brought to the home of Buggit and his wife.

Ah, home as safety. Yes, but the domestic space is heavily inflected by the life of the harsh sea, with its decorations including "designs of lace waves and floe ice, whelk shells and sea wrack, the curve of lobster feelers, the round knot of cod eye," and so on (213). This moment in the narrative, demonstrating the sea's hazard, colors the meaning of more familiar objects like shells, estranging them from their sometimes too domesticated semiotics. Here they are tinged with strangeness, and with the threat of otherness and death, even in the house.

This house, where Quoyle finds his restoration, is Newfoundland in miniature in this book. The home in the immediate scene—and Newfoundland more generally in the book—restore him to life, but in both, the overwhelming otherness of a harsh world looms. The life of the ocean permeates the domestic space like the moisture in the Newfoundland air. The home, soaked in the radically inhuman strangeness of the sea and its life, is uncanny: homesickness, the strange alterity right at the center of subjective space. Human lives shrink in importance against the inhumanity of Earth's wildness, a point, I have suggested, that is strongly reinforced by Proulx's characteristic black humor and her exceedingly rapid, seemingly indifferent movement through descriptions of her characters' lives.

Complex Homesickness in *The Shipping News*

However, in Proulx's largely satirical and harshly realistic body of work, Quoyle's ultimate quiet happiness is somewhat exceptional. He has come home to a place where he and his family can live decently, and by the conclusion, Quoyle begins to enjoy experience itself. Proulx's description of his happiness is as quirky and idiosyncratic as the place that facilitates it: "Quoyle experienced moments in all colors, uttered brilliancies, paid attention to the rich sounds of waves counting stones, he laughed and wept, noticed sunsets, heard music in rain, said I do" (336). Happiness becomes possible in large measure by paying attention, using the senses to contact the world. This thinking differs significantly from a progressivist and aspirational humanism familiar to most of us; like Newfoundland itself, this happiness is more elemental. But these final three clichés—sunsets, music in rain, and marriage—also reiterate Proulx's comic and satirical notion of reduced possibilities in human life, a point reiterated by the novel's final sentence: "And it may be that love sometimes occurs without pain or misery" (337). Elemental experiences can make us happy, but only maybe, sometimes.

Critics differ in their views of Proulx's treatment of human life and possible happiness, revealing distinct interpretive assumptions. For instance, in an interesting essay, Fiona Polack faults the ending for even its trace of human contentment. Polack otherwise celebrates Proulx's consistent exposure of the uncanny in Quoyle's homecoming.[47] On the other hand, Jennifer Denise Ryan argues, in editor Alex Hunt's summary, that Quoyle "overcomes disability, and its social stigma, through his immersion in place-based labor."[48] These perspectives value opposite elements of the book, and I want to suggest that neither of them quite does justice to it, due to their critical frameworks. To make the uncanny an absolute value, as Polack does, ignores the real changes in Quoyle's life, changes underscored by Ryan. Quoyle's life has genuinely improved, and that improvement makes a difference. But it strikes me as overstatement to claim, as Ryan does, that Quoyle "overcomes disability." These two approaches rely on sets of critical assumptions—that the uncanny conflicts with happiness, or, conversely, that disability should be understood as something to "overcome"—that distract us from some of the nuances of Proulx's work. These nuances can appear more fully in a different critical apparatus. Although Quoyle does find a place as a worker and community member in Newfoundland, Proulx also insists on the weak and marginal position of human identity even in this relatively ideal situation for Quoyle. He has come home in both good *and* bad senses, evincing what I am calling this peculiar kind of homesickness, in which the desire to inhabit a known place is mixed with awareness of the faults and weaknesses of one's ancestry, home geography, and selfhood. This is mortal life.

Hunt, discussing resignation to fate, and determinism and possibilism, raises questions about an emphasis on "overcoming," an approach more akin to this chapter's.[49] Proulx's account of human selfhood is not triumphalist, even if it includes small improvements. Immersion in place through labor, though valuable, should not reify the excessively agential human self, the "overcoming" subject. This is one of the fundamental arguments presented by Derrida in his critique of ability, when he unpacks the importance of Jeremy Bentham's question about animals, "Can they suffer?" which orients my argument throughout this book.[50] As Derrida explains, "The question is disturbed by a certain *passivity.* It bears witness, manifesting already, as question, the response that testifies to a sufferance, a passion, a not-being-able. The word *can* [pouvoir] changes sense and sign here."[51] In Proulx, similarly, inhabiting a region exposes a person; Quoyle can dwell in Newfoundland, but that includes a not-being-able in the face of a harsh, wild place. He must come to terms with that reality; inhabitation also involves suffering. "Overcoming" ice and death is not possible.

There are additional reasons for caution about the "overcoming" reading. Quoyle does find a relatively decent job in Newfoundland, Ryan's "place-based labor," but just how able does that make him? He does not—cannot—overcome other large realities that impinge on his work, such as global commerce. Marxist critic David Harvey reminds us that the local is often deeply infused with global capital and other forms of international activity.[52] Similarly, Ursula Heise insists on the need for a planetary approach to environmental problems, criticizing the "self sufficiency" dream in regionalist movements.[53] Disability studies, animal studies, regionalist studies, class studies, and others: all reveal how the independent, self-sufficient subject is a fantasy, and often a very harmful one. Proulx's skepticism and irony are thus incisive reminders of human weakness, the "sickness" dimension of homesickness, which checks against notions of a triumphalist subjectivity.

But to be clear: I am not arguing that Quoyle's place-centered labor regime is undesirable. I am claiming that we need a both/and approach here. Assuming a regional identity and a more stable life are helpful steps that, ideally, should be accompanied by a cosmopolitan awareness driven, in part, by recognizing individual weakness and vulnerability. Nobody, really nobody, goes it alone in this world. Or, to use the register emphasized by Ulrich Beck and employed by Heise: we need awareness of shared global risk.[54] The feeling of complex homesickness involves both of these sensibilities—the desire to have a real and distinctive cultural identity and the desire to recognize shared planetary identity.

Ryan's argument about overcoming is useful here to further demonstrate how a posthumanist reading approach leads in different directions than her more familiar humanist interpretive procedures. For instance, Ryan notes that Quoyle's ability to listen leads him to "success as a newspaper editor."[55] Ryan's accent here is more on "ability" and "success"; my accent is more on what this particular achievement means in a larger sense: listening is a kind of homesickness. It is a passive form of action, or it is an action that unsettles our ideas of action, much as Derrida argues that suffering changes our notions of selfhood. Listening essentially produces a place, as if out of nowhere, where someone else can "produce" themselves. The character of such exchanges reiterates how a homesickness is at the core of selfhood—we make ourselves, in such cases, in others' ears.[56] We are not already whole ourselves, but we must wish to make ourselves coherent to the others to be coherent to ourselves. Wolfe, discussing Ralph Waldo Emerson, refers to this structure of identity as a kind of "active *passivity,*" a selfhood focused on "reception" of the not-me but one that still requires a kind of active engagement.[57]

Ryan goes on to show how Quoyle "becomes a successful narrative agent" through his labor.[58] Again, this is important as far as it goes, but in light of posthumanist homesickness, we must also track the ways in which this very landscape that enables Quoyle's rise to prominence and community membership mocks and estranges the humans who inhabit it. In that frame, Quoyle's labor in this book appears as a cryptic form of figuration and self-presentation, like Proulx's prose, a scratching on paper that is deeply ironized by the setting and its harshness. Indeed, as I suggested about the story-within-the-story of the half-skinned steer, the very nature of narrative comes into question here when we consider Quoyle's trajectory. To the extent that Quoyle's life has improved, we have a standard narrative of growth and development. But that narrative depends essentially on place, and place is clearly shown here to disturb and upset human lives as well. Thus, to adequately understand Proulx's work, especially for its posthumanist effects, we need both recognition of human fallibility and weakness *and* allowance that some types of human life are preferable to other types. In other words, we need both valences of homesickness, of the desire for place: a hope to have a meaningful life and a recognition of uncanniness and frailty.

Ryan recognizes that some regionalist texts can be understood to disrupt the familiar narratives of subjectivity. For Ryan, this resistance to plotting is a sign that a character like Quoyle needs to resist abuse and neglect, to instead make himself a "citizen-subject."[59] True enough, though I reiterate the opposite point too: A clearer focus on place can tend to make human life less significant altogether. Human plots just dissolve. While that may sound like an insult, it is also potentially very freeing from the excessively strict and absurdly self-serious reality television show of individualist subjectivity.

Proulx often approaches fiction along these lines, emphasizing place over plot. Hunt's essay "The Ecology of Narrative: Annie Proulx's *That Old Ace in the Hole* as Critical Regionalist Fiction," for instance, identifies this pattern, as he notes that the novel loses its direct narrative movement, turning instead into a history of place.[60] This change also occurs in Proulx's oeuvre more broadly, as her plotting tends to become more absurdist moving from *The Shipping News* to her subsequent three volumes of Wyoming stories. Many of these Wyoming stories practically refuse to narrate, offering absurdist vignettes or blackly comic prose poems. Then, Proulx moved beyond fiction entirely, writing *Bird Cloud,* a kind of geographical history/memoir of southwest Wyoming even in the midst of her winning acclaim as a fiction writer.[61] Her most recent work of fiction, *Barkskins* (2016), achieves similar results with opposite means: the huge novel treats more than three hundred years of history, rendering *individual* human agents as small and fleeting against the sweep of time and the prevailing presence of the forests they encounter. Yet Proulx underscores the *cumulative* power of human actions as the novel's characters steadily destroy the wild trees of North America, which at first seemed inexhaustible.

Additional details from *The Shipping News* bear out this understanding of Proulx's work. Ryan, relying on humanist protocols of narrative and reading, suggests that Quoyle and Newfoundland become "sources of familial health and community coherence" in the novel.[62] This is certainly part of the story. But a lot of noise and incoherence remain. For one, there is the great destructive force of the party in Newfoundland described in the book, culminating in the drunken mob thrashing and sinking their friend Nutbeem's boat so he will not leave the community, the very opposite of health and coherence (256). Settling in Newfoundland means experiencing this distinctively local form of wildness and disorder, and even being trapped in it, like Nutbeem. Further, in the novel's larger frame, it was death and loss (of Quoyle's wife, Petal Bear, and his parents) that motivated Quoyle's move. So health is put into a larger context of mortality in this book, as in most Proulx works.

And what about family? Ryan reminds us that Quoyle's effort to come to grips with his family identity in Newfoundland involves facing his mad cousin. But again, a humanist/posthumanist question revolves around how to see that relationship. In Ryan's words, "Quoyle needs to move past this legacy before he can enter fully into the new community of Killick-Claw."[63] I would quibble with the phrasing "move past," urging instead "recognize," "acknowledge," or "witness." In practical terms, I take Ryan's point about getting on with life, but the logic of motion and action in this version of subjectivity is one of the central problematics *Homesickness* revisits. These emphases, often undergirding the logic of cosmopolitanism and other similar modes of Enlightenment thought, are clearly part of colonialist and imperialist histories as well as being the targets of much Proulx satire. Although Ryan does not describe it this way, this confrontation with an unhinged heritage is a clear example of the homesickness I have been discussing. Quoyle must acknowledge the sickness in the home of his ancestral selfhood, in terms of both literal place and blood relations and history, before he is able to assume a new version of himself. Homesickness upsets the very possibility of some kind of pure agency or an overcoming, a moving past. Sickness remains. Quoyle must accept it, live with it.

In many approaches to reading, this fact of sickness would muddy the argument. An emphasis on the need for dignified labor, for instance, might drive a reader past Proulx's observation of the waste and ineffectual nature of much human work. But especially in the age of the Anthropocene, when so much of our work has proved destructive, we need to recognize both of these realities—the use *and* the futility of labor. A key moment in Ryan's interpretation further clarifies this point. When Quoyle submits a column criticizing oil tankers, his editor, in a moment of black comedy, changes the story to praise. Quoyle expresses outrage: "You cut the guts out of this piece! You made it into rotten cheap propaganda for the oil industry. You made me look like a mouthpiece for tanker interests" (203). Ryan calls this "the narrative's strongest statement on the worth of personal agency."[64] In her reading, Quoyle is advocating the value of local interests, showing that he has become a capable person. This is all true, to a point. But the wry humor that attends Proulx's whole description of this episode prevents us from embracing "personal agency" too vigorously. After all, Quoyle is merely fighting for a measure of respect in a remote newspaper office where he has just been directly undercut and mocked by his managing editor. It is a pretty small triumph. And, more generally, this passage recognizes the power of vested interests in the real world to generate propaganda even via reputable media, a sobering echo of the limits of heroic personal agency.

At issue in this episode are also aesthetic values about contrasting economic and intellectual systems. Quoyle defends the aesthetics of the fishing fleet, aesthetics that are themselves satirized to some extent by Proulx.

Quoyle's original piece begins by describing a photograph of fishing boats, "beautiful beyond compare." He then contrasts those boats with "the low black profile of an oil tanker," going on to note, "Some are old and corroded, structurally weak." This description helps him earn the concluding sentence: "Nobody hangs a picture of an oil tanker on their wall" (201–2). The skillfully made and skillfully sailed fishing boats, signs of regional identity, are replaced by the sinister "low black profile" of huge ships transporting oil, perhaps the most important and transformational commodity of modern times, enabling not only massive mobility but also, of course, global warming.

In other words, it may seem easy to share Quoyle's aesthetic sensibilities. But oil and its attendant mobility have been essential to producing contemporary forms of cosmopolitanism, for good and ill. Wholesale rejection of modern technology risks a simplistic nostalgia, the kind roundly criticized by Raymond Williams in *The Country and the City.* Indeed, this scene reiterates the difficulty of articulating a positive regionalist vision without falling into a kind of narrow complacency. Proulx's regular escape from this problem relies on caustic irony, what I might call a deeper posthumanist skepticism. Fittingly, then, her treatment of the aesthetics of boats cuts both ways: fishing boats seem quaint in a postmodern world of forceful oil tankers, but, conversely, oil tankers really are not very pretty. Quoyle has a point: we do not customarily see oil tankers aestheticized in pictures, but that leads to questions about aesthetics more generally. Do we want merely a pretty aesthetics? Morton mocks that approach in *Dark Ecology,* as I noted in my introduction; he resists simple and pat treatments of place as "villages, the organic, slow time, traditions."[65] We should instead complicate our aesthetic standards and read the oil tankers in the register of the postmodern sublime, as more ambivalent emblems of the Anthropocene.[66] Does that leave room to appreciate beautiful old technologies? I think so, but differently.

Physical agency gets mixed together with the worth of labor in this scene, and both are at stake together. Ryan insists that this moment is the quintessence of the book's valorization of "face-to-face contact" and even of "physical potency."[67] In his anger about the editor's transformation of his piece, Quoyle does in fact frighten the unlikable editor right out of the office (203). But we should be careful not to rush back into a masculinist and ableist notion of identity.[68] It is precisely labor, even physically potent labor, that led to the existence of the oil tankers (and all they imply). Proulx's novel shows hard-luck labor practices sometimes getting Newfoundlanders literally nowhere, a point Ryan also recognizes when she notes that "unrewarded work is a staple of life in Newfoundland."[69] Proulx grudgingly allows that people need some measure of self-possession of the sort Quoyle develops, but her lacing of irony prevents us from too readily or completely embracing the grand narratives of selfhood by way of "physical potency" and trusty labor. Such skepticism can be aligned with disability theories like those of Rosemarie Garland Thomson and Lennard J. Davis, who show how often agency and self-control are risible fictions, or flimsy fantasies.[70]

Proulx's posthumanist literary style—caustic, ironic, and darkly humorous—registers and reiterates much of this skepticism, pointing to meanings and emphases other than Ryan's "overcoming" interpretation. In short, Proulx's style is a sign of homesickness. She cannot rest in the pretty vision of a quaint if difficult life in a fishing village. Rather, this novel's picture of a good life in Newfoundland appears only by comparison with the rest of an often-miserable world. As always, this argument must be made carefully in a world only too full of people who have not attained citizen-subject status, whose needs are ignored or actively subverted, not to mention the needs of nonhuman life (i.e., the ongoing Sixth Extinction event).

Ryan's argument, emphasizing the need for people and other forms of life to gain recognition and value, could better register the excesses of that humanist logic of subjectivity, which can too easily become part of the problem. One reason so much life persists unrecognized is precisely that the dream of potent agency remains too strong. It is reinforced practically everywhere: It justifies militaristic insistence on national potency; it underwrites hypermasculinity; it perpetuates self-aggrandizing hyperconsumerism. And so on. Many of us who can, do purchase more selfhood for ourselves, prosthetically expanding our persons and our reach in space.[71] We thus press forward the global capitalist system, driven on huge oil tankers, be they ugly, sublime, or both. All these potencies have their uses, but the broader perspective emphasized by Proulx's corrosive irony is essential to undermining these forms of subjectivity when they go too far, as they routinely do.

Proulx's style functions as Hunt suggests: it resists an easy or blasé form of regionalism, instead putting place into dialogue with a cosmopolitanism and postmodernism. Her use of language also distances—perhaps only slightly—the human self from its technology of language, marking failures of representation by exaggerating them. In this way, Proulx resembles Hemingway, who typically uses elision, understatement, and repetition to signal this distance between word and thing, a likeness Tracy Whalen also recognizes.[72] The fragmented and "paratactic" style in *The Shipping News* signifies Quoyle's unsettled position in life and Proulx's larger approach to reality. Yet, here again, Ryan argues otherwise. Following Whalen, Ryan claims that Quoyle's language moves from sentence fragments to complete sentences, urging that this is a sign of his greater agency in life. This argument is interesting, but to my reading, the sentence style does not markedly change over the course of the book. Instead, much as I claim about Hemingway's *Garden of Eden* and his style more generally in chapter 4, Proulx's work tends toward a larger unsettling of conventional humanist agency.

Masculine-informed notions of human agency are also at stake in Proulx's most famous Wyoming story, the harsh and heart-rending account of lovelorn cowboys in "Brokeback Mountain."[73] While a fuller exploration of that story is beyond my purview here, it is worth briefly showing its similarities to *The Shipping News.* Here again we find characters trapped by social, geographical, and mortal circumstances that are beyond their control. The story's final sentence, in Ennis's unspoken internal voice of mourning, uses a Wyoming register to sum up this vision of life: "There was some open space between what he knew and what he tried to believe, but nothing could be done about it, and if you can't fix it you've got to stand it" (285). The phrase "open space" evokes much: the nature of human love and desire, the reality of brutal prejudicial history, and more. Ennis's love for Jack in a deeply homophobic place and time is a forbidden form of emotion, and Ennis must endure it in a subjectivity of suffering and witnessing.

However, the gap between desire and power runs two ways in "Brokeback Mountain." I have been arguing that a posthumanist approach helps us recognize human weakness as a facet of life. We all must "stand" that to some extent. But the "open space" is not only room to suffer. Embodiment is not just an apparatus for pain. The structure of desire here—for Ennis, for the story, and for culture more broadly—also goads people and society to change. Forbidden loves—homosexual, cross-racial, or class-defiant—have increasingly become accepted by the social body. Social change begins in what may at first seem to be merely unrealistic desires. One of the lasting appeals of a cosmopolitan orientation is that it permits such ostensibly strange ideas and practices to come into view, to be tested in the light of reason and sympathy. So although I am contending in this book that a pure cosmopolitanism is impossible, I am embracing the value and richness of a cosmopolitan structure, in which various new cultural practices and beliefs can be considered, engaged, and attempted.

Proulx's work tends to downplay the significance of such changes. While I have quibbled with Ryan in terms of what constitutes a just reading of Proulx, I do not mean to minimize the importance of narratives of improvement. Of course, humans and other animals do have real needs. Some experiences and forms of life are better than others, as Proulx admits. So Ryan's emphasis corrects against the dark hazard of reading Proulx, exemplified by Polack, mentioned above: an embrace of pure irony and uncanniness. Proulx's style and her framing of human life against much larger realities are often on the edge of nihilism. Instead, a complex homesickness allows us both to recognize real needs and to have a broad perspective on human life. Part of that sensibility, especially for Proulx, is ironic and comic. She achieves her satirical effects temporally, in part, bashing characters through the main events of their lives very quickly, sometimes skipping huge swaths of time, rendering characters with a black comedy that foregrounds human weakness in the way a Wyoming storm might. In that sense, her work can be accused of the same thing that Hemingway's character David accuses his wife, Catherine, of in *The Garden of Eden*: being rushed, as discussed in chapter 4. Proulx's fiction starkly insists on our weak mortality and our entrapment, only glancingly evoking life's pleasures. Her posthumanist black humor shrinks the value of human life down to almost nothing, to a "finger-snap," to a "chip."

But we misread Proulx if we forget the perverse *pleasures* of satire, black comedy, and literary style, which alienate and orient us at the same time. Humor, even black humor, can have a warmth, a generative mirth within it. It disabuses us of fantasies of power and offers a perspective by which to adjust our sense of place in the world. Importantly, furthermore, literary style itself, to be effective, assumes our nuanced sense of home, place, and culture. A homesick style only works if we recognize the complexities of the home it is sick of. We must identify the particular habits Proulx describes—of an insular Wyoming, of a remote and wary North Atlantic—to appreciate her satires of human life. It is neither utterly bewildering nor naïvely faithful about progress. It expresses a complex homesickness.

Dying at/as Home, Lost in Our Own Skin

Proulx's black humor and compelling style perhaps find their greater refinement, and a more fitting formal home, in her short stories about Wyoming. The "shortness," I have suggested, is often part of her point. So to conclude, I return to the story that haunts this chapter, "The Half-Skinned Steer," to draw out its take on the fundamental weakness of mortality: Mero's nearly lifelong escape from the harsh and uneasy ground of his roots is undone by the inevitability of weakness, of sickness, of death. His life assumes its final form in the very place he quit as a youth and tried for all his years to reject. In the end, then, readers know Mero as a man who is born in, leaves, and returns to Wyoming. His time in the East scarcely appears in the story at all. Mero's overpoweringly regional identity is consonant with his human limitations, his mortality, and his "ability" to suffer and perish. Going home is dying, and vice versa. I noted above that Proulx reveals the reality of weakness step by step. First, she satirizes (or just realistically depicts) Mero's return from Massachusetts back to Wyoming, a journey Mero sees as another demonstration of his economic and physical fitness. Not only can he complete the cross-country drive in his advanced age; he does so in a Cadillac! But, in fact, the trip brings him face to face with the death of the near other, his brother, and then with his own death, a sequence very much like Quoyle's in his near-drowning scene discussed above.

A series of unfortunate but ordinary events slowly unravel Mero. He has a relatively minor car crash en route, but he can afford to buy another Cadillac. Then there is the snowstorm that gets Mero's replacement Cadillac stuck, leading this successful man of the world to confront the consequences of accumulated errors. Mero's ultimate disability, his mortal weakness shared with animals, finds expression in the figure of a partially killed steer who becomes the story's image of death. Animality literally signifies mortality in this story. It is a mortality connected to the region, the roots, and the home Mero cannot escape. Thus, the story's ineluctable regionalism comes to represent the untamable wildness of mortality itself. Death demonstrates that our lives are particular, always local even when driven by cosmopolitan desires.

Mero's vegetarianism, his octogenarian exercise routines, and his potency in general ostensibly stand in contrast to the incompetent Tin Head, flaccid wienie afly, who can do nothing properly. Yet Mero, riding in his expensive automobile, an artifact "promising motion and escape" (37), turns out to share the fate of his cars. The symbolic economy of consumer society, in which our products represent us, gets pressed to its logical conclusion here by Proulx. The first car is quickly dispatched in the accident; the second, coursing the familiar landscape of the ranch, "is reduced . . . to a finger-snap" (31). The dread of weakness, of stupid incompetence, depicted in quintessence by Tin Head, is a kind of homesickness. Mero's whole life is driven by his desire to escape the lousy ranch and all its significances, the lying yet compelling girlfriend of his father, the corrosive effects of the hard land, represented in part by the tin-eating Tin Head's brain. His desire to escape is akin to humanism's desire to escape the confines of embodiment and animality. But in the end, Mero is drawn back by his human decency, by respect for family and for the dead, which exposes him again to vulnerability, weakness, and suffering.

On this point, Proulx is consonant with recent theoretical work on animals. Most notably, her insistence on the power of death recalls Jacques Derrida's crucial critique of Heidegger's writing regarding death, for example in *The Animal That Therefore I Am.* While both Heidegger and Derrida insist that death is essential to understanding and interpreting the meaning of human life, Heidegger uses death to reinforce the conventional difference between humans and animals. Heidegger believes that it is human beings' knowledge of death as such, as a general reality, that separates us from animals. Derrida rightly counters, however, that death is meaningful precisely because it is absolutely other. We cannot properly know death, and death cannot ever be properly owned by the self or the ego. Cary Wolfe discusses this idea in *What Is Posthumanism?,* noting that while Heidegger had appropriated and thereby familiarized death in his account, in fact death is, as Derrida puts it, a "radical passivity," "something that never arrives in the ego's time."[74] For Derrida, then, as Wolfe notes, the "relation to death is always mediated through an other."[75] This idea lends importance to Proulx's plotting, since Mero approaches death through two others—his brother and then the figure of death in the steer. Readers similarly access death here via an other, the human artifact of story, something uncanny, both foreign and familiar. The exuberantly strange, gothic nature of this and Proulx's other Wyoming stories further underlines this alterity.

Formulated this way, death becomes a crucial example of otherness *and* proximity. On the one hand, death is utterly intimate—it constitutes our sense of time, it is always imminent within us, and it takes us from within as it were, pulling us down by way of the very vulnerabilities that make us up. On the other hand, death is completely other and unknowable, like other posthumanist realities with which we are intimate and yet also always distant. We might say that mortality is always local, but it is a locale that, like Thoreau's twenty miles around Walden Pond, we can never fully know. For this reason, to figure or represent death, we must resort to language and to metaphor—or to metonymy—as with Proulx's vision of the half-skinned steer.[76] This arresting image in Proulx's story is the product of Mero's father's girlfriend, who is, we are told, "a total liar" (32). The steer tale is a fiction within a fiction, a double lie—complete bullshit—and yet it is in a sense the truest part of Proulx's story, truer still in its peculiar way because Proulx has so extravagantly owned up to the lying possibilities of fiction. Death is figured with the steer as an excessive and impossible metaphor that is true, a vision that haunts the main character, Mero, as it haunts Proulx's reader. That is the haunting of homesickness, an impossible or incomplete truth, an unending desire.

The half-skinned steer is an image that readers also internalize but cannot ever domesticate or tame, a local mortality, a death inside us that dominates us more the more we are paying attention as we read the story. It reminds us that language, as Wolfe insists, is a fundamental prosthetic, that images are radically other. The more we inhabit our readerly selves, then, the more we recognize how we lose ourselves—indeed the more we see that our selves have never been properly ours. To get more local in ourselves is to get more lost. In Proulx's final line, Mero recognizes that he is lost at home as he walks from his car, stuck in the snowstorm, at the time of his brother's funeral: "in the howling, wintry light he saw he'd been wrong again, that the half-skinned steer's red eye had been watching for him all this time" (40). And for us.

2

Burning Down the House

Weak Agency and the Self Unhoused

If it wasn't for the looting, we wouldn't get the attention.

—Unnamed commenter on the 2014 demonstrations in Ferguson, Missouri, reported by Tanzina Vega and John Eligon in "Around St. Louis, a Circle of Rage"

Going home, as we saw in chapter 1 with the case of Annie Proulx's Mero, can be strange. But the home itself, despite its intimacy and familiarity, is also stranger than we commonly recognize. The home shelters a vast number of ideas and things: nonhuman bodies and materials in wood, stone, and more; heritages of craftwork and aesthetics; accumulations of labor, capital, and innovation; and rich sets of meanings, all fastened, nailed, glued together into a single whole. How can anybody "own" a home? The concept of ownership is already violent, legible alongside the notion of owning people in slavery and animals in husbandry. In *Owning the Earth,* for instance, Andro Linklater suggests these concepts are mutually informative, having arisen together in the same historical period. He shows how the concept of ownership was applied to the newly reencountered continent of North America after Columbus and profoundly impacted subsequent events; it is widely reported that Native American peoples rarely had a concept of "owning" land, for instance.[1] In *Militarizing the Environment: Climate Change and the Security State,* Robert P. Marzec similarly locates the rise of private property in a history connected to the British enclosure movement of the seventeenth and eighteenth centuries, which for him led to the development of "more atomized formulations of protoneoliberal human subjectivity" and the rise of militarized treatments of land.[2]

Similarly, in the even wider framework of *Dark Ecology,* Timothy Morton argues that "agrilogistics," the norms and protocols of life since the agricultural revolution, first took shape some twelve thousand or so years ago. Then, "private property emerged, based on settled ownership and use of land, a certain house, and so on. This provided the nonhuman basis of the contemporary concept of self, no matter how much we want to think ourselves out of that. Agrilogistics led rapidly to patriarchy, the impoverishment of all but a very few, [and] a massive and rigid social hierarchy."[3] In sum, private property and home ownership are familiar stories we tell to organize our cultural, political, and ontological relationships with a vast number of entities. The concept of owning property performs powerful cultural and political work, but it is not inevitable or universal.

Homes, often seen as innocent, pure, comfortable, and unified places, are in fact complex, more-than-human assemblages, with politics built into them. In terms of meanings, the home may be the most powerful anchor in contemporary life for notions of stable selfhood, investment in place, and the like, a sense reinforced—or made manifest—by the sheer materiality of the house itself: safe as houses. But the reverse view remains persuasive: the mature person must leave home. Home is fleeting and temporary. This notion has taken on particular intensity in American culture, a national tradition, as the cliché has it, of immigrants, with a history rife with relocation in pursuit of better economic opportunities and in escape from religious, racial, and ethnic persecution. In such cases, the home that was abandoned was insufficient or harmful or both.

Holding in view these opposed perspectives on the home, this chapter studies complex homesickness in Marilynne Robinson's *Housekeeping* and Peter Hedges's *What's Eating Gilbert Grape*.[4] These novels emphasize sickness-at-home. They dwell on the ways that place can entrap, centering on characters who are oppressed by their culture's norms and by the limited opportunities of their lives. Far from being comfortable, house and home become uncanny for the characters, reinforcing their sense of unease, dissatisfaction, passivity, and mortal weakness. In both novels, the house in particular is a constant reminder of the conflict between characters' desires and their inherited positions. Their houses come to represent their entrapment even as they reinforce it in mundane daily life; the houses are structures, both literal and semiotic, reinforcing a past and a present that characters resist. While the narratives differ in the nature and form of this resistance, both are organized around its intensification, culminating finally in characters' attempts to burn down their houses. Yet these texts do not treat this act as freeing in any simple way. Instead, burning down the house is deeply ambivalent: is it a form of self-destruction or of liberation?

In this chapter, I argue that it involves both. Burning down the house is a vivid enactment, and sign, of limited agency. In particular, it evinces frustration with prevailing economies and ontologies, that is, with dominant ways of organizing our attitudes toward reality and our place in it. It reveals deep frustration with the confinements of place but also suggests an inability to create a more constructive or desirable alternative. Complex personal and local histories cannot be easily unwound or forgotten. The characters are homesick in the sense of being sick at home, or sick of home. Their reliance on the artifact, the structure, or even the prosthetic of the house, instead of demonstrating human ability as Heidegger argues in "Building Dwelling Thinking,"[5] reinforces human dependence and weakness in a posthumanist sense. And it is due to weakness, to a sense of deeply limited options—but not utter impotence—that the characters in these novels decide to destroy their houses. Destruction, after all, is an act and requires some agency.

Burning down the house is a highly localized form of material signification, reiterating (and exemplifying) how our communicative acts are always placed. We are too weak to entirely leave the local. The texts and signs we read are material, impacting our bodies and minds, our habitats and companion species. We do not stand outside the material world in a position of disembodied reason. The drama and power of burning houses underscore this fact profoundly, since they are frightening, unnervingly forceful displays of meaning that also have inescapable effects on lived reality. Burning houses remind us how potent signification can be.

This chapter first explores homesickness in these novels, then concludes by aligning the texts with similar forms of unrest, of resistance to cultural entrapment, in the 2014 events in Ferguson, Missouri, where demonstrators protested against their sense of racial oppression and injustice following the killing of an unarmed black teenager by a white police officer. In Ferguson, as in these novels, a metaphorics of burning down the house evoked this sense of being sick at home and revealed a powerfully felt resistance. Yet the demonstrations in Ferguson, like the conflagrations in these novels, were ambiguous in terms of the degree of social change and liberation they wrought. Burning down the house as an image and as a reality evokes all of this.

House burning is a cluster of signification that also evokes the age of the Anthropocene and the problem of self-destructiveness wrought on a vastly larger scale. Burning houses are iconic of posthumanist traumas, much as Annie Proulx's arresting image of a half-skinned steer is iconic, as described in chapter 1. Indeed, the use of fire, Stephen J. Pyne writes, is a distinctive human behavior, flickering through the history and prehistory of our species.[6] According to anthropologist Richard Wrangham, it was likely the human use of fire in cooking rather than hunting that *first* made available extra calories sufficient to increase our brain size and free up time to change human culture in a range of ways. Because "cooking increases the amount of energy our bodies obtain from food," Wrangham notes, "the first cooks . . . survived and reproduced better," leading to "changes in anatomy, physiology, ecology, life, history, psychology, and society. Fossil evidence indicates that this dependence [on fire] arose not just some tens of thousands of years ago, or even a few hundred thousand, but right back at the beginning of our time on Earth, at the start of human evolution, by the habi-line that became *Homo erectus*."[7] In *Throwing Fire,* Alfred W. Crosby accounts for human power and influence on Earth by connecting human recruitment of fire with our adeptness at ballistics—the use of projectiles such as rocks, arrows, and finally bullets and bombs.[8] Fire, this loosing of energy from matter, also characterizes the Anthropocene. Human work with fire, Timothy Clark notes, is largely responsible for releasing the tons and tons of carbon that have led to climate change.[9] Activity with fire is a strange kind of cooperative agency in which a small human act can set forth forces latent in nonhuman entities. Then fire and its conspirators of oxygen, wood, and matter take over.

Fire is perhaps *the* quintessential example of the agential reversals posthumanism insists on, in which humans are unjustly credited with possessing powers that reside, instead, to a very large degree in nonhuman forces and things. The Anthropocene offers a much wider frame in which to interpret this strange and powerful form of cooperative agency at the planetary level. Humans may seem to control the fires of our hearths and machines, but we have not been able to control fires' effects on the larger, global scale. Thus, the Anthropocene is frightening as arson is frightening: the destructive force is very real, real enough to expose the survivors to much larger forces that are far more difficult to control. The fire of climate change has long since been lit, but it will require a radical reworking of concepts and practices of agency to stem its tide of destructive force. Studying the more local uses of fire in these novels is important not only to register trauma, human destructiveness, and the entrapments of place, though. These fires reveal a powerful force of desired change latent even in unsought places, a resistance and a desire that can be better cultivated into a freer and more satisfying practice of house and home.

Homebound Posthumanism

In a posthumanist frame, the symptoms and symbolizations of homesickness reflect misalignments between structures of power and personal desires, between social meaning and individual truth. Much posthumanist theory recognizes that our hopes, our expressions, and our performances of selfhood all rely on large and complex environments, networks, and systems. Resistance to a particular imbrication in these realities has various results: it can inspire larger changes, but it can also register as an idiosyncratic or even bizarre symptom; this is how destroying one's own home is often perceived. Yet the scenario of weak but real agency that drives it is in fact common in at least two senses. First, human agency is nearly always more limited and distributed (among other agents and forces) in its enactment than we tend to recognize. Second, the pyrrhic destruction of self and tool that is home burning is far more pervasive than we often admit, such as in the history of war. Because these realities underscore human limitations, they tend to be treated nervously or repressed altogether by humanist cultural orientations.

A central task of this chapter is to draw out these repressions by putting my posthumanist reading of these novels into dialogue with readings from other, more humanist frameworks, especially the many feminist readings. While posthumanism and many feminisms have much in common, often there are signal differences organized around assumptions about human agency in particular. Many feminist readings of these novels attempt to rehabilitate conceptions of human power and ability; I suggest we should dwell longer on their exposure of human weakness. In the end, that effort can deepen feminist approaches to these and other texts by undermining masculinist notions of selfhood.

Of course, the experience and metaphorics of being homebound especially recall gender oppression. A prominent and germane example is the "madwoman" locked away in Charlotte Brontë's *Jane Eyre,* a figure brought into sharper focus by Sandra M. Gilbert and Susan Gubar's landmark study

The Madwoman in the Attic: The Woman Writer and the Nineteenth-Century Literary Imagination.[10] In the end, *Jane Eyre*'s plotting hinges around Bertha Mason, Rochester's "mad" Creole wife, burning down the house Thornfield, and then committing suicide. The novel suggests that insanity runs in Mason's family, with her mother institutionalized for it. Yet, from another perspective, both mother and daughter are victims of oppressive patriarchal and racist norms, epitomized by Rochester's imprisonment of Mason. Her entrapment can therefore be blamed for her destruction of the house, a complex display of powerful and pyrrhic agency, an approach developed by Jean Rhys in *Wide Sargasso Sea,* her response to *Jane Eyre.*[11] More recently, Jane Blocker's work on home and house, as it connects to women, follows this important interpretive thread. She underscores the persistent danger, despite the many advances of feminism, that "woman and the home become . . . so conflated" that they can seem to be "very nearly one and the same."[12] Blocker recalls architectural discourses that are patriarchal, discourses that use the structure of the home to reinforce masculine power.

Blocker is clearly right to point out this problem. Much cultural and political work still needs to be done to disentangle femininity from an ostensibly fixed, natural relationship to the domestic. But doing so does not necessarily mean freeing women from the house into the realm of mobility, as is too often concluded; it can also mean, for one thing, freeing women in the house. We can be more or less free at home *and* in mobility; the push for mobility, often taken as the obvious alternative to repression in the home, can itself be harmful. To recognize this hazard, we must complicate dominant humanist ideologies of freedom. In other words, I am contesting the (often masculinist) fantasy of the autonomous subject, roaming at will, commonly implicit in notions of mobility, which involves a disavowal of dependence not only on other people but also on tools and other human constructions. Instead, I am suggesting that the condition of being associated with one's dwelling is a synecdoche for culture itself, for men and women. For humans, having culture has long meant relying on our homes—of whatever sort—as we do other artifacts and constructions.

This chapter interrupts and questions not so much the human dependence on home, then, but rather its gendering as feminine. *Homesickness* emphasizes how human weakness and mortality mean everyone is, in both literal and metaphorical senses, housebound. But such human limitations are often denied or projected onto others, such as women or ethnic minorities, as Susan J. Matt shows in her history of homesickness (addressed in my introduction).[13] This argument that we are all in a sense housebound is likely to provoke alarms of determinism and concerns about human potential, so it requires some immediate clarifications.

I do not mean to justify or naturalize practices that limit human rights, be they racist, patriarchal, ageist, speciesist, or the like. I also do not mean we should lock ourselves in the house. Indeed, as suggested in the introduction, I endorse an eco-cosmopolitanism that encourages a free mobility, to the extent that this is possible and decent. But there is the rub. Such freedom is only delusion—or risks becoming another tacit imperialism—unless it seriously and genuinely engages with the realities of hierarchical power and mortal weakness. A decent, ethical freedom must be, in Emmanuel Levinas's formulation, a difficult freedom, cognizant that in a finite world, for necessarily limited, mortal beings, we cannot avoid being placed, local, or temporal ("Difficult Freedom" titles a collection of Levinas's essays).[14] Further, "freedom" is often not the value to measure human actions against. That does not mean surrendering cosmopolitan desires; it means recognizing them *as* desires, and tempering our hopes with the human and nonhuman realities of mortality and fallibility.

The fantasy-laden notions of freedom to move often themselves rely, in their essence, on hierarchical social systems that distinguish the free from the not-free, as discussed in the introduction. One person's mobility often directly relies on another's entrapment. In order to abolish or weaken those free/not-free distinctions, we must work to recognize the meanings of our mortal limits, to bring our limitations home, as it were. In *Homesickness*, this effort is achieved partly by a complex regionalism. I understand the region in part to signal the necessary limitations of being mortal, of having an actual, particular history, as I argued in chapter 1. Having an identity, in other words, means coming from a particular place and time, bearing the biases, partial awarenesses, and idiosyncrasies that result from that locale. But identity is even more material than that, as attention to houses and other intimate artifacts shows. This complex notion of placed identity reinforces critiques of abstract subjectivity—conventionally white, masculine, self-determining, rational, and so on—made in disability theory, posthumanism, poststructuralism, and feminism.

Robinson's Homesickness as Second-Order Observation

Much of the writing treated in the first half of this study—Proulx, Hemingway, and Hedges—grows out of unsettled notions of home, an uncanny home. The work of Marilynne Robinson might at first seem to be the opposite, appearing to celebrate home in a more traditional sense. For example, her third novel is titled, simply, *Home,* and on a superficial level it can seem to treat that theme conventionally.[15] However, closer inspection reveals that her work consistently engages more complex notions of homesickness. For instance, in an essay on wilderness, Robinson explains that she "started writing fiction at an eastern college, partly in hopes of making my friends there understand how rich and powerful a place can be."[16] The book that resulted from these early efforts, *Housekeeping,* is saturated with place but in a compellingly peculiar fashion. Its imagined resurrection of Robinson's youthful home in Idaho is refracted both through fictional invention and across the distance of the North American continent, so the book's very existence actually testifies to displacement and to the force of homesickness as a desire that yet, ironically, unhouses us from ourselves.

Indeed, this situation for the production of texts—writing from a position of remove—is a recurrent theme in Robinson's oeuvre. It is the structuring principle of her Pulitzer Prize–winning book *Gilead,* in which an elderly father writes a narrative intended for his young son, to be read when that son has grown into mature adulthood. Place-love in *Gilead* is magnified and estranged by distance, memory, nostalgia, and loss.[17] The plot of *Housekeeping* also reinforces this particular brand of longing in loss, as the home place, the house, proves very difficult to "keep" both in the plot itself and, as I noted, in the scenario of the novel's production. The book therefore underscores what Robinson claims in her essay "Wilderness": "All love is in great part affliction. My bond with my native landscape was an unnamable yearning, to be at home in it, to be chastened and accepted, to be present in it as if I were not present at all."[18]

In Robinson's case, as in others studied in this book, desire for home is sharpened by its absence, by a cosmopolitan mobility. Loss and injury sharpen awareness even as they show awareness to be a kind of symptom as well as a knowledge. This structure of learning and of experience is posthumanist in Cary Wolfe's sense, as developed particularly in his chapter of *What Is Posthumanism?* on Emerson. There, working from Emerson's essay

"Experience," Wolfe underscores a notion of selfhood in which self-possession is, paradoxically, self-evolution, change, development, and growth. He reads Emerson's key phrase "self-recovery" to mean *not* the "recovery of a primordial, pre-existent self" but "the onwardness of the self's movement."[19]

Very much in this vein, Robinson's expression of love for her birthplace appears because she has left it. The paradoxical, and even contradictory, power of this structure of feeling is intensified by the particular story Robinson has to tell in this novel, in which housekeeping means homewrecking in a strict sense, as the protagonists of the story attempt to burn down the family home near the book's end. To know and express her love for place, Robinson, the author, surrenders that place.

This is another moment to pause and clarify, however. While I am arguing that loss, weakness, and unrest are in some sense natural to human animals, that does not mean all their forms are natural or inevitable. Death is also natural, but that does not mean we accept all its forms. I do not mean to imply that everyone who loves a place must burn it down. A simplistic or naïve naturalizing of homesickness is dangerous because it can excuse all sorts of potentially unnecessary actions—not just professional mobility like Robinson's but systematic displacement of the poor, structural violence against the dispossessed, and much more. Identifying homesickness as part of life should not imply simple acceptance of it, then. Instead, as with a Foucauldian recognition of power as a force, homesickness should give us additional vocabulary to ask new questions. Is a given regime of mobility actually necessary and good? Must love of place be seen "in great part [as] affliction," as Robinson understands it? And so on.

There are two other relevant likenesses between Robinson and Emerson. First, Robinson's particular expression of love for her home, her desire to be "chastened and accepted, to be present in it as if I were not present at all," closely resembles Emerson's famous "transparent eye-ball" experience in *Nature,* in which he claims, "I am nothing; I see all."[20] Like Emerson, Robinson dreams of being so entirely at home in place that she disappears. Of course, that is not possible. These impossible terms—immersion to the point of disappearance—are common to many treatments of place, especially Romantic ones. Second, in a strange way, this desire is the mirror image—the reverse image—of idealized cosmopolitan desires, in which the observer (or learner, or student) can denature the self so entirely that he or she can confront, understand, or learn from entirely different cultural realities but, even further, can *become* them, all of them, in key ways. That is what the identity "cosmopolitan" often names. In both the disappearing Romantic self and the cosmopolitan identity, the particularities of the self would disappear, and the self would be absorbed into its environment (natural or cultural or both), ceasing to be a self at all. This subjectivity is impossible, however, and dreams of its enactment risk either imperializing or simply disappearing. Indeed, put this way, cosmopolitan dreams seem more hazardous and impossibly ambitious than Romantic ones, with which they often overlap.

Wolfe's analysis of the structure of perception in his book *What Is Posthumanism?* offers a way to better understand these scenarios. As discussed in my introduction, Wolfe draws from and explicates Niklas Luhmann's structuralist theory, which underscores the blind spot necessary to all observational systems. In brief, the blind spot names the fact that a system cannot perceive itself internally *as a system*; to be seen as a whole system, it must be viewed from the context of another system, in a second-order observation.[21] The structure of feeling in homesickness is a second-order observation: that is, while in first-order observations of home we learn the particulars of place by inhabiting it and watching it closely, by leaving a place we become able to observe those first-order observations from a further remove. As noted in my introduction, second-order observations of home involve a sense of loss as well as insight. A second-order observation of home is only possible because one has left, disabling a person from reinhabiting home in a naïve, innocent way. Thus, all second-order observations of home are partly traumatic woundings.

Robinson's life and work offer a compelling example of this problem. The existence of her fiction, as noted above, begins in her painful remove from Idaho, and her next three novels, Pulitzer Prize–winning *Gilead* and its companion pieces, *Home* and *Lila,* all center around her adopted midwestern home in Iowa.[22] There are complex dynamics of place in play here, but much of the criticism focuses on other issues. Several treatments of *Housekeeping* have read it within a framework of feminist fiction and patriarchal critique. For instance, Marcia Aldrich compellingly discusses a women's writing not necessarily in opposition to men's but as simply other-than-male.[23] Aldrich recognizes the remnant patriarchal power of Grandfather Foster in *Housekeeping.* He built the family's house and brought them to their home place, beginning the process of what the characters Ruth and Sylvie feel to be their alienation and dislocation, their growing sense of *unheimlich.* Yet, importantly, this novel also undermines the pretense of power for Grandfather Foster, or for any other human. The existence of this story in the wake of patriarchal power testifies to a different kind of selfhood or subjectivity, one marked by weakness, loss, traumatic memory, and even derision.

The novel is thus melancholic but also at times slyly, even gently, satirical of fantasies of power. Consider, for instance, its opening allusion to and recasting of *Moby-Dick*'s first line. Robinson begins her novel, "My name is Ruth," while Herman Melville opens, "Call me Ishmael."[24] Robinson's diction is notably lower-key, humbler, and not declarative but conversational. The tacit suggestion is that Robinson's novel pursues an inquiry parallel to Melville's but with a group of girls and women who are largely trapped at home rather than risking their lives on the world's oceans. The critique of such pioneering male efforts is emblematized in *Housekeeping* by the remembered episode of the train crashing into the lake, as though the dreams of human technology, progress, and freedom are swallowed by the inhuman, local particularity of this place, Fingerbone, Idaho.

These dynamics are exactly the reverse of those in Melville's novel, in which waters become a vehicle for global travel and cosmopolitan questioning, as well as the home for whales, and finally a place of danger—the *Pequod* does sink, after all. Robinson's characters go almost nowhere; Melville's go almost everywhere. *Housekeeping* is about entrapment; *Moby-Dick* is about excessive pursuit. In the end, both expose human weakness in similar ways, with waters swallowing human striving. Robinson reveals the wild strangeness of place, much as Melville shows the robust nonhuman presence of the sea, in stark contrast with Ahab's monomania. That Robinson's train crash is a remembered incident in the novel, or a haunting, formally reiterates its humbling view of humanity, since the train is simply gone, beneath the lake's surface, testifying to the invisible depths of that nonhuman presence of water, while this quiet town persists in its idiosyncratic, inhuman-inflected wildness. Like the train, Melville's whaleship, in the end, similarly exists only in Ishmael's memory. The fact that these stories are told from a remove, as second-order observations, in other words, deepens their critiques of human ambition. Both narratives are hauntings, demonstrating the homesick, posthumanist structure of interpretation and subjectivity, in which we must reckon with a past we neither own nor control in order to have some sense of who we are.

Robinson's quietly satirical spirit also surfaces near the novel's conclusion, when Ruth is barely able to suppress her laughter as she hides in the orchard just before she and Sylvie set the house ablaze. In general, and particularly in this case, laughter both exerts and undermines human power simultaneously, much as fire does. Indeed, the grandfather also reveals this sort of complexity regarding agency. As Kristin King notes, although "he fulfills the patriarchal role of planting his family in Fingerbone . . . , he is also the man who gathers fragile flowers in the early spring, loves to wander, builds a house tuned to its surroundings, paints dreamlike and out-of-scale landscapes, and seems to have already vacated his life long before his death."[25]

Wild Housekeeping

A key scene in *Housekeeping* demonstrates its emphasis on human frailty and signals much of this chapter's argument about the book. Near the end of what Ruth understands to be her last summer of childhood, she and her sister, Lucille, take a fishing expedition, stay out too late, and are forced to sleep in a ramshackle hut they throw together. Robinson describes the small shelter—"low and slovenly," "random and accidental"—as though it were a simpler version of the out-of-square home their grandfather built (114). The girls are amateur carpenters like their forebear. Robinson even uses the word "domestic" to describe this daytime-comfortable but finally frighteningly wild place, unsettling the meaning of that word in a way that is consonant with the rest of the novel. The temporary, tenuous nature of the girls' fort, the sense of it being a rough encampment, exemplifies the lives of these characters more generally. They are profoundly alone both in this moment and in the world generally, without most of their family, and on this night they inhabit the very edge of their youth. It is a truly liminal moment. To manage, the sisters also build a small fire, which shores them up against the darkness of night like the hearth fire in a home, but their position is only a more clear example of what Robinson seems to understand as fundamental to the life of the flesh—an exposure to the radical otherness of time, darkness, loss, and the utter inhumanity of the lake, the forests, and the cold.

The sisters arrive at their predicament, having to sleep on the shore, because of their immersion in the "rituals of predation," in Robinson's phrase; having caught and eaten "considerable numbers" of the small perch in the pool there, they "suddenly realized" they "had stayed too long" (114). These predatory undertakings affiliate the sisters with the other forms of animality that surround them. Robinson explains, "Coyotes cried, and owls, and hawks, and loons" (115). As they must sit through the quietly gathering night, their senses grow keener to that other life around them. Shorn of their safe and familiar domicile, the girls' animality appears as a familiar strangeness, as *unheimlich*.

Confronting this situation, the two sisters respond very differently. Lucille defends her sense of self, and her sense of their shared selfhood. When "creatures came down to the water within a few feet" of them, "Lucille began to throw stones at them" (115). She paces, whistles, and sings songs. By contrast, Ruth is more "accepting that all our human boundaries were overrun" (115; see also 172). Ruth then goes on: "Lucille would tell this story differently. She would say I fell asleep, but I did not. I simply let the darkness in the sky become coextensive with the darkness in my skull and bowels and bones" (116). Ruth's quiet openness to this place in this moment, to its dark ecology, gives her a glimpse of her material self, beyond the mind and ego. She sees her very person anew; she is estranged in her humanity and homesick in her body. But in being so, Ruth seems to join the cosmos itself, to become profoundly, even frighteningly, engaged with a much larger reality.

The emphasis on interiority, embodiment, and darkness here may seem the opposite of Emerson's transparent eyeball, but perhaps it is merely its logical extension or its dark twin. To become an all-sensing being is to disappear into the world entirely, to become a kind of material darkness. For Robinson, this experience offers access to a deeper-than-ordinary truth. She goes on to write, in a point akin to critiques of excessive reliance on visual sensing, "Everything that falls upon the eye is apparition, a sheet dropped over the world's true workings" (116). Instead of mirage and visual tricks, Robinson offers darkness as a more fundamental reality, which she calls "the only solvent." Darkness here is more absolute, a different order of matter. It is utter immersion, without "relic, remnant, margin, residue, memento, bequest, memory, thought, track, or trace, if only the darkness could be perfect and permanent" (116). It resembles death, or perhaps a kind of blank version of heaven.

But, we might reply, living people cannot long remain swallowed in darkness. The other possibility *Housekeeping* offers is the partial, idiosyncratic, accidental character of real, individual human life, the humanity of odd memories, desires, and the realities of change. Lucille clings fiercely to an orderly and conventional version of this humanity, and thus, "When the light began to come . . . Lucille began to walk toward Fingerbone" (116–17). Soon enough the sisters walk back from this touch with alterity and death to "ordinary day" (117). Lucille's more conventional attitude in this moment correlates with her insistence on orderly housekeeping at home. Ruth, on the other hand, continues to live with more of this darkness about her life and her person.

Housekeeping in such scenes functions partly as a metaphor, or synecdoche, for subjectivity: the way we keep house reveals our sense of the world and our beliefs about place or placelessness in it. This book does not forget Lucille's and Ruth's ordinary human needs as children for parenting, protection, and guidance, offering a persistent, quiet criticism of Sylvie. However, Lucille's rigorous insistence on normalcy does not appear as the obvious answer to Sylvie's truancy. Robinson insists that Sylvie and Ruth have access to a deeper understanding than Lucille. The novel itself is her testimony to that effect. Sylvie's exaggerated wildness and even animality only clarifies something that Robinson reminds us is central to all actual life, or actual housekeeping: the dust in the corners, the mice living alongside us in spaces we claim as ours, and the slow chaos of aging and disrepair. Because of this family's intense trauma, its posttraumatic status, such realities are outsized and less easily escaped. Indeed, these traumas disable Ruth and Sylvie from having ordinary lives. But, on the other hand, these traumas bring difficult posthumanist realities into view, aligning *Housekeeping* with the accounts of human selfhood and agency in disability theory and suggesting that gender is certainly a central theme but not *the* theme of *Housekeeping*. To say so is to misread the larger statements Robinson makes about wayfaring in this changing world. Gender inflects the characters but does not entirely account for them.

The girls' housekeeping on the shore foretells the ultimate destruction and loss of all such homes, however well built, and so actually positions the girls alongside their grandfather, as I implied above. In the unseen spectacle of their grandfather's train crashing in the lake, the water swallows the signs of a particularly masculine notion of movement, progress, and control. But that is not all; Robinson's argument is much broader. In her account, humanity in general is humbled, or exposed in its weakness. The train is just one example. When it flies into the cold water, it disappears in a vortex of loss, a whirlpool. Later, near the novel's end, Robinson amplifies the resonances or ripples of this whirlpool: as Ruth and Sylvie escape backward on the train track, over the bridge that first brought their people to this place, as though they were unstitching the events that led to their own lives, Robinson notes that the stars "pulled through the dark along whorls of an enormous vortex—for that is what it is, I have seen in pictures" (211). This pause to add the personal testimony of witness—I have seen these vortices; they are real—emphasizes the importance Robinson finds in this factual observation; vortices, or constant movement, unhouse the very substance of the universe. Matter, like human lives, is ultimately in a swirl of change, what we often think of as loss. Another way to put this is to say the universe is "wild" and, in a sense, weak, never holding to final form.[26]

Sylvie embodies this kind of wild selfhood, and she reproduces it in her extravagantly distracted form of housekeeping. Robinson writes, for instance, that Sylvie lives in a "millennial present," in which everything, even rapid deterioration, should be "allowed its season" (94). Sylvie thoroughly, even excessively, accepts the inevitability of loss. In her sense of the present moment, the Real is already invested with its coming alterations; mortality and change are always in view, estranging attention to the present and radically revising what literal reality means. It is akin to recognizing that "our" own human bodies are completely infiltrated with other biota, bacteria, and so on. But in Sylvie, this form of attention often reads as a kind of casual weakness or indifference to conventional values—she's a wonderfully and traumatically strange character, recalling Melville's "Bartleby, the Scrivener."[27] In a universe of loss and weakness, the empowerments of subjectivity are radically diminished, like the small lights of Fingerbone on the shore of the dark lake, in the dark night. As the novel's imagery shows, this reality can be observed or experienced in the world—we do not necessarily need to use disability theory or posthumanism to recognize it.[28]

But I do not think Sylvie fully exemplifies what it means to live in a posthumanist sensibility. As a character, she is between modes of being; she is a posttraumatic figure who registers the radical difference of new forms of selfhood without being able fully to inhabit them. This is partly why Robinson relies on notions of darkness, for instance, as a solution to the problems of trauma and homelessness that the novel raises. There are not ready answers to these issues in familiar ways of thinking.

This difficulty—how do we read Sylvie?—registers in the criticism. For instance, Kristin King notes that "*Housekeeping* has been claimed as feminist work on the grounds that it rejects a symbolic, patriarchal order and the primacy of male characters."[29] King complicates that view, arguing instead that "the novel's feminist charge" relies not on surrendering the symbolic but instead on reworking it. She applies this logic to the novel's discourse of the house, for instance, quibbling with critics who understand the crashing phallic train and the burning house as destructive of patriarchal structures. Instead, King writes, "the text's feminist strategy uses patriarchal structures as much as it undermines them." She continues, "Although it may be naïve to suggest that feminists can use patriarchal structures without being used by them, it may be more naïve to assume we can simply dump the old structures without amputating our access to power." King instead emphasizes the ways that Ruth and Sylvie inhabit the house and language differently: the novel offers "not an escape from language but a recreation of it to affirm multiplicity and indeterminacy." For King, this means skepticism about ostensibly "transparent . . . narratives of fact" without surrendering facts themselves.[30] It means a more complex approach to meaning.

My argument is consonant with King's, but I find her opening claim that Ruth "has mastered rather than abandoned a symbolic order" puzzlingly overstated, running contrary to the orientation of the rest of her article.[31] Mastery seems like the wrong standard here, both for this novel and for Julia Kristeva, whose work King engages. Robinson and Kristeva account for agency in more nuanced ways, beyond the master/slave dialectic. Kristeva's work can be aligned with disability theory, offering ways to negotiate loss, inability, and suffering, unsettling notions of human "mastery" of any kind.[32]

Again, there is no question that gender norms are a dimension of *Housekeeping,* but its engagement with loss does not end there; it demonstrates human frailty and imperfection in the face of a difficult world. Masculine codes have tended to efface or resist this reality, often externalizing it by understanding others, including women, as weak. When we recognize the human individual, generally, as weak in this specific sense—as mortal and exposed to constant change, never holding final form—we undermine that masculinist gender code and the scapegoating system at its root. In chapter 1, I made this same case about the othering of Tin Head, whose weakness eventually comes home to Mero and to the reader, rendering Tin Head uncannily familiar and strangely kin. Christine Caver's work moves in this direction, beyond the tendency to read *Housekeeping* purely as a feminist victory over the housebinding forces of patriarchy, seeing it also as a mourning text, or a literature of trauma. As Cathy Caruth shows, trauma undermines the stability of human knowledge itself. Dwelling on trauma makes mastery impossible.[33]

Metaphysical Homesickness: Christian and/or Posthumanist?

Robinson's account of estranged selfhood, of disorientation and homesickness, relates to her sustained focus on questions of knowledge. Indeed, the disorientation likely intensifies the search for accurate bearings or moorings, and then vice versa. Thus, Robinson repeatedly insists on her story's worldly precision, its veracity, even though it is haunted by ghosts and metaphysical inquiries. That structure of inquiry—rigorous veracity that points beyond the empirical—has been given new life by object-oriented ontology, new materialism, and other such approaches that radically reframe human knowledge. In *Hyperobjects: Philosophy and Ecology after the End of the World,* for instance, Timothy Morton demonstrates how the present becomes strange, even inaccessible, from what I would call a posthumanist perspective. This notion of experience accords closely with Wolfe's reading of Emerson, discussed above.

Structurally, a posthumanist awareness of the world's complexity resembles a Christian focus on the world beyond this one—in both cases, our ordinary sense of reality is rattled. Robinson's discussion of darkness, quoted above, as an entirely different order of meaning is one of many moments when the novel seeks a solution to problems of epistemology and ontology. Her resolution, time and again, relies on traditional Christian metaphysics. Both orientations—Christian and posthumanist—respond to feelings I am calling "homesickness." Of course, which interpretive approach we apply—Christian teleology or posthumanist complexity—can have significantly different implications. But they need not be seen as antagonistic. A posthumanist rethinking of these questions could refigure how understandings of Christian teleologies work, and vice versa. Ultimately, however, such an inquiry is beyond the focus of this book. For my purposes, I simply want to emphasize the estranging effects of Robinson's approach to experience.

A sense of knowledge as partial and frail is especially appropriate to *Housekeeping,* which works along many of what Robinson calls the "puzzling margins" of human life (4). The novel emphasizes mystery—not mastery—in experience, not only with its recourse to dreams, nighttime, memory, and life's liminal periods but at the epistemological level. Robinson makes this explicit near the novel's conclusion, when she has finished giving the details of the story: "All this is fact. Fact explains nothing. On the contrary, it is fact that requires explanation" (217). The gap between sheer reality, that unknown wild, and what we say of it haunts language, subjectivity, and texts, including this one. That gap explains the ghosts that thickly populate the book, including the nonhuman ghost of Lake Fingerbone at its former levels. A cosmos of constant change is haunted by its own past, and Robinson aligns this recognition with fundamental narrative patterns of loss in biblical stories of Cain and Abel, the Garden of Eden, and more, writing, to sum up these stories: "The force behind the movement of time is a mourning that will not be comforted" (192).

Robinson's insistence on the poverty of human life in the world also recalls the Puritan conceptions of earthly life in North America, discussed in this book's introduction. From a posthumanist stance, the puzzles and obscurities of selfhood are just parts of the world's complexity well beyond human knowledge and ego. In place of the sparkling kitchen counters of humanism's rational order are the dusty corners of the home's history, the suffering it has hosted, the loss that contributes to the making of the mature self. "Housekeeping," as a word glossing the maintenance of subjectivity in a human-created space, takes a much different valence in this traumatic story. By estranging house and home, Robinson helps us recall that houses are nonhuman, including once-living and still-living organisms, from the wood framing to the slate roof, the mice in the walls, and the mold in the basement. Housekeeping thus means a radical intimacy with the nonhuman and with the forces of loss.

This intimacy, and Robinson's insistence that her expressions of it are true, truer even than simple fact, change how the plot works. It goes beyond rhetoric of blame. Time itself is the cause of mourning. This idea must be balanced against the more personal dimensions of culpability in the plot, as when Ruth is consistently hard on her grandfather for bringing her and her family "to this bitter, moon-pulled lake, trailing us after him unborn" (149), to take a key, melancholic formulation. But for Ruth, as we saw in the overnight episode with her sister, the darkness has its own compensations that Robinson insists on presenting and aestheticizing. The metaphysical valences of this story are especially clear in the strange trip Sylvie takes Ruth on, later in the novel, to the abandoned house on the other side of the lake.

Haunted by the Future, Visiting No-Place, Inhabiting Absence

The abandoned house episode is like a visit to the distant future of Ruth's own house, like an encounter with her own future ghost, or proof of the smallness of a single human life. Everything about the scene is uncanny and inverted. It involves not housekeeping but homeless surrendering. When they arrive, Sylvie does not watch over Ruth but instead leaves Ruth alone. So Ruth begins searching for the lost children whom Sylvie says live there, and whom Ruth does not actually expect to find, as she later admits. Instead of other children, Ruth finds a haunting absence, which proves to be herself, as an abandoned child in this moment. Robinson writes, signaling her expansive sense of this episode's meaning, "Perhaps all unsheltered people are angry in their hearts, and would like to break the roof, spine, and ribs, and smash the windows and flood the floor and spindle the curtains and bloat the couch" (158). Ruth, Sylvie, and the missing children are all kin in this sense, members of an unsheltered people, and this collapsed structure is their nonhome.

As the scene proceeds, Ruth intensifies her backward housekeeping, or her destructiveness, as she further unravels the wreck in an "angry" fashion, "pulling loose planks out of the cellar hole . . . for all the world as if I had some real purpose or intention." Vigorously proceeding only to avoid "the embarrassments of loneliness," Ruth "worked till my hair was damp and my hands were galled and tender" (158). This is uncanny agency, a powerful rereading of human work more generally as a form of merely keeping busy in the face of our embarrassing exposure to mortality. Work here is a form of small ego noise, reached for in desperation, much as Morton understands the advent of agriculture, discussed in the introduction, as desperate. Fittingly, Ruth's thoughts turn to mourning, clarifying her likeness to the ghosts of those lost children.

> I imagined myself in their place—it was not hard to do this, for the appearance of relative solidity in my grandmother's house was deceptive. It was an impression created by the piano, and the scrolled couch, and the bookcases full of almanacs and Kipling and Defoe. For all the appearance these things gave of substance and solidity, they might better be considered a dangerous weight on a frail structure. I could easily imagine the piano crashing to the cellar floor with a thrum of all its strings. (158–59)

So we might all say of our homes. "Home" appears here via a metonymic chain of things, material objects that lend home a false permanence. We are at home with our stuff, but once we recognize this fact, it becomes strange, we become estranged, and "solidity" turns "frail." The passage goes on to clarify the terms, that in this talk of ghosts, Ruth is also exploring her own sense of loss and melancholy: "I knew there were no children trapped in this meager ruin" (159). Talk of ghosts is a way of externalizing and generalizing her own mourning (as in *Hamlet,* perhaps).

Thus, in this strange place, and still actually alone herself, Ruth sits on the grass, letting the cold grip her, much as she had done in the night of temporary homemaking on the shore with her sister: "I thought, Let them come unhouse me of this flesh, and pry this house apart. It was no shelter now, it only kept me here alone, and I would rather be with them, if only to see them, even if they turned away from me" (159). Finally, loosened from her own physical being, Ruth turns her thoughts to her lost mother, "taken" by the lake, whose presence haunts the scene: "She was a music I no longer heard, that rang in my mind, itself and nothing else, lost to all sense, but not perished, not perished" (160).

This dark, ghostly, *unheimlich* reverie is interrupted by Sylvie's touch, returning Ruth to her body and to Sylvie's strange routine of care. Sylvie puts her tattered coat on Ruth, and Ruth describes being "angry that she had left me for so long, and that she did not ask pardon or explain." Ruth thus "wore her coat like beatitude" because it is an example and representation of Sylvie's truant methods of care and of Ruth's losses (161). But here again, Robinson refuses to stop at this critique of Sylvie or to locate the book's theme here, centered on the issue of proper care for children. Instead, Ruth generalizes her condition, worrying as they cross the lake about capsizing: the "bitter" lake resumes its traumatic pull, leading her and Sylvie both back to considerations of the drowned.

Hazard is a condition of the *material* world—of water itself—not just as a result of poor caretaking. Robinson thus reinforces the breadth of her inquiry by jolting out of her narrative of Sylvie and Ruth's return trip from the abandoned house: in one sentence Sylvie is describing the beautiful day; in the next, Robinson suddenly writes about the biblical "Flood" at its "apex" and then "the day of divine relenting." She imagines "Noah's wife" looking out "upon a morning designed to reflect an enormous good nature," transforming beauty into message, into metaphysical meaning. The nice day means God has relented from the punishing flood, but it also means, Robinson writes, that "the waters were full of people." She wonders whether Noah's wife felt the traumatic pull of the water, whether she "might have wished to be with the mothers and uncles, among the dance of bones, since this is hardly a human world, here in the fatuous light, admiring the plump clouds" (172). Somehow Ruth and Sylvie do not get pulled in.

But Ruth and Sylvie do become disciples of the world's vast, inhuman otherness. Having spent so long on their errand in the wilderness, Sylvie and Ruth finally walk home, through their own town, like strangers; their "dishevelment was considerable" (173). They pass by Lucille, who questions Ruth, but Ruth's journey has deepened her status as alien in her own home. Although Ruth "wished very much, in fact, to tell Lucille exactly where I had been" (174), the power and strangeness of the trip defy ordinary narration. Thus to sum up the meanings of the abandoned house journey, the chapter ends in a dream, a discourse like fiction in its uncanny relationship to "reality." Ruth dreams that she and Sylvie "were drifting in the dark, and did not know where we were, or that Sylvie knew and would not tell me" (174). These homeless souls circle over the lake as if in flight, "looking for the children there, and though we heard them we could never find them. I dreamed that Sylvie was teaching me to walk under water," not on the water. The chapter closes by clarifying how distant Ruth has become from her sister and her home: "It seemed Lucille was talking to me. . . . I believe she mentioned my comfort." But, Ruth ends, "I could not hear a word she said" (174–75).

In *Housekeeping,* there is no innocent return from this kind of travel. Instead, there must be a radical reworking of values. Robinson writes, "Need can blossom into all the compensations it requires. To crave and to have are as like as a thing and its shadow. For when does a berry break upon the tongue as sweetly as when one longs to taste it?" From this claim, she concludes: "And here again is a foreshadowing—the world will be made whole" (152). Robinson's Christian teleology underscores her intention not to offer a criticism of patriarchy so much as to evoke the homesickness of the life of the flesh. That is, the grandfather's leadership of the family inflects ensuing experience, but more fundamentally, Robinson sees the partial, fleeting, imperfect reality of this world as a shadow of the coming redemption.

The collapsed disorder of the abandoned house in this scene signals the life of fallen humanity that is key to Robinson's perspective, as she makes clear in her book of nonfiction essays *The Death of Adam* and as she has discussed in interviews.[34] Robinson therefore is not critical of the wild, inhuman landscape; she acknowledges its strange harshness and interprets it as one more sign of the work of God. For her, that wildness is everywhere, including in the house, and even more intimately, in the bonds of familial lineage and loyalty. Ruth and Lucille's mother's suicide, their father's absence, and their grandfather's questionable migration to Lake Fingerbone all demonstrate the possible disorder and waywardness we are exposed to in life on Earth. The imperfect coldness of the world, in its contrast with our desires, appears for Robinson as a sign of millennium. This situation, like Robinson's view of the stars as a vortex of loss, positions the physical world as a sign of the metaphysical, the completely other. Her Christian framework offers one way to make sense of this otherness; work in new materialism and object-oriented ontology has shown that such metaphysics can also be situated *in* this world. The strangeness of ordinary objects, their withdrawn character, is a form of radical alterity, and in object-oriented ontology, humans are also objects.[35] This point estranges us from ourselves, makes us homesick in our persons, like Robinson's characters.

When Robinson's next chapter opens, we learn that ordinary, worldly outside pressure is mounting, due explicitly to the fact that Sylvie and Ruth were seen riding the freight cars on their return from the abandoned house. The chapter's first sentence declares, "In the weeks that followed the sheriff came twice" (176). The town of Fingerbone also responds to the family with charity—a charity that Robinson casts into doubt. Likening the town to a creature of mud and muck, she presents its ministrations as an effort at self-preservation. Sylvie and Ruth are an embodied affront to a town's order, which, in Robinson's account, is a kind of thin veneer over a wilder reality: "There was not a soul there but knew how shallow-rooted the whole town was. It flooded yearly, and had burned once. Often enough the lumber mill shut down, or burned down" (177). Thus, the town's help, offered "in a spirit that seemed at first sight pity or charity," might be better understood as "an attempt to propitiate the dark powers that have not touched us yet" (178). As this external pressure mounts, Sylvie is forced to answer to the town's women, who, Ruth surmises, want "to keep me, so to speak, safely within doors." They worry that Ruth "would be lost to ordinary society," that she "would be a ghost," "like a soul released" (183). Under this social duress, Sylvie shows resilience, insisting to the women, "Families should stay together" (186). She cleans up the house, combs Ruth's hair, and begins conventional-style cooking.

Further, in a believable scene, Sylvie proves to have remarkable, communicable insights when she tells her female visitors from town of the sorrows and loss in her family. Her words resonate with the women, who answer her first with long silence and then with echoes of agreement (186). All unite in a kind of communal mourning in acknowledgment of the difficulties of life. For a moment the absolute alterity of loss and death, their wild otherness, meet with complete normalcy here, even if that alterity is somewhat difficult for the women of Fingerbone to face. The "dark powers" do touch the town. But only briefly. All understand, but Sylvie lives with this awareness more permanently in the foreground. The others, in rejecting Sylvie's behavior, are rejecting the dark news she seems to carry about her person like her old clothing.

The difficulty of Sylvie's truths, embodied and spoken, is a key driver of Robinson's plot. Though this has often been overlooked in the more rigorously gendered readings of the book, the community women play an important role in forcing Sylvie and Ruth to leave Fingerbone. Their ostensibly kind and polite meetings, bearing casseroles and other "feminine" gifts, ultimately reveal an intolerance for difference or for the wildness of melancholy and loss. Women possess power in these scenes because they align the forces of social convention against Sylvie and Ruth, who therefore feel they have no option but to leave their inherited home.

Robinson's narration of this final step in the plot is compellingly accidental and vital materialist. Sylvie turns suddenly from her attempt at normalcy, working to keep the family together, to her effort with Ruth to burn the house before escaping over the railroad bridge. It is a surprising yet fitting sequence. It begins with Sylvie's small, orderly fire in the orchard, burning old boxes and magazines to purge the house and restore conventionality (199), but it is as though that fire has a life of its own, as though its subtle destructive force is contagious. Here is the agency of the force of fire. First Sylvie puts out the orchard fire, but then Ruth seems to catch its wild puckishness, hiding from her aunt. Perhaps she imitates the Sylvie she has known, the old Sylvie who would simply disappear, even though Sylvie herself has continued to behave more conventionally at this moment. Sylvie's evasive, fleeting, *unheimlich* character has itself spread like a force of nature. Ruth hides in the orchard—out of doors—while Sylvie searches for her around the house, illuminating room after room, so that finally "every one of its windows [was] lighted." Robinson writes, "It looked large, and foreign," a near final step in this book's ever-growing estrangement between the home and its occupants (203). The bright lights bring the sheriff once again, who offers Ruth an escape to his comfortable home, with his grandchildren and apple pie (206). She rejects this offer, and from that point, there is no return.

Testifying to that logic, the next and final chapter begins with a matter-of-fact account of Sylvie and Ruth's attempt to burn down the old house, and their nighttime escape over the railroad bridge. Robinson writes of the decision: "Sylvie and I (I think that night we were almost a single person) could not leave that house . . . to be pawed and sorted and parceled out among the needy and the parsimonious of Fingerbone. Imagine the blank light of Judgment falling on you suddenly. It would be like that." A few lines later, the paragraph concludes: "In the equal light of disinterested scrutiny such things [as those left in the house] are not themselves. They are transformed into pure object, and are horrible, and must be burned" (209). These dynamics regarding the objects in their home are the same as the dynamics regarding the community's opprobrium of Sylvie's methods of care. In both cases, the powers of the community, shambling and human though they are, invade the intimacy and privacy of the house and the family, step by step driving the pair to their final destructive act. Their lives and their things become uncanny, *unheimlich,* or homesick, and the logic that they should be burned is apt.

In a different novel, the house's destruction would be complete. But in this book, so permeated with awareness of human imperfection, the house is only mildly burned, despite the dramatic popping of windows. If the fire displays the women's power, that power is not much more potent than Ruth's grandfather's power to frame and build a perfect structure in this wild place. The house no more finishes burning down than it was perfectly finished in its construction, to be reoccupied by figures Ruth and Sylvie only imagine, never meet or confirm, a "someone" (216). This is yet more uncanny—strangers in their own home. Thus, like other migrants, Sylvie and Ruth become complete outcasts, refugees from human society. Robinson insists in the end that they "are not travelers" (216)—they are more dislocated than that. In the concluding paragraph, Sylvie and Ruth's absence is a haunting, a presence of nothingness. They become ghosts that are more trying because they do *not* pursue Lucille, with whom they never reconcile. They are "nowhere," "no one," and, in the novel's final sentence, they are not sought: Lucille "does not wait, does not hope, and always for me and Sylvie" (219). Loss is redoubled, since it is too deep for Lucille even to register it. (This point resembles the discussion of loss at the end of Toni Morrison's novel *Beloved,* treated in chapter 4.) Indeed, Lucille's repression of these difficult truths of loss and human weakness resembles, even models, conventional humanist repressions. Robinson, writing this novel, brings them into view.

Like many migrants, these characters recognize the dark side of dislocation. Their presence unsettles the eco-cosmopolitan dream, rendering it uncanny. In the age of the Anthropocene, our work is to engage these truths without succumbing to despair and without becoming mere ghosts ourselves, easier said than done.

Housebound Selfhood in *What's Eating Gilbert Grape*

In Robinson's plot, "housekeeping" finally means destroying—or attempting to destroy—the grandfather-built, out-of-square family home. A similarly pyrrhic victory is a plot end point of Peter Hedges's 1991 novel, *What's Eating Gilbert Grape,* made into the compelling 1993 film of the same title by Swedish director Lasse Hallström (this chapter treats the film and the novel).[36] Indeed, Hedges's narrative plays out feelings of homesickness using the symbolic resources of the American house and home along several lines closely parallel to Robinson's 1980 book, *Housekeeping.* Both involve regions distant from the metropoles and include characters whose lives and social positions prevent them from having much mobility. In this sense, remote regions signal a form of geographical determinism akin to that in Annie Proulx's works, discussed in chapter 1. *What's Eating Gilbert Grape*'s plotline is also structured by trauma—actually, a set of compounding traumas. The core event is prior to the story's present: the father hanged himself in the basement of the family home. The mother, Bonnie, formerly a beauty queen, mourns by eating excessively, eventually growing vastly, morbidly obese.

Much as *Housekeeping* reframes male adventure stories such as *Moby-Dick,* underscoring the melancholy of human weakness and loss, Hedges's novel inverts many of the conventions of coming-of-age tales, gently satirizing fantasies of human independence. This story of the Grape family is organized around the disabled, or alter-abled, brother Arnie's eighteenth birthday. As the novel's climax, this event gains special significance because doctors deemed it unlikely that Arnie would live that long. This uncanny eighteenth thus redoubles the novel's insistence on human frailty, since it takes a conventional marker of independence and makes it instead a sign of near mortality for Arnie and, it turns out, of actual death for his mother. She dies on his birthday. Yet Arnie's dependence is only a more pronounced version of every person's needs. He embodies human weakness, slightly exaggerated. Thus the family works very hard to surround him in an envelope of care, something every person requires, if often for a briefer time than Arnie, as Martha C. Nussbaum argues regarding disability in *Frontiers of Justice.*[37] It is primarily Arnie's brother Gilbert who cares for Arnie. He bathes him, he brings him to work, and he insists repeatedly, in various ways, "nobody hurts Arnie" (291). To some extent, Gilbert thus stands in for Bonnie Grape as caretaker, reversing gender stereotypes, as I suggested in chapter 1 is true of Quoyle in *The Shipping News.*

Like Arnie, Bonnie embodies human disability. In the novel's characteristically harsh diction, first-person narrator Gilbert first describes his mother as a "porker." She has become sheer body, with a weight greater than any "household scale," and she lives in front of the TV only to eat and smoke cigarettes (22). Her highest hope is mere survival. Gilbert tells readers, "If you were to gripe to my mother about her weight, or express in any way any fear you have about her steady growth, she would say, 'Hey! I'm here! Alive! I didn't cop out like other people we know!'" (22–23). Mother and son both patina over deep melancholy with these brutally direct pronouncements. Hedges's decision to use the slur "retard" with reference to the disabled younger brother, Arnie, is similar: even a cursory reading of the story shows the powerful self-condemnation involved in characters using this word, especially Gilbert. The insulting diction externalizes Gilbert's self-regard, a point made clearest perhaps in an episode late in the novel when Becky, his love interest, holds a mirror to Gilbert's face. Gilbert, literally seeing himself and Arnie in a single reflected image, tries to break the mirror (288). The moment reads somewhat melodramatically, but it is credible enough. Similarly, Arnie's refrain throughout the story, beginning in the first chapter, that Gilbert is "shrinking" (18) reinforces the story's physical logic: melancholy makes this narrative's men disappear and women grow corpulent. This logic of self-destruction points toward the novel's ending, with a purging fire that is rendered powerfully in the novel and the film. As Jane Blocker argues, the mother figure is particularly associated with the house, so it is macabre but fitting that she is consumed with the house by the final fire.[38]

Burning the house is a rejection of the family's entrapment in their lives, in this geographical place, and in their cultural station more generally. The drama of this final destructive episode stands out, since most of *What's Eating Gilbert Grape* is profoundly ordinary. Its events are self-consciously small-town, and small-scale. Not so the ending's ferocious fire. As a material signifier, the fire enacts a range of contradictory feelings and meanings: it underscores the limited agency of the family to correct its woes; it declares powerful resistance to that entrapment and those limitations; and it insists, combining these two feelings, on the dignity of a deeply injured and compromised person, Bonnie Grape, the obese mother who is lost to her mourning after her husband's suicide.

The narrative builds tension by underscoring the family's unrest in life. Gilbert has resigned himself to staying put in this place and caring for his brother Arnie. Gilbert (Johnny Depp in the film, in an early success) works in the local—and failing—grocery store, surrendering bigger dreams he might have had, until he is distracted by Becky (Juliette Lewis in the film), who awakens Gilbert from his small-town Iowa stupor. Becky is a cosmopolitan from Ann Arbor, with professors for parents and a broader perspective that helps loosen the Grape family's entrapment. The film portrays Becky's cosmopolitanism in a believable register, using a somewhat homely Airstream trailer caravan that brings Becky to the town to suggest a greater level of mobility. In both film and novel, Becky's character is persistently affiliated with movement, as she first appears riding another modern tool of transportation, the bicycle (51). The novel also uses the bicycle to reveal Becky's surprising youth—she's only fifteen, despite her precocity.

In the novel, Gilbert meets Becky at the Dairy Dream, bringing together the book's discourse on eating with its preoccupation with mortality and weakness. When they meet, Becky is studying a pair of praying mantis on the restaurant's outer wall, and her first words to Gilbert reveal a particularity of these insects: the female eats the male after they mate (52). In a book about consumption, about how the weakness of the animal body can collapse families, and in which men disappear and women overconsume, it is an appropriate relationship opening. It is accented by Becky's no-nonsense explanation that she is in small Endora, Iowa, to stay with her grandma, who, she says to a stunned Gilbert, is "old, her hair is blue, and she'll die soon" (52). Becky has an uncanny habit of frankness out of sorts with her youth. In this conversation, Becky goes on to justify her smoking habit and then calmly admit her own mortality: when Gilbert admits that he finds her beautiful, Becky says, "I might be now, but one day I'll have blue hair and blotched skin and plastic teeth and maybe one breast left. If the thought of that appeals to you, then we might talk about hanging out. But if you're into the surface thing, the beauty thing, then I might just have to turn around, snap off your head, and eat you" (52).

Such sentiments align well with those of the Grape family, the turbulent reality beneath the seemingly staid midwestern surface. Arnie expresses the family's unrest in a direct and evocative way: by repeatedly climbing up the town water tower. In the Midwest, these towers often bear town names, signaling their presence to travelers, so they are small-scale cosmopolitan signs (Figure 2). They are both outward signals and, aptly, reservoirs of internal identity, supplying much of the very substance of the townspeople, water being the dominant component of human bodies. Arnie's climbs are emblematic: it is as if he is trying to escape not just Endora, Iowa, but the limitations of the terrestrial world and its difficulties. Yet his climbs are suffused with familiar, repeated futility, since they only take him to jail. Like the novel itself, then, Arnie goes to the heart of small-town symbolic resources and exposes their limits.

Arnie expresses the family's suffering in other ways too. His often-anguished cries and moans, present in the novel, are better revealed in the medium of film, which makes their poignancy more palpable, especially in Leonardo DiCaprio's compelling performance as Arnie. Arnie is often the family's most sensitive member, or at least the most visibly and audibly responsive, for instance, to death and to its incomprehensible character. Arnie knows that something horrible happened in the basement, where the

Figure 2. Trying to escape the limits of the earthly. Arnie, scarcely visible partway up, climbing the water tower in Endora, Iowa, as the town gathers to watch the spectacle in the film *What's Eating Gilbert Grape.*

father committed suicide, but his sense of it is vague and monstrous, more truly registering the horror of suicide than would a literal, conventionally abled account. Similarly, while the novel has Gilbert and his sister Amy present at the moment of Momma's death, in the film it is Arnie who finds Momma after she dies. In this scene, his disability or impairment accents the strange mystery of death and our inability to grasp it: Arnie tries to wake Momma up, slowly realizing that she is not sleeping. His gradual recognition dramatizes and makes visible the puzzle of death, without breaching the realism central to the film. In other words, the film underscores death's resistance to representation and knowledge. Thus Arnie's disability functions as an ability of a sort: his presence accents the meaning of death in the film. Indeed, this moment further undermines the ability/disability distinction since it heightens our awareness that the disability of death is a human universal.[39]

Arnie's distinctive position in the world—his alter-abilities—often enables him to focus on events and to perform actions and say things that shed new light on familiar issues and problems. He dramatizes not only death but the difficulties of routine care that constitute life. Even the good, if discontented, character Gilbert proves fallible in his caretaking, breaking his own rule that no one may hurt his brother. As the eighteenth birthday approaches, Gilbert repeatedly tries to bathe Arnie in preparation. He is tricked once (270) and stymied several other times. Near the novel's end, first confronted by Becky with his own mirror image, mentioned above, then seeing a frosting-covered reflection of Arnie in the mirror, Gilbert finally cracks. He tries (unsuccessfully) to break the mirror. Then he drags Arnie into the kitchen to confirm that Arnie has dug his fingers into his own birthday cake, saved for the next day. A physical exchange escalates believably, and Gilbert heartbreakingly, though not ruthlessly, beats his own brother (288–91). Gilbert has failed his central role: "All my life it's been: 'You don't hit Arnie. Nobody hurts Arnie.'" Gilbert then confesses, "I am beyond hate for myself" (291). Gilbert's horrible failure, driven by his own exhaustion with everything, also grows out of a simple lapse of attention, a job imperfectly done, akin to several other scenarios discussed in other chapters of *Homesickness*: Sylvie, Tin Head and Mero (chapter 1), and Sethe (chapter 4) all reveal ordinary human limitations by failing to complete undertakings central to their identities and to the narratives that explore them. Gilbert's breakdown evokes that of the Grape family more generally.

Gilbert's failure, a piece of self-destruction, like a small suicide, echoes other themes central to this story. Earlier in the novel, Arnie is plucked from the top of the water tower and taken in by the police, rousing his mother from her depressed stupor to spring Arnie from jail. In her first foray into public since her husband's death, she is ridiculed and mocked. Her grief has kept Momma housed in private, so the town is shocked by her abject person, "dressed for winter" in the summer heat (137), reeking of body odor for a lack of bathing (138), and vastly overweight. Since she had once been a beauty queen, the town women relish her new status as "Endora's own Loch Ness Monster" (140). As in *Housekeeping,* Bonnie's appearance produces a communal show of charity, laced with the town's dread and aggression. The town council sends "a basket of diet books, wrapped like baby Moses," and the Elks Lodge takes up a small collection of cash that the family rejects (141).

Uncanny Food

The tacit assumption that deep depression can be cured with a diet is part of Hedges's larger exposure of modern food as *unheimlich* in this novel. Eating is connected to a perverse form of life: for Bonnie, eating is a symptom of loss and entrapment, and it is thus a fitting metaphor for the title, which names Gilbert's misery as a form of being consumed. This plot transforms an essential element of the good life—eating—into an act of misery, just as action, when used for the father's suicide, becomes an uncanny, horrible power. Hedges's treatment of eating is akin to a key scene in Marilynne Robinson's *Home.* In that scene, Jack's sister Glory prepares a chicken meal for him after his suicide attempt, and the food and the eating are flooded with melancholy, marked in that text by Glory's thoughts of the chicken's life (253).

In such cases of trauma and loss, eating is less the practice of the good life than a forced activity constrained by circumstances, even a symptom of bodily animal weakness. Much as we can be trapped in place, we can feel forced to eat to stay alive, a point Annie Proulx makes about her character Tin Head, discussed in chapter 1. This idea lends additional significance to the disappearing men in Hedges's plot. Arnie repeatedly tells Gilbert that he is shrinking away, or disappearing. But Hedges suggests that eating has been tainted not just for the Grape family but for the culture at large. Food culture in this story is presented as increasingly routinized, so that food laborers seem either robotic and absurd or simply anachronistic and doomed—the latter exemplified by the Lamson Grocery, where Gilbert works, slowly being driven out of business by the newer, larger Food Land. In this sense both labor and eating, central elements of home and identity, are disrupted, or unhoused, by the everywhere-apparent modernizing and globalizing process. These corrosive trends align with the story's focus on disability, as the characters in the story, particularly Gilbert, must more realistically come to terms with the disabling, automated industries from the wider world invading their hometown, making it uncanny to them, rendering them strangers.

The limited options for work are dramatized by Gilbert's friend Tucker, who needs a job and so is eager to work at Burger Barn, where the modernizing process leads to animal-like labor for people even as it depends very directly on the countless deaths of industrial animal agriculture.[40] Tucker, played comically by John C. Reilly in the film, is Burger Barn's apostle, praising the restaurant's efficiency to friends. The aesthetic and emotional consequences of this kind of laboring are represented by the quietly satirical grand opening of the restaurant, with the crew adorned in matching fast-food uniforms, looking like a self-parody (Figure 3). The Burger Barn plot again combines food and labor—both key methods of demonstrating agency and identity—into a single institutional framework. As Eric Schlosser writes in his 2001 book, *Fast Food Nation,* McDonald's represented "the first time [that] the guiding principles of a factory assembly line were applied to a

Figure 3. Unhomely food. The grand opening of Burger Barn in the film *What's Eating Gilbert Grape,* looking like a parody of fast food and prefabricated architecture.

commercial kitchen."[41] At Burger Barn, both our work and our food become commodified, part and parcel of international capitalism.

These distortions of food and work are powerful drivers of ordinary homesickness in modernity. A corollary to this: fast food is uncanny. As Michael Pollan argues in *In Defense of Food,* "The fast-food hamburger has been brilliantly engineered to offer a succulent and tasty bite" but little more. Pollan goes on: "This is a hamburger to hurry through."[42] Instead of a deeply nourishing product of compelling culture, such food is like a tourist's bauble, an easily accessed and easily forgotten gimmick. It is virtual food, or *unheimlich* food. Pollan, Schlosser, and others have shown how this form of eating is profoundly interwoven into a certain capitalist system of production that flattens particularities—of places, cuisines, flavors, and laborers—into homogenous systems that can be transplanted around the globe (with perfunctory adjustments for cultural differences). Hedges also notes the routinized construction of the fast-food building itself: "each Burger Barn is identical to the others" (154). Food, labor, architecture, and cityscapes thus all fall under the homogenizing force of Mc-development, making fast-food restaurants triply *unheimlich.*

Criticisms of fast food may seem unnecessary today. But Hedges's comparatively early satire (1991) shows the difficulty of escaping or revising these systems of production. Since Food Land, Burger Barn's kin, is also driving Gilbert's employer Lamson Grocery out of business, this narrative demonstrates how these neoliberal, globalizing systems can trap people in particular places and in narrow roles, a problem that has become more pronounced in recent political debates in the United States and elsewhere. Most recently in the real world, the big grocer is Super Walmart, pushing out even the Food Lands of the United States. Workers in fast food and at Walmart are notoriously underpaid (even though minor improvements took place in 2015, as businesses raised wages slightly),[43] compounding the problem of urban food deserts along lines of race and class. Ever-larger-scale corporations are driving the locals out of business, a trend affecting Iowa and U.S. farm country more generally. As small farms grow fewer, the face of labor, and therefore the presentation of human agency, changes in the Midwest and in the United States more generally, demonstrating the complexities and ambiguities of embracing a global or planetary cosmopolitanism. We must ask, Whose cosmopolitanism? Which cosmopolitanism? In Hedges's story, one realistic response to such circumstances is resistance. Gilbert despises and relentlessly mocks Burger Barn, which is one step. But the action of the novel's concluding fire takes a further step, rejecting entrapping places and the cultures of food, labor, and more that abide in them, and leaving a resonant image—a house on fire—that we are working now to better understand in a homesick mode of interpretation. There is a terrible and real energy in that fire.

Embodying Homesickness

If Gilbert and his siblings have a chance of escape, their parents remain victims of this town, of this form of life. Our view focuses especially on Bonnie, the mother in the story, a point that Jane Blocker's analysis underscores. As noted above, Blocker argues that the narrative conflates Bonnie with the house that she dies in, reiterating how female domestic roles have entrapped women. This is an important concern. However, Blocker's analysis risks exaggerating the gender dimensions in this case. For one thing, as Blocker recognizes, the father figure was no image of perfection: the house is badly built, again recalling *Housekeeping*, and he himself, in Blocker's words, "seemed to lack direction,"[44] a point underscored, of course, by his suicide. So while patriarchy may lend him a measure of power, the other systems of class, labor, region, and so on seem to victimize both parents, as well as their children.

So how do we read Bonnie Grape in this story? Gilbert provides one view, with what Blocker calls his "open hostility" toward his mother, citing incidents when he calls her names like "beached whale" or when he helps children look at her and laugh. However, I understand his attitude toward her as more complex. He clearly names and rejects her obesity and abjection, but Bonnie feels the same way about herself. Her self-hatred actually resembles Gilbert's hatred of her and, for that matter, his own self-hatred. Rather than setting family members against each other, the novel seems to recognize their *shared* unfortunate circumstances, which they all despise in various ways.

Instead, Gilbert's loyalty, his refusal to leave the family, and his defense of his mother's dignity in death must be factored into his complex attitude. Gilbert is deeply aware of fundamental human weaknesses, of abjected and repressed dimensions of human life. In fact, his harsh language about Bonnie's present state distinguishes him from other characters in the narrative. He defies what Blocker calls a common "gentleman's agreement to pretend not to know that which is manifestly true, to pretend not to see the abject," in this case Bonnie specifically.[45] Rather than pure hostility toward his mother, then, I read in Gilbert's character a kind of accurate comprehension; his harshness indicates the difficulty of the truth she embodies.

As Blocker signals, moreover, the medium of film encourages a more general recognition of Bonnie's embodiment of sorrow in the actress who plays her, an actress who was new to Hollywood at that time and who "is barely distinguishable from the character she portrays."[46] The fictional character Bonnie in this movie therefore opens a window directly into one form of maternal domesticity, and one form of subjectivity more generally. In this context, as Blocker aptly observes, "Bonnie Grape's relationship to the gaze is contradictory; she undoes the viewer at the same time that the viewer controls . . . her."[47] Texts work on readers and viewers, who are passive to some extent in reading, an element of knowledge work that tends to be underemphasized in humanist frameworks that privilege agency, control, and rationality. Bonnie's extreme condition thus only clarifies the more general reality that reading unhomes us from ourselves, exposing us to uncanny difference. I suggested this model of reading as haunting in chapter 1, and I extend this account of the reading/textual transaction in subsequent chapters, especially chapters 3 and 6.

Bonnie is a powerful semiotic figure, especially in the film, but more should be said about what exactly she embodies. Blocker resists a Jean Baudrillard–style reading, which would take her obesity as symbolic of excess consumption in capitalism. I agree that would be too simple, but I do not agree with Blocker's simple reversal: she instead sees Bonnie as a "heroine."[48] We need more nuance. Blocker is right that Bonnie behaves heroically at several key moments, especially in retrieving Arnie from jail, and several characters recognize it. Betty Carver says, "I admire her" (147), and Becky pronounces her "courageous" (161). But seeing Bonnie purely as a "heroine" insults her potential. A significant dimension of Bonnie is her role as a traumatic witness, more than either a heroine or a mere symbol. She has incorporated—in the form of obesity—the misery of her family's way of life. Like Melville's Bartleby, she prefers not to, resisting nearly all conventional forms of behavior. Much as I argued in chapter 1 about readings of Proulx, Blocker's heroine reading risks reifying an overly optimistic humanism organized around heroes and heroines, and thereby flattening some of this novel's complexity.

Instead, I suggest that Bonnie embodies homesickness. She demonstrates how consumption in capitalism is often profoundly *disconnected* from the good life, from happiness, and from home. She signifies perverse or uncanny consumption, a consumption that can seem compulsive, miserable, or even murderous; it is one more trap, one more route into unhomeliness. This is not the same as arguing, presumably *pace* Baudrillard, that she simply represents overconsumption, which would imply only that she should consume less. Her circumstances are worse than that. Consumption for Bonnie is not an excessive acceptance of cultural norms; it is an embodied rejection of them, a satirical exaggeration of the whole set of norms and values. She is a casualty of a misguided cultural system that needs redirection, and she and her family seem to have few alternatives. Her consumption is actually proof of her deep injuries. In that way, Bonnie embodies a critique much akin to the one I argue Proulx presents in the character of Tin Head in "The Half-Skinned Steer," as I addressed in chapter 1.

Bonnie's state of abject misery is visually reinforced by the film's extended treatment of the house. Many scenes focus on the creaky floor, bending under the weight of the mother, who is bloated with the family's loss and melancholy, and the film frequently screens the house's peeling paint and general decrepitude. The burning of the house is thus a symbolic destruction of the family's grief and shame, which the house embodies, and in that sense the fire denotes a partial escape of geographical and social determinism. But the house fire is also a traumatic, dramatic signifier of the family's shame, injuries, and loss. What will it lead to? It is not clear from the narrative. For a comparatively poor family, destroying their most valuable piece of property may make things even harder. For all these reasons, the burning house signifies a form of real but limited agency.

Home Burning as Weak Agency

As a demonstration of weak agency, house burning is a close parallel to suicide, not only in this plot but in Robinson's work as well. Suicide and home burning are dramatic signs of rejection and discontent, declarations of a woefully insufficient life. They are so powerful partly because they have an uncanny resemblance to more positive forms of agency. They demonstrate an ability to act even as they underscore—as profoundly as just about any other action—ultimate human weakness. The melancholic narratives studied in this chapter circle around this human vulnerability, from Ruth's brave, desperate confrontation of a harsh world—"come unhouse me of this flesh"—to the self-destructive actions of several members of the Grape family.

Suicide and its cousin signifier home burning powerfully reveal human weakness and mortality, recalling Jacques Derrida's discussion of ability in *The Animal That Therefore I Am*, treated in previous chapters and centering partly on the famous question raised by Jeremy Bentham about questions of ethics: "Can they suffer?" Bentham, resisting an ethics hinged on other forms of ability such as speech, argued instead that exposure to suffering should orient ethics. The question is not, Can a being speak? But can it suffer? As Derrida explains about this argument, "The question is disturbed by a certain *passivity*. It bears witness, manifesting already, as question, the response that testifies to a sufferance, a passion, a not-being-able. The word *can* [pouvoir] changes sense and sign here."[49] This focus on suffering, weakness, and exposure radically changes how we think of selfhood and agency.

This reading of the destruction of one's own home as a sign of weak agency is reinforced by the events immediately preceding the fire. After Momma's death, the elder sister, Janice, repeatedly insists on calling an ambulance. Gilbert resists, with increasing vehemence, first saying, "I just need more time to get used to the idea of Momma gone." Then he adds, "It doesn't sink in. It just doesn't sink in, does it?" (328). Death is bewildering, and haunting. It undermines familiar orientations, a point further underscored in this moment as Gilbert is forced to use the same word, "buddy," to encourage both his successful, worldly older brother, Larry, who has come home for Arnie's birthday, and his disabled younger brother, Arnie, to have a family talk (329). These otherwise radically opposite characters are stunned and confused in the same way in the face of death, and both need the same coaxing under the same sign of identity, "buddy." Gilbert, almost always able to have an ironic and observant distance from events, is completely overcome too. As he searches for younger sister Ellen to tell her the news of Momma's death, he says, "I keep repeating 'Momma's gone' in my head, hoping that it will sink in" (326). These are stark repetitions in a narrative that persistently highlights Arnie's verbal repetitions, labeled those of a "retard," in Gilbert's characteristically harsh diction. Yet now Gilbert, facing the traumatic truth of suffering and death, is likewise reduced to stuttering incomprehension. This is language not as ability but as murky sign of impairment.

The family takes time for Momma's death to register, listening to music she loved and talking through memories. Then they return to the refrain of this concluding section of the novel: "time to call" the ambulance, to have

Momma's body removed before the sun comes up (331). They do not want to have this done in the light of day, for fear of making Momma a spectacle one more time. Yet Gilbert continues to resist, finally yelling, "SHE IS NO JOKE! THEY'LL LAUGH AT HER AND POKE AT HER AND JUDGE HER! DO NOT LET THEM DO THAT!" (332). A moment of family indecision is followed by Gilbert "ripping the phone away" from Janice, unplugging it, and then carrying two of his dresser drawers outside to the front yard. The siblings are confused, but the sympathetic sister Amy understands, saying, "Gilbert's right. It's gonna take a crane to get her out." She goes on: "'Gilbert's also right—they will laugh and judge. And, yes, Momma deserves better.' She takes her stuff down the stairs and out onto the front lawn" (333).

Faced with these limited options and under the burden of Momma's embodied display of absolute weakness, Amy, like Gilbert, moves from verbal protest to concrete action. But her display of agency is uncanny, zeugmatic, and oddly ordinary in light of the momentous occasion. Responding to death by moving drawers? Yet, as she takes "her stuff down the stairs and out onto the front lawn," she renders those things strange, much as Ruth and Sylvie in *Housekeeping* feel their belongings become uncanny under the threat of social opprobrium. In the ensuing three hours, the Grape family has peeled the second skin of their desired belongings away from their house, piling them on the lawn. Then, using gasoline, that essential fuel of mobility and movement, they light the home on fire. Gilbert's narrative voice reports, "With my back to the house, I watch my brothers and sisters watch the fire grow. The light brightens their faces. I feel the heat on my neck. The downstairs must be in flames" (334). Hedges thus underscores how the meaning of this event for Gilbert is refracted through the experiences of his whole family, how the house on fire is culmination of this chapter of the whole family's narrative (Figure 4).

As in *Housekeeping*, the decision to light the fire seems as strange, sudden, and inevitable as death itself. Arnie says of the rapidly growing fire, "Scary, scary," which is perfectly apt. Gilbert as first-person narrator tells readers a paragraph later, "The fire is beautiful," but the final images of the family are those of mourning. Larry's "eyes are full and about to drip," "Ellen's got her eyes closed—she's listening to the fire," and the book's final paragraph reads this way: "The sirens [of approaching police] fill the air, the walls in Momma's room fall down in flames, and Amy says, 'Yes, Arnie, look

Figure 4. Burning down the house. The Grape family home burning down, with Momma's body inside, in the film *What's Eating Gilbert Grape.*

at the lights'" (335). Here, as at many other moments in the story, Arnie stands in for the rest of the family and for readers, positioned as observers of this final trauma, the ambiguous fire, which is both a freeing force and a revelation of suffering and entrapment.

As the novel's final page suggests, the fire has not freed the family from being a spectacle: "the police and newspaper people" will soon arrive (335). The question is what kind of spectacle they will be. Unlike the indignity they fear of removing Momma's body with a crane, the fire signals not only trauma but agency—if nothing else, protection of Momma's dignity—and hope for a new beginning. The characters unhouse themselves, forcing them to build new lives, and new selves.

Even if the burning of the house portends possible positive changes for the Grape family's future, it is important not to imagine that future as entirely free of the past. The tendency in Enlightenment subjectivity to forget or abject suffering, passivity, and loss—all conjured by suicide and home burning—is understandable for daily psychological functioning but harmful for deeply understanding the place of humanity in the cosmos. As so often in Anthropocene analyses, personal frames of meaning run counter to wider frames. We need a posthumanist version of subjectivity that recognizes human fallibility without getting lost in it. That is, as Timothy Morton argues in *Hyperobjects*—as noted earlier in this chapter—we must simultaneously recognize "a new human phase of *hypocrisy, weakness,* and *lameness,*" a phase deeply aware of human fragility in ways that Morton unfolds regarding these terms; but we cannot surrender all notions of human agency.[50]

Ferguson, Missouri, and "Burn[ing] Down Our Own House"

Burning down one's own house, like Bonnie's overeating, is a form of strange, even perverse, consumption, a kind of property suicide. The resonances of these episodes in fictional texts derive to some extent from the persistent importance of similar demonstrations in history. For example, many puzzled, often-conservative commentators have made this critique of urban "riots" in the United States, such as Watts (1965), Detroit (1967), Chicago (1968), and many others, generally failing to recognize that the prevailing modes of law and order are harmful to those protesting. That is at least one of the meanings of their destruction. It says that this form of social being, and these rules, are worthless—or worse, damaging—to me, to us.

In these demonstrations, many of the dynamics addressed in this chapter were also in play, as they were in the 1992 Los Angeles riots after the acquittal of police officers involved in the Rodney King beating, which occurred just after Hedges's book's publication. The August 2014 demonstrations in Ferguson, Missouri, near St. Louis, after a white police officer killed Michael Brown, an unarmed, black teenager, also follow these patterns. The demonstrations resulted in the destruction of a number of buildings, and they grew out of a history of racial injustice, intensified by what many condemned as the militarization of many American police forces following the 9/11 attacks.

I underscore again how clearly these concerns center on prevailing forms of social and material organization of life; racism is present in the very structure of the segregated city, in the dispensation of social force by way of military tools. But such profound elements of resistance can be difficult to register in more mundane debates about how to regard demonstrations. Thus, as *New York Times* reporter Alan Blinder noted in his coverage of these events, the Highway Patrol took over for the local police as matters escalated, and the person in charge, Captain Ronald S. Johnson, who became something of a hero, remarked, "We have to make sure that we don't burn down our own house, that we don't go down there and vandalize our own buildings."[51] While Johnson was a calming and well-meaning presence, his comment fails to recognize that this idea of "our own house" is radically questioned by the demonstrations, given that this form of ownership is so constrained by the larger history of racism (and capitalism). That history calls the very idea of "ownership" into question, exposing it less as possession or sovereignty (both synonyms for "ownership") and more as a forced, defensive action, weak agency in response to a larger history. Even "owners" of these buildings are constrained to play by the larger rules of property in a racist and segregated society. "Ownership," as I suggested in the beginning of this chapter, needs to be read in the context of slavery in these demonstrations, which are a short historical distance from the Thirteenth Amendment's abolition of slavery in 1865. Indeed, if we think more broadly, these demonstrations are not distant from slavery along a historical line of progress but part of the *same long moment* materialized in various ways, making that "history" of slavery persistent or present.[52]

Here again, then, the word "house" is densely metaphorical and semiotic, representing literal and symbolic structures at the core of the identity of the demonstrators. It matters that Captain Johnson "grew up in the area," as Blinder reports, and that he is African American, like many of the demonstrators. Identity, agency, and justice are all at issue in such episodes. Burning down one's own house is a dramatic mode of expression, signification, and control that earns the attention of major media organizations (and of cultural critics like me). These actions derive from the desperate frustration of being trapped in structures both literal and political. On this point, a *New York Times* article reporting on Ferguson by Tanzina Vega and John Eligon quotes a man who declines to give his name: "If it wasn't for the looting, we wouldn't get the attention."[53] We can add the fires and the demonstrations to this statement: They all reveal the failures of more conventional forms of social change—the failures of political agency—but they *are* significant actions. They exemplify weak agency.

Weak agency complicates the story of "rioting." As Janet L. Abu-Lughod argues in *Race, Space, and Riots in Chicago, New York, and Los Angeles*, discussing early twentieth-century riots in Harlem, "Rioting, albeit combined with astute political organization, achieved results that boycott alone had failed to do."[54] The rupture of civic peace and order brought by riots, then and today, brings much more attention to issues too often swept aside. But here again, the local and the particular matter: Abu-Lughod distinguishes the results of riots in New York City from those in Los Angeles by saying that the better political organization in New York meant that riots led to changes there, whereas in Los Angeles, "the 1965 and 1992 riots seem to persist in a time warp: the uprisings did not achieve their ends but cycled back to equivalent levels of powerlessness."[55]

This point about a "time warp" coordinates with my suggestions about time above. It also underscores how agency is always shared or distributed; no person, by her- or himself, has the power to upend long-term historical and material realities. To make change, people must activate whole networks and help them shift their function. That is weak agency. This point is not merely theoretical or academic; it is practical. To better resist the violence of racism and its damage to individual lives, we have to more self-consciously embrace the fact of weak or distributed agency, recognizing that demonstrations matter but that their context, their reception, and their affiliations matter too. One context is the long and important history of justice. Viewed within the longer history of race riots and ethnic violence, the events in Ferguson, Missouri, are another example of human rights, personal dignity, and desire for legal justice trumping the concern for private property as construed by modern capitalism, much as in the novels analyzed in this chapter. The preference for justice over property is at the heart of (at least one version of) the national story of the United States itself.

Rioting, home burning, suicide: these potent, embodied forms of signification both protest injustice and testify to weak agency. Yet they also insist on a form of dignity held by those without other recourse to express unrest. They are actions, and they often indicate more than mere destructiveness. In Hedges's novel, it is defense of Bonnie Grape's personal dignity that motivates the family to burn down their house rather than have her suffer embarrassment in death. Those dynamics make it more difficult for outsiders to understand the house burning, since the family does not want others to know the details. It is much the same situation in *Housekeeping*, where the town's invasive meddling drives Ruth and Sylvia to attempt to destroy their home rather than be forced to inhabit it in a fashion not of their choosing. Similarly, protestors in Ferguson and elsewhere insist—with fire!—on being treated with dignity and humanity, when it is so challenging for them to be heard otherwise. Aligning Hedges's novel with so-called race riots in urban centers underscores how trauma and economic marginalization, even at the domestic scale in the case of the Grapes, can produce similar consequences across the segregating lines of "race." Rural, "white" Iowans resort to unusual measures in defense of dignity, much as "black," urban Missourians and others do.

This fact corrects against implicitly racist notions that only "ethnic" groups protest in these ways. Like protesters expressing outrage about unjust power structures, the Grape family and Sylvie and Ruth all know they cannot fully control all the events that matter to them, and that very lack of control leads them to feel unhoused from themselves. In their attempts to reverse this dynamic by unhousing themselves with dramatic statements in fire, they expose the limits of individualist agency. Sylvie and Ruth are thereby rendered homeless ghosts, while the Grape children, one hopes, will rise from the ashes and make better lives. But any new beginning for them will necessarily be, as Haraway puts it, a becoming-with.

While there are clear likenesses among these fictional and historical examples of weak agency, it is important to reiterate the differences as well. Gender, racial, and class oppression are intersectional, but they are also distinct, with particular causes and symptoms that I do not mean to collapse into a singular or simple homesickness. Similarly, while I understand the house on fire as a kind of icon of the Anthropocene, like any image, it risks obscuring differences and particularities precisely in being representational. Nonetheless, and running that risk, in concluding I want to zoom back out and reiterate a wider point at the scale of the Anthropocene, an epoch legible as a kind of burning down the house of Earth. Thinking at wide scales helps us recognize that the impact of fire reaches deeper into the past than even the very species *Homo sapiens,* as noted above. So the kind of cooperative agency that fire facilitates is far from novel or accidental. Our very species itself became-with fire, and we have continued to cultivate that strange force in our engines and machines. Indeed, our Enlightenment-inspired dogma that we do all this alone, as ostensible kings (owners? sovereigns?) of the planet is precisely what the Anthropocene calls into question. The traumas and changes to nonhuman ecologies and climate systems remind us with special force that everything humans do is accomplished with shared agency. That crucial point ought to be reentered into considerations of law and property, ownership and selfhood, recognizing that the Anthropocene is akin to a riot of the planet, a material demonstration that prevailing modes of human culture are causing astonishing harm. Musing and mulling the icon of houses on fire is one way to engage this problem at a broad scale, but the effort to more deliberately embrace our becomings-with will also require us to home back in to much finer, more local scales with situated and particular responses, distinctive in every case.

3

The Elephant in the Writing Room

Hemingway's Travels, Eco-cosmopolitanism, and the Desire for Africa

> I had been a fool not to have stayed on in Africa and instead had gone back to America where I had killed my homesickness for Africa in different ways.
>
> —Ernest Hemingway, *Under Kilimanjaro*

Chapter 2 studied place and home as entrapping, featuring characters and people who resist their limiting circumstances with demonstrations of fire. This chapter, focused on Ernest Hemingway, investigates the opposite extreme: privileged and even destructive travel. Hemingway himself traveled an extraordinary amount. He traversed Europe regularly; he went to Africa, China, Canada; and he took frequent cross-country trips in North America, mostly in an age before comfortable air travel and user-friendly interstate highways. Hemingway lived in Cuba for much of his adult life (1939–59), longer than any other place, although during those years he often spent summers in the Rocky Mountains of Wyoming and Idaho. It hardly needs recounting that he is perhaps as famous for his connections to Pamplona, Cuba, and Paris as he is for his writing. In short, Hemingway was a savvy traveler, a cosmopolitan, renowned for exploring interesting places and cultural experiences. He wrote compellingly about many of these locales, attentive to their nuances, finding different ways to make himself happy in many of them.

Kevin Maier, writing in the *Hemingway Review*, summarizes that Hemingway sought "the authentic both off the beaten path and in vibrant cultural centers."[1] Maier underscores that Hemingway's journeys took place as transportation technology was rapidly modernizing. These changes created a world in which the transatlantic trip to Europe, for instance, has become much more accessible. In her 2011 history titled *Homesickness,* Susan J. Matt writes generally on this topic: "In the early nineteenth century, the trip from Western Europe to America took between four and six weeks; by the end of the century, it took only seven days."[2] Today, on an airplane it is only a matter of seven or so hours.

It is worth dwelling for a moment on the orders of magnitude in these changes—from weeks to days to hours. In a world of such drastic changes in transportation technology, it has indeed at times seemed as if, in Thomas L. Friedman's phrase, the world has become flat.[3] But I have insisted that such seeming ease in mobility can blind us to the very real and persistent difficulties of travel, not just in terms of logistics and movement—even on an airplane—but more particularly in terms of engaging with, and adapting to, new places and cultures. Such challenges make cosmopolitanism more difficult than it first appears, and this book investigates what those difficulties mean to human life more broadly. Hemingway—because of his fame, his significant travel experience, and his privileged status—is a particularly compelling figure to study in this light. His life and work clarify not only the challenges of cosmopolitan identity but also the imbrication of all human identity in nonhuman realities, both ecological and technological. In short, Hemingway's life suggests what it might mean to be posthumanist.

One route into an eco-cosmopolitan, posthumanist reading of Hemingway begins with his first transatlantic trip in World War I, which established a template for many of his later travels and for much of his later life more generally. This trip, though voluntary in a thin sense, clearly demonstrated Hemingway's *subjection* to a traumatic set of international circumstances, intermingling a cosmopolitanism with exposure to personal harm and to cultural and existential crisis. In this way, his experience was typical of the many millions involved in the Great War. The limits of Hemingway's agency in World War I were both personal and systematic: his eyesight difficulties prevented him from joining the military effort in the fashion he preferred, leading him instead to join the Red Cross, where, as an ambulance driver in that large, complex organization, Hemingway's agency was necessarily limited and imbricated in social networks and more-than-human networks;

then, a few weeks after going to the Italian front, he was seriously injured by a mortar shell.[4] This is hardly the pure dream of a cosmopolitan mobility, and the experiences of this trip permanently marked Hemingway's selfhood. His ensuing sensibility can be understood as posttraumatic, frequently leading him to frame experience (reductively) in terms of killing or life and death, as in the epigraph of this chapter. This reality underscores the problem that I address more directly in chapter 6: the difficulty of relating wartime subjectivity with that of peacetime. The selfhood of war, especially modern war, is so radically other to peacetime selfhood that veterans commonly feel radically alienated from their homes and their old selves. Hemingway's story "Soldier's Home" is an early exploration of this kind of homesickness.[5]

And a second recalibration: Does it make sense to regard Hemingway as American? The norms and protocols of literary interpretation have tended to corral writers into national designations. In Hemingway's case, this can be particularly jarring, as when his home in Cuba is understood as a key endangered site, specifically, of American historic places.[6] The move—need it be said?—smacks of imperialist appropriation, in which the work of a profoundly internationalist writer, whose writing relies on the lives and realities of places well outside America, is collapsed back into hegemonic American culture, along with his very home itself on foreign soil. Of course I am in favor of preserving Hemingway's house in Cuba, but this example demonstrates how the nationalist frame of interpretation can fail in striking ways.

Instead, it seems more fitting to understand Hemingway as postnational, as cosmopolitan or even eco-cosmopolitan.[7] His unusual combination of place-love, careful observation, and durable mobility led him to feel homesick for many of the places he visited. It is all too easy to dismiss these feelings as either sentimental or privileged or both. They *are* in fact both, but that is essential to what makes them useful and telling. Hemingway's feelings about place clarify what it means to live in an ever-increasingly mobile world, where, paradoxically, love for and defense of particular places, of particular forms of life, has become even more important, precisely because of mobility and the vast changes it, and the associated carbon regime, has wrought.

Hemingway's pattern was to establish a kind of psychological home in a place, and ever after, that place became a resource and a focus of desire for him in a retrospective structure of the sort I detailed in the introduction. It may seem tempting to call Hemingway's homesickness imperialist appropriation or “imperialist nostalgia” and leave it at that, a charge Louise H. Westling makes in *The Green Breast of the New World.*[8] But that critique fails to register the complicity with structures of power that many of us share with Hemingway. This dismissal also tacitly conceives of morality as a system of beliefs that is never in doubt. Yet Derrida, and before him Levinas, exposed the problems with that view of ethics, emphasizing especially the importance of doubt to any ethics worthy of the name.[9] Hemingway understood ethics in a similar way, suggesting, for example, in *Death in the Afternoon* that “what is moral is what you feel good after and what is immoral is what you feel bad after.”[10] Furthermore, I am arguing that Hemingway’s habit of feeling about a range of places actually demonstrates a structure that is essential to all human subjectivity, exposed to mortality and the passing of time. As I argued in the introduction, subjectivity is always too late, and always retrospective. Further yet, when we acknowledge in a posthumanist way that the human self is always already coconstituted with its many others, animal, material, geographical, then homesickness—an uncanny alienation from the self often appearing as a desire for the familiar—becomes an inevitable result.

Hemingway’s unusual privilege in movement, intensified by the advance of transportation technologies in his lifetime, simply accented this larger structure of selfhood. His trauma-driven compulsion to encounter new places and to take risks further deepened his insights into this strange sense of homesickness. He regularly mentioned feeling “homesick” for these places, though calling them “home” stretches our conventional understanding of the term (in a way he very much intended). Hemingway felt at home—or tried to feel at home—in places that compelled and interested him, in short, rather than at home in his native Oak Park, an early Chicago suburb. Miriam B. Mandel argues compellingly that, although he aimed to live a “liberated” modern life that indulged in “lots of travel, reading, hunting, fishing, and safaris,” Hemingway nonetheless also felt a contrary tug of conventional moral purpose. Mandel suggests, “He was still struggling against the concept of home, whose values diluted or undercut his pleasure in the lifestyle he had chosen.”[11] In other words, at issue in Hemingway’s thinking about “home” are precisely the norms and expectations of a good life. If for William Wordsworth, famously, “all good poetry is the spontaneous overflow of powerful feelings,” about which the poet has also “thought long and deeply,”[12] for

Hemingway, homesickness was likewise a powerful cluster of feelings and desires recollected in comparative tranquility. These terms—"homesickness" and "poetry"—do similar work for these two figures, gathering together something like the most essential desires and emotional truths from their lives.

The difference in terms reflects not only the difference in personalities but, more importantly for my purposes here, the differences between their historical moments. In Hemingway's period, and especially in his social class during the years of the world wars, fixed and familiar ideas of home were seriously reworked. He lived through the radical changes of worldwide mobility and, if you like, deterritorialization, culminating in what many now call the Great Acceleration after 1945, with the carbon economy exploding. Deterritorialization indeed. Partly due to his mixture of intelligent sensitivity, brazen and exaggerated masculinity, and class and race privilege, Hemingway experienced more mobility than most. The corollary: his homesickness was especially intense, especially as it mixed in his sensibility with the traumas of modern life and experience in war. It seems fair to say, recalling chapter 1 of *Homesickness,* that Hemingway was haunted both by the ghosts of places he loved and places he hated and dreaded, ghosts that peopled his mind and his writing. Hemingway's homesickness epitomized his posttraumatic desires, which continue to resonate in readers in complex ways. A haunting image evoking all these feelings is the one he conjures, via memory, in *The Garden of Eden,* of an elephant the protagonist's father helped murder in Africa. This specific animal—his power to command Hemingway's imagination, memory, and sympathy—is a synecdoche of the overwhelming nonhuman presence in human language more generally, despite the fantastical claims of humanism to stand above the rest of creation. It is the elephant in the writing room, writ large. But before I investigate that complex image and novel, it is important to detail more of Hemingway's own homesickness and its cultural context.

Hemingway's Early Homesickness

I noted above that Hemingway's intellectual and authorial life tended to follow a pattern largely set by his first major life trauma, his injury in Italy working in the Red Cross ambulance corps in World War I. The importance of that injury was noted during his lifetime in the criticism of Philip Young.[13] Hemingway resisted Young's assessment—or, perhaps, psychological diagnosis—insisting on preserving the sense of control over his writerly identity.[14] In any case, that first injury, followed by a long hospital stay, helped establish the pattern of overwhelming experience followed by analysis, assessment, and aesthesis about those experiences—that is, followed by writing. Running parallel to that process was often a feeling of homesickness derived from his time thinking about the past.

Thus, when Hemingway was laid up injured during World War I in a hospital in Milan, he and his heartthrob Agnes von Kurowsky talked of making a "home" of their shared stay in the hospital.[15] That structure of understanding—making a home in companionship even in very temporary locations—appears in much of Hemingway's fiction too, as when in *A Farewell to Arms* Henry is able to see Catherine again and they "come home" to their hotel.[16] Similarly, during a period Hemingway spent in Piggott, Arkansas, in 1928, as his second wife, Pauline, prepared to have their child, Hemingway felt "homesick for northern Michigan and the scenes of his boyhood," though he also mentioned in letters to his friends from this time that he felt "homesickness for Wyoming, Zaragoza, Key West, and Paris."[17] In 1932, likewise, when he was living with Pauline in Key West, he wrote to painter Waldo Pierce, his friend, that "home for guys like us is a place that should be left in order to come back to."[18] This pattern is perhaps most prominently displayed in his famous fictional memoir, *A Moveable Feast,* which includes the following epigraph: "If you are lucky enough to have lived in Paris as a young man, then wherever you go for the rest of your life, it stays with you, for Paris is a moveable feast."[19]

Memoir is a genre of homesickness, and memoir in various forms dominated much of Hemingway's late writing. He was still at work on *A Moveable Feast* when he committed suicide (scholars dispute how complete the book was), and he had spent significant time working on the manuscript that became *Under Kilimanjaro* (first published as *True at First Light*), which is also a kind of fictionalized memoir.[20] This style of writing, bridging genres, had long appealed to Hemingway. He completed both *Green Hills of Africa* and *Death in the Afternoon* in the 1930s, which mix fiction and nonfiction to some extent, though the former is more properly like memoir than the latter.[21] In *Under Kilimanjaro,* which treats Hemingway's second and final safari in East Africa in the 1950s, Hemingway articulates his intense interest in and love for Africa. At one point in the text during lunch, the Hemingway character recalls his earlier time spent in Africa, thinking, "I had been a fool not to have stayed on in Africa and instead had gone back to America where I had killed my homesickness for Africa in various ways" (205). This feeling of homesickness for Africa proves very complex, evoking larger cultural trends of primitivism and colonialism, in ways the remainder of this chapter explores.

Homesick for Africa

Hemingway's interest in Africa has provoked criticism in terms of colonialism and racism. For instance, in her book *Playing in the Dark: Whiteness and the Literary Imagination,* Toni Morrison argues that Hemingway understands Africa as a "blank, empty space" open for conquest.[22] Morrison's charge is part of her nuanced, compelling study of how American literature relies on a black African and African American presence. She exposes many moments in which a structure of power hinges on the presence of subjugated black people, and she convincingly shows how that structure operates in many Hemingway texts. Still, Morrison's study of Hemingway could recognize more fully the complexity of his treatment of power dynamics. She notices, for instance, that in many cases in Hemingway's work, "black men articulate the narrator's doom" and "disturb, in subtle and forceful ways, the narrator's construction of reality." But Morrison calls such moments "slips of the pen."[23] That dismissal is too easy. I agree that Hemingway's racial discourse is uneven and at times deeply reliant on an Africanist presence in disturbing ways. Quite often, however, I believe Hemingway embraces the disruptive views of his works' black men. Sometimes that embrace is even his main purpose.

Morrison's claim that Hemingway's Africa is empty also simplifies both Hemingway's attitude toward Africa and the problem of place, mobility, and cosmopolitanism more generally.[24] He had already begun to explore this problem in *Green Hills of Africa* (1935). In a famous, often-quoted section near the end of that book, he both criticizes imperial/colonial interventions *and* insists on the necessity and even right of people to move. First the critique: "A continent ages quickly once we come. The natives live in harmony with it. But the foreigner destroys, cuts down the trees, drains the water, so that the water supply is altered, and in a short time the soil . . . starts to blow away. . . . The earth gets tired of being exploited" (284). While this account may oversimplify things, particularly in its idealization of "natives," which evokes the reductive myth of the noble savage, its general shape has often proven true. Its first-person plural ("we come") self-consciously positions Hemingway squarely within the colonialist behavior he challenges. Hemingway continues in this vein: "We are the intruders and after we are dead we may have ruined it but it will still be there and we don't know what the next changes are" (284–85). This is a notably skeptical, even pessimistic, attitude toward imperialist cosmopolitanism. Death is important here, since acknowledging it permits Hemingway to articulate concern for the future—"we don't know what the next changes are." This is a posthumanist gesture in its humbling of the stance of the individual and in its insistence on the value of "the earth," of place, of nonhuman life, in acknowledgment of their massive importance. But what costs will have been paid by the place and its inhabitants, human and nonhuman?

At first in this section, Hemingway insists he would inhabit Africa differently: "I would come back to Africa but not to make a living from it." The passage continues, "I would come back to where it pleased me to live; to really live. Not just let my life pass" (285). Hemingway's homesickness for Africa involves his desire to inhabit a place where the human animal can live well, a desire that has driven human mobility throughout history and before. But in this context the desire is tempered by awareness of individual limitations and death. The value of the land goes two ways, then: to understand the land's value means living in a way that is not purely exploitative, requiring devotion to place; but it also means going to a place where the "land" remains a nonhuman presence worth engaging. Go and stay. This structure of feeling is the direct result of modernity's facilitation of movement via machine ensembles—and modernity's ensuing depredations of places.

As the passage continues, these complications regarding home and mobility multiply: "Our people went to America because that was the place to go then. It had been a good country and we had made a bloody mess of it and I would go, now, somewhere else as we had always had the right to go somewhere else and as we had always gone" (285). After several more sentences, this expression of place desire turns into a specific list enumerating reasons for his love of Africa: "There was game, plenty of birds, and I liked the natives. Here I could shoot and fish" (285). Here again, the discussion contradicts itself, as Hemingway seems to recognize. He admits that "our people" had hurt the landscape and ecology of America, which was part of why Hemingway desired Africa. He has also named interests that, if everyone pursued, may well lead—have often led—to the ruination of other places. Yet he also expresses his desire not to just "make a living from" the land, connected to his disdain from those who fail to put human life into a broader perspective. These criticisms are directed partly at Hemingway's own cultural heritage and even at himself.

The passage offers a proto-ecological perspective on human life that is essentially shaped by awareness of human mortality and ephemerality, and that recognizes human weakness in the theoretical sense as well. That is, the human is always composed to some extent by the environment, whatever that environment may be; the boundaries of the human are "weak," permeable. This is a moment of homesickness in this study's richer sense, then; homesickness is both this desire to inhabit a place well, to live fully, and the awareness that human life can be very damaging to the places we love. We make our homes sick. Hemingway's later works in particular highlight regrets about how he and his progenitors lived, and this is the more negative notion of homesickness—the recognition that home never was what it seemed to be, that one's own native cultures have been regrettable in key ways. Such mixed feelings about his own selfhood and Africa take canonical form in his short story "The Snows of Kilimanjaro," with its mixture of self-condemnation and desire.[25] That story is worth exploring more in these terms, though I lack the space to do so here.

On his second African safari (1953–54), Hemingway extends and solidifies many of the lessons he learned on the first safari, constantly underscoring the value of deep inhabitation, of robust, self-conscious engagement with nonhuman and human elements of particular places. This is reflected in the opening of *Under Kilimanjaro,* which highlights the tensions of the Mau Mau rebellion in Kenya during the 1950s in a series of paragraphs that do not appear in the earlier edition of the book, *True at First Light.* As noted by the editors of *Under Kilimanjaro,* Robert W. Lewis and Robert E. Fleming, "The Mau Mau was a secret society of Africans (largely Kikuyus) whose goal was to expel white colonizers from Kenya."[26] This set of local and political concerns is put into the foreground immediately, self-consciously marking a contrast with Hemingway's earlier safari book *Green Hills of Africa,* which opens with a much more narrowly focused, more self-involved scene about the dynamics of Hemingway's own hunting, revealing him perhaps more as tourist than traveler or cosmopolitan. The text of *Under Kilimanjaro* is clear that much of this difference is due not only to Hemingway's better sense of the politics of colonialism but to how "things had changed very much in East Africa" (2). That is, African resistance to colonialism has forced a more general change. This translates to routine naming practices on safari, for example. Discussing his hunting assistants, Hemingway notes the racist and colonialist norms that permitted calling them "boys" in the 1930s (he does not use the terms "racist" and "colonialist"). By the 1950s, however, "you did not do it. Everyone had his duties and everyone had a name. Not to know a name was both impolite and a sign of sloppiness" (6).

Personal relationships on this second safari, however, are complicated, eliciting much debate among critics about their dynamics. Jeremiah M. Kitunda, for example, describes Hemingway's "treatment of African reality and people as complex to the point of contradiction: generally sympathetic, but sometimes sarcastic, superficial (as in the matter of the Mau Mau), and even falling into the easy romanticism of travelogues."[27] I would note, though, that this description applies well to Hemingway's treatment of most people everywhere, throughout his writing, including himself. Kitunda also faults Hemingway for failing to truly register the environmental tensions in Africa of the 1950s.[28] When critics read *Under Kilimanjaro* more affirmatively, it is often in the context of Hemingway's own personal search for meaning. Mandel underscores a measure of personal and biographical liberation that Hemingway found in Africa as part of his effort to justify and theorize his life preferences, efforts he describes as a search for a "new religion."[29] I suggest more fully below that this is a far-reaching inquiry into the norms and purposes of life, and I think it is cosmopolitan in the sense of being inspired and enabled by cultural and geographical difference, but it is also deeply problematic in the ways Kitunda signals.

The book exemplifies, then, the particularity and individuality of cosmopolitan searching and thus, in a sense, the inevitable failure to be fully cosmopolitan in a pure or absolute sense. In that regard, it can read as parallel to, or perhaps mirroring, the case Njabulo S. Ndebele makes in "Game Lodges and Leisure Colonialists."[30] There he describes his experience as a black African staying at a game lodge in South Africa, feeling a tension between being pulled back into colonial and racial (racist) roles and inhabiting his postcolonial professional identity as a customer. His work to forge a new and distinct identity has to overcome the friction of the past, a past that surrounds him to a large degree at the game lodge. Similarly, Hemingway's

Under Kilimanjaro, whatever the author's intentions, often feels caught in the larger gravity of colonialism, imperialism, and racism, signaling that the haunting presence of that history cannot easily be escaped. To be reductive, Hemingway tries to go native but ultimately cannot, while Ndebele's cosmopolitanism is encumbered by the persistence of the colonialist past.

This dynamic perhaps feeds Hemingway's already strong tendency to focus on the nonhuman in places, be they Kenyan, American, Cuban, or the like, a tendency that is especially pronounced in Africa. Here again, the ecocosmopolitan impulse is double edged. The very focus on the nonhuman, perhaps ostensibly apolitical, is in fact deeply political. As Achille Mbembe notes in opening *On the Postcolony,* Africa can seem ineluctably caught in "*negative interpretation.* Africa is never seen as possessing things and attributes properly part of 'human nature.' Or, when it is, its things and attributes are generally of lesser value, little importance, and poor quality. It is this elementariness and primitiveness that makes Africa the world par excellence of all that is incomplete, mutilated, and unfinished."[31] It can seem easy to collapse Hemingway's writing in and about Africa into this trap, and sometimes that is deserved.

I recognize these problems in Hemingway's work, but I also look to what is enabling, productive, and distinctive about it, under the premise that this is a key function of criticism, alongside pointing to shortfalls in a writer's work. Indeed, this chapter argues that Hemingway proves both more circumspect about the problem of racism than we might guess and much more serious about nonhuman animals, which involves a serious politics too. This combination becomes more visible in light of Hemingway's robust and radical critiques of modernity more generally—capitalism, the commodification of everything, and the world wars. Read in light of this radical skepticism, Hemingway's attempts to rethink what it means to be a human animal perform important work. Via an ostensible leisure practice (safari) that ends up crossing back into labor (publishing), he complicates one of the most powerful logics that drives capitalism, the labor/leisure distinction. He replaces faith in progress and work with an ethics of self-experimentation, or perhaps with a self made by experimenting with ethics. In the big picture, his love of and desire for the primacy of experience in a more-than-human world of animals and danger can contribute to one of the projects Mbembe advocates: questioning the teleologies of "social evolutionism and ideologies of development and modernization."[32]

One key passage in the second safari account explores Hemingway's awareness of place in terms of the animals who live there, a common mode for him.

> I thought how lucky we were this time in Africa to be living long enough in one place so that we knew the individual animals and knew the snake holes and the snakes that lived in them. When I had first been to Africa we were always in a hurry to move from one place to another to hunt beasts for trophies. If you saw a cobra it was an accident as it would be to find a rattler on the road in Wyoming. Now we knew many places where cobras lived. (*Under Kilimanjaro*, 116; *True at First Light*, 97–98)

Here again is a strikingly paradoxical homesickness. This passage criticizes excessive mobility, the "hurry to move from one place to another," in order to praise careful inhabitation of an Africa that is manifestly not Hemingway's home. He is there because modernity has ruined the chance to live this way in many other places. These two safaris referenced in the passage might be distinguished as tourism in the earlier case and travel—or even as something else, wayfaring?—in the second.[33] Maier reminds us that the distinction between traveler and tourist was emerging in the early twentieth century as "travel became more accessible and travel guides directed ever-larger groups of people to the same popular sites." As this occurred, "Hemingway sought to differentiate his mode of travel from tourism."[34] Hemingway's retrospective criticism of his first safari trip can be read as part of that desire.

The more localized and particularized awareness on the later trip—manifested in terms of animals—seems tied to the claim Hemingway makes in the paragraph that follows the one quoted above: "The time of shooting beasts for trophies was long past with me." Instead, he "was shooting for the meat we needed to eat and to back up Miss Mary and against beasts that had been outlawed for cause" (*Under Kilimanjaro*, 116–17; *True at First Light*, 98). Although the paragraph goes on, oddly, to mention an impala that he did in fact shoot "for trophy," Hemingway clearly marks out a critique of wasteful killing here, as critics have suggested. In place of the recreational pursuit of animals that is trophy hunting, Hemingway emphasizes his experiences, his engaged knowledge of place.

Such interests suggest that Hemingway can be seen as a new form of regionalist writer, sharing some allegiances and disposition with Sarah Orne

Jewett, Willa Cather, and others but expressing them through the machinery and nonhuman ensembles of a much more mobile, carbon-intensive mode. He is particularly interesting in this light because he seems so manifestly cosmopolitan yet was so powerfully interested in the local and the particular. In this way, he compellingly demonstrates my claim in this book that every writer, no matter how cosmopolitan, is also a local writer. We might even go as far as Morton in *Dark Ecology,* where he suggests that "art, in an ecological age, will melt into kitsch because there will be no single, authoritative scale from which to judge."[35] Critiques of the universalist presumptions of cosmopolitanism, discussed in the introduction, already suggest such a debasement or radical relativizing.

Of course, Hemingway's desire for Africa is part of a larger modernist primitivism, which reached beyond the art of Pablo Picasso or Paul Gauguin to impact the whole intellectual climate, including the sciences and politics. On this latter point, Suzanne Clark's *Cold Warriors: Manliness on Trial in the Rhetoric of the West* offers many rich examples, such as her discussion of Teddy Roosevelt's interest in hunting and its impacts on his explicitly political stances. Clark connects Roosevelt's time leading a "strenuous life" in the Dakotas and eventually in Africa to his beliefs about American imperialism: "Progress was not equated with more and more civilized behavior, but rather with strenuous effort. . . . The narrative of modernity equates evolutionary progress with *fitness.* The Roosevelt/American version of progress thought not in terms of reproduction of the species, but in terms of manly striving that reproduced an American individual."[36] That is why, faced with depression after the loss of his wife, Roosevelt left the U.S. East Coast for the Dakotas, where he could remake himself—reproduce himself—in more virile form. That (onanism?), roughly, was Roosevelt's prescription for global political concerns as well. Clark underscores, "At a time when linguistic philosophy began to think in terms of structures that carefully distinguished logical truths from claims about reality, Roosevelt collapsed the distinction between representation and reality by emphasizing the reality/truth of the act."[37] Roosevelt, in short, espoused a kind of naïve realism epitomized in the powerful and virulent male person.

Surprisingly, Clark shows not only that Hemingway resisted this simple mode of thinking, despite stereotypes of him (often fueled by his own actions); she also shows that Hemingway's resistance exposed him to harsh criticism after World War II. Hemingway unsettled oversimple valorization of war, for example, and tended to write in a way that underscored the difficulties involved in representation more generally. In other words, Clark's chapter on Hemingway and Roosevelt in *Cold Warriors* offers a sophisticated reading of what is often understood as Hemingway's primitivism, which she distinguishes from Roosevelt's. Clark recognizes that Hemingway was influenced by Roosevelt, but she notes that this influence was also complex, with points of resistance.[38] I suggest that if Roosevelt offered a prescription of American dominance through the ideal of the strenuous life, Hemingway's strenuous life often flipped back around to reveal human vulnerability and complexity. His homesick writing procedure noted above, with periods of strenuous activity followed by a serious and committed analysis of it via writing, drove Hemingway to difficult admissions about human fallibility and weakness. This structure is perhaps a version of Anthropocene awareness in miniature: vigorous enactment of a cultural logic followed by wary recognition of the culture's flaws and cultural revision.

A key difference that too often disappears in readings of Hemingway centers on the function of foreignness in his work, a foreignness, I noted at the opening of this chapter, very much at the center of his oeuvre. Clark resists critics who flatten Hemingway's treatment of difference into simple dominance. She underscores that when Hemingway writes about "American Indians, Spanish bullfighters, the gypsies, the Cuban peasant fisherman of *Old Man and the Sea,*" there is an estrangement effect; there "is always a political doubleness about such frontiers and contact."[39]

I heartily echo this point because we need models for encounters between self and other, between the familiar and the unknown, that go beyond what often seems an unavoidable dominance. Otherwise we are locked into a narrow isolationism, a nativism, a xenophobia. Despite his reputation, much of Hemingway's work presents an entry into useful considerations about this type of complex eco-cosmopolitanism. Indeed, especially because many view Hemingway as the classic modern example of a domineering, imperious masculinity, it is valuable to see how his work was in fact more nuanced. For Clark, these elements in Hemingway's work, in texts like *For Whom the Bell Tolls,* open alternatives to contemporary capitalism and militarism. Yet Clark shows how the political climate of the 1950s United States effaced such possibilities and made large parts of Hemingway's work illegible or even invisible. Indeed, Clark notes that the intensity of attacks on Hemingway made it more difficult for him even to *publish* his later writing, and probably "also had a silencing effect" on him, likely preventing him from writing as much as he might have. Clark admits that "no one can assess the extent to which these conditions kept Hemingway from writing at all," but that we do know from his letters and such just how much he was adversely affected by the critical climate.[40]

Difficulties writing are mostly invisible, but Hemingway's hunting in Africa connects to major American cultural norms and institutions that are very visible, like New York's Museum of Natural History. We must read carefully his engagements in these activities or risk losing their nuances. Both Hemingway and his predecessors saw their trips to Africa as uncommonly significant. In this vein, Donna Haraway's trenchant reading of the Museum of Natural History in *Primate Visions,* cited by Clark, highlights Roosevelt hunting animal specimens in Africa and his followers, like Carl Akeley. Both names—Akeley and Roosevelt—adorn essential parts of the museum still today, and the Akeley Hall, according to the museum's website, "is considered by many to be among the world's greatest museum displays."[41]

Haraway does not seem to disagree with this assessment in general, particularly with regard to the gorilla group in the museum, which she says "stands out from the others."[42] She explains that this exhibit displays "the scene that Akeley longed to return to. It is where he died, feeling he was at home as in no other place on earth."[43] This display includes "the lone silverback gorilla," the Giant of Karisimbi, who was killed to "inhabit Akeley's monument to the purity of nature."[44] For Haraway, this gorilla is presented as a "double for man," memorializing Akeley as "the fulfillment of a sportsman in Teddy Bear Patriarchy."[45] Haraway highlights the deep irony of this system of masculinist identity: "Man is the sex which risks life and in so doing, achieves his existence. In the upside down world of Teddy Bear Patriarchy, it is in the craft of killing that life is constructed, not in the accident of personal, maternal birth."[46] Further, as Haraway emphasizes in opening her chapter, the Akeley exhibit, in the American Museum of Natural History, thereby resides in what is "a monumental reproduction of the Garden of Eden." That building, in turn, lies in New York City's Central Park, "the urban garden designed by Frederick Law Olmsted to heal the overwrought or decadent city dweller with a prophylactic dose of nature."[47]

It seems impossible to overstate the significance of these locations and constructions. One of the world's great urban centers, a profoundly cosmopolitan place, has at its heart a monument that rejects cities, technology, and, at least in a sense, cosmopolitanism. Haraway reminds readers that the natural history movement of the late nineteenth and early twentieth centuries, with its unease about urbanization, also ran in league with eugenics and nativist anxieties about immigration. Yet Central Park houses a museum that expresses these concerns with a return not to a white Europe, say, but to Africa and the Garden of Eden. Indeed, this is where Akeley understood himself to be most at home! Ironies are thicker than tourists here. The hope was to escape the perceived decadence and corruption of the present. Haraway suggests that "in [the] immediate vision of the origin, perhaps the future can be fixed. By saving the beginnings, the end can be achieved and the present can be transcended."[48]

Haraway's account unforgettably exposes the contradictory ideological work of the museum. But the power of her analysis can make it too easy to reject entirely the questions about ostensible civilizational development that animated Akeley and Roosevelt. From our perspective in the Anthropocene, it is possible to accept some of Roosevelt's cultural critiques while condemning the masculinist, imperialist, eugenic thinking that accompanied them. Further, and most especially for this book's argument, Haraway's suspicion about the nostalgic effort to secure a fixed past is too easily joined with the more general, default rejection of nostalgia common to contemporary Enlightenment and cosmopolitan subjectivities.

My case here, on the other hand, is that acknowledging this homesick structure of selfhood can run in the opposite direction, answering to Haraway's concerns: instead of "saving the beginning," complex homesickness reiterates the openness and complexity of life and evolution. Complex homesickness, that is, undermines the larger framework that would aim to purify contemporary social structures by fixing in place an imagined past. Instead, this homesick selfhood, with its posthumanist acknowledgment of human interdependence with so many others, facilitates a more open, ethical, and hopefully enjoyable mode of life, akin to modes Haraway advocates. Although Roosevelt and Akeley often expressed their longings in violent and contradictory ways, it is possible to see how even their desires to be among animals in a place far less marked by human presence actually has something in common with conceptions Haraway articulates in texts like *When Species Meet.*[49] Perhaps even more fundamentally, I am arguing in this book that a measure of nostalgia—or at least backward-oriented interpretation of subjectivity—is inevitable.

Furthermore, the many ironies and contradictions that accrete around "Africa" recall Morton's argument in *Dark Ecology.* Morton interrupts the possibility of returning to some innocent condition early in human history in two ways. First, he underscores the stunning point that in two foundational religious texts, Genesis and *The Ramayana of Valmiki,* the establishment of religion is associated precisely with the origin of sin, a contradictory scenario.[50] This undermines the possibility of a return to religious innocence. Second, and related to this first point but put in more general terms throughout his book, Morton argues that the anxious desire to end anxiety, the hope to fix human life in a condition of permanent comfort, is itself ironically the cause of the Anthropocene, the biggest human-wrought instability in the history of the planet.[51] This is homesickness at the global scale. He writes, "About 12,500 years ago, a climate shift experienced by hunter-gatherers as a catastrophe pushed humans to find a solution to their fear concerning where the next meal was coming from."[52] From this contingent condition began the agricultural revolution, which Morton calls "agrilogistics."

At first glance, it might seem that, like Akeley, we should wish simply to return to an innocent state before agriculture. But Morton compellingly shows, along lines akin to Haraway's case treated above, that the desire to escape history simply re-creates the problem. That does not mean there are no steps to take. Indeed, *Dark Ecology* makes a number of suggestions about what to do now, many of which involve not ending agriculture but changing it.[53] But Morton's analysis is more fundamental: he shows that the desire for a single, permanent fix is perhaps the essential problem, spurring an ongoing epistemic and ontological violence, which he calls, again, agrilogistics, "the slowest and perhaps most effective weapon of mass destruction yet devised."[54]

Homesickness in/for *The Garden of Eden*

While Hemingway participated in at least parts of the same ideological matrix that drove Akelely and Roosevelt, one important difference is his treatment of the idea of the Garden of Eden. While in the museum that garden is re-created, fixed in time and place to rescue decadent contemporary civilization, for Hemingway in his novel by that name, the Garden of Eden figures the *impossibility* of reclaiming an imagined perfect past. (However, Hemingway's novel does express a homesick longing for the lost past of his marital relationship.) This is an important difference. Akeley and others aimed to fix an imagined past; Hemingway only mourned its passing. Hemingway's stance registers much more fully human mortality, weakness, and exposure to death. Our mortality also implies human fallibility, our inevitable exposure to error. Hemingway is more willing to accept that weakness, while the logic of museums, fixing the past in safety forever, seems to deny both loss and fallibility.

For Hemingway, that homesick structure of subjectivity also connects us with animals, as in the Museum of Natural History, but again with a difference. Hemingway keenly recognizes that humans share our mortal vulnerability—of which homesickness is a sign—with animals. His thinking about animality, that is, further emphasizes how Hemingway departs from his forebears Roosevelt and Akeley. Such departures from patriarchal forebears are one of the central themes of his novel *The Garden of Eden.*[55] Indeed, despite his ardent, lifelong hunting practice, Hemingway did not think of animals in conventional ways. And while critics have widely recognized a more complex Hemingway, especially following the publication of *The Garden of Eden,* signs of this version of Hemingway appear throughout his writing. I write elsewhere, for instance, about the intimate place domestic animals have in Hemingway's sense of himself and his relationships with other people, and how often he relied on encounters with wild and domestic animals to confront difficult truths in this life.[56] One of the most arresting episodes in this pattern appears in his ambitious, surprising, and unfinished manuscript, published partially as *The Garden of Eden,* a text facilitated in part by his thinking about and experiences in Africa, particularly on the second safari. Mandel notes how the mobility and freedom of safari facilitated Hemingway's more open exploration of "his first breaching of monogamy" and of "a variety of sexual matters . . . that had been hidden or excluded in the earlier work."[57]

The published novel *The Garden of Eden,* it should be said, is less than half as long as the manuscript and is considerably sanitized.[58] Hemingway scholar Carl Eby aptly calls it "bowdlerized."[59] In its title, which signals its ambitions, *The Garden of Eden* both evokes mythic dreams of an ideal place and, by recalling the narrative of human expulsion from the garden, signals their impossibility. Although the novel exposes the fault lines of such innocent dreams, it is part of a larger move in Hemingway's late work that is not purely critical of them. In this way, the novel shares much with Morton's argument in *Dark Ecology.*

Hemingway's expression of the allure of Edenic fantasies and of a perfect nature, in my view, evokes his larger resistance to much of modernity, and his work refuses to surrender what good may come from the radically other perspectives made available by engagements with African nature and nonhuman nature in general. Hemingway has long been recognized for his serious interests in the nonhuman, in nature, in animals, even in ostensibly inhuman human behaviors—violence in ritual and war; feats of endurance in fishing, walking, and drinking; breaches of cultural and social taboos. But critics have been too quick to label these interests merely primitivist or simply insignificant; Harold Bloom characterizes the topic of *The Old Man and the Sea* that way, as insignificant, in his introduction to a set of critical essays on the text.[60]

Posthumanism offers a better route into these elements of his work. Too little sense of Hemingway's complexity has registered in criticism of him (beyond the comparatively small coterie of Hemingway scholars), too little awareness of how thorough and considered were his studies of culture—not just of literature but of museums, politics, sports, and so on. He is no naïve innocent nature lover, but he recognizes many of the deficiencies of modern, Enlightenment-inspired life, including some of the problems with the Euro-American presence in Africa and its effects on the indigenous peoples there. Although many of the texts he produced later in life were unfinished, they bear the signs of even greater complexity. Indeed, given his reluctance about freezing vitality into artifact, a reluctance not so different from Haraway's criticism of the logic of the museum display in *Primate Visions* (which also turns complex nature into fixed displays), the very status of his late texts—incomplete—can be read to testify to his complex ideas about representation and reality.

Moreover, Hemingway's lifelong interest in nonhuman nature underscores the vital presence and alterity of the nonhuman more generally. As Christophe Bonneuil and Jean-Baptiste Fressoz claim in *The Shock of the Anthropocene,* the planet has increasingly been subject to "a radical internalization" to human systems. They continue, "This internalization is expressed in the efforts to measure ecosystemic functions in terms of financial flows, making a nature that is liquid and capitalizable even in its most intimate processes. Internalization into the market is backed by the ontological dissolution of nature by constructivist philosophies that deny its alterity in relation to humans."[61] In much of his work, by contrast, Hemingway clarifies the radical alterity of the nonhuman from human economic systems. That is one of the key arguments of *The Garden of Eden.*

The Elephant in the Writing Room: Sympathy and Weakness in Hemingway's "Masculine Text" The Garden of Eden

Criticism of *The Garden of Eden* has frequently noted the book's richness and its many interlaced themes.[62] Hilary K. Justice reminds us of Hemingway's 1950 statement to interviewer Harvey Breit that his writing had "moved through arithmetic, through plane geometry and algebra," and on to "calculus."[63] This complexity derives in part from *The Garden of Eden*'s self-reflexive nature; it is a book about making books, "a novel about a writer writing."[64] However, readers have disagreed about what the novel finally means to say about writing, about producing language, which is not surprising regarding so sophisticated a text. For example, James Nagel, focusing especially on the elephant tale in the text, understands the story to value artistic language above all else.[65] But in *The Bones of the Others,* Justice takes a different approach. She widens her investigation to include more of the published novel and its manuscripts, thereby complicating a reading like Nagel's. She shows that *The Garden of Eden,* especially in manuscript form, betrays great anxiety about writing, and especially anxiety about what kind of writing to undertake. For Justice, the core question Hemingway confronted was "whether or not to make public that which was private."[66] These differences in critical focus produce different conclusions about language.

Many critics join Nagel in attending to the elephant tale nested in the larger narrative of *The Garden of Eden.* In that story, the child David finds himself identifying with an elephant, across the boundaries of species and against his father, whom he criticizes sharply. In his anger, David disavows language itself, thinking to himself, "Never tell anyone anything ever. Never tell anyone anything again" (181). David's sympathy for the elephant crystallizes his feelings about his father's philandering and elephant killing, leading to his vow of silence. But one of the debates—for Hemingway and for his critics—centers on how to understand this boyish vow. Does it reflect an insight? Is it a moment of childish naïveté?

Like Rose Marie Burwell and more recently Robin Silbergleid, Justice believes that the elephant resembles David's adult partner Catherine in the story. Justice claims that both Catherine and the elephant have "been betrayed by their natures."[67] This formulation, in essentially blaming Catherine and the elephant for their misfortunes, echoes a critical consensus that Catherine is unraveling and that David rejects her. Indeed, Justice, reinforcing Burwell, further argues that writing the elephant tale permits David to "avoid the neurotic, intrusive female presence" of Catherine. But Justice also notes that David "strongly" identifies with the elephant,[68] and that point introduces a complex wrinkle into the story.

While these readings rightly recognize the importance of David's encounter with the elephant, more should be said about the tension between empathy, connected above to silence (about the elephant), and making language. The remainder of this chapter, focused especially on *The Garden of Eden*'s theory of language and (like Silbergleid's article) working outward from the elephant tale, claims that David's radical questioning offers a new interpretative approach to many other elements of the book, modeling a posthumanist reading more generally. David's youthful experiences on the elephant hunt should be read not only for their personal significance, teaching him "to protect things—the elephant and his own feelings—through silence."[69] These experiences should also be read to extend Hemingway's career-long, increasingly sophisticated skepticism about key elements of Western civilization, including how we understand knowledge and the function of language. In other words, the book explores Hemingway's negative homesickness, richly understood, his growing dread of certain parts of his cultural heritage. This skepticism was fueled by Hemingway's interest in non-Western cultures and locations like Africa,[70] by his complex experimentation with traditional gender roles, and by a lifelong and growing sympathy for animals, anticipating posthumanism. As Cary Wolfe makes clear in his book *What Is Posthumanism?* and elsewhere, such considerations have powerful impacts on our ideas of language.[71]

The famous passage in Hemingway's *A Farewell to Arms* condemns "abstract words such as glory, honor, courage, or hallow" (249), and later texts such as *The Garden of Eden* enrich this critique. Distrust of abstractions grows into fuller resistance to the ways of life those abstractions represent, and into the wariness about language noted by Justice. Thus, in *The Garden of Eden,* language appears not as the pure, idealized medium of immortal truth or the marker of humanity's towering reason but too often as an instrument of petty, greedy, and brutal power relationships. It is therefore particularly appropriate that David confronts his father and his heritage by swearing off human language in the face of a suffering animal. I argue that in this text, such scenes dramatize the insufficiency and the weakness of language, which is not all it is sometimes anthropocentrically assumed to be. Such scenes also underscore Derrida's insistence that much of what counts in our responses to life should be oriented less by "capability" and more by, as Jeremy Bentham put it, the question of whether a being can suffer.[72]

Foregrounding the elephant scene in *The Garden of Eden* also clarifies the importance of sympathy to Hemingway. Empathy is a strange kind of weakness that is also a strength. It involves feeling for others, imagining their situations, and thus expanding the self, but feeling empathy also opens the self and makes it vulnerable. Even when engaged self-consciously, it is a way of deliberately estranging one from oneself; commonly empathy overtakes the rational self, exposing how humans are much more than rational beings. Further, empathy often engenders awareness of our limitations both to know and to help others. Such is the situation of Catherine's and David's experiments in this book, I argue. They make more of themselves—more selves—by changing their hair, their gender roles, their marriage roles, and by producing second selves textually via writing, and these experiments depend on empathy. But they press their desires beyond the breaking point, reminding us that empathy too has limits, as they both slip back into empathy-destructive, self-protective selfhood in the face of the novel's several traumas. I find that *The Garden of Eden* exposes and criticizes this excessively expansive selfhood, this excessive desire, a problem that runs through the hunting story as well as the marriage story, and a problem that too often drives human hubris of many other kinds. Hemingway marks the line of too much desire, plainly enough, at the point where others get hurt. But being fallible, mortal creatures, we humans often find that line retrospectively, via a homesickness, after a trauma has already happened, as David and Catherine do.

This fallibility appears at the chronological beginning of the events in *The Garden of Eden*, when young David is out walking at night in Africa with his dog. In the published novel, very much as in the story "Get a Seeing-Eyed Dog," the animal narrative connects to an investigation of a failing love relationship between a newlywed couple, David and Catherine. Their happy honeymoon is interrupted by David's need to begin writing again, which leads Catherine to begin her own artistic experiments with her body. The pressures on their relationship become very intense, fighting ensues, and in the context of this growing wreckage, David thinks back to his experience as a boy on the elephant hunt with his father, mentioned above. The collapse of

David's adult union with Catherine provokes his remembered loss of closeness with his father.

David's memory of this episode proves very intense, and he regards the writing of it as very difficult. Still, he begins working on the story, driven in large measure by the challenges he is facing in his current marriage with Catherine. In the opening of the remembered boyhood story, a dog appears again as a kind of sensory supplement for human weakness, even for human disability: young David "was waiting for the moon to rise and he felt his dog's hair rise under his hand as he stroked him to be quiet and they both watched and listened as the moon came up and gave them shadows. His arm was around the dog's neck now and he could feel him shivering. All of the night sounds had stopped. They did not hear the elephant and David did not see him until the dog turned his head and seemed to settle into David" (159). This story proves to center around this elephant, and the first sign of its presence comes through the dog's senses and more particularly through David's relationship with his dog. So in this story as in the larger novel, certain profound truths become more accessible through relationships, between and among humans and animals.

Those dynamics—relationships helping to unveil truths—connect to human language and to human sympathy for animals as this elephant story proceeds. It happens that this elephant David encounters in the night is a much-prized animal with enormous tusks, tusks that are very valuable to the ivory trade. David reports the presence of the elephant to his father and his father's friend Juma, who are elephant hunters, and they bring David along as they pursue this animal. The pursuit is exhausting for David, and it forces him to recognize his own youth in contrast to the mature strength of the men, so this is one insight. But when they finally come closer to the elephant, David confronts several other truths.

The novel's architecture, with the childhood hunting story nested inside the adult story, implies that this traumatic memory was not fully understood by the boy. The adult David uses retrospection—homesickness—to revisit those childhood events. I have called this attitude "complex," but that word does not do justice to the scenario, which is fundamental to life, human and otherwise. The homesick structure of subjectivity reveals the complexity of reality, its wildness, its resistance to knowing. Morton reminds us that this kind of account of knowledge traces back to Kant and correlationism, the idea, in Morton's gloss, "that when I try to find the thing in itself, what I find are thing data, not the thing in itself."[73] Morton, for simplicity's sake, refers to "the thing in itself," but of course his gloss explains all perception, which can only ever involve data. Retrospection, rethinking, writing—all these enable more robust engagement with that data. This retrospective or homesick structure of subjectivity is built into *The Garden of Eden,* with the first traumatic hunting tale located inside the longer traumatic novel, so that the forward movement of the story leads to a backward movement, a recollection, or what Morton calls a loop.[74] Hemingway's title indicates that this relationship to origins and temporality is precisely the theme of the work. It is about homesickness and expulsion.

Language in The Garden of Eden

The Garden of Eden tests human relationships in terms that often hinge on language, especially on tensions between producing saleable, consumable stories and living the intimacy of a marital relationship. To rehearse the plot briefly in terms of this tension: The story begins with the joyous honeymoon of David and Catherine, only to show their marriage unraveling under the stress of David's need to write. Yet David's writing includes the account of his and Catherine's increasingly troubled relationship, which Catherine insists he produce. Meanwhile, Catherine undertakes a series of experiments with hairstyle and self-presentation that involve David and that amount to an embodied answer to and critique of David's writing, which he sees as his "enforced loneliness" (14).[75] We can read this "enforced loneliness" as the (re)production of a laboring subjectivity in specialized capitalist structures. Then, in this rapidly building spirit of experimentation, the couple has an affair with another woman, Marita, and the situation spins out of control.

Under the pressure of these traumas, the narrative fractures. David begins to recall and to write about the childhood trauma of the elephant hunt, mentioned above, and the two stories—childhood and adult—become intermingled in the novel. The hunting story describes David's father and his father's friend Juma killing an elephant whose presence David reported to them. Crucially, David feels he has "betrayed" the elephant (181). As the tension in that embedded story mounts, Catherine burns all the stories David has been working on, including the elephant story, sparing only David's narrative of their relationship. The published novel ends with David rewriting those burned stories, with greater clarity than before.

Many critics have read the plot as a conflict between the value of masculine art and the ostensibly corrosive effects of the bodily and the feminine. For instance, Rose Marie Burwell's chapter on *The Garden of Eden* is subtitled "Protecting the Masculine Text," and she cites several instances in which the text—particularly the unpublished manuscript—seems to make the creation of art exclusively masculine.[76] Similarly, Nagel underscores the idea that "David has been able to transform the difficulties of his present life into significant art. As David realizes more and more as the novel progresses, it is only in his writing that he truly lives." Nagel calls this insight the "most significant" of the book.[77] In one sense this seems true. However, I believe that the novel also confirms some of Catherine's feminist critiques of writing. Catherine's uneasiness in her gender role closely parallels David's uneasiness, his homesickness, as a producer of language and as a descendant of his father. Neither has found a stable home for their identities. Indeed, precisely because David identifies with Catherine, and because their identities are evolving in parallel, her unease can be read as a mirror of his own.

Anxiety about producing language is revealed, for instance, in a complex early scene just after David has begun writing again. Catherine has left him alone to work. When David finishes, he finds *Catherine*'s writing: "He opened the note which said, David, didn't want to disturb you am at the cafe love Catherine. He put on the old trench coat, found a *boina* in the pocket and walked out of the hotel into the rain" (38). The passage alludes to the concluding line of Hemingway's *A Farewell to Arms*: "After a while I went out and left the hospital and walked back to the hotel in the rain" (332). In that novel, these words mark by mood and understatement the gulf of Frederic Henry's loss (his lover Catherine and their child die in childbirth). Hemingway labored famously over the ending to *A Farewell to Arms*, producing forty-seven variations before settling on the published version.[78]

In *The Garden of Eden,* the sentence, again signaling loss, appears early in the narrative and interprets the significance of Catherine's writing and writing in general. Her underpunctuated, unpretentiously direct statement of their separation is not set in quotation marks in the novel, so formally it can also be understood as David (and/or Hemingway) speaking. This hybrid, shared speech thus stands exactly at the moment in the book when producing saleable text begins to upset more fully embodied marital life. Catherine's note is a stand-in for their lived union, signaling their expulsion from the garden. Their writing, David's and Catherine's (and Hemingway's), marks the end of the honeymoon period in which "everything was free" (31). Writing marks the loss of innocence, much as use of language in the hunting scene—discussed more fully below—is a regrettable "betrayal" of the elephant and the beginning of David's own loss of innocence and his "knowledge of loneliness" (201). The remainder of the novel tries to sort out what this loss and separation, this homesickness, means.

Catherine's Body Language

As the narrative proceeds, Catherine begins to experiment with her self-presentation in parallel to David's work with language, as has been noted by critics like Burwell and Kathy Willingham. Burwell, for example, urges that Catherine's embodied arts function as "acts of protest" against David's writing.[79] I would underscore that Catherine pushes her inhabitation of the gendered body to its limits and then beyond, into "unknown country." Her first dramatic haircut, "cropped as short as a boy's," we are told, "was cut with no compromises" (14–15). Catherine's unrest in her gender position leads her to this writerly gender revision presented as a concise statement, shorn of its excesses. Bodily material is cut away, leaving only her innovative message. Catherine says, "Stupid people will think it is strange. But we must be proud. I love to be proud." David, in support of her art, agrees: "We'll start being proud now" (16). Her clipped and foreshortened style of communicating recalls Hemingway's own understated style.

Not only gender conventions are at stake here, but more broadly, what counts as meaningful in human life—products or relationships, art or lived reality, text or embodiment. In my view, *The Garden of Eden* can only elaborate these dilemmas, failing to resolve them. In this sense, I depart from Burwell's reading. Although she maintains that Hemingway decides against Catherine in the book, the published text and the manuscript are clearly invested in showing the sophistication of Catherine's position. Burwell acknowledges that "Catherine's is the most complex characterization of the novel" and that she offers "a striking analogue of the history of women's creative struggle," but Burwell nonetheless insists that these elements of the book do not indicate Hemingway's ultimate stance.[80] Instead, she repeatedly urges that "David symbolically kills" Catherine by abandoning the honeymoon story, and that he "shrives" his father of guilt in the elephant killing by rewriting the African stories.[81] Given that Hemingway did not himself decide on an ending for the story (as Burwell notes), it seems necessary to take a more agnostic position about Catherine. Even if we agree that David abandons Catherine by abandoning the honeymoon narrative, Hemingway's own position differs at least insofar as he, contra David, wrote *The Garden of Eden*. As Burwell herself explains, "The entire novel is part of the honeymoon narrative."[82]

Furthermore, it is not clear that the rewritten stories "shrive" David's father. That interpretation hinges on several statements in the novel that I find to be quite ambivalent. For instance, as he rewrites the stories, David says that he feels "fortunate, just now, that his father was not a simple man" (247). But the African stories, even rewritten with "more dimensions" than before, remain full of uncertainty and tension. These dynamics appear in the key scene mentioned above, when David's curiosity about the elephant and his friend leads him to inquire about them.

> "How long do you suppose he and his friend had been together?" David asked his father.
>
> "I haven't the faintest idea," his father said. "Ask Juma."
>
> "You ask him please." [David replies.]
>
> His father and Juma spoke together and Juma had looked at David and laughed.
>
> "Probably four or five times your life he says," David's father told him. "He doesn't know or care really."
>
> I care, David thought. (180–81)

David's rejection of his father and Juma in this brutal scene is double—he refuses their position regarding the elephants, and he refuses even to tell them anything further. (David's "I care" response is internal; it is only "thought.") This silent rebellion is reinforced by the end of this inset hunting story when, returning after they kill the elephant, David agrees, dishonestly, to make peace with his father. Afterward, David thinks to himself: "He knew this was the start of the never telling that he had decided on" (202).

The elephant spurs David's alienation, or his sickness at home, helping him better know and then reject parts of himself and his father. Thus, David is simultaneously estranged and renewed with regard to the classic attributes of human distinctness—language and ethics—by his confrontation with an animal other. While the capacity for ethical behavior is often used to mark the difference between humans and nonhuman animals, in *The Garden of*

Eden the elephant shows signs of complex feelings that move David, even though he is still a child, to criticize his father's inhumanity, his *brutality.* In the scene about the elephant's friend, spoken language itself proves to be an exercise of power, used to humiliate David and to aid in the work of killing the elephant, whom David will later call "his hero" (201), whose eye "was the most alive thing David had ever seen" (199). Thus, language is used here much as it is in many scenarios of war, as I discuss in chapter 6. Rather than revealing deep inner rationality and human goodness, language appears instrumentalized, as a tool that facilitates human violence in unprecedented ways. It thus exemplifies the hazards of human prosthetics and technology in the Anthropocene more generally.

David's sympathy for the elephant separates him from his father, and even from his own species identity, but it also teaches him much more about this particular place in Africa and about its animals. Knowing the animal places in Africa is a kind of shorthand in later Hemingway work for place more generally. Deep fractures in the cosmopolitan dream appear in this moment because it is an emotional allegiance and a muddying of species boundaries that intensify David's local knowledge. In other words, the power of a highly localized empathy—an empathy for the animal directly in front of him—teaches David. Knowledge is not the opposite of emotion. Moreover, his more intensely local orientation causes David to forcefully reject other ways of being. Cosmopolitan tolerance conflicts with local empathies and knowledge.

Furthermore, David's recognition of, and identification with, the bull elephant mirrors the elephant's recognition of his dead friend in a crucial scene.

> The tracks of the old bull led to it. It was a skull as high as David's chest and white from the sun and rains. There was a deep depression in the forehead and ridges ran from between the bare white eye sockets and flared out in empty broken holes where the tusks had been chopped away. Juma pointed out where the great elephant they were trailing had stood while he looked down at the skull and where his trunk had moved it a little way from the place it had rested on the ground and where the points of his tusks had touched the ground beside it. (180)

The marks and signs of the living elephant investigating the skull show his concern, his suffering, and his mourning. David, looking backward on his traumatic childhood memory of this scene, sympathetically recognizes the elephant's mourning through the prism of his own collapsing marriage. Moreover, the scenes of recognition, with their marks and traces of language, resemble each other: the elephant's writing on the ground with his tusks, suffused with pathos in Hemingway's presentation of it, mirrors and helps produce its double that is *The Garden of Eden,* also a story of loss. How we read this scene depends fundamentally on our awareness that, as Cynthia Moss (among others) reports in her study of elephants, these animals do in fact mourn.[83] It is a strange displacement for David, as he is driven more deeply into himself, into his empathetic identification with the elephant's losses. That identification also drives him out of who he thought he was before. This scene reiterates the book's conflict between life and commodity, with the "empty broken holes" from the tusks recalling that the elephants were killed for salable ivory.

The exposure of David's father's (ostensibly adult) ruthlessness carries into the passage that immediately follows it in the published novel, when David comes "out of the working room and he was happy and empty and proud" (203). How could such pride in having written well not be tinged with irony, following as it does upon a story that concludes with the necessity of not telling? The description of David as "happy and empty and proud," with its echoes of postcoital bliss, is even more ironic when we recognize the novel's larger architecture, the impending failure of the whole experiment with Catherine and Marita. David's efforts both in writing and in relationships do not prevent his expulsion from the garden of marital happiness or from the garden of innocently observing the elephant. Even Jenks's (the novel's editor) sunny ending cannot make the reader forget the loss of the elephants and of Catherine.

Thus, it is hard not to listen keenly when Hemingway gives voice to Catherine criticizing the African stories: "The worst thing was the dirt and the flies and the cruelty and the bestiality. You seemed almost to grovel in it. That horrible one about the massacre in the crater and heartlessness of your own father" (223). David replies first by asking that they not talk about this topic, and when Catherine insists, he tells her, "Write it out" (223), an insult he repeats and intensifies: "You can tell it to somebody who can write it down" (224). This comment alludes mockingly to the creative structure of their shared narrative. Writing here is equated with the *failure* of any authentic, intimate exchange between them.

Then, when Catherine repeats that it was necessary for her to burn the stories and says, "I'm sorry if you don't understand," David returns to the unspoken discourse that forms the novel's deeper level of truth and admits silently to himself, "He had understood really" (224). That is, he *does* understand Catherine's destructive criticism. David then further condemns himself for falling into "rhetoric" in his fight with Catherine, rhetoric that he "disliked" in classic Hemingway form. Moreover, David's silent soliloquy includes his consideration of "how untrue it was that everything that was understood was forgiven" and his recognition that he must solidify "his own discipline" in order not "to lose control" (224).

In this series of events, David admits to understanding both his father and Catherine but explicitly distinguishes understanding from forgiveness. He has very little ground to stand on; his honest appraisal of his father and Catherine permits comprehension but causes greater loneliness, homesickness. This traumatic scenario corresponds frighteningly well with our awareness of the Anthropocene, and for the same reasons. The Anthropocene, perhaps especially if we regard it as beginning with the advent of agriculture, which connects to the origins of written language, mythologized as sin and loss in the Genesis story of the Garden of Eden, is homesickness at a global scale.[84] As Morton writes in *Dark Ecology,* the Anthropocene is like a noir fiction in which "I'm the detective *and* the criminal."[85] David likewise finds *his own* heritage and identity deeply objectionable. In this story, that is epitomized as his father's violent actions in Africa, to which David contributed. These are the same concerns we see Hemingway beginning to air in his earlier work, *Green Hills of Africa,* noted above.

Knowledge of Death, Knowledge as Death

David and Catherine are driven into these difficulties by their excessive experimentation, by their sympathetically but dangerously open practice of selfhood. Their desires—to write, to know others intimately, to know at all—are essentially bound to trauma and mortality in this book, hence its title's biblical allusion. (In the biblical Garden of Eden story, curiosity and temptation lead to God punishing humans with, among other things, mortality.) Not only does the manuscript send Barbara to suicide, but it includes one plot that would potentially have David and Catherine carry out suicide together.[86] In that version of *The Garden of Eden,* David's sympathy with

Catherine is so strong that he wishes to share all her plight, even unto death. Suicide becomes the horrible, final shared artistic experiment, expressing the absolute limits of intimacy and the hazards of human desire. Similarly, it is human desire, expressed in a hunt with all its resonances of masculine power, sexuality, and animality, that drives the elephant to make his own marks and signs of loss.

More generally, producing signs in this story connects to a kind of animal mourning: it is essential to the complex plotting of *The Garden of Eden* that Catherine and David's experimentation drives his writing of the elephant story backward toward the strangely familiar memento mori of an elephant skull with gaping holes where its ivory tusks once were. When David makes a kind of reluctant trophy of his experience in the form of stories, he turns away from living the intimacy of his marriage, rendering it, like the elephant, into commodity and corpse. The presence in the text of Catherine's fierce criticisms makes this transformation more visible. At stake in this scenario is not just a romantic relationship; it is commodification more generally and the framework of a laboring subjectivity, which via guilt and aspiration drives David back to writing. It is modernity.

Modernity, as Philip Armstrong demonstrates in *What Animals Mean in the Fiction of Modernity,* has been produced in dialogue with ideas of animality and in engagement with the bodies and lives of actual animals.[87] The elephant to whom David leads his father and Juma, and whom all three pursue, has fled back to the scene of a previous trauma, where Juma killed the elephant's "askari," meaning "soldier," but also for Hemingway implying "friend."[88] His father and Juma remember the place: "Juma had looked at David's father and grinned showing his filed teeth and his father had nodded his head. They looked as though they had a dirty secret, just as they had looked when he had found them that night at the shamba," where they had cavorted with married women (180). The men's shared knowledge, "the dirty secret," goes without saying in these gestural exchanges. Their body language parallels the elephant's tracks and traces next to his friend's skull, noted above, which signify his memory of the place. Thus, the elephant has led the human trio, via tracks, to this recognition scene. As we have seen, reading all this, David surrenders his place among the humans, aligning himself as a vulnerable third member of the elephant group, as Cary Wolfe has noted.[89] At the center of the scene is the empty skull, shorn of its ivory appendages, so that the elephant has "written" a narrative line that David's story follows to this place, the elephants' *querencia,* the place where they settle down to defend themselves against killing.[90]

I have noted that David identifies with the elephant, against his father and Juma; recognizing his heritage is tantamount to rejecting it, made clear in the many occasions when David refuses to speak. David also delivers that rejection to his father in perhaps the most taboo of curses, one on the edge of language and pronounced so quietly that he must repeat it: "Fuck elephant hunting" (181). Burwell notes that this diction connects ivory hunting with the "orgiastic scene" where David had found his father and Juma with married women.[91] Both these indulgences pervert the activities of consumption and reproduction—sexual and cultural—by extending them beyond necessity, at the expense of others. Hence David's critique: "My father doesn't need to kill elephants to live." And "Juma," David thinks, "will drink his share of the ivory or just buy himself another god damned wife" (181).

From here we can better see that David's curse names paternity with an overstated version of what fatherhood is, like an oversized shadow, an uncanny double. "Fuck" mocks excessive sexuality just as David understands his father to be mocking it, and that concern has clear implications for the adults David, Catherine, and Marita. We know the youthful David has stepped out of his former bounds when his father first asks, "What's that?" in response to David's curse, and then revises and returns the curse: "Be careful you don't fuck it up" (182). David immediately thinks, "He's not stupid. He knows all about it now and he will never trust me again. That's good. I don't want him to because I'll never ever tell him or anybody anything again never anything again. Never ever never" (182). These mutual recognition scenes turn around a word, and language itself. David's sympathy with the elephant leads to his vow of silence. He puts that decision to himself, in the passage just quoted, in a language that testifies to language's insufficiency with its repetition and overstatement. These failures in language are exactly parallel, furthermore, to the living elephant's walk to the empty elephant skull: both track and drive toward some final recognition scene that is ultimately only muteness and death, holes in a skull, a swearing off of communication in silence. The scene radically refigures language not as a towering force of superrational humanity but as an animal competency that is dwarfed by the deeper truth of radical vulnerability that is more-than-human.

The youthful David's use of forceful language followed quickly by his rejection of language altogether presents in miniature what becomes Catherine's dramatic critique of David's writing. She begins with David's clippings and public persona, but then dismisses more and more of his work, ultimately burning all the stories except their honeymoon narrative. David's writing, leading toward death and emptiness in the elephant story, couples with Catherine's "writing" out the death of writing, in fire. Hers is a dramatic, embodied form of signification. Moreover, in a move important for the position of the word and the practice of relationships, Catherine, the avowed nonwriter, actually pens a letter to David to explain her actions.

David reads this letter twice, underscoring its importance, thinking, "He had never read any other letters from Catherine because from the time they had met . . . they had seen each other every day" (237). Again, the very presence of writing signals a failure of intimacy. Catherine's letter reiterates the novel's questions about reproduction in a metaphor that compares burning the stories to killing a child in a car. But even such figurative language fails, as Catherine concludes by saying, "I did it and I knew I did it and I can't undo it. It's too awful to understand. But it happened." Language and understanding cannot account for the world's traumatic events. The next sentence, opening a new paragraph, redoubles the claim to incommunicability: "I'll cut this short" (237). Echoing the many cuts of this narrative—hair, news clippings, ivory tusks, relationships, the published novel itself—these words help explain David's understanding of events: Catherine is "Hurried," he tells Marita (230). Catherine's desire to completely understand desire and subjectivity leads her to rush to the end of things and, in effect, to cut things short.

Crucially, though, cutting things short is exactly what David's beginning to write again does to the happy honeymoon. Life's brief and tenuous nature is a common focus of Hemingway's work, so it is not easy to reject Catherine's hurry toward understandings and endings. Early in *The Garden of Eden,* for instance, David and Catherine discuss the problems of experience, art, and mortality. Catherine worries about preserving the singular feelings provoked in her by the countryside: "'There's nothing except through yourself,' she said. 'And I don't want to die and it be gone.'" David assures her that she has the memory of that country, a kind of homesickness, but Catherine forces him to acknowledge that death ends memory: she says, "But what about when I'm dead?" He answers, "Then you're dead." Burwell reads this answer as a "brutal riff in the masculine style" that shows Hemingway's defensiveness.[92] But the whole dialogue seems to me an *agreement* about the imponderable reality of everyone's shared mortality. Indeed, I understand Catherine to present the upshot of their talk: "'When you start to live outside yourself,' Catherine said, 'it's all dangerous'" (53–54). This statement aptly glosses a kind of open, eco-cosmopolitan subjectivity, recognizing the appeal and the vulnerability of its unavoidably permeable boundaries.

In this scene, David answers to Catherine's concern by encouraging patient, conscientious inhabitation of the embodied self, saying of death, "Don't let it happen till it happens. Look at things and listen and feel" (54). But David also knows that is not so easy. In *The Garden of Eden*'s architecture, as in the above passage, endings cannot be escaped, only sometimes delayed. Honeymoons must end. Writers must go back to their work, which means finishing—ending—stories, as David insists: "Finishing is what you have to do, he thought. If you don't finish, nothing is worth a damn" (108). A mature writer finishes, but a mature writer's work is therefore tinged with death; as Michael Reynolds reports, this is how Hemingway "felt about his writing: each book a little death."[93] Likewise, in the elephant story, David's use of language to reveal or "betray" the elephant leads to the elephant's death, just as his insistence on writing as a solitary activity contributes to the death of his relationship with Catherine and to her equally potent artistic evocation of death in burning the manuscripts (181). Yet Catherine ultimately writes her letter. David insists on continuing to write. Hemingway wrote this novel, although compounding these complexities is the fact that we do not have a finished book in *The Garden of Eden,* since Hemingway could not decide how to end it. The manuscript therefore embodies Hemingway's deep and complex reluctance about not only its characters but its very existence.

Too Weak Not to Kill

Along this line, even though it registers the trauma of death, the novel does not dismiss actual killing entirely, not even in what David later calls his "very young boy's story" of the elephant hunt (201). As the threesome pursues the elephant, David himself kills "two spur fowl" with a slingshot without guilt (172). Wolfe reads this moment as an example of the "novel's humanism" because David fails "to establish any ethical linkage between the multiplicity of animal others he encounters in the novel, such as the 'two spur fowl.'" Wolfe asks how David could both kill birds *and* feel such sympathy for the elephant. Wolfe continues, "This systematic parsing of the animal other into quite different and discrete ontological and ethical categories would in turn evince the obsessive hierarchization and classification of the other so central to the Enlightenment project."[94]

Wolfe may have a point about Hemingway's interest in elephants, but his account neglects the necessarily tenuous, circumstantial quality of ethics. In this sense, his version of ethics is too universal, too abstract, at least in this case.[95] Wolfe worries that recognizing some animals as worthy of ethical consideration while ignoring others simply restores a humanist or anthropomorphic understanding of them. However, we see in the terms of David's condemnation of the elephant hunt an implicit expiation for his killing of the spur fowls: his own necessity. He was too weak not to kill the birds, in a sense. The party was low on food, and having enough energy simply to cover the miles was very much at issue for David, whereas his father and Juma patently did not need the wealth from more ivory. The ethical task is both to recognize this human animality and weakness and to sustain a possibility of ethical action. That reading of ethics is in keeping with much of Wolfe's work, as when, for instance, he discusses Zygmunt Bauman's *Postmodern Ethics.* Wolfe underscores Bauman's point that morality is "*not universalizable.*"[96]

Under Kilimanjaro corroborates this view of a hunting ethics increasingly attentive to particular, concrete, local contexts and actual animals. In that book, I noted above, Hemingway explains that he has stopped trophy hunting and restricts his shooting of animals to meeting the camp's need for food, to supporting his wife Mary's hunting, or to hazards or dangers involving specific animals, ones "that had been outlawed for cause" (116–17).[97] Though he does not disavow killing animals, he crowds such actions with an ethics that hinges largely on necessity, much as we see in *The Garden of Eden*'s hunting story.

This specific, situated approach to making judgments reiterates my questions about eco-cosmopolitanism in this book. It also provides a new way to understand the bodily play that Catherine and David and eventually Marita undertake. Wolfe reports that this play, especially the obsessive tanning, is often read as part of the return-to-Africa plot of *The Garden of Eden,* a kind of colonialist going native. While Toni Morrison argues that Hemingway understands Africa as a "blank, empty space" open for conquest,[98] as noted above, Wolfe rightly complicates this reading by showing that David does not think of Africa as empty, and further, that David stands against such conquests. Wolfe compellingly argues that by recognizing the discourse of species operating in the novel (David's allegiance with the elephant, against his father and Juma), we become better able to read the book's critique of colonialism and racism.[99] Indeed, we can connect this fierce critique—"fuck elephant hunting"—to Hemingway's uneasiness about imperialist mobility already visible in *Green Hills of Africa,* discussed above.

Attention to species discourse is necessary in Wolfe's view because the novel otherwise seems to espouse sameness. For instance, he reads Catherine and David's tanning and their shared hairstyling as tending to reduce difference, to disavow the complexity or heterogeneity of the self.[100] For him, this is true also of their trading sexual roles. They look and act more and more alike. That reading, true in a sense, minimizes the complex relationships that enable the tanning and bodily play to go forward. While David and Catherine (and eventually Marita) are presented as looking alike, the narrative reveals their different responses to that apparent likeness. In fact, because each responds differently, the whole radical experiment in shared selfhood collapses. It is crucial to recognize this because it shows how narrative itself can complicate the seeming mimeticism of the word or image.[101] Narrative—and the historical function of the novel more generally—reveals individuality, difference, uniqueness; it reveals local truths. Narrative reiterates, indeed, that reality is uncanny, that it transcends our epistemological and ontological framings. Thus, despite the threesome being in the same "racial" category and undergoing similar experiments with their appearances, marking their bodies with some of the same external signs, their internal differences upset notions of homogeneity, racial or otherwise. In this sense, narrative reveals an important theme of *The Garden of Eden*—the difficulty of unity—perhaps the key lesson from the story in Genesis.

Failures of Language

Language, like signs marked on bodies and hair, communicates and unites imperfectly. Near the end of the published book, in what seems the triumph of the written word to some critics,[102] David is actually forced to recognize the impossibility of absolute success in writing. When he first begins penciling the hunting tale, David states the fundamental challenge: presenting experience as though it could "be lived through and made to come alive" again (108). He is attempting to conjure up a ghost, we might say. Later, in the midst of writing that story, he thinks how

> he tried to make the elephant come alive again as he and Kibo had seen him in the night when the moon had risen. Maybe I can, David thought, maybe I can. But as he locked up the day's work and went out of the room and shut the door he told himself, No, you can't do it. The elephant was old and if it had not been your father it would have been someone else. There is nothing you can do except try to write it the way that it was. So you must write each day better than you possibly can and use the sorrow that you have now to make you know how the early sorrow came. And you must always remember the things you believed because if you know them they will be there in the writing and you won't betray them. The writing is the only progress you make. (166)

This final sentence seems to suggest the triumph of the word only if we ignore what precedes it, which makes it clear that David cannot "possibly" write as well as he must. Words do not suffice; words can only begin to do the work of conveying loss, so central to this story, *The Garden of Eden*, when we acknowledge the gap between what we desire of them and what they do. Good art knows the limitations of art. Without this sense of language's insufficiency, writing is only a "betrayal." This unsettled, homesick position of language is registered formally by nesting the hunting story in the larger narrative, hybridizing its genre, complicating and multiplying its meanings in Hemingway's "calculus," and likening it to elephant tracks, to animal signs in the larger nonhuman world.

Trauma's disconcerting penetration of the ordering text is presented concretely in the above passage. That is to say, the rarefied story is locked away in the drawer, the door then closed upon the room, doubly encasing it, but David is nonetheless immediately pierced by the consciousness that his safekeeping has failed: "No, you can't do it," he thinks. The attempt to protect his interpretation of the past, like young David's desire that the elephant not die, is contradicted by the larger narrative in which even these stories end in ashes, only to be rewritten. This rewriting, of course, has its biographical explanations in Hemingway's own life—his first wife, Hadley, lost his manuscripts in the 1920s and his mother burned his father's natural history specimens.[103] But the burning and rewriting of manuscripts also dramatically renders the insufficiency of texts, their inability to capture the world's complexity, a point also echoed in Hemingway's practice of writing in pencil, not ink, which David follows in this text. Hemingway's sophisticated approach to writing—his well-known iceberg principle, his serious revisions, and his understated style—testifies to his keen awareness of the weakness of language. Language is incomplete, fallible, and mortal because its users are.

The best of such artistic language can remind us of the experience of the past, but in a literal sense that past is lost beyond recovery, as David admits. Recognizing that the elephant in *The Garden of Eden* shows traces of a similar consciousness of mortality enriches Hemingway's evocation of loss and emphasizes that the experience of loss is not the exclusive domain of humans. Reading the elephant's marks in the dirt also reminds us that human language is embodied, contextual, and physical, undermining the distinction between human and nonhuman communication systems. The elephant's traces pointing toward his dead friend's skull are figures for and examples of language, gesturing at, and weak before, the mystery of death. And in that magnificent skull, we find a memento mori not only for the soon-to-be slain elephant and for Catherine and David but from our current perspective for Hemingway himself.

Much more broadly, the murder of elephants in Africa also today evokes the larger realities of the Anthropocene's global extinction crises, which require us to face the practically unimaginable traumas to nonhuman life and world wrought largely by humans. We need eco-cosmopolitan ideas to better understand these planetary losses, but our empathies are most fully developed when we access the real bones of loss and the marks of suffering one local narrative at a time.

4

"124 Was Spiteful"

Forced Mobility and Unhomely Care

> And suddenly there was Sweet Home rolling, rolling, rolling out before her eyes, and although there was not a leaf on that farm that did not make her want to scream, it rolled itself out before her in shameless beauty.
>
> —Toni Morrison, *Beloved*

> It was not a story to pass on.
>
> —Toni Morrison, *Beloved*

Hemingway's privileged travel has an important root in the traumas of the Great War, a war that tested and exposed the logic of modernity. The millions of lost lives accompanied massive human dislocation and geographical revision, with national borders shifting and lifeways radically changing. Such traumatic disruptions have been essential to modernity. Indeed, contrary to cosmopolitan ideals of movement, for many millions, mobility and migration have been anything but free. A huge portion of mobility has been forced; another large portion, even if somewhat more deliberately selected by migrants, has been desperate.

The experiences of slaves in the transatlantic slave trade are perhaps the clearest and most severe example. With reference to both slaves and other forced migrants, Susan J. Matt notes, as I quoted in my introduction, "Between 1607 and 1789, roughly half of the 600,000 Europeans and all 300,000 of the Africans who landed on American shores were not free, arriving either as servants or slaves. . . . Their lack of autonomy influenced how they thought about the places they left and the journeys they made."[1] For blacks, this pattern persisted until the Civil War won them a greater measure of agency. But Jim Crow and the ensuing experiences in the twentieth-century

Great Migration of the United States, in response to racial terrorism and apartheid in the American South, as well as economic opportunities in the North, demonstrate the ways that mobility is profoundly conditioned by human vulnerability and exposure to violence, as well as by choice.[2] The Great Migration (approximately 1915–70) involved the movement of "some six million black southerners," reports Isabel Wilkerson in *The Warmth of Other Suns: The Epic Story of America's Great Migration.*[3] As a consequence, Wilkerson writes, by the 1970s, "nearly half of all black Americans—some forty-seven percent—would be living outside the South, compared to ten percent when the Migration began."[4] While most of these migrants ostensibly chose to move in a sense, it was a drastically and violently constrained choice.

Such forced and often violent mobility is not just in the past. Again, as noted in the introduction, "more than 70 million people" were forced migrants worldwide in 2015, reports Mark Tran in *The Guardian.*[5] A growing proportion of these migrants move because of environmental risk: in *The Shock of the Anthropocene,* Bonneuil and Fressoz note that, currently, 20 to 30 million people are dislocated annually because of natural disasters, and the authors report that the United Nations expects there to be some 50 million people dislocated each year due to environmental disturbance, including climate disturbance.[6]

These harried forms of migration raise serious questions about cosmopolitan hopes. But the case I make throughout this book is that the dream of a free mobility has always been something of a delusion, one that is tightly braided with humanist fantasies of autonomy and self-control more generally. Persisting in an innocent embrace of it, and in an automatic rejection of nostalgia and homesickness as sentimental, perpetuates the harmful fantasy of an independent but thereby isolated subjectivity. More particularly regarding the topic of this chapter, naturalizing movement as some scholars do risks reinforcing a technique of power that has facilitated much damaging dislocation and homesickness throughout history—not just the slave trade but indigenous peoples' displacement worldwide as well as countless other local episodes. A more specific example: the razing of poor neighborhoods to make room for interstate highways in 1950s America, a move that tended to impact African Americans disproportionately, not unlike what Georges-Eugène Haussmann did to make modern Paris.[7]

Toni Morrison's *Beloved* wrenchingly exposes the violent traumas of slavery, relating them to the ensuing forced mobility, showing how both movement and violence then infect ostensibly safe house and home. Sethe and her family settle at 124 Bluestone Road in Cincinnati; this home becomes both a register of, and agent in, their unrest, as marked in Morrison's first sentence: "124 was spiteful."[8] Morrison's *Beloved* thus defamiliarizes and estranges the place of home; it undomesticates the domestic, a term that is the very figure for comfortable inhabitation in place and in culture. Sethe's experience of slavery's brutality and dehumanization had already led her to flee the ironically named Sweet Home. The horrors of her experience there are so absolute that, when faced with the imminent capture of her and her family, she decides to kill her children instead, succeeding only in the case of her baby girl.[9]

Thus, I argue, Morrison's novel hinges on a complex and unsettling form of protection-as-violence within the inconceivably destructive system of racial slavery. Sethe's love for her children is so profound, and the norms of racial slavery so vile, that she refuses to permit them to live in it at all. Here, then, mothering care becomes uncanny and unhomely specifically because Sethe viscerally rejects the *place* slavery makes for her and her children in the world. Sethe's act is uncanny and terrifying in the novel, not merely unconscionable, because we know that Sethe deeply loves her children. Readers are forced to reckon with how undergoing this crucible of uncanny love might feel. The haunting motif of the novel further demonstrates that Sethe, once she has been driven to this decision, has had her sensibility and her home infected with the ghosts of loss. Sethe's violence dislocates her from her surviving children and from her very self, echoing the historical trauma of being owned by another person in slavery. She cannot own her self. In other words, the novel's harms result from a contest in ownership, a bloody fight around the core logic of private property referenced at the opening of chapter 2 of the present book. Sethe, unable to escape this ownership logic, caught in its power, destroys in order to escape. The shock of her acts, while finally too horrible even for Sethe to entirely face, are also made familiar and somewhat comprehensible by the narrative, producing a horrible, powerful uncanniness for readers regarding the history of slavery and its impacts.

Sethe's attempt to kill her children rather than permit them to be enslaved is perhaps the most extreme expression of homesickness as sickness at home. Sethe has a concept and a feeling of home that she has materialized in 124 Bluestone Road—she wants that home, and forcefully insists on it—and she strikes at her own in order to protect her actual home and her concept of home against the violent hierarchy of slavery. But this response, worse than suicide, suggests how she has internalized slavery's hierarchies of power, a point that becomes clearer later in the novel when Sethe revises her response to the seeming arrival of the slave catcher and, rather than harming her own, tries to kill him. These are the terms of action in the property transactions of racial slavery. Sethe's home is consumed from the inside out, the reverse of the burning down the house motif developed in chapter 2. Similarly, Sethe's uncanny sympathy is a more intense version of that felt by David in *Garden of Eden,* discussed in chapter 3. Such homesickness continues to infect the United States to this very moment in the form of de facto segregation, racial profiling, police violence, implicit biases of many kinds, and so on, all of which make home a haunted and damaging place, a place to reject and flee, or even, as we saw in chapter 2, to burn down. The social body of the United States is literally, in this sense, haunted by its past, a past that, as the William Faulkner line goes, "is not dead. It is not even past."[10]

That is to say, this uncanny homesickness must not be confined to the novel alone: Morrison ends the text by reiterating the general challenges of traumatic historical memory. That final section of Morrison's novel is a kind of coda, but one unmarked as such; it is lonely, dislocated, uncontained, and homesick language floating out beyond the edges of the narrative itself, like the footprints of Beloved discussed on the final page. It defies categories or genres. It is a ghost language. Morrison registers there the reverberations of the extraordinary horrors of slavery, the persistence of that injustice. She thus makes a kind of place for the utterly placeless, the lost, using the character of Beloved to focus her point: "Although she has claim, she is not claimed" (323). In this final section, Beloved is a traumatic truth that cannot be kept: "Remembering seemed unwise" (324).

And yet the novel is a memory, of a particular kind. It is a mark, a registration of the horrors of the history of slavery, one that cannot be fully understood or rendered canny. It remains uncanny, homeless, and homesick. Sethe can only survive it, not fix it. The cultural body, however, must register that horror in order to begin to do justice at least to the memory of the lost, and to Sethe and her kin, and all survivors.[11] Thus, under Morrison's hand, American literature itself becomes uncanny, as does human language. At the core of the American story are events that resist telling—the trauma of slavery—events that are too terrible to tell, yet must be. Exactly this sickness is one home of the American story. Morrison's technique of literalizing—

making Beloved a real ghost, personifying their house as angry, and so on—dramatizes the specificity and material reality of this sickness. Her technique also evokes the posthumanist notion that the nonhuman powerfully impacts the human in a range of ways.

The novel demonstrates the violence of denying autonomy—self-naming—to slaves. But this does not mean that we need simply to reiterate humanist notions of identity. Instead, I understand those humanist exaggerations of (white) autonomy as relying for their coherence on the subordinated status of black slaves. While granting autonomy to slaves was obviously an important step in the framework of humanism, it simply restages its hierarchical logic of dominance in the framework of species. We find a more robust critique of that logic of dominance in various theoretical movements highlighting intersectionality. Posthumanism extends that critique beyond the human, and an emphasis on homesickness underscores the way that identities of any kind operate in Derrida's concept of the trace structure, with identity dispersed and eternally deferred among other concepts. That is, the concept or identity of anything relies on how it contrasts with other concepts and identities. Our sense of self in homesickness is crossed up with "home," with the material and technological realities that surround us, and our relationship to them all is itself recursive, backward referencing, so that identity is a structure of weakness, or of openness and desire. This is a posthumanist structure partly in being more resolutely material, borrowing much of its content and behavior from the nonhuman inside and around us, and this is part of why it opens such radically different ways of being and thinking. These patterns of identity and meaning appear in *Beloved* more clearly because of the pressures and intensifications of trauma.

Real Ghosts

The magical realism of the novel, or its supernatural character, is a dramatic statement of the limits of the literal and the rational. Sethe's horrible act is not easily comprehensible, even if suicides and infanticide are common historical occurrences in catastrophic scenarios like slavery, the Holocaust, and so on.[12] The novel thus relies on a kind of metaphysics—ghosts, the supernatural—to expose the intensity of slavery's horror. However, while the events of *Beloved* are extreme, the novel's structure of haunting, I contend, evokes a more general reality visible in a posthumanist framework: the strange evanescence of the Real, and of the just. Jacques Derrida makes this general point early in *Specters of Marx,* his inquiry into questions of justice, where he analyzes the fundamental problem of how to live. In a sentence that can clearly be applied to *Beloved,* Derrida insists we learn how to live "only from the other and by death."[13] He notes that this form of learning entails "a strange commitment," a coming "to terms with death" that necessarily means "*talk with* or *about* some ghost."[14] Because death cannot be domesticated, thinking about it requires dealing with ghosts, with that which extends beyond the known or knowable, the present or the living. He further explains, "It is necessary to speak *of the* ghost, indeed *to the* ghost and *with* it, from the moment that no ethics, no politics, whether revolutionary or not, seems possible and thinkable and *just* that does not recognize in its principle the respect for those others who are not yet there, presently living, whether they are already dead or not yet born."[15]

In this passage, Derrida wrestles with the same problem of absent presence, of a looming other who is "not yet" or "no longer" that Morrison treats. But crucially for the argument of this chapter and for our culture's readings of *Beloved,* this problem for Derrida is not only one of exceptional scenarios. For Derrida, this is *the* problem of life. How do we live? I underscore this here because it is too easy for an entrenched humanism to evade the difficult questions Morrison and Derrida pose about human life. A common move is to push such questions out to the margins of life, connecting them only with explicitly posttraumatic texts. Another dismissal can be accomplished via a simple and reductive treatment of history, making it seem neatly bound and located in a past that does not touch the present. But for Derrida and Morrison both, to ask questions of justice—to be humane, human—is instead to undergo this haunting. The past infects and afflicts but also renders valuable the present. Already, then, even before we say so, as Derrida might argue, these ghosts, real ghosts, swirl in this chapter.

Beloved's haunting hinges on a central paradox: it is Sethe's insistence on her humanity and the humanity of her children that drives her to commit one of the quintessentially inhumane acts: infanticide. Perversely, Sethe is condemned even by the African American community for permitting herself to be too human, for having too much love for her children. Her acquaintance from Sweet Home and eventual lover, Paul D, thinks, "Very risky. For a used-to-be-slave woman to love anything that much was dangerous, especially if it was her children she had settled on to love" (54). He tells Sethe her "love was too thick" (239). This same hazard—claiming too much humanity, too much vitality, too much life—earns Sethe's mother-in-law, Baby Suggs, condemnation too. When a celebratory party emerges somewhat spontaneously twenty days after Sethe successfully escapes from Sweet Home, becoming a massive feast and joyous party, it finally makes the community "angry. They woke up the next morning and remembered . . . and got angry." "Too much, they thought. Where does she get it all, Baby Suggs, holy? Why is she and hers always the center of things? How come she always knows exactly what to do and when?" the community wonders (161).

Their jealousy is partly the result of ordinary human tensions, but it is clearly also a result of the dehumanization of slavery, which has degraded community expectations of life. In his telling of the events that day—the Misery, Sethe's attempt to kill all her children—community leader and agent of the Underground Railroad, Stamp Paid, urges that this jealousy, a kind of "meanness," prevents the community from giving Sethe and Baby Suggs a warning about the arrival of schoolteacher, which was part of why his arrival took them by surprise, contributing to the catastrophic events. Thus, similarly, years later, when Paul D arrives at 124 Bluestone Road and asks Sethe to have a child with him, Sethe feels fear, thinking, "Motherlove was a killer" (155). In these circumstances of life, precisely the power of a mother's love is something too dangerous to embrace.

These doubly entrapping expectations issued first by the white power structure and then reinforced by the black community's need to survive produce the paradoxical result of love leading to killing, and they endanger the strong characters like Sixo and Sethe. These perversions of life damage the self, making it sick, befouled, victimized. At the novel's close, Paul D helps Sethe see a route out of her disappearing self by insisting, "You your best thing, Sethe. You are" (322). This proclamation of her dignity, her value, is not just a reassertion of familiar discourses of human rights, since in this novel familiar notions of the human have been radically shaken.

Instead, I argue that we must understand this idea of Sethe's dignity against the backdrop of the extreme trials of her mobility, her unhomely life, and her being rendered as a slave, a form of fungible property. In slavery and oppression, her identity becomes deeply withdrawn, her selfhood a black hole of loss. This attribute is expressed in a physiological register by Paul D when he first arrives at 124 Bluestone Road. He remembers Sethe as "Halle's girl—the one with iron eyes and backbone to match" (10).[16] But eighteen years later, in the novel's present, Paul D describes Sethe's face as "softer," but "too still for comfort." He notes this suspended character in her eyes particularly: "Her eyes did not pick up a flicker of light. They were like two wells into which he had trouble gazing" (10).

These black holes of Sethe's life trace back to the arrival of schoolteacher after Mr. Garner's death, who, Paul D remembers, "broke three more Sweet Home men and punched the glittering iron out of Sethe's eyes, leaving two wells that did not reflect firelight." After a paragraph break, Morrison continues with Paul D's account about the novel's present: "Now the iron was back but the face, softened by hair, made him trust her enough to step inside her door smack into a pool of pulsing life" (11). This "life," of course, is the force that later manifests as Beloved, a ghost not only of Sethe's past but finally of the general history of slavery. Sethe's determination has returned, but it is a force so strong that it makes Paul D nervous. He is willing to confront the ghost in the house only because of "the face, softened by hair." This moment from early in the novel reiterates the fundamental brutality of slavery that Sethe's character exposes with special clarity: that strength and independence become *liabilities*. It is exactly Sethe's iron will, her fierce determination to protect her children, that leads her to try to save them by killing them. The violence of slavery makes that strength into a deeper wound. And her partially recovered strength nearly prevents a robust reunion with Paul D.

Such stories complicate an account that emphasizes the importance of freedom of movement, because for Sethe movement is always haunted by the experiences she has undergone. Freedom to move her person, then, is not a real or an absolute freedom. This is so in at least two senses. First, more simply, mobility in Sethe's case is always haunted by the dehumanizing violence of slavery; even her choice to flee Sweet Home cannot be seen as unfettered. And second, as I noted in the introduction, her very idea of freedom bears within it the material and historical reality of slavery. A free and mobile subjectivity has always had slavery to contrast against, as argued by Morrison herself in *Playing in the Dark* and by Jennifer Rae Greeson in "The Prehistory of Possessive Individualism."[17]

Sethe's experience reveals that all forms of mobility entail a measure of subjection, weakness, and loss, even if they are disavowed, a claim central to the argument I am making in this book. Indeed, Sethe's aggrieved and haunted shock is a greatly intensified version of a dimension of all subjectivity: loss and mortality mean that one dimension of the self is nonrational, suffering flesh, even scar tissue. We cannot fully understand our losses; our visceral and emotional needs drive far more of our actions than we generally acknowledge; our future is far less in our control than we tend to admit. These are accounts of our weakness. I argued in chapter 1 that Annie Proulx demonstrates this reality clearly with the more privileged form of mobility exercised by her character Mero in "The Half-Skinned Steer." The history of Enlightenment subjectivity has scapegoated these realities of weakness onto women, animals, and the ostensibly nonsentient to varying degrees, but posthumanism insists on better coming to terms with them. This means not only performing a rational analysis of these realities, as I am attempting here; it also means acknowledging this weakness and inscrutability as essential to life itself. This is why we are all homesick.

Trauma as Placed in *Beloved*

The homesickness produced by the violence of slavery is perhaps most clearly rendered by Sweet Home, which is a very complicated place for the slaves who lived there. Nancy Jesser describes it as "the reference point through which Sethe makes her decisions about the future."[18] Sweet Home is inescapable for her and others in that sense, since it organizes their past, however violently and harmfully. Thus, when Paul D first arrives at 124 Bluestone Road, he and Sethe immediately find a companionship that derives from their shared history in that place, a companionship that is the first step back from the social isolation Sethe and her daughter Denver inhabit after the killing of Beloved. It is important to underscore this paradox, because it is typical of the novel more generally, and of the larger argument of *Homesickness*: it is only with this return to memories of the horrible place Sweet Home that Sethe and thereby Denver can begin to recover from their ferocious traumas. Indeed, from a posthumanist perspective equipped to accommodate more complex understandings of the roles of the nonhuman in human life, this moment in the novel can be understood as a kind of haunting *by* the place Sweet Home; *it* becomes a partial agent, drawing out buried realities from the past.

In her foreword to recent editions of the novel, Morrison writes that this effort to disorient the reader is exactly the point of *Beloved*: "I wanted the reader to be kidnapped, thrown ruthlessly into an alien environment as the first step into a shared experience with the book's population—just as the characters were snatched from one place to another, from any place to any other, without preparation or defense" (xviii). She further argues that the novel's opening sentence is designed to mark this house as the sponsor of a very particular kind of experience: "There would be no adjectives suggesting coziness or grandeur or the laying claim to an instant, aristocratic past. Only numbers here to identify the house while simultaneously separating it from a street or city—marking its difference from the houses of other blacks in the neighborhood" (xviii). This particularity is also, I am arguing, precisely what makes Morrison's story general: all memory is this focused, this specific, or it is not memory at all. Its hold on us is its reality, its immediacy, even though of course all memory is also misremembering, or perhaps better, a reworking.

From that perspective, we can also read the entire novel as a kind of metafiction about the power of places and our experiences in them, as though the whole story's supernatural character attests to this otherworldly—or, more exactly, uncanny, *worldly*—power. While the conventional—and important—discussion of memory in *Beloved* typically connects it to trauma, the strange, haunting effects of Sweet Home are an extreme version of the way past experience informs present understanding in general, a structure of experience I have been calling "homesickness."[19] The strange perversity of memories of Sweet Home make this surprising reality clearer than is common, but memory commonly tends to work this way. The fact of temporality—the fact that, in effect, our encounters with places and other realities extend across time beyond the actual event of the encounter—signifies the power and the alterity of the nonhuman. In all experience, we are haunted by the past as we continue to reassess it. Because our experiences are crossed up with the others of places and beings, experience too becomes less scrutable and more foreign to us. Our experiences are homesick inside us, uncanny to us, and memory exposes us to them again and again, even as the physiological act of remembering also changes the memories themselves.[20] These memories, the very stuff of our selfhood, are changing strangers within us.

We can read the entire novel as a kind of metafiction about how memory haunts us. In that strange reading, Paul D's appearance at 124 would derive not from plot, which becomes more incidental, but from the involuntary character of memory, to which this novel is powerful testimony. In this reading, Paul D too is a kind of ghost. Indeed, the whole novel, with all its characters and narratives, is a haunting by unsettled ghosts from the traumas of slavery. And they cannot be contained within the novel's pages or frame. They haunt us now, in reality. They should haunt us. While most of my remaining reading of *Beloved* in this chapter will treat it in more conventional, less metafictional terms, I think it is important to conjure the ghost of this other reading and accept that it haunts us. It is this haunting—the refusal of the story to remain safely fictional and contained—that makes this novel, and narrative more generally, political. Narratives have a presence, like Beloved, that does (unpredictable) work in the world, to readers, to cultures, and to the nonhuman: haunting.[21]

Beloved dramatizes this reality with special force, as Morrison notes in the passage about the reader being kidnapped. This structure of experience is entirely contrary to the cozy, reductive, and dismissive accounts of memory and nostalgia, which tend to reduce both to a simple circularity in which we confirm a subject that is not really in doubt. But in truth, these actions of memory are akin to Timothy Morton's general argument about human weakness, in *Hyperobjects* and *Dark Ecology* especially. In the latter, for instance, he understands the history of agriculture to reveal not just ability and agency but also desperation, as noted in my introduction.[22] That is, we reach for memory precisely because the present of the subject is inchoate and unstable, always, necessarily. We rely on the past—often with a kind of (disavowed) desperation—to reaffirm our sense of ourselves. Again, as I argued in the introduction, I suspect this tremendous power of memory over us, inside us, and this sense of our own being unmoored in time, constantly, helps facilitate the wholesale rejection of nostalgia. The humanist fiction of the sovereign self requires repression of the power of the past and of the other(s). Beyond simplistic nostalgia—beyond a reductive account of how the past informs the present—be dragons. Easier to call them fantasies and ignore them. Stay on the petroleum-sponsored map. But in *Beloved*, Morrison bravely goes out to countenance them. In making this case, however, I certainly do not mean to naturalize or in any way excuse the kinds of traumas that Sethe and her family experience. Racism is not inevitable or somehow "natural." Instead, I am showing how their experience of memory at the very limits of what is possible for humans helps clarify the more general reality of memory.

Thus, to note that this is a posthumanist structure of subjectivity and memory is not at all to leave aside questions of race and racism. In fact, quite the contrary. Much as I argued in chapter 1 that using a posthumanist tack to rethink questions of gender has the power to deepen feminist critiques, posthumanism can clarify the power of Morrison's critique of slavery and its inhumanity, for several reasons. For one, the account of memory as a stranger, as an other, precisely inverts the long history of xenophobia that tends to undergird racism. "They" (whoever "they" might be) are not the only strangers in this account; we too are strangers. We are strangers to ourselves. The strange, the uncanny, thus appears as central to life, all the more so in the age of modernity, as humans have been increasingly exposed to difference and strangeness in the forms of new places and peoples encountered via new technologies, technologies that themselves brought out new dimensions of reality that were strange to us. Modernity has exposed us to all sorts of alterity. Indeed, a key word in modernity, the "Anthropocene," demonstrates how nonhuman entities and forces that have often been regarded as familiar and subject to human control, forces commonly gathered under the abusively singular word "nature," are far less controllable than has been imagined.[23] The Anthropocene names the strange otherness of the "natural" world we live in, making us homesick on/for a planet we thought we knew.

Ethnic and racial difference, then, is part of a larger experience of alterity in modernity, which requires an ethics of hospitality to the stranger.[24] I am arguing here, however, that this need characterizes much more of our lives than we commonly admit, putting novels like Morrison's *Beloved* not on the margin of human experience in modernity but at its center. Morrison dramatizes the power of the not-us (even the not-us that is inside us) and offers a kind of example (not to say "program") for how we might be more welcoming of it.

Commonly, we welcome the other at home. Narrating the background of the house at 124 Bluestone Road, which sponsors this novel's activities, Morrison underscores the power of strange traumatic memory, a powerful and unpredictable visitor. Baby Suggs, for example, mourns her inability to remember much of her eight children, all "gone away from me," she says (6). Of her firstborn, she mourns, "All I can remember of her is how she loved the burned bottom of bread. Can you beat that? Eight children and that's all I remember" (6). Sethe responds by naming one of the central themes of the novel, and more particularly of Sethe's own memories: "That's all you let yourself remember" (6). Sethe herself "worked hard to remember as close to nothing as was safe," particularly of her two boys, who had been chased out of the house by the ghost, by the traumas of history hanging over the place.[25] However, Morrison continues about Sethe, "Unfortunately her brain was devious." The slightest "something" would stir her mind,

> and suddenly there was Sweet Home rolling, rolling, rolling out before her eyes, and although there was not a leaf on that farm that did not make her want to scream, it rolled itself out before her in shameless beauty. It never looked as terrible as it was and it made her wonder if hell was a pretty place too. Fire and brimstone all right, but hidden in lacy groves. Boys hanging from the most beautiful sycamores in the world. It shamed her—remembering the wonderful soughing trees rather than the boys. Try as she might to make it otherwise, the sycamores beat out the children every time and she could not forgive her memory for that. (7)

This account underscores a complex subject at odds with itself, a posthumanist self we cannot entirely control in the involuntary action of memory. For Morrison, this involves for Sethe a kind of shame. The shame is twofold. First, it is pointedly about responsibility for and to these particular events, the damage and the injuries caused by racism and slavery. Second, in the text, Sethe feels shame for her misbehaving memory. This too is a strange shame, since her response ought to model our own. Her work of historical recovery (and Morrison's work) is synecdoche for our work. Reading *Beloved* ought to fill us with a form of shame that can drive historical change. The shame is therefore political. The novel's title is a metonym for all those who have been lost to the world-shattering violence of slavery and the slave trade. That Morrison has chosen that word—"Beloved"—is crucial to the power of the novel because it humanizes those victims with a term of endearment. But, as Morrison's novel clarifies, the shame is not purely political goad or functional response. It also verges on debilitation; indeed, it *should* include a measure of debilitation that is part of mourning, a stillness like that which Paul D sees in Sethe's eyes when he first arrives at 124. That is one of the tasks of this novel: to mark out a place of mourning for the lives that are gone and that cannot be restored. Hence Morrison's dedication: "Sixty Million and more."

If we turn this novel *merely* into a condemnation of racism, we misread it; we miss its crucial mourning work. So reading *Beloved* properly should make us feel pity and shame that cannot be erased.[26] That relates to the second dimension of the shame we share with Sethe, which derives from the power of these memories over us. That is part and parcel of our larger weakness, our inability to redirect the world's traumatic events in general. In *Homesickness,* I am arguing that at some level, this weakness is unavoidable. I am calling that weakness "mortality." That is not to say, of course, to reiterate, that racism is inevitable! But our inability to keep alive all the creatures and people we love is inevitable.

As in the passage quoted above about Sweet Home, that shame is placed. The beauty of the plantation is particular; they are real sycamore trees populating an actual place that Sethe recalls. The perverse and upsetting power of these memories hinges on this reality and particularity, which is again why approaching trauma through place is important. Sweet Home is ironically named; it names homesickness of the deepest kind. Memories of it not only displace Sethe's memories of her boys; they make memory itself, the home of the subject, a source of pain and grievance. Further, by infecting the beauty of the world and the richness of parenting and family with the disease of abuse, memories of Sweet Home turn the world itself terrible. Homesickness is sickness at home. Morrison names it perfectly: hell. It is so much the worse, more vicious, and, again, perverse, for being beautiful. As Morrison notes, "Fire and brimstone all right, but hidden in lacy groves." This sentence uses a spatial example, a geographical, ecological, and aesthetic register—"lacy groves"—to evoke the surfaces of memory, the ostensibly placid outsides, like Sethe's eyes, inside of which lurk "fire and brimstone," the hells of vicious histories.[27]

The uncanny haunting by Beloved works in the same way, dealing with the homely realities that should make life pleasant and enjoyable: a "kettleful of chickpeas," "soda crackers," a "cake," each of which is used to haunt the house on the opening page of the novel (3). This is where trauma lives. Not in the abstractions of "psyche" or "history" but in the immediate and the particular; hence the need for narratives. Trauma infects these nourishing foods, making them poisonous to Sethe's boys, Howard and Bulgar, who can take no more of them, leaving behind only memories, their ghosts that Sethe ignores as best she can in order to survive. Sethe refuses to name her loneliness, steeling herself against it with her iron eyes, but Paul D's appearance provokes words from Denver that begin to help her and Sethe move on with life, a process that takes the entire novel and, we surmise, more.

Paul D's arrival, expressed and made legible with the semiotics of Sweet Home—that is, with reference to the shared history of that particular place and its meanings—brings Denver's humanity back to the surface. Coming down the stairs to see Paul D, Denver "was suddenly hot and shy. It had been a long time since anybody (good-willed whitewoman, preacher, speaker or newspaperman) sat at their table, their sympathetic voices called liar by the revulsion in their eyes" (14). This revulsion is precisely the challenge of confronting the real legacies of slavery (and more specifically of the Fugitive Slave Law): a loving mother, like the historical figure Margaret Garner upon whom Sethe is based to some extent, whose very love drives her to kill her children. To turn the abstraction of slavery into this particular act, and to ask readers to confront it, is essential to this novel's power. Slavery means, among many other things, *this* action, this destruction of humanity, something so horrible that even well-meaning people, "good-willed" people in Morrison's wording, cannot readily countenance it. These visitors are turned against themselves, made uncanny to themselves, offering sympathy in their voices and revulsion in their eyes.

After her initial heat and shyness, Denver then experiences anger as she feels excluded from the sudden collaboration and community present between Sethe and Paul D. Again, and aptly, Morrison terms this with particulars: "They were a twosome, saying 'Your daddy' and 'Sweet Home' in a way that made it clear both belonged to them and not to her. That her own father's absence was not hers" (15). So Denver is lonely not in a general sense but in a particular one; she is removed from intimacy with her father (and, thereby, with her mother): homesickness, or sickness at home. Of course, this too derives directly from the violence of slavery, undergirded by the racism that understands humans as property. Denver's loneliness gives her understanding of and language for Beloved's, and leads her to express a critique of the past more explicitly: "How come everybody run off from Sweet Home can't stop talking about it? Look like if it was so sweet you would have stayed" (16).

Morrison details the suffering of Sethe, Stamp Paid, Paul D, and many others in explicitly spatial terms, revolving around "place." Paul D's response to Beloved, for instance, considers her in light of his own suffering of placelessness. She comes to epitomize—but also intensify and extend—his suffering. Paul D thinks, "This girl Beloved, homeless and without people, beat all, though he couldn't exactly say why, considering the colored people he had run into during the last twenty years." First, it is important to pause and register his uncertainty here, because it speaks to Morrison's larger treatment of history and understanding. Beloved functions in this novel as a mystery, as a force difficult to understand or categorize, precisely because she embodies a history that is beyond recovery. She is the lost. This sentiment, that Paul D "couldn't exactly say why" she "beat all," evokes the difficult reality she represents, a difficulty that goes well beyond even the hell that Paul D had seen in his time. He describes that hell following the passage just quoted.

> During, before and after the War he had seen Negroes so stunned, or hungry, or tired or bereft it was a wonder they recalled or said anything. Who, like him, had hidden in caves and fought owls for food; who, like him, stole from pigs; who, like him, slept in trees in the day and walked by night; who, like him, had buried themselves in slop and jumped in wells to avoid regulators, raiders, paterollers, veterans, hill men, posses and merry makers. . . .
>
> Move. Walk. Run. Hide. Steal and move on. (78)

For Paul D, the world itself becomes no-place, a dislocation that is worse than disorienting because its forces are designed to actively pursue and harm him. He must wrest his living from animals, as Morrison accents, because the only other place afforded him and others by humans is in slavery, a fate that is worse than death for many, as Sethe's attempt to kill her children dramatically testifies.[28]

This larger history establishes the conditions to which the ghost Beloved responds, and her expression of desire and need in the lyrical chapters late in the novel hinges on finding a *place* in the world. Beloved thinks, "Sethe's is the face that left me Sethe sees me see her and I see the smile her smiling face is the place for me it is the face I lost" (252). Again, Morrison's writing registers the challenges of putting a lost history into language, as Beloved speaks a searching and unconventional language, one that is both metaphorical and excessively literal, like the novel as a whole. The ghost in the novel becomes real—literal—yet the power of the novel relies precisely on the metaphorical, synecdochal structure. Thus Beloved stands for the much larger losses of many like her. The placelessness, literally, that Beloved experienced in being killed is beyond even the horrors that Paul D so compellingly and horribly details. Being without place, strictly speaking, is to entirely lack a language: to disappear; to be invisible. In his article "The Question of Reading Traumatic Testimony: Jones's *Corregidora* and Morrison's *Beloved,*" Abdennebi Ben Beya expresses this idea this way: "Disaster precedes the word, it precedes and transcends expression. Disaster is silent."[29] Morrison, working along that outer edge of what can be written, has Beloved speak a strange and evocative language, if only to begin to bring the invisible back into the visible, to begin to address the historical wrongs that escape notice in the seemingly ordinary world.

In this way, Beloved comes to *embody* these lost stories and this *dis-placed* history. This is what makes her a presence, a character in the novel. Morrison handles this effort carefully, however, working between the constraints of realism that the novel insists upon and its "magical" or supernatural elements, for lack of better terms. The haunting ghost is accounted for in several literal ways. Stamp Paid, for instance, thinks she might be "a girl [who had been] locked up in the house with a whiteman" (277), while Paul D wonders about what she could be (276). Denver, asked by Paul D if Beloved is "sure 'nough your sister," responds, "At times. At times I think she was—more" (314). That reading of Beloved, as the criticism has recognized, is buoyed by the passages in Beloved's own voice, in which she gives expression to experiences beyond her own, such as the Middle Passage (248–52), so that she comes to represent the larger traumas of slavery. Thus Jean Wyatt notes that "Beloved also has a collective identity: she represents a whole lineage of people obliterated by slavery, beginning with the Africans who died on the Middle Passage."[30]

Beloved is synecdoche, part for whole, of African American heritage, but she is also a kind of synecdoche for fiction and especially historical fiction. She embodies the past and brings the past into the present, in person, first in the particular, dramatic role she plays within the world of the novel. For instance, she asks Denver to tell the story of Denver's birth. Denver obliges, giving the story texture, life, and complexity by including various details about the "whitegirl" who helped with Denver's delivery, including the whitegirl's hair, the set of her face, her character; she also adds specifics about velvet, about Baby Suggs, and more (90–91). As Denver tells, responding to Beloved's "alert and hungry face," her "downright craving to know," Denver herself "was seeing it now and feeling it—through Beloved. Feeling how it must have felt to her mother. Seeing how it must have looked. And the more fine points she made, the more detail she provided, the more Beloved liked it" (91–92). This moment of metafiction, a commentary on how fiction works for both teller and auditor, reiterates the challenge of accessing the past in a robust fashion, justifying the second-order perception that historical fiction embodies (second-order because, as fiction, it stands at a remove from direct observation). To really begin to grasp the past, we need its specific nuances, its textures, moods, and particular significances. This moment also reiterates that Beloved embodies the past, that she takes in the past like food, like nourishment in her "hunger." She grows bigger and bigger with the past as the novel proceeds.

Beloved's hunger for life overcomes 124 and especially Sethe, who cannot deny her as the novel proceeds. Sethe loses her job and surrenders her pragmatic judgment, giving Beloved anything she could: "lullabies, new stitches, the bottom of the cake bowl, the top of the milk. If the hen had only two eggs, she got both" (282). Sethe "cut[s] Denver out completely." Then, in Sethe's desperation for Beloved, "the thirty-eight dollars of life savings went to feed themselves with fancy food and decorate themselves with ribbon and dress goods, which Sethe cut and sewed like they were going in a hurry. Bright clothes—with blues stripes and sassy prints" (282). Beloved, an embodiment of historical trauma, swallows not only stories and food, then, but the economic means for the future and even the aesthetic realm—colors, clothing, craft, style. Beloved's pregnancy further suggests that she incorporates the biological possibilities of the future, appropriating them for herself. She is reclaiming all that was denied her—and by extension denied to African Americans more generally—reversing history.

Near the novel's end, Denver looks at the pair and thinks, "The thing was done: Beloved bending over Sethe looked the mother, Sethe the teething child. . . . The bigger Beloved got, the smaller Sethe became; the brighter Beloved's eyes, the more those eyes that used never to look away became slits of sleeplessness. . . . Beloved ate up her life, took it, swelled up with it, grew taller on it" (294–95). For Sethe, there is no appeasing the past; Sethe's experience in this episode evokes the larger realities of African American experiences in and after slavery, through Jim Crow, redlining of real estate, and so on, as the traumas of the past undermine the possibilities of the present.

The only solution to Sethe's guilt is the intervention of the community women, spurred by Denver's search for help. And again, Beloved's presence—her appearance as a manifestation of prior events—calls forth the women's own specific pasts. When the thirty women arrive at 124, "the first thing they saw was not Denver sitting on the steps, but themselves. Younger, stronger, even as little girls lying in the grass asleep." The paragraph goes on to detail their specific memories of this house—tastes, sounds, and sights associated with its better days, during Baby Suggs's life (304). Ella, who helps Stamp Paid on the Underground Railroad, is key to organizing the effort of these community women. As Morrison makes clear by recounting Ella's own traumatic memories of rape (301, 305), these women, in helping Sethe and Denver, are also confronting their own pasts and working to heal them. Beloved is a ghost that haunts them too in a dynamic that resembles Sylvie's confrontation with community women late in *Housekeeping*, discussed in chapter 2.[31] The women's whispered talk outside the house turns into song, and their singing brings Sethe and Beloved to the front door: "For Sethe it was as though the Clearing had come to her with all its heat and simmering leaves" (308). Again, Morrison underscores how places like the Clearing organize a whole range of meanings and experiences. But the power of place also has a negative valence: as Mr. Godwin rides toward the house, Sethe is drawn back into the traumatic memory of "the Misery" that happened under similar circumstances in this exact place, 124 Bluestone Road, and she attempts to kill the white man arriving in his cart, reversing her earlier response, aiming her violence not at Beloved but at the man she thinks is coming to take her child. Morrison's novel repeatedly models such historical reversals.

Jesser similarly emphasizes how this effort to recuperate and respond to the traumatic past plays out in terms of places, places that can both enable and obstruct, as is clear in that dramatic episode just recounted. Jesser highlights four places that perform these roles: Sweet Home; Alfred, Georgia (where Paul D works on the chain gang); the Clearing; and 124 Bluestone Road. Her focus on the power of these places to organize the novel is consonant with my own, but a posthumanist approach to the novel permits us to understand the function of these places somewhat differently. Jesser reads them in the framework of utopia and dystopia, arguing that "calls for the return to home and to community are both nostalgic and utopian."[32] This approach seems to limit the value and application of questions about home to texts explicitly treating those themes. I would suggest that "place" is not just a *thematic* element of texts. Instead, place is a sine qua non of all human meaning, though this reality is often minimized in humanist orientations.[33]

Thus "calls for the return to home" are actually much more fundamental; they underlie the call of subjectivity itself. The subject is always interpellated in terms of home and the past. This difference is crucial, again, because there is a risk of understanding the placelessness, the homesickness of *Beloved* to be only a consequence of trauma. In effect, homesickness is thus ghettoized.

That move can be doubly harmful; it can quietly reaffirm both the misguided humanist sense that the familiar home of subjectivity remains safe and knowable for most of "us," and thus it can deepen the differences between oppressed and, to simplify, nonoppressed communities, reproducing divisions derived from racist histories.

For these reasons, I believe it is important to supplement the crucial readings of *Beloved* in the context of the African American tradition with posthumanist readings, alongside texts from other ethnic literatures (including "white" texts), which is not at all to suggest these are mutually exclusive modes of criticism. For instance, in "Ecomelancholia: Slavery, War, and Black Ecological Imaginings," Jennifer C. James evokes the way that the "earth is a site of black memory" for authors such as Charles Chesnutt, Zora Neale Hurston, and Toni Morrison. James suggests that "'natural memory' represents a belief in organic proximity and reciprocity; the lines separating humans from nature, the living from the dead, are scarcely determinable."[34] While James also emphasizes the hazard of an ecophobia that registers "the legacies of trauma and injustice" in natural spaces for blacks,[35] her point about natural memory conjures the strange power of place along the lines pursed in *Homesickness.* Similarly, Jesser notes that one of the essential strategies for imagining a place and a world beyond Sweet Home is to think about and plan to reach the "Magical North." That way of thinking of the North, Jesser argues, is not a final answer, however, since in fact the North "offers little to combat the racist institutions, whether in the form of chattel slavery or the brutal enforcement of the Fugitive Slave Law."[36]

This is an important historical point, one that resonates long after slavery too. It is a recurrent theme in Wilkerson's *The Warmth of Other Suns,* for instance, as African American migrants to the North and West find less freedom and more racism than they hoped or expected.[37] However, this demystification strategy may obscure the heterogeneous (and nonhuman) complexity of places. Reducing a place to the dominant power hierarchy in it not only reinscribes a reductive humanism; it forecloses very real affordances present in places like the North, which can provide a way out. Part of what facilitates Paul D's escape, for instance, is precisely his ability and willingness to associate with elements of the landscape, of the Real, that lie outside conventional human experiences and understandings. Sethe likewise hides in nonhuman, "natural" spaces in her escape from Sweet Home, and of course the Ohio River is itself a powerful nonhuman force that facilitates hiding and escape even as its presence determines the boundary between free and not-free states. We might even defend thinking about the North as a kind of magical place as a compelling shorthand for the way that places gather a cluster of realities difficult to isolate or fully understand rationally. All places, in this sense, are "magical."[38]

Denver's thinking about places—and her tendency to personify 124 Bluestone Road—can be read in this framework too. For instance, Denver finds companionship in "five boxwood bushes planted in a ring" that had grown "to form a round, empty room seven feet high, its walls fifty inches of murmuring leaves" (34). Similar to the compensatory houses of Ruth and her sister, Lucille, in *Housekeeping*, discussed in chapter 2, this alternative space is both human ("planted in a ring") and nonhuman. It is "first a playroom (where the silence was softer), then a refuge (from her brothers' fright), soon the place became the point. In that bower, closed off from the hurt of the hurt world, Denver's imagination produced its own hunger and its own food, which she badly need because loneliness wore her out." The boxwood gave her a place away from the house, which she regarded "as a person rather than a structure. A person that wept, sighed, trembled and fell into fits." Dismissing or demystifying that attitude toward her house denies the reality that human experiences, emotions, and memories commonly anchor in nonhuman places, relying on their presences and the affordances they provide, like shelter. In the boxwood, where "the place became the point," by contrast, Denver found other possibilities: "She felt ripe and clear, and salvation was as easy as a wish" (35). Perhaps because of her traumatic experiences, Denver has discovered a posthumanist insight: that places, richly engaged, become a central point, of life, of experience.

In other words, there is an outside to the seeming omnipresence of racist human realities. Jesser also points to this outside. Not only individual escaping slaves but entire resistance communities rely on what we might call the affordances of these nonhuman places. While she does not make this point in this posthumanist register, Jesser does, for instance, recognize that Paul D's escape from Alfred, Georgia, and the chain gang is facilitated by the Cherokee, "a band who 'removed themselves' from history by retreating into the Blue Ridge Mountains."[39] Allowing that the affordances of the natural world are not entirely controlled by the white, Euro-American power structure, and further that some whites such as Mr. Bodwin use their property to help Sethe and her family, denaturalizes slavery and the violence that attends to it, returning them to a history that is subject to dispute and to change. Denaturalization has long been crucial in the resistance to the evil institution because one of the essential strategies of racism has been, and continues to be, naturalization: the idea that there are plain, natural differences among people, differences that ought to translate into social roles. Recognizing that nature does not align with the white power structure undercuts these absolutist narratives.

One such place outside the white power structure in *Beloved* is the Clearing, mentioned above, which Morrison describes as "a wide-open place cut deep in the woods nobody knew for what at the end of a path known only to deer and whoever cleared the land in the first place" (102). There, Baby Suggs leads the community in prayer and healing before "the Misery." Morrison notes of Baby Suggs preaching in the Clearing, "She did not tell them to clean up their lives or to go and sin no more. She did not tell them they were the blessed of the earth, its inheriting meek or its glorybound pure." Instead, she encouraged her listeners to reclaim their persons: "'Here,' she said, 'in this here place, we flesh; flesh that weeps, laughs; flesh that dances on bare feet in the grass. Love it. Love it hard. Yonder they do not love your flesh. They despise it'" (103). Jesser importantly emphasizes that this form of care is "not sustainable in the constricted and categorized world of white Cincinnati and white America" (332). I further emphasize the power of particularity in this entire scene, a power that runs contrary to the generalizing and systematizing of harmful racist dogmas. Instead of the blanket policies enabling harm to black bodies, Baby Suggs suggests a love for each distinct body. Personal love *is* precisely that kind of particularity and specificity, and in this scene, it is enabled by the particular place called "the Clearing." If the Clearing had other attributes—if it were less well hidden, if whites continued to use it, and so on—it would not be available to enable these sessions of community healing. The affordances of the natural world give this community a space to be other than what white racists require of them.

Black Bodies at Risk

Sethe's own life is every bit as much at stake as were the lives of her children. In this status, she and Beloved both represent what it has meant to be black in the United States. This same problem arises in Ta-Nehisi Coates's National Book Award–winning text, *Between the World and Me* (2015), written as a letter to his son.[40] One of his central themes is the profound vulnerability of the black body, and the extraordinary economic implications of this exposure. Coates writes, "At the onset of the Civil War, our stolen bodies were worth four billion dollars, more than all of American industry, all of American railroads, workshops, and factories combined, and the prime product rendered by our stolen bodies—cotton—was America's primary export."[41] The violence of this system and its results echo through culture at the level of the body today, shows Coates, expressed by hip-hop artists who assert, "against all evidence and odds, that they were masters of their own lives, their own streets, and their own bodies." For Coates, the unspoken undercurrent of this bravado is "fear" of violence,[42] an uncanny sense of one's own person as strange: "Disembodiment is a kind of terrorism, and the threat of it alters the orbit of all our lives and, like terrorism, this distortion is intentional. Disembodiment. The dragon that compelled the boys I knew, way back, into extravagant theater of ownership."[43] This unrest in one's own self is violent and results from violence, which reproduces itself in black-on-black crime that is kin to Sethe's attempt to kill her children.

Such violence has too often been described as caused by problems internal to black culture, itself a racist gesture that reproduces the apartheid logic of Jim Crow, forgetting the fact of interbraided white and black histories. In Coates's book, as in *Beloved,* the vastly degraded status of black lives leads directly to these surprising measures of self-protection as violence. For Sethe, the only way to save the humanity of her children is to kill them. In the horrible reality of slavery, death is sometimes a better option than life. In this regard, attaining a measure of dignity in life can literally lead to destruction, since dignity cannot endure the degradations of slavery. This is a homesickness of the most severe kind, going beyond suicide to infanticide. (Note in this context that many of the other texts treated in *Homesickness* regularly approach the threshold of suicide in response to a related sense of despair.) Similarly, in the inhumane, circumscribed lives of so many black communities, where agency is profoundly curtailed, violence is a way to reassert one's agency and selfhood.[44] The refusal simply to accept the massive slow violence of multigenerational, persistent racism involves "extravagant theater of ownership," a performance of homesickness.

Likewise, in both the place of the Clearing and in embodiment, there is a homesickness for self and place that animates the community. They desire a place to be what they can imagine, and doing so involves engaging the strange mysteries of physicality, the alterity of our very selves. Owning the self in this account is not simply a transfer of title deed or the like; that very concept of ownership, instead, is the problem. Racism reduces the complexity of people to the ostensible simplicity of objects, objects that are misrecognized as fixed in their identities, as self-similar, what Morton calls in a different context "Easy Think" objects.[45] In fact, not even objects are so simple. Thus, for Baby Suggs, reclaiming selfhood involves the mysterious practices of laughter, tears, and dance.

That mysteriousness is reinforced by Morrison in the larger novel in two key ways. First, at the conclusion, Paul D echoes Baby Suggs's earlier effort in preaching to encourage auditors to reclaim themselves. Paul D insists that Sethe reclaim herself, saying to her, "You your best thing, Sethe. You are." Sethe responds with surprise: "Me? Me?" (322). Arguably, those are the novel's final narrative words (the subsequent final chapter does other work, I suggest more fully below). Ending this way, Morrison emphasizes the challenge and the mystery of this return to self, a complex homesickness, notably distinct from an easy or simple homesick structure of selfhood. The complexity is earned by the novel as a whole, which demonstrates how difficult it is for Sethe to be a self. But the evanescence of the self is also marked by Morrison in the final chapter, which I see as outside the narrative, a necessary ethical comment on the whole story. It also reiterates another key point of the novel, that Beloved represents the lost. She is a vacuum, a gulf, a loss that cannot be recovered. In this novel, the homesickness of selfhood involves precisely this acknowledgment, one that none of us is free of. We are all inheritors of this absence; it marks us from the inside, not only by way of lost and even unknown ancestors but in terms of dimensions of our own selves that we deny, repress, will never, even can never, bring to consciousness.

The power of mourning in this text, and more generally, undermines notions of individual sovereignty and is emblematic of risks in humanist recuperations of selfhood, as I argued in previous chapters. Even Jesser's piece, which attends to these questions, does not fully recognize the import of mourning. Jesser notes that in Sethe's efforts to reclaim herself and her story, she ends up adding new traumas to her consciousness: "Halle's face smeared with butter and clabber. His being broken by the sight of his wife assaulted by teenage boys becomes part of her story." Jesser then suggests, "Sethe and Paul D cannot secure the future for each other because neither has yet integrated their whole pasts into their presents. They have not reckoned with the dead or their own deadness."[46] While I agree that integrating the past into the present is central to the characters' work in the novel, it is not possible to integrate the "whole past." The past resists us, and some of our "own deadness" cannot come back to life. I believe Morrison's novel registers these human weaknesses, unavoidable dimensions of being alive at all.

But at stake in this question is not just a robust account of what it means to be human; it is also the cultural reception of novels like Morrison's. The common tendency to assume selfhood is about fully digesting our past is, I contend, often precisely what animates resistance to texts like *Beloved.* Morrison's novel draws out realities that have *not* been sufficiently confronted by our culture, the brutal and persistent realities of racism that haunt the present. Similarly, the defensive refrain often heard regarding questions of racism—my ancestors did not own slaves, or the like—simplifies how the past impacts the present. Such defensiveness urges an innocence to subjectivity that is selectively material and selectively historical, ignoring the fact that the legacy of racism persists in the contemporary material reality in a range of ways, from segregated communities and schools, to differences in wealth ownership, to the powerful impacts of implicit bias on a range of activities, including job applications, promotions, social reputations, and much more: white privilege, in brief.[47] Being a self in a racist culture, whatever one's personal feelings or mentality, is to depend on or suffer from these unjust realities, or both. A posthumanist account of the self can help bring out our dependence on many more partnerships both within and without our species than we keep in our conscious mind. Indeed, the very concept of "implicit bias," which underscores that "actors [i.e., people] do not always have conscious, intentional control over the processes of social perception, impression formation, and judgment that motivate their action" accords with posthumanist theory more generally.[48]

This gap or fallibility in human rationality calls for skepticism not only of the misguided confidence that we have moved beyond racism but to larger political systems such as eco-cosmopolitanism, which is also exposed to being unselfconsciously racist (and problematic in other ways). As I argued in the introduction and elsewhere in this book, eco-cosmopolitanism can tend to be undergirded by excessive faith in systematic rationality. Rather than regarding eco-cosmopolitanism as a saving program for a planet in peril, I suggest that it is better understood as a kind of guiding light, like the North Star for escaped slaves and others, that both orients our actions and remains distant, no matter how long we approach it. This stance makes more room for the radical alterity—of stars, places, people, and more. These often inhabit a different realm at another scale, much as do the various forms of being that humans depend on, from the microbiome in our guts to the bacteria on our skin, from the activities of plants making oxygen to the minerals that permit plants to grow. We depend entirely on these realities, though we rarely keep them in mind. Deepening our appreciation for what we fail to keep in consciousness is thus important to answering to humanist fantasies and to the fantasy that racism is over because, perhaps, fewer people *consciously* bear racist animus in their minds.

Weakness of Self, Uncanny Weakness of Language

In *Beloved,* these realities play out in individual terms, with persons exposed to harm by systems of racism. These scenarios clarify human weakness in two related ways: at the level of the body and in language. Language has often been understood to reveal human capacity, to distinguish humans from all other animals. We observe the political work of this human/animal distinction in the novel when schoolteacher attempts to animalize Sethe by having his pupils separate her "human characteristics" from her "animal ones" (228). Clearly, one response to schoolteacher's intellectual violence, intended to justify his physical violence, is to insist on Sethe's humanity. That crucial step can be strengthened with recourse to a posthumanist reorientation of language: is language exclusively human? In a much-discussed passage of his essay "Eating Well," Derrida argues that language can better be understood as a system of marking that is akin to many other natural systems of marking.[49] In effect, this move undermines the very distinction—human/animal—used to produce violence against black bodies, rendering actions like schoolteacher's even less tenable. Those actions appear even more clearly to be a pure, vicious violence, justified by horrible nonsense.

But where does this leave us in our conceptions of language? *Beloved* offers compelling routes into this question too. In trauma, language becomes both more crucial and less effective. As I suggested above, a central task of this novel is to expose loss, to register a gulf or an absence where destroyed lives might have been. That work requires admitting our *inability* to know what is gone. Too much presumption of knowledge would abuse the lost.

Thus, at the novel's conclusion, Morrison insists repeatedly that "this is not a story to pass on" (324). What does this mean in light of the fact that these words come at the end of a novel that seems to pass on this story? Does Morrison mean we should not reproduce this story in the world, or that we should not even tell the story? Perhaps both, paradoxically. Morrison voices here the double-bind of traumatic narrative: the need to tell and the need to admit surpassing horror, lest we suppose too much familiarity with it. This talk to and with ghosts, this language at the limits of the self, reaching across the gulf of death, exposes human limitations. We are perhaps too weak, too susceptible to reproducing this story literally, in reality, so we must tell it in narrative form as a kind of inoculation.

I underscore what happens to concepts of human agency here. It becomes much more complex, muddled, and far less vaunted, and it does so around one of the preeminent tools of human beings: language. Further, this is not just any language but the more rarified artistic language, literary language, long taken to signify human distinctiveness. At its limit, such language attempts—but fails—to fully narrate the world's traumas. In this way, Morrison's novel is doing social and cultural work similar to what Hemingway attempts in *The Garden of Eden,* discussed in the previous chapter. In both cases, in order for language to engage with the profoundest and most challenging of truths, it must admit its insufficiency. To evoke these fundamental traumas as the traumas they are, we must mark the failure of language to account for them. The traumas surpass our accounts. In the Anthropocene, I think we are to apply precisely this structure to our understandings of human beings more generally. The trauma of the Anthropocene requires humans to admit our weakness and dependence on the nonhuman. Our failure to do so precisely puts human life in jeopardy. That is exactly the situation of Sethe. She must come to terms with her story enough to be able to change it, to move on from it; that involves reckoning its trauma. We, like her, are too weak to hold on to our former conceptions of ourselves and must accept what is required to go on living. In that sense, the ordinary concept of change already demonstrates that subjectivity is something different than we commonly take it to be: fixed, clear, and functional.

In such cases, humanity becomes uncanny; the language-using animal that is the human being loses its grip on one of the central functions of language, narrative. Language as an ability is undercut, humbling it and us and complicating the too-absolute human/animal distinction. And here again we face the notion from trauma theory that the horrors of terrible truths undermine our very ability to have sure knowledge. If we cannot readily know or understand fundamental stories, stories about life and death, because they utterly challenge our reason and our understanding, then we are far less capable of knowing than Enlightenment rationality suggests. We are, in other words, returned to the scenario Morton describes, as discussed in the introduction: unable to access or produce any kind of metatruth or metalanguage but therefore all the more required to cope with the world that we see as best we can.[50] In Graham Harman's sense, we must become more sincere, not less.[51] A postmodernist irony does nothing to answer to the real traumas of the world, traumas of slavery, violence, and destruction. Instead, we must find ways to ameliorate them. We must become more serious.

Morrison's treatment of traumatic narrative is this kind of excessive seriousness. There is an irony to the need both to tell and not tell, but it is not exactly postmodern in our usual understanding of that term. It goes further, exposing fractures in language and human systems of meaning, splitting open humanism from within. In Jean Wyatt's now-classic argument from 1993, "Giving Body to the Word: The Maternal Symbolic in Toni Morrison's *Beloved,*" she draws out this element of the novel not in posthumanist terms but in something like postpsychoanalytic ones. Wyatt applies Margaret Homan's notion of "literalization" in language to *Beloved.* Wyatt quotes Homan in a note to explain the term: it "occurs when some piece of overtly figurative language, a simile or an extended or conspicuous metaphor, is translated into an actual event or circumstance."[52]

Wyatt demonstrates several examples of literalization in the novel, but one she does not mention involves the house itself: it is personified in a literalizing movement that treats the home as sick. This is announced in the novel's first line: "124 was spiteful." It was angry, vengeful, and upset about the past in a way very much consonant with my sense of the word "homesickness" in this book. Indeed, to consider 124 haunted by Beloved in the context of this novel is to understand the house itself to be possessed by the traumatic history of Sethe's family, and by the larger traumatic history of slavery, of which Sethe's story is part. Again, as Wyatt underscores in a quotation from Morrison herself: "The purpose of making [the ghost] real is making history possible, making memory real—somebody walks in the door and sits down at the table, so you have to think about it."[53]

So literalization of the ghost requires readers to confront history; it is a *political* gesture. But it is also crucial to underscore the challenges of representation that attend to traumatic events and that contribute to defamiliarizing strategies like literalization. That is, at stake in this scenario is the status of language more generally. Wyatt underscores that Sethe, in her infanticide, "extends her rights over her own body . . . to the 'parts of her' that are her children, folding them back into the maternal body in order to enter death as a single unit (though she succeeded in killing only one of her daughters)."[54] Referencing Morrison's own thinking about the event, Wyatt glosses this effort as revealing "the ultimate contradiction of mothering under slavery."[55] Wyatt then argues, "Sethe's sense of continuity with her children also makes it difficult for her to take the position of narrating subject and tell her story."[56] Wyatt underscores that Sethe's own subjectivity is incomplete and that she cares much more for her children than for herself, that she is even willing to let herself die were it not for her children. Sethe's status, her lack of distinct selfhood, Wyatt contends, "precludes putting that act [infanticide] into words." Instead, Sethe thinks, "She could never close in, pin it down for anybody who had to ask."[57] This problem of not being able to explain, Wyatt suggests, might be understood by deficiencies in "the language available to her," to Sethe.[58] The infanticide, at the center of the novel's central events, evades representation. As Wyatt notes, "Readers learn about the infanticide a bit at a time from different perspectives."[59] A clearer representation of it comes not from Sethe but from schoolteacher and the sheriff, "a collective white/male perspective."[60]

But why? I would emphasize that the trauma is much, much more severe for Sethe than for the sheriff or schoolteacher. This failure of language and rational systems of meaning to account for this horrible event in the world is a theme related to homesickness that I have returned to again and again. In Sethe's experience I think we see the worst, most powerfully traumatic event of any discussed in this book. No wonder she cannot explain it. No wonder Morrison cannot explain it. No wonder I cannot explain it. Indeed, "explaining" it requires precisely the kind of admission offered by Morrison, that we cannot fully explain it, *that inexplicability is at the center of what this event is.* Morrison's literary work to evoke this complex reality takes her text out beyond the narrative near the end, to words that stand alone in the space of the pages, like the difficult-to-reconcile traumas themselves, which seem to be out of time and space, to be uncanny or unreal. We can also understand Morrison's use of multiple perspectives to reveal the infanticide as aligned with this world-shattering fact of trauma.

At issue here is, literally, the world, and our use of language to relate to it. As Wyatt explains, for Jacques Lacan, "To move into a position in language, an infant must sacrifice its imaginary sense of wholeness and continuity with the mother's body."[61] It is precisely this kind of separation that Beloved's haunting *presence* undermines; indeed, Sethe refuses the separation, instead insisting on a literalist connection both to her lost child and to her children more generally. They will all remain directly in touch. Sethe's being stuck at this stage, Wyatt argues evocatively, accounts for another dimension of the novel: "The plot—present time—cannot move forward because Sethe's space is crammed with the past."[62] The passage from the novel that Wyatt quotes to support this view expresses Sethe's sense of oppression in terms of the house, redolent of oppressive memories: "When she woke the house crowded in on her."[63]

It is important to pause at this moment to recognize that Sethe's situation is an especially severe form of a general reality for victims of historical oppression and violence. Being trapped in place, in poor communities beset with violence and danger, where social and professional opportunities are constrained, is this kind of experience. The plot of life cannot move forward because the places are literally conditioned by the past. There is continuity between Sethe's life circumstances and those, say, of people living in West Baltimore or the South Side of Chicago. In such places, people's lives are literally crowded and trapped, haunted by the ghosts of racism, ostensibly past but altogether too present, too painfully present.

Morrison's novel is thus synecdoche rather than symbol: it is a *part of* the larger reality of racism that continues to manifest materially, in segregated housing, racist police practices, and omnipresent violence. Racism is exactly material practices, segregation, unequal access to property ownership, and so on. To put this in temporal terms: the racist past is still literally present in these material facts, which are forms of homesickness, or sickness at home, at the heart of American identity. I do not mean at the heart of African American identity, to be clear; I mean American identity more generally. Since slavery and its accompanying economic systems literally made the United States what it is, since these practices continue to materialize in the lived environments of the country today, racism is one of the most powerful forms of sickness at home at the heart of who Americans are. But it is also important to recognize the continuity of these forms of life with the forms discussed in earlier chapters of *Homesickness*. The sense that one cannot move forward, that one's own home presses in, I have discussed with regard to Robinson's *Housekeeping*, Hedges's *What's Eating Gilbert Grape*, and Proulx's work, including the short story "The Half-Skinned Steer."

The very fact that histories, structures, homes, and the like can be enabling necessarily also entails its opposite: those forces and presences can be disabling. In fact, they are all necessarily always both, since one form of enabling means opportunity cost; it means, that is, *not doing* something else. This argument is a way of refiguring notions of ability in rhetorical rather than absolutist (or logical) terms, an approach I draw from both disability theory and animal studies. In the former, disability is exposed to rely on social constructions and norms, and also on the built environment, which caters to certain kinds of abilities even as it hinders other kinds of abilities. Disability is partly in the material and ontological structures that surround people. Likewise with nonhuman animals: the simplistic, binary, humanist notion of ability has been built via the opposition to animality, whereby the concept of humans as upright (in several senses), rational, ethical, and so on is opposed to animality rendered as horizontal, carnal (or embodied), and instinctual. But that distinction does not hold, since humans, like other animals, are also carnal, instinctual, and much less upright than we commonly imagine; even as other animals have also been proven to be more rational, ethical, and even linguistic than convention has held. In other words, these theoretical approaches underscore our need for a much more rigorous and situated conception of ability, one that does not indulge racist, humanist, sexist, or other fantasies. Ability is not a superpower; it is a competency that has specific uses in specific scenarios, uses that not only can be undermined but that can play against the user.

That insight is powerful for a range of reasons, and it changes the way we read texts like *Beloved*. For one thing, it changes the way we understand Morrison's treatment of language and narrative. As Wyatt underscores, Sethe is stuck in her traumatic condition partly because she cannot separate from her lost child; she cannot use language to describe the loss. Part of the reason for that may be the very terms of self-ownership itself, which make slavery possible and find their echo in Sethe's insistence that she will take her children back, unmake them, to prevent them from being enslaved again. Wyatt emphasizes that Sethe's challenge stretches across the whole of the novel, beginning to find some resolution in its conclusion, particularly aided by Paul D's loving assistance. This assistance is specifically and importantly embodied, involving his gentle, intimate caresses and his offer to bathe Sethe, which, Wyatt accents, puts Paul D in "the restorative maternal role once occupied by Baby Suggs."[64] While I agree this role has been "maternal" conventionally, both in the novel and in the culture more generally, it perhaps perpetuates that harmful form of gendering to understand it that way, since doing so erases the significant amount of caretaking performed by men, and suggests that such male caretaking is an exception rather than a fundamentally human (and humane) action, as I would insist it is, or should be.

Nonetheless, Wyatt shows that Sethe's effort to make a sufficient peace with her past fundamentally relies on bodily as well as narrative practices. She needs not only to begin to tell her story but to be sustained in a loving home of companionship. This approach significantly revises the conventional psychoanalytic account of subjectivity, Wyatt emphasizes: "Morrison thus rewrites the entry into the symbolic in terms that retain the oral and maternal, challenging orthodox psychoanalytic opposition between a maternal order of nurturing and a paternal order of abstract signification."[65] Putting this point slightly differently, Wyatt later writes, "Replacing Lacan's vision of the move into language—a move away from bodies touching to the compensations of abstract signifiers—Morrison makes physical contact the necessary support for Sethe's full acceptance of the separate subjectivity required by language systems."[66]

In the context of my argument, this resistance to abstraction has many crucial ramifications. It points to the need to account for physical structures like homes in our descriptions of subjectivity, a point already evoked above. More generally, it points to the need to include the mesh of the nonhuman world, often described as "nature" or ecology, in our understandings of human subjectivity. While the conventional psychoanalytic account of subjectivity tends to take all such matters for granted, delivering a "developed" or "mature" person into the world as independent, I have been insisting throughout this book on the fact of human *dependence*. Morrison shows how Sethe is able to begin to recover, to attain more (if not absolute) independence, precisely by exercising her dependence on Paul D and on the community of women who help expel the ghost Beloved.

So this is a paradox of life: a measure of independence won only via dependence. It is plain enough at this point in *Homesickness* to recognize that this is the reality for all of us, who were after all reared in our utterly helpless infancy by loving parents, however imperfect, and who will, eventually, succumb again to dependence in injury or infirmity in old age. More generally, of course, we also must recognize our dependence on a planet and its complex ecologies that permit our existence. This approach to selfhood as a form of dependence and cooperation sets up an important contrast to the dream of the independent subject too easily drawn from conventional psychoanalytic accounts and from humanism more generally. The sense that the subject must, precisely as subject, leave home—home as house, home as mother, home as relation—and stand alone in the world is at the root of these accounts. That bogus and fantastic logic is at the heart of so many contemporary harms: ecological collapse, slavery (dislocating millions), hatred-inducing abstractions of many kinds. By contrast, Morrison shows how we are always instead "becoming-with," to use Haraway's term, discussed in the introduction. Rigorously understood, that concept involves not only a new level of humility and appreciation but also responsibility. Since mutuality is the condition of life, it cannot be escaped. This means that the heritages of slavery and racial injustice are our responsibility to confront. They are our ghosts, ghosts we should speak to and with, to echo Derrida. They are haunting us.

5

Shopping as Suffering

Neoliberalism's Slow Violence, Walmart, and the Fallacy of Free Choice

"You can never go home again, Oatman . . . but I guess you can shop there."
—Martin Q. Blank in *Grosse Pointe Blank*

Assuming new cultural practices in a foreign land, à la Hemingway, is one test of eco-cosmopolitan ideas in light of the peculiar form of homesickness this book describes. Another cultural practice with a new form in the early twentieth century presents a different test: shopping. Like "homesickness," "shopping" is a word freighted with meanings particular to carbon-intensive modernity. It spells so-called materialism (in the ordinary sense of excessive desire for purchased products), capitalist freedom, women's liberation or escape, or the response to sheer need. And much more. Its dynamics have been studied not just by marketing departments working to influence human behavior but by cultural critics who bemoan its ill effects. A truism that recurs in this literature is that, at least in its ideal form, shopping is an expression of agency, of will, even of democracy. In her conclusion to *Cheap: The High Cost of Discount Culture* (2009), Ellen Ruppel Shell urges that, if we as shoppers are only well-enough informed, we will stop being "slaves to the low-price imperative" and become "free to make our own choices."[1] For her, this is how we must answer to the "sober responsibility" that attends globalism.[2]

This perspective, sensible within a humanist frame of rational individualism, fails to acknowledge realities I am framing in this book as posthumanist. For one thing, that approach fails to address structural problems with structural solutions. Instead, Ruppel Shell insists largely on an individual morality, common to neoliberal thinking. But, of course, an individual's "moral" decisions can only go as far as a given structure or framework will permit. If the question is, How can we consume responsibly? other questions get pressed aside. As political scientist Anne Norton writes of this structure of consumption, "It is . . . impossible to register one's rejection of the commodity" more generally within it.[3] Those who refuse to consume simply disappear from the legible (and often from the serious, ironically enough). This problem is especially important in Norton's critique of consumption scenarios because she concludes that many of them, studied closely, "subvert the connection between capitalism and democracy."[4] Instead, too often contemporary capitalism undermines authentic democratic choice.

Furthermore, even taken on its own terms, Ruppel Shell's book describes in considerable detail how many factors undermine our ability to be deliberate in our shopping decisions in the way she advocates. She quotes behavioral economist Daniel Ariely, who notes, "We are all much more emotional about the present and more rational about the future."[5] Similarly, we can adduce the argument of psychologist Daniel Kahneman in *Thinking, Fast and Slow*.[6] He presents two systems for human thought: the first is rapid, emotional, and centered on intuition; the second is slower and more logical. The first system tends to dominate many of our shopping decisions—all the more so in spaces designed to encourage more buying—undermining rationality and revealing compulsion. An important implication of such assertions about human behavior is that rationality, like other human desirables, is evasive. It is a luxury we may not be able to afford, not just economically but culturally, temporally, and ethically. In the context of this chapter, focused in particular on an emotional novel about an extremely poor young woman and the appeal of Walmart more generally, the opportunities for longer-range rational thinking, particularly thinking connected to larger class interests, are not nearly as accessible as immediate savings in a discount store.[7] This fact dramatically exposes the limits of the rational consumer framework, a point made clearer yet in the context of posthumanist theory.

As Cary Wolfe notes in a touchstone passage for *Homesickness*, posthumanism "names the embodiment and embeddedness of the human being in not just its biological but also its technological world, the prosthetic coevolution of the human animal with the technicity of tools and external archival mechanisms (such as language and culture)."[8] This reality, though it radically undermines fantasies of human independence, also foregrounds how alliances with other species and other materials make us who we are, an enriching insight that reverses conceptions of existentialist solitude. The universe looks far less lonely in this framework. Nonetheless, this structure of subjectivity also exposes our weakness, reiterating the porous boundaries of selfhood. Consumer capitalism takes advantage of this weakness. Its ideology, expressed in commercials and advertising campaigns, product designs and commercial spaces, and much more, hinges on our recognition that we are not ourselves. We must complete ourselves with the goods of the world. Therefore, we must buy. Of course, critics of capitalism too often throw out the baby with the bath soap, so to speak: that is, they take to decrying "materialism," as though humans make any sense as a species without our things, our prosthetics, and our own embodiment and materiality.

If we view this familiar problem from an oblique angle, compelling insights emerge: in consumer capitalism, the self is othered. We are alienated from ourselves. Commonly such estrangement is decried as the result of modernity, a problem to solve, and it clearly is in part. But it also evokes the structure of subjectivity I map in this book. To be a self is necessarily to be out of phase, to orient one's identity around partly assimilated experiences from the past. Subjectivity and consciousness, I have argued, are forms of homesickness. Wolfe's accounts of posthumanism, likewise, can be read as distinctive ways to interpret the much-maligned feeling of alienation. That is, posthumanism, with its recognition of prosthetics and weak subjectivity, offers tools to read the sense of self-as-other in a more affirmative light. But precisely at this point, work is required. We cannot excuse all forms of homesickness as somehow natural. Instead, we should investigate which forms are just and desirable, and which forms are not.

From this position, we can more readily name and criticize a key capitalist trick: instead of making the insight of self as other, as uncanny, a cause for developing a sophisticated ethics of selfhood in which we consciously embrace our need to define ourselves cooperatively, consumerism makes us craven for the next gimmick. This is a commodification of alterity. In such a scenario, it seems clear that consumption is compulsive, neither rational nor robustly satisfying. Worse, since such consumption is generally couched in a rhetoric of independent and autonomous selfhood, it contradicts its ostensibly animating logic. This recognition therefore undermines one of the fundamental planks of Enlightenment subjectivity along the lines that Wolfe explores in *Before the Law*, and in chapter 3 of *What Is Posthumanism?*, "Flesh and Finitude: Bioethics and the Philosophy of Living."[9] In the latter text, Wolfe engages and extends arguments from Cora Diamond, Martha Nussbaum, Peter Singer, and others: that the subject of rights is distinct from the subject of interests (or, in Jeremy Bentham's original formulation, the subject who suffers). Wolfe quotes Singer on this last point: "The capacity for suffering and enjoyment is *a prerequisite for having interests at all.*"[10] This fundamental basis for selfhood is widespread among nonhuman life. Thus, when we emphasize a subjectivity of interests and suffering, we leave human exceptionalism behind, opening new vistas on human selfhood as kin to other nonhuman animal selves. Wolfe continues in this direction in *Before the Law,* borrowing Foucault's distinction between the notion of a sovereign self and a self with interests. A self with interests is one that makes choices out of its "capacity to feel (and the desire to avoid) pain," which differs significantly from the fantasy of a purely rational subjectivity.[11]

While the Enlightenment paved the way for a capitalist self, a rational being whose choices ostensibly maximize good for himself (the self is traditionally male in that framework, of course) and the culture simultaneously, Foucault and others reveal the deficiencies of the model. Their approach offers a critique of the capitalist faith in choice, right at the foundation of capitalism; the belief in choice is revealed precisely as a faith, a dogma. While the general outline of this critique is familiar, accenting its politics of *species* and the related posthumanist implications in terms of house and home opens new perspectives. This chapter emphasizes how the subject in this structure is profoundly dislocated from itself, so that shopping, rather than consolidating and affirming a selfhood, diffuses and disperses that self. In recent decades, with the hollowing out of other social and cultural institutions in U.S. neoliberalism, the expression and performance of subjectivity is increasingly *constrained* to consumption and consumerist logics. In that light, shopping appears partly as a form of suffering, a slow violence against other forms of human (and other-than-human) potential, particularly for the poor. Human biological and cultural life and reproduction are subjugated to commodity production. The self becomes a widget, a deracinated object designed by and for consumer capitalism, and the structure of feelings and relations in consumer capitalism is more resolutely naturalized, making us homesick. But I also suggest this very status, the self as a kind of object, bears within it radically other, posthumanist potentials for reworking subjectivity.

Where the Heart Is: Walmart?

Billie Letts's sentimental novel *Where the Heart Is* (1995), a selection of Oprah's Book Club and a best seller, begins both in its inception in the author's mind and in the movement of its plot with the omnipresence of Walmart.[12] There, choice and compulsion are conflated in the quintessential enterprise of American neoliberal capitalism. At an Oklahoma Walmart, the poor, pregnant, seventeen-year-old protagonist Novalee Nation is deserted by her deadbeat boyfriend when they stop so she can empty her baby-crowded bladder and buy a pair of shoes. Is this a choice? Not really, certainly not in the idealized sense that undergirds capitalism. Instead, this scenario is homesickness in the extreme. Novalee is entirely without a place, without a home. Abandoned at Walmart far from her undesirable home in Tennessee, she lacks a familiar social network and even basic geographic orientation. She is a kind of refugee of capitalism, an internal refugee, a stranger in her home country. Even her body is not entirely her own, as it is rendered unfamiliar and uncomfortable by pregnancy. This novel thus reveals Novalee's subjectivity beneath choice, a suffering subjectivity, the "reason beyond reason," as Cary Wolfe compellingly puts it, that orients any decision she might make.[13] Her exposure and vulnerability set the stage for the emotional homesickness—the desire for a home—that drives the plot.

Willy Jack, Novalee's escaping boyfriend, proceeds west toward their once-shared destination of California, reiterating that familiar westward-oriented narrative pattern in U.S. literature and culture. Indeed, Letts's name for her character, Novalee Nation, makes her iconic of the United States (or, in Letts's terms, of "America") in important ways right from the start, and this is why the novel's selection for Oprah's book club and its best-seller status are relevant to this chapter, as they demonstrate the novel's resonance in the culture it describes. Letts's allusions to the westward migration of earlier American history appear in the first few pages, with Novalee snapping photographs and planning to tell her children about her own foundational journey to California, a microcosm of the national story. These moments quickly turn from melodrama to realism—or satire—since Novalee never gets any farther than Oklahoma (and her fleeing boyfriend experiences far worse misadventures in the West), an evocative treatment of the gap more generally between national myth and reality. Letts's novel focuses mostly on what happens to those left behind the westward travelers, much as Robinson's

Housekeeping explores the private and domestic life undergirding the pioneering, west-driving family. Novalee, despondent in her abandonment, unsure of what to do, spends her day and then evening in the Walmart browsing, eating its fare of popcorn, chili dogs, candy bars, and soda, and ends up, serendipitously, in the women's room vomiting this junk food as the store closes. The novel captures this moment by interspersing the loudspeaker announcement that the store is closing—sounding "tinny and distant, like a bad connection"—with Novalee's growing awareness that she is about to get sick. She feels "lightheaded," then "something surged in her chest," and she tasted "cold chili" before racing to the bathroom (29): homesickness.

It is a fitting opening to a story that, author Billie Letts explains in an interview included in the book's appendix, was inspired when she "was in Wal-Mart one day and the thought came" to her "that someone could probably live there for weeks, months . . . years, maybe, without ever having to go outside" (366). Such is life in consumer capitalism. The bathroom scene can be read as a comic parody of a feeling familiar to many inhabitants of the so-called postindustrial West, and maybe particularly the United States: gorging in the happy, practically intoxicating utopia—the placelessness of the box store, filled with more products than the shopper could possibly explore, all at cut-rate prices. Such experiences of gleeful excess are often understood—if they are even registered in political or social discourse—as one of the benefits of the age of globalized mass production. Or they are decried as "materialism." Neither framework adequately accounts for Novalee's experience in the store; instead, hers is a kind of suspension of disbelief about her own dire circumstances, utterly poor, deserted by all, and crowded in her very body by a life she alone must bear responsibility for. She is truly, like a contemporary Blanche DuBois, dependent on the kindness of strangers. The falseness of her soda and chili dog solution is implicit in the sickness it produces. The tinny and remote announcement underscores her—and our—tenuous connection to community in the age of (often forced) mobility. It is the background realism of such a situation that adds piquancy to the comic escapism that Letts uses to describe the Walmart day Novalee has spent. That is key to this chapter: although Novalee seems to be an extreme case, in many ways she simply exemplifies the conditions under which most of us live in neoliberalism.

That Novalee uses the Walmart as a kind of *escapism* is not a point strongly insisted on in the novel, though it is implicit from this early scene to the critical moment much later in the book, when Novalee begins to feel labor pains as she is camped illegally in the store (she is an illegal migrant in that sense). Recognizing these pains for what they are, Novalee acknowledges that "she wasn't ready." She begins to worry about what she will do, how she will manage the birth. She then springs into a moment of self-recrimination: "Why, she wondered, had she waited until the last minute? Where had the time gone? Two months had passed since Willy Jack had dumped her—and she had done nothing. She hadn't looked for a place to live, hadn't figured out how to make a living. She hadn't even picked out a name for her baby" (84). Her extended camping trip in Walmart had been an escape, a suspension in a troubled life. If in more extreme form, Novalee's experience is akin to that of many shoppers, especially contemporary recreational shoppers, wherever they may be.

But in neoliberalism, such moment-to-moment desperation—making due and making a life from whatever is at hand—is exactly what constitutes many people's practice of home, wherever they are. Tenuous inhabitation of a rental home with poor lifelong work prospects, in a place often rendered inaccessible or unstable by the creative destruction of capitalism, is home. This is how and where we live. Further, even the fortunate, whose claim to property and stability may be stronger, live entirely uncanny lives, saturated with media productions, artificial climate, globalized food and product supply chains, and so much more. When the wealthy are at home, they dine and recreate with much of the world. Again, Walmart also evokes all these uncanny realities.

In *Where the Heart Is,* the escapism does not—cannot—last, and Letts reminds us even in the passage just quoted about the trials of extreme poverty. Indeed, awareness of poverty is part of the appeal of this book: it truly reckons with the gritty life experiences of someone like a Novalee Nation. The novel resolutely concentrates on her homesickness, on her desire to establish roots in a place, to have a decent life, and all of this is symbolized by the possession of—or lack of—a house. Letts does not hide from other, darker elements of the lives of impoverished single mothers, such as when Novalee's friend Lexie and her children are violently and sexually assaulted by a sexual predator masquerading as a potential life partner. However, Letts persistently puts such experiences into a personal framework, ignoring or even celebrating the larger structures that often reinforce such realities. Most obvious among those larger structures is Walmart. From this first moment of actual sickness in the Walmart, the plot relies on happy accidents and lucky good fortune to rescue its protagonist.

Indeed, a kind of irrational fatalism—marked by Daniel Ariely and cited above as typical in human behavior—is announced as a central principle in the novel's opening sentence, which characterizes the protagonist as inhabitant of an unfortunate time in an unfortunate place: "Novalee Nation, seventeen, seven months pregnant, thirty-seven pounds overweight—and superstitious about sevens" (3) would receive the (implicitly) bad news of her abandonment by her boyfriend Willy Jack a few pages later in the form of an unlucky unit of change in a Walmart, $7.77 (16). Receiving this change, she shouts, "No," and throws the money "across the floor." Letts goes on, "She knew he was gone, knew before she reached the door" (16).

This monetary figure, $7.77, is a profoundly mixed sign, I suggest, at once highly precise and thereby evoking Enlightenment rationality, and, conversely, made meaningful by Novalee's irrational superstition. The fact that Novalee's reading is correct signals the mystification central to the novel's inquiry into poverty and economics. Although it compellingly explores the personal experiences of Novalee, any investigation into the larger, systematic politics of poverty is precluded by a relentless treatment of agency as personal, as character-driven, or as purely accidental. As I suggested at this chapter's opening, such thinking is characteristic even of Walmart critics, who rely on familiar humanist frames of interpretation. Letts presents Novalee as completely at the mercy of fate and those benevolent strangers, many of whom she begins meeting right after her abandonment. Their relationships are personal and apolitical, driven by emotion.

Novalee's trust in kind strangers links to the pathos that is the explicit center of the book and film *Where the Heart Is,* signaled in the title. As has been widely observed, pathos is often treated as a mere symptom in the Enlightenment, secondary to rationality.[14] Typically, only in B-grade (or worse) artistic fare can "heart" be the organizing principle of discourse. Letts's book and other such texts insist on the importance of "heart," of emotion, and do so by narrating a romance, but at the expense of rational and critical frameworks. In other words, though the novel seems to challenge the privileging of reason over emotion, it actually accepts their separation, that dogma of rationalism, and simply accepts its status as sentimental and superstitious. Yet I am insisting in this book that we should better recognize how emotional and rational belief systems are always woven together, and this braiding often appears in terms of house and home. Part of what makes *Where the Heart Is* compelling is its exploration of the subject's imbrication in commercial frameworks, though it does so through the ostensibly low-brow discourse of the sentimental. While its title insists on "heart," its plot insists on housing.

It is a novel about a distinctive form of migration, then, about the isolation of the neoliberal subject. Novalee's problems are not linguistic or cultural ignorance, the more familiar challenges to migrants; they derive from her solitude. She presents a pure form of the ostensibly independent self, reiterating the flaws of that Enlightenment concept. Again, Letts does not write the novel in these terms, however. She instead deals pragmatically with realities around us in contemporary America, resulting from these neoliberal ideologies. In any case, in effect Letts reveals the delusion of these conceptions of solitary selfhood by having Novalee immediately pursue community. That this seems like "common sense" in the novel, like an apolitical move, reveals how depoliticized thinking has become normalized in the relentless personalization of reality in neoliberalism—the ostensible postpolitical period.[15] Her solutions are only practical, not political.

Walmart and Queering the American Family

Novalee is displaced and abandoned in Walmart (a good synecdoche for neoliberal theory—it abandons us to Walmart and its kin), but she quickly begins to assemble a new social network. She is saved by this strange new kind of community in many ways, her alternative, queer family all organized around Walmart, the de facto heart of this rural community in eastern Oklahoma. Letts explains, in the book's Reading Group Guide, that she came up with Novalee's story while shopping at Walmart (366), and she presents Walmart as a kind of Mercado of contemporary life, "the most likely place for Novalee to encounter" a range of different people. Novalee meets a Native American boy; she is led into photography, which becomes a consuming interest, by Moses Whitecotton, an African American who lost his own child to drowning; and she is housed and cared for by the recovered alcoholic and Bible promoter Sister Husband. She meets Moses and Sister Husband at Walmart and is helped in innumerable ways by the many other members of her new community in Oklahoma. In this way, the book fulfills an element of what some Southern studies scholars call for—greater recognition of the complex ethnic and racial realities in the South, a reality quite different from the common simplification of southern culture as primarily white and heteronormative, which critic Tara McPherson warns against in "On Wal-Mart and Southern Studies."[16]

These queered conceptions of family and community are compelling and likely central to the novel's appeal, though their importance contradicts the largely unchallenged neoliberal individualism that drives the bigger culture. In other words, the novel's popularity is likely a sign of the *contradictions* of neoliberal frameworks, which degrade the social in favor of the personal and the economic. If the social does appear, it is dismissed as sentimental, as inferior, and thus relegated to the realm of "fiction" or even "chick lit." We might also read this popularity as a sign of what Fredric Jameson calls "the ineradicable drive towards collectivity that can be detected, no matter how faintly and feebly, in the most degraded works of mass culture."[17]

This developing ad hoc community contrasts with Novalee's ongoing experiment in solitude. Following the lucky incident of Novalee's sickness at closing time, enabling her to spend the night in the closed store, she realizes she can live in Walmart. She hides each night when the store closes and so, for two months, inhabits a kind of limbo, surviving in the interstices of this capitalist institution. She sleeps in a Walmart sleeping bag, which she hides "at the bottom of a shelf" each morning (52), and she dresses in clothes from Walmart's stock. It is clear that her independence is in fact already dependent on the store. Indeed, I suggest that Novalee herself comes to resemble the objects for sale in the store, as a product of Walmart's mode of production, a radical posthumanist flattening of human identity and a deeper queering of the family (the goods are like her siblings—more on this below). During the day, she leaves the Walmart and occupies herself in the small town, eventually finding her way to the library, where she meets Forney, her love interest, presented in the novel as a genius waylaid from great things by his responsibility to care for his alcoholic sister (67).

The film (2000) made from the novel presents these scenes effectively.[18] Following the book closely, the film shows, in compressed fashion, Novalee's two months of living at the store as an extended, quintessentially postmodern camping scene. Novalee, played by Natalie Portman, makes camp on a rectangle of Astroturf, with a borrowed tent and sleeping bag (Figure 5). Like the historical pioneers, like Thoreau, like the pseudo-pioneering American camping movement and the American Scouting movement of the nineteenth and twentieth centuries, Novalee Nation—her surname hardly accidental—is fronting the essential facts of life today. She offers an image of motherly desperation, of human reproduction married by necessity into commodity reproduction. Her horizontal position in the still frame, amid the array of products arranged for sale around her, evokes her equality with them as another good of the world. But such a reading is not strongly encouraged by the film. Instead, the scene is softly anaesthetized by the sentimental framework of the story, the fictional genre, and the clever cuteness of the camping scenes and other moments in the store at night. It takes a critical intervention, a jarring visual quote of the film, to facilitate my reading here. The camping scenes, then, present contemporary (post)nature myth, replete in the film with as much bathos as pathos, therefore rendering it more appropriate than its makers likely intended; it signals the seeming absurdities of reproduction in contemporary times. This is the reality of a self inheriting its *consuming* positions, with the box store literally replacing the family home. Though, again, the camping scene probably screens as clever and cute to the film's target audience, it is a particularly effective ironic treatment of the pioneer stereotype. Camping here, instead of signifying self-reliance, is a sign of poverty and desperation. As a form of independence, it is as false as Astroturf.

Figure 5. Posthumanist camping. Novalee Nation, in the film *Where the Heart Is*, camping on the Astroturf at night in a closed Walmart, kept company by the other goods, illuminated by lightning, and fronting the essential facts of her life in neoliberal consumer capitalism.

The irony of the film as a cultural text deepens insofar as it relies on Natalie Portman to play the unwed teenage mother. Portman, even though she performs well in the role, splits the character she plays into competing semiotic figures. Beautiful, elite, well-educated actress, or poor, nearly illiterate, abandoned young woman? Many viewers will see *both* as they watch. The beauty and cultural caché of the actress combines with her reputation as an intelligent Harvard graduate to effectively pierce her cloak of character as Novalee (Portman enrolled at Harvard just after she finished filming *Where the Heart Is*). To further complicate the semiotics of her role in the film, Portman wrote in the *Huffington Post* in 2010 that Jonathan Safran Foer's book *Eating Animals* turned her from vegetarian to vegan, so activism with regard to purchasing decisions is part of her public identity.[19] Thus, when viewers watch her play this gritty role about desperate poverty, the potential impact is complex. In general terms, Portman's celebrity might soften the treatment of Novalee's poverty—we see her merely playing at poverty—better assuring the film's status as mere sentimental entertainment. Yet, especially today as the film continues to be screened on cable television, Portman's own public veganism and conscientious consumerism has the potential to amplify the film's often-quiet politics.

In the plot of the film and novel both, Novalee's desperation culminates, as noted above, when she feels birth pains one night in the Walmart. She attempts to undergo this trial in utter solitude, alone in the domain of the ostensibly rational and powerful consumer. Instead of exercising choice in Walmart, Novalee inhabits a position of extreme passivity. The subject who suffers, subtending the subject who chooses, appears via bodily trauma, the embodied event that makes life possible. However, she is rescued in a moment of melodrama by the kindly and attractive local librarian, Forney, who leaps dramatically through the Walmart window in the film (his entrance is slightly less dramatic in the novel). Forney literally breaks the shell of the box store, which has both protected and effectively isolated Novalee, rescuing mother and child in the process of giving birth (87). That is, Forney must break into the already-broken nuclear family to save its essential elements of mother and child. This structure—rescue at the hands of the elite and the wealthy—is repeated when Sam Walton delivers Novalee $500 in the hospital instead of a scolding.

Novalee is a familiar character type: a poor, innocent woman with a strong moral core, something like a modern Huck Finn. Thus, she keeps a record of all the products she borrows at Walmart with the intention of repaying them. But Walton rejects her promise to pay him back for the products and instead offers her a job at Walmart, which Novalee gratefully accepts. Likewise, her savior Forney evokes the largesse of the Carnegies and other capitalist barons (who often paid for local libraries) rather directly since the librarian is descendent of "an aristocratic family," "Boston Brahmin" originally (319). By contrast, Novalee's mother, who had abandoned her daughter long before, returns, pretending concern after the birth, only to rob Novalee. Broken families remain fundamentally broken, only to be redeemed by corporate beneficence.

Here again the narrative, in both its book and film forms, fails to seriously question labor or consumption patterns—and their relations to community—in contemporary American life. This is symptomatic of much U.S. culture. McPherson recognizes that "Wal-Mart makes manufacturing decisions that impact wages and working conditions through the entire world," underscoring the need to think more globally about these issues.[20] But Novalee shows little skepticism about this corporation. Box stores, postmodern consumption patterns, and increasing class segregation are not to blame for Novalee's homelessness; rather, these are the only reliable forces in addressing it. In that way, commerce becomes the more-natural natural law, while natural spaces become commodified: not only campsites, as per above, but houses and families. Sam Walton becomes naturalized as family and does what in other tales a good grandfather might do. And why would he do such a thing? Although it is consistent with the accounts of Walton himself,[21] Letts offers a more direct rationale, delivered from Walton's mouth: he is getting "free publicity" that is "good for business" (100). Business is the overriding logic here.

Further, in a clever paragraph with an edge of critique, Letts mentions the many well-wishes Novalee received when her Walmart pregnancy made her a celebrity. One was a phone call from a woman suggesting Novalee name her daughter Walmartha and aim to have a son she could call Walmark. Then this woman, a doll-maker, would create dolls by these names and sell them to Walmart in a mutually beneficial arrangement. Such schemes are the way to make it in consumer capitalism—devising some saleable gimmick that marries into the purposes of powerful forces like Walmart. In this plan, commerce runs reproduction and infects the intimacy of naming practices. Or, as Susan Strasser suggests in her historical analysis of Walmart,

"Increasingly, Americans satisfied their needs entirely through the market." She elaborates, "People's daily routines involved making fewer things and purchasing more."[22] The practice of culture increasingly centers on the reproduction of commercial culture. Home and home economics are dislocated and globalized.

This key reversal upsets the biological reproductive patterns of the family while reinforcing commercial reproduction. That is a more negative valence to this novel's particular mode of queering the family. Thus the story's homesickness—the strong desire to have a home and a cultural sense of belonging—is undercut precisely by the terms in which it is presented. Letts is committed enough to social realism to evoke this paradoxical truth. Thus, later in the novel, when the regionally significant reality of a tornado destroys the Walmart (and kills Sister Husband), Walmart decides to rebuild in another town on a larger scale, putting in a Supercenter, precisely what has actually happened in many such places across America. Indeed, as noted by John Dicker in his anti-Walmart manifesto, *The United States of Wal-Mart,* the Supercenter is Walmart's "biggest growth vehicle,"[23] leading to a related problem of abandoned older Walmart boxes gathering dust in the exurban American landscape, creating commercial, postdevelopment wastelands. These shells, echoing with emptiness, represent the homesickness of the neoliberal consumer capitalist regime as well as any reality.

Nonetheless, in a moment of economic and political mystification, Novalee admits to herself that "she wasn't sure why, but she felt a tie to Wal-Mart" that keeps her working there even when she is displaced because the new Supercenter goes in some fifty miles from her adopted hometown (241). When Novalee hears the news of Walmart's relocation, she exclaims, "But this is home. I can't just move" (241). Forney is similarly upset, since he does not want her to move, the solution Walmart has offered to the employees. But Novalee makes clear she has no real other option, asking him, "What else can I do, Forney?" (241). The logic of mobility, so celebrated by many, including eco-cosmopolitans, but which Letts's novel strives against mightily, has found Novalee again. How does she resolve the problem? By driving the five hundred miles a week and keeping her home; by becoming mobile again even as she deepens her roots in place. Of course, this solution, facilitated by the carbon economy, is typical in contemporary American life. Its mundane, familiar status only reiterates how such cultural norms function not only as freedoms but often as compulsions.

More cracks in the social and political logic of the text emerge, with its commitment to realism but its refusal to engage a larger politics, when Novalee further explains why she wants to continue working at Walmart: "the pay's decent" and she has "sick leave, health insurance for Americus" (242), her newborn. Of course, the high cost for employees of Walmart's healthcare program is one of the chief complaints against it. Walmart keeps all its overhead expenses low, including those of labor and of employee benefits, a crucial part of its formula for success.[24] But the loyalty Novalee (and presumably Letts) expresses to Walmart is not unheard of or entirely surprising.

If these narratives ring significant changes on received ideas of culture and of family, it is in a social context that also aims for a strong retrenchment of a certain kind of family values. Walmart plays an explicit part in this debate, presenting itself as pro-family.[25] Indeed, Walmart uses family as a structuring principle of its labor regime. The corporation's infamous resistance to unions often takes the form of a highly personalized approach to employee relations, a (pseudo) populist stance that figures laborers as "associates" and even as family.[26] If its family members have a concern, Walmart has an open-door policy. Workers should take it upon themselves to speak to their managers. Thus, Dicker reports, "workers who vote against unionization are cast as independent thinkers who handle problems on their own,"[27] activating familiar tropes of American individualism and Enlightenment subjectivity. Nelson Lichtenstein writes of the wife of an assistant store manager at a Walmart who defended the company against criticisms on a website. She wrote, "The people at the store work not only as a team but as a family unit. When families in our community have trouble Wal-Mart is there to help." Focusing her sights on the Walmart critic, she continues, "You are only upset because Wal-Mart is Pro-Associate and Anti-Union. And I pray to GOD as a Christian woman that it stays the way it is."[28]

As Bethany Moreton argues in *To Serve God and Wal-Mart,* the connections between God, family values, and Walmart's labor regime are wound tightly together,[29] in the process straining the denotation of the word "family." That strain is not just linguistic. Lichtenstein writes, "The company defends its low-wage, low-benefit personnel policy by arguing that it employs workers who are marginal to the income stream required by most American families. Only 7 percent of the company's hourly employees try to support a family with children on a single Wal-Mart income." Lichtenstein concludes, "Not since the rise of the textile industry early in the nineteenth century, when women and children composed a majority of the labor force, has the leadership of an industry central to American economic development sought a workforce that it defined as marginal to the family economy."[30] Targeting these segments of the population who are ostensibly not central to the family's earning structure not only justifies Walmart's compensation practices; it drastically changes the dynamics of those families themselves. Such jobs are one piece of the larger cultural reality that has moved more individuals out of the home and into the labor force, important to the homesickness studied in this book. Many emphasize how such social trends undermine "family values," whatever one construes those to be.[31]

More generally, while Walmart apologists like Richard Vedder and Wendell Cox urge that "there is no reliable evidence that Wal-Mart . . . has been a job-killer," insisting instead that "the expansion of the discount retail trade has been associated with a net creation of jobs in America,"[32] many other critics suggest otherwise. Ruppel Shell discusses a study at the University of California at Berkeley that found that "the opening of a Wal-Mart store lowered wages and benefits in the surrounding region by up to 1 percent."[33] David Karjanen reports on the difficulty of making a final determination about Walmart or other such stores' *direct* influence on jobs, reminding us to read studies like those quoted above with at least a measure of caution, but he too quotes a study suggesting that one and a half jobs are lost for every one Walmart creates.[34] He is less cautious in insisting that "much evidence, both anecdotal and statistical, indicates that the world's largest company [Walmart] pays wages and benefits that are much lower than the existing grocery industry and even lower than most paid in the discount retailing sector itself."[35]

These debates are part of a larger U.S. context in which, Ruppel Shell writes, the rewards for increasing labor productivity have been going to the very rich. She explains that the years 1947 to 1973 brought a doubling of real median family income and a doubling of "the value of what the typical worker produced." By contrast, from the 1970s to 2008, "the national product tripled" while "medium family income had been flat for years."[36] This pattern is part of the characterization of two distinct labor regimes in the United States, presented by many analysts: the age of General Motors after World War II brought stable and well-paying jobs; while the period beginning since the 1970s or so has tended to erode the middle class in terms of pay, benefits, and stability.[37] Walmart shoppers live in a world that has traded access to stuff for what might have been a more reliable middle-class job and status. In this world, people resemble objects, or animals reduced to bare life, a reality visible in so many modern institutions: zoos, prisons, stockyards and slaughterhouses, and hospitals.

Walmart and Globalizing the Local

These paradoxical realities—Walmart at once serving and undermining poor communities—are typical of capitalism's creative destruction. No one denies that Walmart achieves its business aims effectively: it has grown by leaps and bounds, sells its products at extremely low prices, and has tremendous control over its supply lines. However, to sum up the criticisms assembled in the Nelson Lichtenstein academic essay collection *Wal-Mart: The Face of Twenty-First-Century Capitalism,* cited throughout this chapter: it pays low wages, has a high employee turnover, discourages unions, runs its suppliers through often-destructive reforms of their business practices, increases exurban and suburban sprawl, encourages automobile use implicitly, has been involved with sweat shop labor practices, and so on. In other words, Walmart profits by helping institutionalize and materialize neoliberal economic and political regimes.

Yet, as Walmart executives point out, the business is booming. In the book *The Wal-Mart Revolution: How Big-Box Stores Benefit Consumers, Workers, and the Economy,* Vedder and Cox signal their argument with their title. It is true that even the jobs at Walmart often prove highly desirable to a certain segment of the population. Dicker reports a comment by a Walmart CEO that when a store opened near New York City, they confronted "over 15,000 applicants for 300 jobs."[38] Of course, these numbers signal much more than just the desirability of a Walmart position. They reiterate the desperation of laborers in neoliberalism, where unions have been undercut and the social safety net shredded. And the numbers reiterate the more general prominence of this corporation. It is at the heart of contemporary American capitalist culture. This point is also made repeatedly in the collection edited by Lichtenstein.

But Walmart represents more than the abstraction "consumer capitalism" or neoliberalism. It is important to recognize that this corporate juggernaut has roots in a very particular locale, the U.S. South, at a particular historical moment, and its particular brand of business practice depended crucially on those original local contexts. Lichtenstein explains, "Neither the New Deal nor the civil rights revolution had really come to northwest Arkansas when Walton began to assemble his small-town retailing empire."[39] That reality, he continues, coupled with the changes in American agriculture, "depopulating Arkansas farms, and putting tens of thousands of white women and men in search of their first real paycheck," helped establish a context in which Walmart's business model could get off the ground.[40] Another dimension of this context is the South's "long-standing, business-friendly, antilabor policies."[41] Walmart leveraged these realities, McPherson notes, by locating stores in rural districts not served by other box stores like Kmart.[42]

With these roots in place, Walmart used its ever-improving economies of scale to grow into "the largest corporation in the world."[43] Letts's novel is perched amid this take-off period, with Walmart functioning in the novel in an ambiguous fashion: it is a sign or icon of the region around Arkansas, a local institution; and it is already a large business, gone well beyond Bentonville or any single town. Lichtenstein reports that Walmart had about 1,500 stores in 1995 (the year Letts published *Where the Heart Is*); by 2005 it had more than 4,000 stores and had spread well beyond its original focus in the cluster of states around Arkansas and Missouri.[44] Misha Petrovic and Gary G. Hamilton explain that in 1987 "Wal-Mart was only the fifth biggest retailer in the U.S." but that by 1992 it "had already become the established leader of the industry."[45] The local globalizes. In this way, though, Walmart represents how, frequently, what appears to be local is in fact connected to global realities, and vice versa. As McPherson has suggested about Walmart, it is both the result of a specific history in the U.S. South and deeply imbricated in a world economy.[46] We must acknowledge both of these elements, a point central to the larger argument of *Homesickness.* Indeed, more broadly the South, though it has a long history of celebrating its unique places and culture(s), has long been global. McPherson notes that "the slave trade attests" to this global history.[47]

Clearly there are crucial distinctions between the slave trade and Novalee's mobility—most particularly the legal validation of slavery's enormous and direct violence against black bodies and black families. However, the shibboleth that someone like Novalee, in contrast to slaves, is free to make decisions is a gross exaggeration. Her mobility is not forced in quite the same way as in slavery. She does "choose" to leave Tennessee, at least as presented in the narrative (9–10). But she does so already pregnant and without full knowledge of her partner Willy Jack's plans for their future: he intends to take a job with the railroad but does not tell her of his intended scam to collect insurance money from that railroad company. Indeed, her ignorance stretches even to the basic biology of human reproduction, as Letts later indicates (150–56). So Novalee's mobility is indirectly forced, due to ignorance as well as poverty, and the irony of this condition is further signaled by Letts when she reports of Novalee: "She knew a job with the railroad would guarantee she would not have to live on top of wheels ever again" (10). Earning a living from a quintessentially mobile industry, aspiring simultaneously to efface any signs of that mobility: that connects this novel's treatment of mobility to the reality described in Peter T. Kilborn's book, in which the highly mobile classes are shown to be weary of their own "chosen" moves.[48] Like Novalee, they must follow the logic of an economic system, enabled by fossil fuels, that prizes and requires movement.

In such regimes of mobility, it is as though the logic and the infrastructure run the people, rather than the reverse, a point akin to my argument in the next chapter about war technology seeming to dominate its users. Morton names this notion more generally as agrilogistics; he emphasizes that people can "appear as machine-like components" of the larger technology.[49] The norms and protocols of agrilogistics—in Morton's account continuous with contemporary capitalism more generally—are even more difficult for us to evade or even recognize as norms. Unrecognized, naturalized, those norms have extraordinary power, seeming to run us, Morton suggests, "like a computer program."[50]

In that way, the logic of mobility in *Where the Heart Is* connects to a double-edged economic determinism. Stay in place and miss the train of economic advancement; move and exhaust oneself with it. As Lawrence Buell explains, discussing the dark side of contemporary celebrations of the local, "Reinhabitation presupposes voluntary commitment to place; but not all are free to choose."[51] And though Novalee happens luckily upon a community that she comes to love, she certainly never consciously chooses to live in Sequoyah, Oklahoma. She is deserted there. In that way, we must regard all of the book's local color as ironically tinged. It is a place, a reality, generally unacknowledged as good: flyover country. Novalee is, in a way, the reverse image of idealized, rational cosmopolitan mobility. Her ultimate happiness signifies the flourishing of *undesirable* communities and the possibilities that exist *outside* individually willed actions. Further, my point in opening the introduction to *Homesickness* with Kilborn is to disrupt the fiction that only the poor face limited choices; choice functions in a limited way even for the professional classes.

This brand of "free choice," in which choosing is a symptom of weakness rather than the expression of individual self-determinacy and power, often applies to Walmart history as well. Its business strategy of locating in smaller towns and rural areas has meant, frequently, that once a Supercenter appears and other stores close, shoppers have little option but to go to Walmart. Dicker, in full denunciation mode, makes this point: "As Wal-Mart's growth machine plunders on, regional grocery stores bite the dust at a ratio of two to every new Supercenter. . . . Competing national chains like Albertsons and Publix have packed up from entire markets shortly after Walmart's arrival. People who never chose to shop at Wal-Mart in the first place now have one less place to go."[52]

In this context, choice loses its idealistic force. As with Novalee's mobility, the ostensibly free market, giving itself over to Walmart's competitive practices, becomes less free. In a wider framework, shopping shows more of its constraints too. Read idealistically, freed from need, shopping can appear as a kind of recreational activity, becoming its own value, a good for its own sake. In postmodernist accounts it is entertainment, play; even, we could add, a sort of posthumanist engagement with the nonhuman. But there too it would be a seriously constrained (and hence posthumanist) choice: the overriding logic of consumer capitalism conditions us to remain in that consumerist imaginary, even while capitalism has eliminated both the leisure time and the undeveloped spaces and places that would be necessary for other forms of recreation. Further, it is clear that shopping itself also often slides from a practice of freedom into one of obsession and compulsion, a problem noted at the opening of this chapter.

Importantly, Novalee and Walmart are not just parallel or homological cases. It is precisely the globalized structure of commerce as practiced by Walmart and its cohorts that has, for instance, undermined better middle-class jobs and left people more and more exposed to homesickness and forced mobility. The value of mobility in globalization is thereby tested as human weakness is revealed and people tire of trying ceaselessly to adapt to new places. In such cases, the polarity is often switched; the local becomes the valorized ground upon which to fight against the intruding global force of a Walmart: site fights. Dicker reports stories such as that of Inglewood, California, which successfully repelled the installation of a Walmart.

Yet it can be too easy to demonize Walmart. As Dicker also argues, Walmart has not created all the conditions of its success, nor can it be solely blamed for reinforcing problems like the erosion of a middle class and the like. Real attention to the local actually means treating each place in each circumstance distinctively, recognizing that sometimes a global entity like Walmart can be a force for good. Dicker explains that sometimes Walmart is one of the few enterprises willing to locate in blighted neighborhoods. Dicker presents precisely this scenario as it occurred in South Central Los Angeles, in Hartford, Connecticut, and in west Chicago.[53] Furthermore, David Karjanen—no Walmart apologist—suggests that in such settings, where there is a scarcity of businesses, Walmart does not even seem to drive out small businesses that are there,[54] unlike what occurs in other scenarios. Indeed, Karjanen credits Walmart with helping "invest in undercapitalized communities, regions, and whole nations" more generally, supporting what Walmart apologists like Vedder and Cox argue.[55] However, Karjanen continues, Walmart's "business model can flourish only by externalizing many of its most important social and economic costs, which are displaced onto a . . . supply chain, an underpaid retail workforce, and those many thousand communities" that must "absorb so many of the intangible expenses."[56]

Dicker compellingly argues that Walmart shoppers, or shoppers anywhere for that matter, rarely have full consciousness about all these processes behind the products they buy. Dicker thus satirizes "the idea posited by Wal-Mart and its friends . . . that consumers consciously vote manufacturing jobs offshore every time they buy a foreign-made product." He asks, "Where exactly is the choice?"[57] Indeed, perversely enough, as economic conditions worsen, it becomes more and more necessary for shoppers to pinch pennies and shop at the discount stores. Such scenarios were observed with Walmart predecessor A&P, which actually fared quite well with its discount business model during the Great Depression, Dicker notes. Similarly, he writes, Walmart has continued its advance through the recessions of recent years.[58]

A&P is registered in the canon of U.S. literature in John Updike's story "A&P," about a young man who quits his ho-hum job in the store by that name and is thereby released into his worldly fate, for better or worse.[59] That story and setting may seem quaint next to today's globalization, but it is part and parcel of the same processes as Walmart. As consumer culture historian Susan Strasser explains, the A&P chain grew to national prominence with tactics in the 1940s that very much presaged Walmart's. A&P began a discount division they called "the economy store" and then worked to cut out producers, creating its own line of products that could be sold cheaply.[60] Such business strategies capitalize on structural changes to business models and on human weakness, not just in the face of recession but in general—the individual consumer has much less influence over the marketplace than has the individual policy maker at an A&P or Walmart, who can leverage whole regimes of technology and labor. Of course, consumer groups can and do band together to increase their power over businesses, but the structural challenges to change remain powerful even in such cases.

Walmart's expansion into food in the 1980s drove even other large supermarket chains like Albertson's and Safeway to distraction,[61] and sent many other supermarkets out of business—the likenesses of Food Land in *What's Eating Gilbert Grape,* discussed in chapter 2. Dicker argues that Walmart's presence in the food sales division "is quickly turning an industry that once had room for dozens and dozens of owner-operators into an oligopoly unlike any the world has ever seen."[62] The Updike story "A&P" registers unease about this process. "A&P" turns on the young man, working as a checker, experiencing a visceral (embodied, ethical) reaction against what he takes to be his boss's indecent treatment of the young women who have entered the store in bikinis. In this way, the story gestures at a deeper cultural anxiety about work and identity as American culture began its shift toward postindustrialism. For instance, Moreton shows that before World War II in the South, there had been resistance to chain stores (like A&P) and the kind of labor they entailed, their "reduction of independent workers to feminized men who would never know the possessive individualism of self-command."[63] Walmart, rooted in Arkansas and the South, resolved this problem, Moreton contends, by employing many women as clerks and rewriting "the family sexual hierarchy onto the workplace."[64] But a broad cultural anxiety about what businesses like Walmart have done to American identity and labor still underlies criticisms of Walmart.

Walmart as Localizing the Global

Walmart's initial rise, then, relied on particular conditions of the U.S. South, but its subsequent expansion, though increasingly global, still hinged on distinctive (i.e., local) conditions in various locations, particularly in China.

Walmart has been a humongous importer of Chinese goods to the United States, bringing in some $15 billion in 2004, a much higher amount than the previous year.[65] Hiroko Tabuchi reports in the *New York Times* that by 2013, the value of Walmart's imports from China had risen to some $49 billion. Tabuchi also reports that these imports from China "eliminated or displaced over 400,000 jobs in the United States between 2001 and 2013, according to an estimate by the Economic Policy Institute, a progressive research group that has long targeted Walmart's policies."[66] While Tabuchi also includes criticism of that jobs estimate by both Walmart and some economists, nevertheless, Walmart's current business model clearly depends on the cultural and social realities at play in China. Those include not only the repressive governmental regime but, more importantly for my purposes here, an unprecedented internal migration. As Dicker reports in the early twenty-first century, citing Ted Fishman's piece in the *New York Times*, "The population of displaced Chinese peasants searching for work exceeds the entire working population of the United States."[67] This dislocation inaugurates a homesickness of profound measure and directly contributes to the existence of Walmart (which enforces its own kind of homesickness, as this chapter claims). The larger point is to connect these dislocations to contemporary international labor, trade, and capitalism.

But as Stephen Greenblatt has recently argued, such mobility is not new. Indeed, Greenblatt's book claims that this mobility is not even a reality of modernity but is instead fundamental to human life.[68] He thus unwittingly echoes Walmart's own defense of its international manufacturing system: Lee Scott, CEO of Walmart, said on CNBC in 2004 that "moving offshore started a long time before we [Walmart] got to be the largest sales company in the world."[69] The counterargument to Greenblatt that I have repeatedly made in this book insists on distinguishing among regimes and forms of mobility; prehistorical human movement, for instance, differed radically from the contemporary forms of mobility and dislocation wrought by international commerce. Universalizing and naturalizing movement as he does facilitates enormous violence and harm, both fast and slow.

Walmart leverages the global situation of production at both ends. Although it has often billed itself as quintessentially American, some of the products labeled "made in America" have proved foreign made.[70] A lot of the nationalism connected to Walmart is mere advertising, sloganeering covering over the reality of a very *international* capitalism. Indeed, the mundane fact that Walmart is expanding its operations into foreign nations underscores that this corporation is a contemporary, transnational business rather than a purely American institution.[71] This reality conflicts with, for example, Letts's desire to locate the growth of the newly rising middle class, children of Novalee Nation, as birthed in and from Walmart. Locating identity in this upstart American company *dislocates* identity. To be a child of Walmart is not just to identify with the American social class that patronizes the stores in the United States; it is also to be one, if you like, with this capitalist internationalism.

These realities of globalization illustrate the need for caution in a too-eager embrace of cosmopolitanism. Again, we must ask, Which cosmopolitanism? Whose cosmopolitanism? The local implications of large-scale realities for a Novalee Nation and for, say, Chinese laborers unsettle cosmopolitan programs that are often co-opted by global capitalism. Their homesickness is a fundamental symptom of contemporary human life. Homesickness takes new shapes in different places and times, as the sheer size of this Chinese dislocation makes clear. And it is also clear that Walmart did not, indeed could not, entirely create such a reality, even if it can and does benefit from it. This huge, dislocated population helps keep Chinese wages low, Chinese trade surplus high, and products cheap at American outlets like Walmart. It is also clear that such scenarios cannot be robustly understood as the results of some purely clear, rational process. Chinese peasants, like Walmart shoppers, respond with their own limited agency to a global scenario that offers limited options and that is driven by large forces of biopower and powerful different philosophical orientations in China and the United States.

"Wall-Mart" in *South Park*: Containing Critique with Irony and Entertainment

These international restructurings of labor and the marketplace reiterate the limitations of conceiving of political agency in terms of deliberate consumption practices of the sort advocated by Ruppel Shell, discussed at the opening of this chapter. Instead, texts like *Where the Heart Is* tend to reveal the limited agency of individuals. This cluster of issues, and the symptomatic rejection of alternatives, are effectively presented in an episode of the puerile but often sharply observed animated television program *South Park* focusing on "Wall-Mart" (a deliberate misspelling, no doubt to avoid legal censure).

The episode, "Something Wall-Mart This Way Comes," is about the impacts Wall-Mart has on small-town South Park.[72] It trots out many of the standard criticisms of the Walmart business model, showing how it encourages sometimes absurd purchasing patterns driven by a perverse logic of saving, how it swallows huge tracts of land, and how it undercuts local stores and eliminates locally controlled jobs. The presentation of the deserted downtown South Park is especially funny and apropos here, since it visually depicts the abandoned buildings in disrepair as a synecdoche for what I am calling homesickness more generally. Indeed, it matters that *South Park* is named after and set in a small, rural mountain town in Colorado, near where the *South Park* creators went to college in Boulder. Thus the semiotics of the show incorporate local and idiosyncratic culture and images—regionalism—to engage broader arguments and questions. To solve this Wall-Mart problem, the episode engages and satirizes epic/adventure genres that would have heroes kill the monster (Wall-Mart) laying waste to the community, exposing such genres to postmodern irony. But these young questing knights inspire a further homesickness also in the key of irony: as the boy heroes strive to strike at the heart of Wall-Mart, giving their lives purpose, Stan's father, Randy, drops away from the group, insisting that he cannot resist Wall-Mart's low prices on screwdrivers.

Again, the posthumanist flattening of relationships stands out: Randy's relationship to his son is on the same level—indeed, is subordinated to—his relationship to screwdrivers. While taking nonhuman objects and tools seriously is an important plank of posthumanism, in this case of course that move is exposed as facilitating a commodification of selfhood via a neoliberal and repressive business. Indeed, Randy is presented throughout the episode as lacking the will to stop shopping at Wall-Mart, having quit his work as a geologist to take a job at the Wall-Mart store and even passing out in a fit of exhaustion at home, having shopped himself nearly to death. Beaten, he is depicted wearing on his face like bruises cheap stickers bought at the store. Randy is living in a virtual world, a postworld, with stickers standing in for bruises, excessive shopping replacing excessive labor, all supplanting attention to more fundamental conditions of life and world (in short: shopping instead of geology). The scene effectively captures how the bargain-driven business model works—and how culture falls under its sway. Virtual bruises from virtual labor on an animated (i.e., virtual) program: the Real has gone missing.

But if *South Park*'s treatment of the store is more incisive in these respects than other parallel treatments discussed above, the episode ultimately refuses, as with these other texts, to allow that real alternatives exist. When the town becomes fed up with Wall-Mart's effects on the community, they burn the building down, comically singing "Kum Ba Ya" as they do so. But the store is quickly rebuilt and the town resumes its shopping, only to repeat the same cycle of growing fed up and burning down the store again. Here, as in chapter 2, a burned-down building is an icon of limited agency. And here again, shopping becomes an irrational compulsion, naturalized as inevitable. Indeed, when the townspeople do muster up the collective will to shop at a local store instead of Wall-Mart, that local store quickly grows into precisely the same shape that Wall-Mart had assumed; it is the same store under a different name. The sequence can be read in competing ways. On the one hand, it smartly exposes the risks of demonizing Walmart and other such businesses without addressing the underlying problems they represent and enact. On the other hand, it is classic *South Park*, reducing every issue to irony and undermining any possibility of social and political change.

The prevailing cynical message, then, is that individual weakness prevents communities from taking any kind of stand against corporate policies they dislike. Thus the episode *naturalizes* Walmart's business model, obscuring the constructed and contingent character of consumer capitalist subjectivity. However, the history of successful "site fights" that have prevented Walmart from entering communities offers one counterexample to *South Park*'s logic.[73] And the *South Park* argument is too easy in other respects too, since we know that organizations with business models similar to Walmart's, such as Costco, have been able to offer better pay, benefits, labor policies, and the like, and still succeed in a capitalist framework.[74] Such cases drive alternative conclusions about human frailty than those in *South Park*: rather than making Walmart inevitable, our weakness requires organized movements and larger cultural reorientations to insist on good treatment for workers, humane business practices, and much more conscious and deliberate city planning rather than the laissez faire or even pro-Walmart approach that currently prevails. Beyond that, reconceiving human selfhood in posthumanist terms would involve much more radical reworking of human goals, human labor, and daily life.

"MADE IN AMERICA": Equating Capitalist Selves with Capitalist Products

Randy surrendering his personal commitments and professional career in order to shop at Wall-Mart; the dislocation of Chinese workers, of Novalee, and of others: these are forms of emptying out the subject, of deracination. In this context, add another image to this list: Novalee in Walmart. Novalee's condition is desperate, her life scarcely worth living, a scenario not entirely unlike that in *Beloved,* discussed in chapter 3. Hence Novalee's state of suspension and denial for two months in Walmart as her pregnancy advances. More particularly, Letts offers a resonant image of this reality early in the story, one that may be durable even outside the context of the novel as a kind of meme: when Novalee is abandoned by Willy Jack and forgotten even by the Walmart employees who initially helped her, Letts describes her as a "pregnant girl on the bench by the door, sitting under a red, white and blue banner that said MADE IN AMERICA" (17).

Consider this moment in relative isolation, as an image of an unknown young woman. She is a product who/that is "MADE IN AMERICA." Indeed. The crude and excessively insistent declaration (all capital letters), here in the form of commercial and advertising discourse, is exactly right. Although the larger novel does not offer this sort of critique of Walmart, this image of Novalee is profoundly neoliberal. It is also, potentially, posthumanist, with a human presented as a *product* of global manufacturing like other Walmart goods. In both schemas, hierarchies of value are thus dramatically flattened. Someone who might perhaps have benefited from the General Motors labor regime in the 1950s, earning a solid wage, in the neoliberal age is relegated to underemployment or unemployment, subject to whatever—to borrow the Adam Smith–esque euphemist language—capitalism wills.[75] In this image of Novalee, the idealized democratic Enlightenment individual is far from the locus of value; quite the reverse. The system of production dictates what the individual will be. Hence the sign, yelling in all capital letters. Indeed, as Wendy Brown argues, "equality ceases to be an a priori or fundament of neoliberalized democracy."[76] Instead, she argues, economic inequality becomes "normative," understood as a sign of a healthy, competitive marketplace. In neoliberalism, then, we should expect and even desire people to be in circumstances like Novalee's. Interestingly, this image was left out of the film; instead, at roughly the same moment in the narrative, we see Novalee eating junk food in the Walmart. The same argument, sans the political critique of Walmart, applies: Novalee is positioned as kin to the corn dog and other food items advertised behind her; all of them are deracinated and objectified (Figure 6).

In this "MADE IN AMERICA" image, and throughout the novel, Letts also engages questions of gender, and clearly one reading strategy would interpret Novalee's difficulties in a feminist framework. That approach usefully helps accent specific experiences and hazards women are exposed to, including sexual assault and pregnancy, but in making such points, we must be careful not to reiterate the familiar stereotypes of weakness and exposure as distinctively feminine. As I have shown by engaging the dynamics of consumer capitalism and Walmart, however, the suffering subject with limited choices is not just feminine or female, by any stretch of the hypermasculine imagination. Such a feminization of weakness, besides being false, is a powerful strategy for reaffirming long-dominant masculinist—and humanist—protocols. It needs to be resisted, and posthumanist modes offer one set of tools to do so.

The image of Novalee as "MADE IN AMERICA" also evokes postnationalism ironically, accidentally, exposing the fictions of xenophobia, since many Walmart goods are not in fact made in the United States. Dicker reports a

Figure 6. Novalee, Made in America. Novalee amid other Walmart products—corn dogs, sausages—all deracinated like her potted buckeye tree, next to her, from the film *Where the Heart Is*.

controversy aired on *Dateline NBC* when it was revealed that some products presented in Walmart stores as American-made proved in fact to have been manufactured abroad.[77] What is more, as suggested above, Walmart's expansion and domination of the retail market has included international growth of store locations and increasing public use of international sources for its products, particularly in Asia and especially in China.[78] That means likening Novalee to other Walmart products tacitly admits *her* postnational status. Read robustly, she appears as a kind of postcolonial, posthumanist refugee.

What about Novalee's appearance in this image as a kind of object? The word "object" has at least two competing valences here: it can be a derogation of Novalee in light of the familiar, naturalized humanist hierarchy that places "inanimate" matter on the bottom and humans on the top; or, in object-oriented ontological sense, it is more neutral, since all entities are interpretable as objects in that discourse. In the latter case, as suggested in the opening of this chapter and subsequently, the empty subject of capitalism, the self that can only be completed with the goods of the world, can be aligned with posthumanist notions of self. The risks of that move certainly haunt this whole chapter, as neoliberal capitalism is adept at co-opting such ideas to reinforce the status quo. But, much as Naomi Klein argues in *This Changes Everything: Capitalism versus the Climate* that climate change may perversely offer an opportunity to rethink capitalism as a whole,[79] there may be an opportunity in such reconfigurations to tilt selfhood away from consumer fetishism toward a posthumanism that complicates the subject/object split. We can begin simply with the objects at hand and the objects we are, right in the middle of Walmart. Doing so would restore to identity the importance of the material and the nonhuman, and of the particular and the regional. Since selves are always a becoming-with, our material surroundings and our idiosyncratic locales matter more than we fully allow. This recognition also brings into view the slow violence to the subject implicit in neoliberalism, with its relentless framing of life in economic terms and its fantasy of independent selves that must justify their existence by falling into place in a get-and-spend regime.[80]

In other words, consumer capitalism requires new frameworks of interpretation, including posthumanist ones. In recognizing the heterogeneity, the more-than-human status of human selfhood from the start, posthumanism avoids the contradictory, agonistic relationship to difference that characterizes conservative defenses of Walmart. Walmart is a terrain where nonhuman objects, collected from around the productive world, can be engaged; however, in the traditional, conservative view, that *difference* is subjugated, or obscured and downplayed, by the fantasy of the rational, imperious subject who, participating in capitalism, maximizes his (in the standard theories, his) best interests and therefore reiterates human exceptionalism and humanism more generally. Yet the realities of irrational desire and weak, suffering, open subjectivity, a homesick subjectivity, accord better with new economic accounts of choice and biological descriptions of the human body that are plainly present in the shopping encounter; such truths also liberate crucial affective dimensions of life. As I have argued above, these affective dimensions are what make life worth living, so they are very much in need of rehabilitation.

Flat Ontology and Capitalist Appropriation: Shopping Technology and Posthumanism

Conventional, humanist distinctions among nations and even between humans and products are flattened or blurred by Walmart, and in Letts's story, in large part because of the (less-visible) function of technological innovations in contemporary shopping practices. Walmart thus culminates one strand of a long history of technological change. Ruppel Shell, who draws heavily on the Lichtenstein collection of essays on Walmart that I have repeatedly cited, joins others in emphasizing the development of mass assembly procedures. She dates this development back to gun manufacturing in the late eighteenth century,[81] which was then famously advanced with Ford's moving assembly line. Several authors discuss the importance of the Sears catalog, not only as a force in driving prices down but as a model for the systematized presentation of goods.[82] That innovation presaged the important and powerful bar code system, first used on a pack of gum.[83] The bar code system gave producers and merchandisers much more control over their product lines and affected the way that shopping happens. Further, recent efforts have been made toward radio frequency identification systems of marking products, so that they could be tracked, located, and distributed with even greater efficiency, though these efforts remain faltering for various reasons.[84] These kinds of technical innovations are intermarried with the shifting missions of discount stores, which, in Ruppel Shell's account, turned away from the "venerable retailing practice of offering customers precisely what they wanted" and moved toward offering "customers what was available at the lowest possible price."[85] Price and the pursuit of perceived value trump actual need or conscious want in this schema.

These posthumanist practices, intermixing technology and human agency, are particularly important in an era when more and more people inhabit signifying systems that they buy their way into, as Anne Norton emphasizes, part of a large literature on the topic.[86] People use products, especially branded products, to declare their identities, and even, as Gary Cross shows, to express their nostalgia.[87] In this scenario, Walmart seems again to inhabit a paradoxical position. On the one hand, Walmart makes name-brand goods available, often at the lowest possible cost, permitting shoppers both to confirm their identities with brands and to save money. On the other hand, much of what Walmart sells is remarkable not for its name brand but simply for its low expense. In this sense, it is part of the tradition that stretches back to A&P, which was the first modern merchandiser to manufacture its own generic label of goods to sell in its stores, a practice that is of course quite widespread today.[88]

Whether one buys name-brand goods cheaply or Walmart brand products, the significance of owning products is changed with discount stores. A well-branded product in such a context has different meaning than in a context of comparative scarcity. That is, brands lose some of their panache, and hierarchies of cultural value are flattened. Dicker's suggestion that Walmart's customers shop "for stuff more than status" is also germane.[89] This sheer materiality—"stuff"—evokes the horizontal mode of living advocated by theorists like Giles Deleuze and Félix Guattari.[90] Purchased goods are part of a signifying system that is less hierarchical and more material.

One can defend Walmart on these grounds: does it not offer shoppers more access to the egalitarian American dream, as rendered by contemporary capitalism? Similarly, Walmart's management practices a kind of anti-elitism, what Lichtenstein calls "symbolic leveling," in which all employees are called "associates" and "top executives are put through skits, songs, and vaudeville-like routines that embarrass them before thousands of raucous associates."[91] This performance of populism is powerful, but it belies another reality presented by Ruppel Shell: "Before retiring in February 2009, Wal-Mart CEO Lee Scott Jr. took home in his biweekly paycheck what his average employee earned in a lifetime."[92] Thus—no surprise here—the leveling is indeed "symbolic" only, a patina of populism over a fundamentally neoliberal structure.

Distinctions of cultural capital have not disappeared, then; they have been leveraged by Walmart to help generate commercial success. The newly rising forms of cultural capital can be read, again, as part of capitalism's creative destruction.

Thus, as much as Walmart's hierarchical flattening may expand the possibilities of consumption, it also reinforces inequalities even among consumers. True, purchased objects expand options in life for recreation, employment, and so on, but they do so ever less equally. Likewise, as per Norton, those objects are also forms of speech, and "you can buy as much speech as you can afford."[93] Furthermore, in terms of the economic reality of Walmart and other such discount retailers, this flattening of hierarchies can be connected to the ill effects of this particular form of consumer capitalism. Karjanen points out that such stores are part of a history that "has flattened the job hierarchy and simplified the complex staffing pattern that once characterized full-service department stores like Macy's and Bloomingdale's [and] has eliminated many of the career ladders that once enabled clerks to become higher-wage specialists, buyers, and managers."[94] Thus, embracing an ontology of flatness, like embracing mobility, must be undertaken with caution and always in context. Deleuze and Guattari's *A Thousand Plateaus,* and more recent work to level or refigure hierarchies in object-oriented ontology, new materialism, and related movements, suggests a liberating potential in recognizing humans as objects, but that potential can be turned to various and conflicting purposes.[95] Capitalism is very good at co-opting such moves. As a philosophical principle, the abstraction of flat ontology may be too universal; it risks enabling further injustices and further damage.

"Animal Keening," Eating Animals, and Walmart

A primary route around the universal goes through the particular, the local, and the sentimental or affective; it responds to suffering in real places. I have argued that the plot of Letts's novel reveals the slow violence of neoliberalism, without the benefit of a clear critique in those terms, seeming to naturalize contemporary living conditions. In other words, Novalee is fundamentally and dramatically exposed in her weak human animality, a vulnerability rendered more extreme by her youth, her poverty, and her gender position in this case. Letts briefly accents Novalee's likeness to other animals in the

Walmart birthing scene, when this poor girl, alone and intending to deliver her baby herself, hears her own cries of labor pains as if they were those of somebody or something else: "She heard an animal keening—its high-pitched cry made her throat ache" (89). The animal within her surprises her, and here again, in Walmart the familiar self is rendered strange, but this time not by exposure to the vast production of consumer capitalism in a shopping practice but simply by exposure of individual weakness. Walmart is a strange and disconcerting—terrifying, really—place to birth a child alone.

Letts's self-conscious, stylistically effective rendering of a more-than-human selfhood here is the exception, not the rule, in the larger book. Human animality for Letts, as for the culture at large, tends to be acknowledged only at moments of crisis—birth, violence, war, and the like. Yet the animal keening is one of the clearest expressions of suffering subjectivity in the novel. It is a keening evoking not just bodily pain but the suffering and desire that characterizes Novalee's larger hopes. In the keening, human verbal expression—near language—becomes less distinctly legible and more uncanny, fuzzy, expressing an inchoate desire at the root of all language. It joins many other images and icons treated in *Homesickness* that reveal the posthumanist status of language and meaning—elephant tracks and carcasses, a half-skinned steer, and burning homes. Indeed, Novalee's persistent desire to establish real roots in a place reiterates human embodiment, weakness, and animality—reiterates, that is, her/our posthumanist status, requiring much more robust attention also to place, that more-than-human reality. Letts establishes early on that, because Novalee "had never lived in a place that didn't have wheels under it," she "dreamed of all kinds of houses" (7). Many of these fantasies are deliberately stereotypical, derived, as Letts repeatedly writes, from magazine images (7). One task of the novel is to upend those easy media images, as Novalee ultimately finds a resilient community in a rather less picturesque trailer home—on wheels still, of course—spending time with a quirky, imperfect, economically marginalized but warm bunch of Oklahomans, her queer family in flyover country.

The child brought forth in the Walmart birthing scene, Americus, develops an affection for stray animals, whom her mother tolerates. Their adoptions include a "skittish kitten" (228), a "fuzzy mongrel" dog (229), a "pregnant cat," and "a three-legged beagle" (275), among others perhaps. Americus displays the same sympathy for strays that the community has shown for her mother. But this pity for abandoned creatures, a minor feature of the novel regarding nonhuman animals though major regarding Novalee, does not extend into the products this family consumes. Just sentences after Novalee tells her love interest Forney that she will help her daughter "take in the strays of the world," she sits down to "some creamed chicken" (267). Does that chicken also deserve ethical attention? After all, as the Animal Studies Group reports in introducing their 2006 book *Killing Animals*, "six billion broiler chickens are raised in sheds" in the United States each year, destined for such meals.[96] The National Chicken Council reports that almost nine billion broiler chickens were produced in the United States in 2017,[97] a figure significantly higher than the whole population of humans on planet Earth, and the number of chickens killed is perhaps larger today.

This neglect of the larger biopolitics of food animals in favor of sympathy for individual strays is of course symptomatic of Enlightenment, individualist humanism, and neoliberalism. But the novel can be read to register the tension between humanist and posthumanist frames. There is an ambivalence to be found in this moment of the text, sitting down to "creamed chicken," even if the text does not clearly present that ambivalence. "Creamed chicken" is metonymic of Novalee's own status through much of the story; in her dire circumstances, trapped in Walmart, she resembles the other products sold in the store, like chickens, reduced to deracinated objects. From this perspective, eating creamed chicken is a kind of cannibalism, of the sort discussed by Nicole Shukin in her postscript to *Animal Capital*. Citing Jameson, Derrida, and others, she underscores how "capitalism cannibalizes itself to ensure a future."[98] That is, Novalee's circumstances exist partly because she is subject to many of the same forces and conditions that chickens are, but the rigid, dogmatic human/animal distinction prevents her from recognizing this, a blindness that, in sum, reaffirms her basic entrapment. Of course, a person does have to eat. It has been made clear from early in the novel that Novalee and her daughter need the warm, hearty, home-cooked meals this community offers them. But what food and in what form? When Letts indicates that the family's trials have expanded their sphere of concern to include animals in at least some way, she shows a limited awareness of the similarities between Novalee's plight and those conditions of other animals, but those connections are not pursued directly.

This reference to cannibalism, it is worth noting, functions differently in a posthumanist framework as well. Unnervingly, we cannot so simplistically operationalize the taboo of cannibalism in an intellectual structure that undermines the human/nonhuman animal distinction. Rather, as I just noted, eating animals can resemble cannibalism, and one upshot of this idea is that all of us are at least susceptible, in desperate enough times, to become literal cannibals ourselves. We have seen this in many historical episodes, both distant and recent, some of which have become culturally prominent, such as the sinking of the whaling ship *Essex* by a sperm whale in 1820, followed by some of the survivors resorting to cannibalism to survive. Those events were part of the larger story that inspired Herman Melville's *Moby-Dick* (1851) and that were described in the nonfiction book *In the Heart of the Sea* (2000), by Nathaniel Philbrick, which was also made into a film (2015).[99] Another prominent example was the rugby team that resorted to cannibalism in the Andes Mountains after an airplane crash in 1972, as depicted in the film *Alive* (1993). This hazard of sliding from an ethical eating practice to cannibalism is also explored in the novel *Life of Pi* (2001), again made into a film (2012).[100]

Novalee's eating practices are not at all equated with cannibalism in explicit terms, yet a posthumanist reading strategy can pry open alternative possible readings of the text. Thus, in another instance, at another of the book's most traumatic moments, when Novalee's friend Lexie and her family have been assaulted, Novalee comes across one of the shocked children "keening softly like a frightened animal" (283). This is a terrible and terrifying scene that equates the child with a nonhuman animal exposed to harm or even, at least metaphorically, to cannibalism. The passage thus resembles the strategy used in the film *The Silence of the Lambs,* as discussed by Cary Wolfe in *Animal Rites.* He finds "the heart of the film's trauma" in "cross-*species* identification" that renders Agent Clarice Starling kin to the lambs she pities via traumatic memory but that also makes the cannibal Hannibal Lecter "the postmodern wolf in sheep's clothing."[101] Wolfe insists that in a postmodern context, we cannot so readily distinguish our lives and our eating practices from Lecter's by way of the modernist "discourse of speciesism," which would permit us to say there is a vast difference between eating human and nonhuman flesh.[102] Instead, Wolfe points out how Lecter's strange desires, reduced to a kind of animalistic embodiment, are like our own, which are "generalized in commodity fetishism and consumer culture." For Wolfe, however, the film obscures our likeness to Lecter via a "strategic misrecognition," preventing us from thinking too much about what we share with him.[103]

What happens when the human body is acknowledged as a body and as animal? Do we thereby lose the grounds on which to make ethical decisions and thus facilitate an embrace of "commodity fetishism and consumer culture"? Do we all become merely blind shoppers? A compelling answer to this concern exists also in terms of species discourse. In short, to be animal does not mean being without ethics or without community sensitivities. As Frans de Waal insists in *Primates and Philosophers* and as Marc Bekoff insists in much of his work, morality is an evolved talent of social animals, and being embodied often means, in part, activating this community sensibility.[104] More particular to this chapter, furthermore, desire is not just an active, consuming, even cannibalistic movement. It is also a wariness of suffering, a sense of exposure, and a necessary immersion in the not-me, including an immersion in communities: shopping as suffering.

Such reversals—shopping as suffering—are traumatic to humanist notions of sovereignty. But breaching the humanist enclosures in *The Silence of the Lambs* and *Where the Heart Is,* registering our animality in crises, also reveals new understandings, new self-conceptions. These understandings contain an affirmative potential for recalibrating human life after trauma. Indeed, the traumatic events in Letts's novel, taken together, present a more robust account of what people need in life, such as the queer reality of community that in fact makes possible the imagined, fictional, pure wholeness of the nuclear family, parallel to the way the fantasy of pure and isolated individualism is in fact made possible by cross- and transspecies communities. In Letts's novel, the adopted stray animals become part of an unconventional family, a few degrees off-kilter from the traditional family with its domesticated pet or pets. They make visible new possible ways of sharing the world.

But the treatment of domesticity in this book is otherwise often largely conventional, different from a text like Marilynne Robinson's *Housekeeping,* discussed in chapter 2. The treatment of animals in *Where the Heart Is* works in the vein of Oedipal animals discussed by Deleuze and Guattari in *A Thousand Plateaus*; they are "family pets, sentimental, . . . each with its own petty history," and thus, Deleuze and Guattari go on, these animals "invite us to regress" and "to discover a daddy, a mommy, a little brother."[105] The attitude toward animals is part of the book's larger approach to what I am calling simple homesickness, and the treatment of animals is folded into that domestic context. More systematic investigations are mostly pressed aside: what causes so many strays in the world? If the book offers an answer to that, it is again mostly personalized: we can blame lousy teenage boys like Willy Jack, or horrible mothers like Novalee's, who leave such young women exposed to the world. The novel tends to avoid considering other structures that reveal Willy Jack's own status as victim to some extent and that might make his wandering more legible and sympathetic (his caricatured presentation in the novel forestalls any serious attention to him, making him an easy scapegoat).

For these reasons, one level of response to the novel involves condemning its discourse of animals as typically sentimental, attentive to pets and other domesticated animals but indifferent to animals beyond that immediate sphere. That move repeats the common critique of our culture's treatment of nonhuman animals more generally. To sum up that view, we might think of this novel in the terms of Deleuze and Guattari's general condemnation of pet keeping: "*Anyone who likes cats or dogs is a fool.*"[106]

But this critique exposes another layer of response to this text and the questions it raises: Is it so easy as that, either in the case of this novel or in the case of dogs or cats? This chapter, by engaging with a book that is so clearly and deliberately sentimental and conventional, is built on the premise that such narratives can in fact reveal valuable, underrecognized dimensions of homesickness, animality, and place. An important dilemma here is how to attend to this sentimental novel, or to dogs and cats. Will both be rendered into clear and pure symbol systems? Deleuze and Guattari want to resist turning all thinking back into an Oedipal scenario, but their strike against the living animals that share human space brushes past the fleshy reality of those creatures. Donna Haraway's criticism of their "scorn for all that is mundane and ordinary" and their "absence of curiosity about or respect for and with actual animals" resounds incisively.[107]

Defamiliarizing domestic animals even a few degrees opens vistas about dogs and cats and so much more, as the rapid development of animal studies testifies. But also, by a classic Oedipal triangulation, such estrangements open perspectives ("lines of escape," if you like, in the Deleuze and Guattari formulation) on the human subject, on the home itself and its powerful metaphorics. To have an animal in the home is to make it an animal den and to make it inhuman, posthumanist, a place that we cannot and, in very practical terms, do not possess or own.[108] This is one irony of contemporary "pet" keeping, in which animals have returned to the home, as if in an effort to return to premodern times and the longhouse, where prior to the sixteenth and seventeenth centuries, humans and their cattle often slept under a single roof.[109] More practically, to use a personal example, when I want to write (need to write?) but the dog in the house needs to follow his circadian rhythms and run in the morning, I am pulled in opposite directions. Because of my cross-species commitments, I cannot stay. I must go out the door, and in this sense I am homesick, pressed out of doors, loose in a bigger world, soon to be traveling (this time) in a patch of Eastern North American hardwoods, open to the pileated woodpecker that is in the neighborhood and the many robins and so on.

In what sense am I, then, out with the dog, actually in the city limits of Philadelphia, city of brotherly love, as it is designated in the human maps? We could name this place otherwise. This scenario evokes what it means to be homesick even while at home, to demonstrate a different logic of selfhood. And following from this line of escape (or is it better understood as a route home? a route of home? a practice of home?), how can the suffering of displaced forms of life, nonhuman and human, articulate with high critical theory, or just ordinary cultural criticism? Few of these living beings—the dog in my house, Novalee Nation and her family's adopted stray animals—can readily speak the psychological discourse of Deleuze and Guattari, obviously, but that does not mean their forms of life do not function. Brian Massumi suggests in engaging critical theory like that of Deleuze and Guattari, "The question is not: is it true? But: does it work?"[110] Then how could we possibly ignore the rife, vital, omnipresent forms of life present in "bad texts," in sentimental novels, in dogs and cats, which clearly work in several senses? If theory is to work at all in the actual world, it must do better by those realities than simply to call them foolish. In this regard, I am following the route of Jane Tompkins in *Sensational Designs,* where she seeks to "move the study of American literature away from the small group of master texts . . . into a more varied and fruitful area of investigation," as the book's first sentence has it.[111]

Bad Food and Other Malnourishing Cultural Practices

This approach also warrants renewed attention to the bad food creamed chicken and its surprising implications in debates about the global and the local in food. An animal studies critique of the rhetoric and function of food in Letts's novel might underscore how the suffering and poor treatment of chicken, in effect, sponsors the recuperation of humanist verities by helping rehabilitate Novalee and her family via the comfort food of creamed chicken. As I implied above, one version of a more ethical eating would link the suffering of Novalee with that of the chicken and other victims of the food system. Their entire ways of life have been dislocated and mangled in consumer capitalism. They are homesick, in a much more severe sense even than the half-skinned steer of Annie Proulx, treated in chapter 1.

Another version of this critique would insist on the importance of locally sourced food, locavorism. This approach to eating ethics thinks through the planetary impacts of carbon-intensive food systems and thus argues for the benefits of the local.[112] So it uses a global frame to advance a local conduct. A standard counter to such arguments, however, hinges on class, on people's economic ability to buy often more expensive ethical foods, and on their opportunity to access the arguments and beliefs that might lead them to such an eating practice. The locavore movement, in this sense, requires a nonlocal kind of education about the food industry, not to mention a whole host of arguments and assumptions about what is or is not valuable in life. So the local food movement, paradoxically enough, is eco-cosmopolitan, requiring very sophisticated kinds of awareness not readily available or desirable to many people ("think globally, act locally"). The further paradox in terms of debates about the local versus the planetary is that many eaters default to their familiar dietary regimes and shopping habits that they imagine to be very personal—familial, commonly—and local. Yet, generally today, they are neither really personal nor local. Shopping and eating today are commonly international undertakings, even if the nuclear family and domestic arrangements participate in their perpetuation. It takes special and even strange work to avoid international commerce.

In this case, it becomes clear that a rhetorical contrast between the frameworks of the local and the nonlocal is insufficient, on its own, to enable more careful thinking and practices connected to food. Instead, we need to improve at shuttling between and among scales—local, regional, and planetary—because we have competing forms of (largely) nonlocal forces expressed in local terms: eco-cosmopolitan arguments about food ethics versus globalized supply chains that offer cheap prices. In the latter, a shopper's decision to buy at Walmart is not just economic; it is also a declaration of community identity, an acknowledgment of being a member of the other-than-elite, who does not have time or energy for fussiness about food. This complaint is often legitimate in a sense, reiterating the importance of Daniel Kahneman's argument in *Thinking, Fast and Slow* about the challenge of longer-range (or bigger-scale) rational thinking, mentioned early in this chapter. We all have a harder time doing this than we tend to admit. These anti-elitist social formations—think "deplorables"—are increasingly self-conscious of their identities. Their resistance to nuance and dismissal of arguments about carbon footprints or animal ethics are actually akin to the dismissal of homesickness in contemporary capitalism and cosmopolitan cultures, as noted in the introduction. Historian Susan J. Matt notes that homesickness is commonly dismissed in favor of mobility, which is understood as "natural and unproblematic" and as "a central and uncontested part of American identity." While homesickness, Matt further remarks, had been understood as a sign of sophistication in the past, today it has increasingly been denigrated as a sign of "backwardness" and even "prissiness."[113]

That is, the elite and the populists alike unreasonably and unfeelingly dismiss forms of thought that defy their familiar paradigms. Deplorables embrace a tribal identity and reject fancy arguments; eco-cosmopolitans tout the forces of reason and argument, denying the power and reality of their emotional commitments to real, always local communities. Deplorables and their ilk thereby deny the global and their dependence on it, engaging in what I call a kind of cannibalism, while eco-cosmopolitans repress their own suffering and local selfhood, potentially undermining the very reasons we human animals have for ethical arguments and practices in the first place. To reiterate Singer's point, quoted by Wolfe: "The capacity for suffering and enjoyment is *a prerequisite for having interests at all.*"[114]

I am arguing that the concept of complex homesickness offers a terminology to better engage with these sorts of problems by clarifying the common ground between such positions: the suffering subject. A suffering subject is always incomplete and always to some degree homesick, but that does not mean we should accept all forms of homesickness equally. We need more nuance, more historical and regional particularity in our assessments. And, I have argued, posthumanism teaches us to recognize how the subject is always constituted by its outside, by culture, by the nonhuman, by the global, and by other hyperobjects. We thus confront a kind of paradox akin to Derrida's treatment of human agency. As Leonard Lawlor explains, in an argument that helped inspire *Homesickness,* Derrida's account of the necessary openness of the self to the world, indeed, the self's dependence on the world in the most mundane situations, is a kind of disability, a weakness. We are too weak not to require eating and many other relationships with different kinds of entities. But, Lawlor continues, this weakness means "we are able to welcome others into ourselves."[115] Weakness means ontological openness, not just by choice, an unavoidable openness that also entails opportunities.

Here too there sound resonances about the species partnerships that literally compose the human body itself. Openness is always already built into us.[116] Indeed, our animality, cooperation, and symbiosis would not likely seem traumatic or challenging were it not for the Enlightenment history of regarding the subject as singular, enclosed, and independent. From a position recognizing the mutuality of selfhood from the start, however, the premise of subjective solitude is the traumatic one. To be a self is always already to be responsible for more than one's self. No other conception of life is possible. This is a complex homesickness, and it is, to echo Ruppel Shell's wording quoted earlier in the chapter, sobering. But it is also joyful, even intoxicating at times—especially in the sense of being impure, mutual, and more than narrowly rational.

6

Killing Words in War

Homesick Soldiers and the Shadow of Agency

All you can do is whimper and wait.

—Tim O'Brien, *The Things They Carried*

The head was mine, but not to use, not to think with, only to remember and not too much remember.

—Ernest Hemingway, *A Farewell to Arms*

Chapter 5 showed that shopping can sometimes perform a slow violence against other human and nonhuman potentials. Slow violence: this is a notion that borrows coherence from the reality of what might be called fast violence, and in modernity, fast violence gets faster all the time.[1] Its speed is part of why fast violence is difficult to think about and make sense of, deepening the disorientations produced by war as one of its profoundest effects. War's disruptions are marked at the cultural and social levels by historical periodizing and by concepts like modernism and postmodernism, and in a variety of forms at the personal level. If war is the "theater" par excellence for the demonstration of an agency so potent it kills, then the consequences of war, caught in this powerful logic, also produce disability, inability, or the failure of agency. One's strength, in the zero-sum logic of war, is necessarily another's weakness. However, it is less frequently recognized that even the "victors" often prove weak in other ways. Victory bears inside it grave personal loss, two parts of the same system of subjectivity. Systematic violence begets systematic injury, not only to bodies but to psyches, relationships, and so on, on "both" or all sides of a conflict. Likewise, the cosmopolitan benefits of a soldier's global experience breed a strange new type of homesickness, as soldiers rely on idealistic, nostalgic dreams of home to ballast against bewildering new experiences, only to find upon return that home is not, and never was, what it had seemed. War produces a profound disorientation.

As I noted in the introduction, the very word "nostalgia was coined in 1688 by the Swiss medical student Johannes Hofer" to name what he understood "as a medical disease afflicting Swiss soldiers and mercenaries who had travelled from their Alpine homes to the plains of Europe to wage war."[2] Similarly, in *Militarizing the Environment: Climate Change and the Security State,* Robert P. Marzec shows how the environmental and social disorientation/reorientation of the British enclosure movement of the seventeenth and eighteenth centuries helped found the security state and its warring apparatuses, and that such militarized space contributes more than is commonly acknowledged to our sense of environment—especially environment in peril. He notes, for instance, how hazards of the war machine, writ large, drove twentieth-century environmentalism: "Modern-day ecological 'awareness' thus first develops when scientists involved in nuclear defense projects begin to confront the destructive elements inherent in military-oriented technological development."[3]

War estranges us from our bodies and from familiar places. As Fredric Jameson underscores in "War and Representation," war is always liable to produce "an utter transmogrification of the familiar into the alien, the *heimlich* into the *unheimlich,* in which the home village—the known world, the real, and the everyday—is transformed into a place of unimaginable horror."[4] These transformations attend not only to the horrors of the battles themselves but to wars' results. When territory is "won," a strange new regime may make one's own home place foreign, even monstrous. War is a quintessential producer of homesickness, of the *unheimlich,* accelerating processes more familiar in contemporary life, magnifying them at astonishing scales. Indeed, Jameson emphasizes the grave challenges of interpreting war at all, claiming that "collective realities" like war "exasperate narrative ambitions," that war is "virtually nonnarrative."[5] Yet, while seemingly infinite horrors attend war, it may be that war so clarifies the terms of contemporary social organization and means of production that it permits those means to be successfully challenged.

In her book *Homesickness,* historian Susan J. Matt traces how large-scale conflicts as early as the U.S. Civil War left former soldiers feeling "increasingly alienated from all they had left behind." She describes the problem this way: "On the one hand, they [soldiers] wanted their nearest and dearest to understand what they had gone through; on the other hand, they did not want their loved ones to be damaged by the traumatic events they themselves had witnessed."[6] Furthermore, home seemed different, or strange, because, as Matt explains, it had been changed by the war too, a distinct form of the more general experience termed "solastalgia" by Glenn Albrecht, the feeling of loss when a beloved place changes.[7] So, ironically, despite the common feeling of homesickness among Civil War soldiers during the conflict, the reality of homecoming, in its uncanny strangeness, often delivered yet another trauma to soldiers and their families. Such feelings of complex homesickness remain common among veterans today, in ways that defy easy characterization.

War is a difficult subject for a range of reasons. Despite its outsized impacts on history and culture, war tends to remain at arm's length from humanist modes of understanding. War is central to humanist organizations of time in modernity, for example, as in the world wars demarcating historical periods; but war is marginalized, often taken as the *other* of what humanists really do, which is advance culture, civilization, and so on. War's traumas are typically understood as tragic (sensibly) and as conditions to be cured. But war and homesickness in war are not purely traumatic; they are also instructive. Indeed, many who suffer war stress do not wish to be "cured" of it; they recognize and embrace their new knowledge. This line of inquiry regarding veterans' experiences is pursued by Sebastian Junger, for instance, in his compelling book *Tribe: On Homecoming and Belonging,* discussed below.[8] This is not to say war is desirable in the abstract, however; it is really to complicate what traumatic experience means more generally, since many undesirable experiences are also deeply informing, a point repeated throughout *Homesickness.*

Furthermore, and central to my purposes here: war subjectivity is important to interrogate because it reveals several elements of posthumanism in stark terms: human vulnerability, our deep reliance on technologies over millennia, and our retrospective action of interpretation, which I have been calling complex homesickness. The rapid, chaotic, and contingent actions of war, especial modern war, have sometimes seemed entirely to subsume individual agency, making soldiers appear to be so much fodder for the cannons, as though people served the guns rather than the reverse. This sense that systems of technology and meaning have their own power, momentum, or even agency is, of course, also a prominent dimension of posthumanist views on language and other technologies.

From one perspective, the horrors of war are tightly and directly coupled with the Anthropocene not just in the twentieth century but much more fundamentally. Some historical analyses of war make it roughly coterminous with agriculture (or agrilogistics, in Morton's sense, revisited below), meaning that the past twelve thousand or so years have involved, for many humans, these two related processes whereby places become radically estranged due to humans' own actions.[9] Both agriculture and war radically and suddenly transform places, rendering them strange and intensifying the homesickness of subjectivity. Again, as noted in the introduction, I intend two distinct forms of homesickness in this argument, one existential and the other historical. The former, existential homesickness, is inevitable in some sense because of our retrospective processing of experience. The latter, viewed in this larger historical context of agriculture, permits us to speculate about the existence of a specifically *agrilogistic* or *anthropocenic homesickness* and thus resist the tendency to naturalize or universalize homesickness in war as fundamentally human. That relates to the stance Frans de Waal takes in *The Age of Empathy: Nature's Lessons for a Kinder Society,* where he criticizes the idea that aggression is "the hallmark of humanity."[10] Instead, in light of the manifest ability of humans to cooperate, de Waal urges, "The only certainty is that our species has a *potential* for warfare."[11] We also have many other potentials. Indeed, Alfred W. Crosby notes in his history *Throwing Fire* that the potent human combination of ballistics and fire in weaponry like guns borrows much of its force from the cooperation of groups who use those weapons.[12] Even in our warmaking, then, cooperation is key.

Such thinking about violence is buoyed by other scholarship. For instance, despite the persistence of war in the world, Steven Pinker's book *The Better Angels of Our Nature* argues that a great decline in violence has been underway over the course of human history, offering much data to support his claim. He suggests that "today we may be living in the most peaceable era in our species' existence." Even if we have not "brought violence down to zero," and even though the decline "is not guaranteed to continue," Pinker insists that the overall decline is "an unmistakable development." "No aspect of life," he argues, "is untouched by the retreat from violence."[13]

These ideas should be borne in mind as we investigate the traumas of war, and they must be weighed against the grim realities of the Anthropocene.

Intrahuman violence declines, but extinctions of other species rise precipitously. Human commerce advances, helping slow war (for now), but the planetary ecological system as a whole grows more and more tenuous. These are system-wide versions of the same symptomatics discussed above, in which "victorious" soldiers nonetheless suffer serious emotional and physical injuries. In other words, Pinker's analysis raises the question of what really constitutes violence. His focus on the human species silently ignores the basic biological fact of human interdependence with other forms of life and matter, thereby disavowing the slow violence of biopolitical processes that have increasingly damaged the entire biospohere—and damaged entire domains of human experience too. Humans win the "war" to control the planet, and thereby lose, along with practically every other form of life.

Moreover, commerce in neoliberalism is now causing new divisions and hazards. Srinivas Aravamudan recently reiterated that many believed the end of war would be achievable because "national divisions would eventually be superseded when commerce and cosmopolitan right established peaceful relationality."[14] Precisely such commercial ventures, however, have served to deepen inequality, while cosmopolitan intellectual formations have been increasingly criticized as elitist (sometimes justifiably), contributing to recharging nationalist divisions visible in extreme forms in the rhetoric and actions of Donald Trump, Vladimir Putin, and others. A posthumanist critique offers the chance to advance the benefits of these historical changes while stemming the tide of the destructive ones.

Meanwhile, other ostensible benefits won via the world wars have increasingly come into question. For instance, the existence of the modern suburb, spurred in the United States by the return of veterans of World War II, has been widely understood as central to instigating the Anthropocene. As an organization of space, suburbs depend on the omnipresence of the automobile, and with it the growth of roads and highways that are ecologically expensive both intrinsically (in sheer material) and in the emissions they enable. Suburban development has aided in reproducing a racist geography in much of the United States, an apartheid that impacts education, health, and more. Suburbs also, of course, relentlessly encroach on nonhuman places, as Alisa W. Coffin summarizes in "From Roadkill to Road Ecology."[15]

The marketing of those suburbs also reveals additional ways in which wartime subjectivity is directly tied to thinking about home and place. One answer to the traumas of World War II for U.S. soldiers involved promises of technologically advanced and comforting homes after the conflict (Figure 7).[16] In effect, the same technologies that helped make the war especially miserable would salve the wounds, physical and especially psychological, of the soldiers afterward. Housed in an issue of *Life* magazine full of references to World War II, an advertisement by General Electric expresses that double meaning of homesickness. On one level, the ad shows the soldier's *desire* for home filtered through his war subjectivity; on another level, the ad reiterates how conceptions of home are, henceforth, estranged by the experiences in war. The very house itself, dislocated into the suburbs and made of materials like aluminum that were developed and refined in the war effort, becomes a strange place. As ever, and as discussed in chapter 5 on Walmart, the trick of consumer capitalism is to make that strangeness at/as home into a desirable reality. This advertisement was one way to do so.

One further general point: much of the affective energy of wartime subjectivity is too easily condemned as inherently violent, as a sign of humanity's ineluctable evil. In fact, I join others in contending that affectivity expressed in war is ambiguous and subject to radically other potentials. Sebastian Junger makes this point in his book *Tribe,* where he suggests "how very close the energy of male conflict and male closeness can be," underscoring how the energy pushed into war can be redirected into powerful prosocial attitudes and practices.[17] To facilitate such changes, individuals and cultures could practice what Brian Massumi calls "*affect modulation techniques,*" ways of improvising and adjusting encounters as they occur.[18] Junger's discussion hinges around his observation of an encounter among two Spaniard men and three Moroccans that very nearly became a fistfight. Then, in the midst of the rising tension, one of the Spanish men was able to defuse the situation. By the end of the night, Junger writes, the men were all friends.[19] In that case, near violence was modulated into camaraderie, resolving that confrontation and setting an example for future encounters, an example reinforced by Junger's telling of the story. Summing up, Junger argues, "There seemed to be a great human potential out there, organized around the idea of belonging, and the trick was to convince people that their interests had more in common than they had in conflict."[20]

That is a hopeful episode. However, much of the literature of war moves the other way, focusing on trauma and loss. Aiming at least to gesture toward the range of extant war literature, this chapter explores several U.S. texts, proceeding chronologically from World War I to recent conflicts (even as I

Figure 7. Home as homesickness, commodified. The World War II soldier's reward for war: a technologically advanced home, made out of war-improved materials like aluminum and dislocated into new suburbs. General Electric advertisement, *Life Magazine*, May 10, 1943.

resist a linear concept of temporality), investigating the function of homesickness in them. I show how this sense of estranged selfhood is intensified by war, and I call further into question humanist dogmas about human language and agency by demonstrating how language is much more animalized in war than is commonly admitted. Finally, I show how the very logic and structure of war that facilitates power and agency—even near superpower and superagency—also cast a long shadow, subjecting soldiers to radical reversals in their status as agents. Yet these traumas and the weakness they reiterate open possibilities for creating a more deliberately open and cooperative posthumanist subjectivity, one that can be robustly compelling and satisfying.

Posthumanist Words: Reanimalizing Language in War

These conflicts between human subjectivity and the exigencies of war are treated in some detail by Mary Louise Pratt in "Harm's Way: Language and the Contemporary Arts of War," mentioned in the introduction.[21] For instance, consider the general reality of U.S. soldiers in Afghanistan or Iraq, pressed into a highly unfamiliar scenario, usually without access to local language, with relatively little literacy of cultural norms, and then completely severed from the peace that attends most forms of daily life. They are simultaneously empowered and disempowered, in different ways, and that experience evokes the larger paradoxical reality of agency in war. As Pratt explains, the vast mobility of contemporary warfare strains the resources of military preparation, putting different forms of capacity into conflict with each other. Her article focuses in particular on what appear to be the natural limits of human linguistic competency: "It is not possible to maintain military readiness in all, or even a fraction, of the existing languages."[22] For Pratt, this is because of a "clash of temporalities. The temporality of modern war making is incompatible with that of language learning. It takes years to learn another language, and adults are not very good at it."[23] Modern wars, by contrast, can erupt quickly, suddenly, and practically anywhere. Furthermore, Pratt argues that "the circumstances required for people to acquire advanced translingual and transcultural competence are those that make them security risks." Residents of other countries who might be recruited into military service are likely to have "divided loyalties" at best, while translators are difficult for both sides to trust in a scenario of war.[24]

Those who engage in what might be called such cosmopolitan endeavors as developing translinguistic and transcultural expertise therefore often do not somehow double their world, as we might assume, gathering more identities to themselves. Rather, they become exposed to mistrust and doubt, alienated from origin cultures and from new ones alike. The resulting homesickness, even if it does not become posttraumatic stress disorder, certainly upsets any kind of comfortable inhabitation of "domestic life," whatever that might be understood to mean in such cases. To be sure, a vigorous cosmopolitanism has the potential to make transcultural sensibilities much more positive too; my point is simply that they are not always positive currently, especially in the context of war, which has been perhaps the dominant force instigating migration since the nineteenth century.

Pratt's argument demonstrates various ways in which the logic of war runs counter to the logic of cosmopolitanism at the level of language. She urges that "to be multilingual is above all to live in more than one language,"[25] to inhabit different, complex cultural systems at the same time, but warfare requires the clearest possible distinction between "sides" and loyalties. Her article presents this problem as a kind of fundamental contradiction at the heart of cross-cultural warfare, in which language "is itself a weapon integral to the war making."[26] She discusses, for example, a video taken by Australian photojournalist Stephen Dupont, showing American troops in Afghanistan in 2005. Pratt describes how the video includes a "performance of empowerment and self-identification" as the Americans arrive in a village "in a cloud of dust, sunglasses, rifles in hand, Pink Floyd blaring." The communication in such scenes, she writes, is about declaring power rather than presenting a discrete piece of "discursive meaning."[27] This form of intimidation, Pratt reminds us, is quite old, and is carried out by nonhuman animals as well.[28] These are killing words, killing signs. The linguistic dimension, she further argues, recalls Gilles Deleuze and Félix Guattari's assertion that much of human language use operates this way, not so much as communication but as "interpellation," as establishment or reiteration of one's role in a structure of power.[29]

Particularly remarkable for the present context is the central paradox: human language pressed into such extremes fails even as it succeeds. When used as an instrument of warfare, of force, language is thereby most resolutely connected to human agency, indeed to a whole complex performance of agency that enlists technology, rock and roll, and drama; in this use, however, language fails precisely to be a piece of "discursive meaning," leaking out its internal meanings and taking on a sheer instrumentality. The instrumentality is exactly what makes it so powerful; it is not used for rational debate or engagement. Such strange weakness (as power!) in human language undermines the claims made for it. Human use or possession of "language" is commonly used as evidence of human reasoning, of human superiority to animals, and so on, a humanist paradigm that facilitates the endless violence against animals and other nonhuman life. Yet in war, this ostensibly special competency, ostensibly different in kind from any other animal's ability, seems to be just another animal display, or probably worse. It demonstrates a special *depravity* of human potential derived precisely from our (also vaunted) use of technologies and social organization. Language here is an instrument of powerful force that, precisely in this role, demonstrates the weakness of human rationality and the power of mortality. In the following analyses of Hemingway, Tim O'Brien, Bobbie Ann Mason, and others, these posthumanist treatments of language are abundant and revealing.

Ernest Hemingway, Uncanny Selfhood, and the Dread of World Wars

That modern combat has been globalized in an intensified manner is a truism signified by the labels given to the "world wars," a usage so familiar as to be a dead metaphor. Their numeric ordering, I, II, seems to imply, as many of us have feared, that a III, and perhaps more, must be in the future. This sense of time and historicity is agrilogistic, in Timothy Morton's sense. That term, discussed in previous chapters, is Morton's name for a "twelve-thousand-year machination," "a specific logistics of agriculture that arose in the Fertile Crescent and that is still plowing ahead. Logistics, because it is a technical, planned, and perfectly logical approach to built space. Logistics, because it proceeds without stepping back and rethinking the logic. A viral logistics, eventually requiring steam engines and industry to feed its proliferation."[30] Further, this historicization—World Wars I, II, and III?—is tragic, assuming a sequence of growing severity inching toward apocalypse; Morton points out that tragedy is an agrilogistic mode, one that we ought to rethink in the Anthropocene.[31] And while resistance to a third world war has led to important planetary changes, including especially the founding and functioning of the United Nations, the dominant, progressivist temporality persists all the same. *Homesickness* proposes a radical rethinking of that temporality by recognizing time's backward function, the way that subjectivity is formulated retrospectively and in circular fashion.

Tension between the violent, global temporality of world wars and the more circular temporalities of seasons, ecologies, and subjectivity plays out with special rigor in Hemingway's work. Barely old enough to enter the theater of the Great War, Hemingway became significantly cosmopolitan in his orientation, largely spurred by his time serving in Italy in World War I. His cosmopolitanism involved not only a lifelong interest in international experiences; some capacity in multiple languages, including Spanish, French, and German; and an abiding curiosity about ostensibly authentic experiences. It also involved, as part and parcel of his cosmopolitanism, a profound sense of human weakness and mortality. His oeuvre is inescapably marked by his own injuries in war and by the difficulty of thinking in ways not determined by the logic of war. Indeed, the primary conflict at the heart of *A Farewell to Arms,* for instance, between the soldiering self and the more broadly human or animal self, is synecdoche for that tension throughout Hemingway's own life and his historical period more generally. In that book, Frederic Henry clings desperately to his nonwar self, his embodied self, only to become immersed in a finally tragic domesticity that delivers death in the time and place of birth.[32]

Hemingway criticism has recognized the importance of this trauma from the very beginning, in Philip Young's wound theory studies published before Hemingway died. But debate about what this trauma means, or how to understand it, has persisted to this day. *Homesickness* complicates Young's position and its subsequent influence. In a nutshell, Young urges that Hemingway's war traumas led him to exaggerate his masculinity in other spheres of life, trying to heal or compensate for what was broken.[33] Young is clearly correct that trauma was central to Hemingway's writing and experience, but Young's approach tacitly affirms an overly simplistic notion of the self against which he contrasts Hemingway. That is, Young compares Hemingway to a fantasy, an unrealistic notion of gender identity and of ostensibly healthy or normal subjectivity that we might call "normate," following Rosemarie Garland Thomson in her work on disability studies.[34] With this term, Thomson aims to underscore the constructedness of this category "normal," complicating the logic of what is often seen as "disability." Thus Young's sense of Hemingway's injured subjectivity relies on an unrealistic version of the normal.

By contrast, *Homesickness* has shown how the trauma of loss characterizes much of modern and contemporary life, even if that is often disavowed. Further, Hemingway was one of a whole generation—indeed, several generations—of people profoundly affected by the trauma of the world wars and other conflicts, well beyond veterans, a point that I make most fully below, with reference to the Vietnam War and the novel *In Country*. So with the benefit of greater temporal distance than Young had, I suggest there is a measure of denial at work in Young's wound theory, which effectively reaffirms a simplistic notion of subjectivity by triangulating against Hemingway's traumas. Rather than, or perhaps in addition to being unusually traumatized, Hemingway can be well understood as unusually insightful about traumas, due to both war and modernity's upheavals more generally—war often represents and intensifies modernity's upheavals.

A central trauma of the Great War was the widespread sense of soldiers' passivity and weakness in the face of powerful modern technologies of violence. As Alex Vernon notes, "One historical consensus about World War I is the unprecedented degree to which its soldiers were rendered passive by the new technology of machine guns, indirect fire artillery, and mustard gas."[35] That trauma was redoubled by World War II and especially by the terrifying power of nuclear weapons. Both of these traumas presage—and materially, concretely advance—the massive new shock of the Anthropocene.

Soldiers worked hard then and now to claim some measure of agency. Hemingway's story of Lieutenant Frederic Henry in *A Farewell to Arms* turns on his renewed assertion of a selfhood and agency outside of the military, after his desertion. The book nonetheless displays deep awareness that Henry's agency is always limited, often profoundly so. That is perhaps the central theme of the novel. Consider the full shape of the plot in terms of Henry's agency: it begins with a brief spark of romance interrupted by war that gets Henry hospitalized, where in a much-reduced condition, his and Catherine's romance genuinely blooms. Yet he must return again to the fighting and only deserts when his other choice is being assassinated.

After his escape from near execution, Henry's circumstances convey his utter desperation and weakness, his reduction to what Giorgio Agamben calls "bare life" as a body reduced to seemingly discrete fragments.[36] Henry, bettering his escape by hiding on a train, replays the recent events in his mind. "Lying on the floor of the flat-car," he considers that his new knee

> had been very satisfactory. Valentini had done a fine job. I had done half the retreat on foot and swum part of the Tagliamento with his knee. It was his knee all right. The other knee was mine. Doctors did things to you and then it was not your body any more. The head was mine, and the inside of the belly. It was very hungry in there. I could feel it turn over on itself. The head was mine, but not to use, not to think with, only to remember and not too much remember. (231)

Henry can claim only partial ownership, partial control of his person. His surgically repaired knee is, he thinks, the doctor's, and though Henry tries to reclaim something like his basic self in his mind and stomach, appetite too can be understood as beyond the subject's control.

This is a posthumanist self, even a cyborg self, constructed via technology and medical techniques. Indeed, Henry's recognition that he does not own his whole body is symptomatic or synecdochic of war in general. As noted above, war estranges us from our bodies and from familiar places. In Jameson's terms quoted above, Henry's experience reveals how war transforms "the familiar into the alien, the *heimlich* into the *unheimlich*."[37] It also instrumentalizes humans, making us machinelike parts of the larger war machine ensemble. Henry rejects the politics of this objectification when he mocks his would-be assassins at the moment of his desertion: "The questioners had that beautiful detachment and devotion to stern justice of men dealing in death without being in any danger of it" (224–25).

Henry's account of memory also reverses the familiar hierarchical binary of subject/memory: instead of the subject steering through recollections, recollections pull the subject after them, hauntingly. The memories thus seem bigger and more powerful than the self, signifying the presence of the nonself—in memory—inside the self. Memory is a kind of uncanny self, both utterly familiar and strange. In the passage quoted above, Henry shows awareness of these estranging traumas in a backward way, by insisting he *does* own part of himself. Here is Hemingway's famous iceberg principle, where the large psychological traumas that put self-ownership in doubt loom behind these simple sentences declaring self-ownership. These dramatic failures of self-ownership echo a pattern underscored throughout *Homesickness*, made clear especially in chapter 2 on burning down the house, in chapter 4 on slavery and *Beloved*, and in chapter 5 on shopping.

Read this way, Hemingway is radically reversing stereotypically masculinist notions of a powerful selfhood, though his declarative and minimalist style can make such gestures difficult to see, a difficulty that appears everywhere in the cultural and critical responses to his writing, where, too often, Hemingway's often distressingly hypermasculine persona in real life is read back onto his writing in a way that distorts that work.[38] It is better to recognize that posturing as a sign of a radically estranged, homesick subjectivity seeking new modes of being. Indeed, Henry's insistence that his selfhood involves remembering, but "not too much," strikes much the same note, in practically the same language, as Toni Morrison's Sethe, facing another horrible trauma, as discussed in chapter 4.

In this passage, as in the larger plot of the book, Henry, per necessity, leaves the complexities of war and tries to return to the basics of life outside political and warring identity—eating, resting, and simple and loving companionship. This regrounding of selfhood in the animal body helps save Henry's sanity. Indeed, ironically perhaps, orienting himself more simply in his body helps *rehumanize* him after the brutality of war. This posthumanist gesture—reconceiving embodiment and human animality as heartening—offers a model of hope and learning in Anthropocene trauma. But even here he cannot dispense with the past; his knee is not even his own, and his memories must be warded off.

That otherness inside the self also appears in the hunger that Henry tries to own for himself and to mark as distinct from his repaired knee. "The head" and "the inside of the belly" are his, he claims, but the phrasing "hungry in there" and "I could feel it turn over on itself" points to appetite as a force that has its own kind of power within the heterogeneous subject, like a cramp. Hunger is another fundamental example of homesickness. We do not own it. It belongs instead to a physiology that long predates and continues to supersede *Homo sapiens*. Hemingway's concrete account of the strange and estranging reality of hunger, pulling us out of any kind of neatly bound self, significantly reworks what it means to be human, an insight made more possible precisely by the uncanny sense of selfhood that follows traumatic experience. The strangeness of hunger is kin to the strangeness of traumatic experience. Indeed, considered carefully, all experience is strange or uncanny because actual experience is not a concept; it is an undertaking.

Similarly, the dread of too much memory points to Henry's limited ownership of his thought. This limitation is easier to see in trauma, but in fact none of us entirely owns our thoughts, since they are imbricated in a much larger network of understanding that includes language and its nonhuman technicity. That technicity includes mechanisms of writing, recording, archiving, distributing, and so on, all of which condition how language and memory function for us, a dimension of posthumanism accented by Cary Wolfe in *What Is Posthumanism?*, as noted in my introduction. Indeed, as Wolfe remarks, our thoughts take shape not just from language and culture but from the biological context we have evolved from and depend on.[39] In effect, even memory, I suggest, is more-than-human because it involves and relies on the world.

Henry *wants* to own stomach and mind because, even though they also do things to him, like war to some extent, they participate in a more fundamental economy of the subject that is not as corrupted by injustice. The passage reveals, via style, an intersubjectivity, or more robustly, it reveals what Donna Haraway calls "sympoiesis," the reality that each person and each creature of whatever kind is always necessarily making life together with the world, with other people and animals, with minerals, oxygen, and so on.[40]

The central question of *A Farewell to Arms*, we could say, is what kind of sympoiesis will be pursued, one inside or outside the war effort. Henry persists in his war selfhood out of a sense of duty until it becomes a clear question of life or death. Upon deserting, his relationship with Catherine genuinely blooms. That relationship is thus positioned in stark contrast to the violent and objectifying selfhood of war. The contrast is sharper than is sometimes recognized. Vernon underscores, for example, the strikingly unconventional gender logic that animates their developing relationship: "Frederic falls in love with her in Book II only after his wounding, after finding himself in her care—after, that is, he finds himself in a passive position, which in Hemingway's time was associated with the feminine and, in men, with the homosexual."[41] Much can be said about these dynamics, but for my purposes here, suffice to underscore that Henry's deep and direct acquaintance with the ultimately unavoidable truths of weakness and mortality enables an embrace of love and intersubjectivity. That same movement characterizes Hemingway's larger thinking about nonhuman nature. The traumas of the Anthropocene can function similarly, I have been claiming, encouraging and even requiring a redefinition of ourselves as posthumanist partners in care with the nonhuman.

Emphasizing the interimplication of Henry's injury and his romance with Catherine, the novel turns to her immediately following the passage about Henry's knee. Again signaling how aggrieved and delicate memory is in his condition, Henry allows that he "could remember Catherine," but not too much or he "would get crazy" with missing her (231). The right measure of memory weighs against, in Hemingway's metaphor from *For Whom the Bell Tolls,* the spinning "flywheel" of his thoughts.[42] But they nonetheless commence to spinning in this critical moment of the book. Henry considers that he "did not love the floor of a flat-car nor guns with canvas jackets" but that he

> loved some one else whom now you knew was not even to be pretended there; you seeing now very clearly and coldly—not so coldly as clearly and emptily. You saw emptily, lying on your stomach, having been present when one army moved back and another came forward. You had lost your cars and your men as a floorwalker loses the stock of his department in a fire. There was, however, no insurance. You were out of it now. You had no more obligation. (*A Farewell to Arms,* 232)

This vision's clarity derives from comprehension of the individual's place in modern war. Henry recognizes himself as a mere body in the conflict, a pawn who had "been present" in a larger scheme. This sentence's passive construction, which is followed by an abstract account of the movement of armies that does not delineate allegiance, marks the reduction to bare body, as does the seemingly zeugmatic simile that likens losing men and cars to losing "stock." Henry's awareness of his fragile bodily status, moreover, is sharpened by his physical position as he thinks in this passage, lying on his stomach, still at risk of death.

Trauma has brought the self/body alterity—a kind of homesickness—into view here, and has driven a narrative that reclaims the self by way of a reestranging internal monologue that works to comprehend bewildering war experiences of the past.[43] He is thinking retrospectively. Henry recognizes himself anew as a physical body, and that helps him free himself in a kind of postwar baptism: "Anger was washed away in the river along with any obligation" (232). Even though he is still in the conflict zone, he has consciously left the war. Continuing to work backward into Hemingway's narrative (in a homesick fashion), we can thus revisit the novel's previous chapter, when Henry escapes into the river. Physically performing his separation from the war effort, Henry offers a radically posthumanist description of himself, his person, as flotsam among other objects in a great river: "I was lucky to have a heavy timber to hold on to, and I lay in the icy water with my chin on the wood, holding as easily as I could with both hands. I was afraid of cramps and I hoped we would move toward the shore. We went down the river in a long curve" (226).

Mentally catching up to rapidly unfolding worldly events—and again thereby demonstrating the lag time between events and their comprehension, the homesickness of subjectivity—Henry understands himself here in terms of his physical position. He is on the level of the timber he is floating with. Its company—this status of company is signaled by the repeated pronoun "we"—contrasts with the human, military companions he has just left. Trauma forces Henry into this recognition of sheer human materiality, or bodily weakness, but also companionship and solidarity with the nonhuman. That is, "we" ironically reinforces the sense that the human situation could not be endured. His only friend is a piece of driftwood. Henry escapes the war by relying on a primitive tool, which shows his status as another mere body, exposed to the river's current like driftwood.

This is technology at its most fundamental, but it calls up posthumanism with all its complex freight. The saving company of "objects" here functions like the company of language, which can also be seen as a mere object. That is, we should take this "we" seriously as well as ironically. Hemingway has recognized the war's lesson that the human can be reduced to mere body and is always partly body, but he refuses the haphazard and at times unjust application of this principle in war. The river flows beyond these human injustices, these imperfections, just as hunger and sexual desire partake of another economy of the human. But immersion in the river, as well as the surrender to hunger and desire, also admit the alterity and physicality of the human.

This moment evokes the fundamental tension in much of Hemingway's work between a conventionally masculinist, war-produced self and a radically other selfhood that finds companionship, for example, in the nonhuman floating timber, the Gulf Stream, Wyoming and Idaho forests, and so on. In *The Old Man and the Sea,* Santiago's passionate fellow-feeling for the marlin he hunts is an example,[44] as is the striking experimentation with gender, sexual, and species identity in *Garden of Eden,* a kind of experimentation that many critics have increasingly noticed also in the earlier work. Thus, for example, Vernon, cited above, applies some of the new insights about Hemingway's especially complex gender performances, insights provoked by the publication of *Garden of Eden,* to the earlier novel *A Farewell to Arms,* underscoring that Henry eroticizes his own injured passivity.

Henry escapes the brutal war to an ostensibly more simple, reliable form of life with Catherine, but Hemingway redoubles the trauma of this narrative when the small spark of life Henry helps nourish is extinguished—his and Catherine's child is stillborn—and Catherine hemorrhages to death from the birth as well. At the book's end, as these events dawn on Henry, he recognizes again the profound passivity of selfhood, turning to the panicked internal monologue Hemingway often uses in his oeuvre to evoke trauma. Having just learned of their child's death, Henry thinks:

> Now Catherine would die. That was what you did. You died. You did not know what it was about. You never had time to learn. They threw you in and told you the rules and the first time they caught you off base they killed you. Or they killed you gratuitously like Aymo. Or gave you the syphilis like Rinaldi. But they killed you in the end. You could count on that. Stay around and they would kill you. (327)

The deaths of Catherine and child are not just random, then; they exemplify the other events in the story. Exposure to massive systems of warfare turns individuals into meaningless victims, accenting—but, I would add, exaggerating—what is a basic fact of mortal human life. Our exposure to mortality, moreover, is something "you never had time to learn." We cannot catch up with the flux of events in time; we are homesick as subjects. Henry reads these deaths in the framework of war, generalizing and naturalizing them as inevitable. But the larger thrust of Hemingway's oeuvre relentlessly seeks other modes of being and other ways of framing experience. Often condemned as apolitical or antisocial, his deep, abiding interest in pursuits like hunting, fishing, skiing, and the like are better understood as attempts to escape the overpowering impacts of war on the social during his lifetime. In that way, they are not only deeply political; they are also useful models for rethinking selfhood in the Anthropocene.

The soldier's struggle to maintain a meaningful sense of agency, a sense of worthwhile control over his own life, is also an organizing principle of

Hemingway's *For Whom the Bell Tolls,* his novel about the Spanish Civil War in the late 1930s. We can thus read this novel as a renewed attempt by Hemingway to come to terms with the subjectivity of the soldier, to name it, locate it, and thus possibly enable other ways of seeing life, efforts that genuinely bloom in the next decade of his life in his writing about his second African safari, his rethinking the dynamics of fishing in *The Old Man and the Sea,* and so on.

Generally, *For Whom the Bell Tolls* investigates the Civil War by focusing on a small group's efforts to resist the fascists. This structural decision implicitly emphasizes that the human scale of value is generally much narrower than the scale of the larger war. That is, the book's basic parameters reiterate how war often dwarfs individual value, a point powerfully underscored by protagonist Robert Jordan's death at the book's end, and by the novel's first and final sentences, both of which position the protagonist as lying flat on the ground. Still, Hemingway seeks meaning and value in what Jordan does. To do so, the novel takes as one of its purposes, to borrow Robert Jordan's words, telling "what we did. Not what the others did to us" (134). That is a succinctly Hemingwayesque definition of agency. This task is carried out perhaps most clearly in Pilar's famous, self-consciously horrible account of mercilessly killing the fascists in their village (103–30). In Pilar's telling, the behavior of the townspeople erodes until they become a mere "mob" (121), each feeding on the brutality of the others, with no one in control. Thus, again, individual agency is undermined.

Hemingway's exploration of the realities and limitations of individual value in war is also apparent in Jordan working to accept his role in the conflict. He considers, "You're a bridge-blower now. Not a thinker. Man, I'm hungry, he thought" (17). He is trying to convince himself to focus. For him, the abstraction "war" equals the specific task "bridge-blower." Carrying out his particular duty, with few delusions about its significance, returns Jordan to the body and hunger, which are regular sanity-saving provinces in Hemingway, especially in the face of debilitating circumstances. Robert Jordan persistently works to sustain the focus required to complete his assigned task, in the face of a gnawing, repressed awareness of his larger insignificance. To prevent himself from facing this insignificance, a fact that might lead a thinking person like Jordan to stand aside from the war entirely as Frederic Henry ultimately decides to do, Jordan repeatedly, forcefully narrows his attention back to local and embodied circumstances.

In other words, one accomplishment of this novel is its revelation of the constant effort required to produce a soldier's mentality. It underscores the need for paring away other parts of one's humanity to maintain the necessary focus. Hemingway carefully sustains this depiction of a soldier's selfhood through the book's conclusion, where he puts Jordan on the edge of an inevitable and immediate death, waiting to perform one "thing well done" a final time. He is "completely integrated" into the mountains, and in the novel's final sentence, "He could feel his heart beating against the pine needle floor of the forest" (471). As a rendering of death, this scene calls to mind Greek accounts of war as risking "a sort of ontological collapse into the ground itself," in Mary A. Favret's terms.[45]

Earlier in the novel—continuing my homesick method of analysis, moving backward in the text—the night before the attack and the bridge-blowing that are central to the plot, Jordan's internal dialogue registers anxiety about his wartime role, which modulates into worries about becoming pure stuff, about ontological collapse, about, that is, dying. In a moment reminiscent of the passages from *A Farwell to Arms* discussed above, Jordan is quietly panicking. He is self-conscious that this is happening, that he has "been concentrating so hard on something" that his "brain gets to racing like a flywheel with the weight gone" (340). He encourages himself to "remember something concrete and practical. Remember Grandfather's saber, bright and well oiled in its dented scabbard. . . . Remember Grandfather's Smith and Wesson" (336). But this effort works imperfectly. Those memories return him inevitably to the trauma associated with the Civil War in which his grandfather fought with this sword and gun, and to his father's suicide with the same pistol. In other words, he is drawn back to facing the same core concern about the flimsiness of individual selfhood, its expendability, especially in war. These traumas, reaching well beyond his subjectivity and his own temporality (that is, beyond his lifetime), nonetheless essentially make and condition who Henry is. The novel displays that psychological process, that production and reinforcement of Henry's selfhood.

Another way to put this is that Jordan is shifting between the local and the general. The limits and the materiality of the bodied life show both in the content of the memories themselves and in the *desire* to remember something physical, which is described as a sanity-saving practice. Jordan's metaphor—"like a flywheel with the weight gone"—presents this accurately. "Weight" evokes sheer matter, and the need for this weight, like thinking about hunger, allows him to play the role he feels is required of him by his world. "Weight" brings Jordan back to the real, palpable, material world at hand, where he can actually perform an act, even if he knows it is not very significant in the broader scheme of things. Recognizing the materiality of the self enables situated action. Henry has to localize his sense of self to have any impact or agency. In the broader terms of *Homesickness,* action, even when oriented by larger, possibly planetary purposes, is always also local and material.

Jordan is clearly aware that he is tricking himself to some extent. He recognizes the desperation, even the absurdity, of the whole set of circumstances.[46] Does this one act of bridge-blowing *really* matter? This self-consciousness can therefore be read as a social critique, or more pointedly as a critique of war, especially modern war. Broadly speaking, this critique is quite clear when Hemingway, as detailed by biographer Carlos Baker, describes himself going to Spain as an "anti-war war correspondent."[47] That trip, on which he would write journalism reports,[48] led him to eventually write *For Whom the Bell Tolls,* and seemed only to confirm his antiwar beliefs. On that point, Baker quotes an article Hemingway wrote for *Esquire* on the approach of World War II; Hemingway argued that modern war resulted from "demagogues and dictators who play on the patriotism of their people to mislead them into a belief in the great fallacy of war when all their vaunted reforms have failed to satisfy the people they misrule."[49]

Despite his profound skepticism, though, Hemingway, not unlike his character Robert Jordan, embraced war when doing so seemed necessary, admitting he even took a guilty but significant pleasure in his involvement in it.[50] The version of selfhood Hemingway thus displays is complex. He recognizes fully how warfare can entirely efface the value of the individual, can destroy lives for corrupt reasons, and so on. The thoughtful, moral, and cosmopolitan dimension of Hemingway thus rejected war. But another side of him acknowledged that humans are mortal creatures caught in the sometime necessity of war. This too is a moral position. He inhabits both of these divergent beliefs, often uneasily.

Consider the larger narrative of Hemingway's war writing for further evidence of this mixed attitude. Jordan's story ends in death, and Henry reducing himself to an individual body is no final cure, in light of the novel's many other traumas. Indeed, in Hemingway's oeuvre, the earlier book *The Sun Also Rises* reveals what might happen to a Henry, since it follows chronologically

Henry's story. *The Sun Also Rises* treats the postwar experiences of people confronting their broken worlds and broken selves. Hemingway's oeuvre thus functions in a homesick fashion, with the earlier novel treating later events, and vice versa. His characters do not fit in any longer; everything has become strange or uncanny for them. Their alienation from the usual roles is perhaps most clearly signaled by Jake's war injury, which disables the potential story lingering at the edges of that novel: instead of a romance plot between Jake and Brett, we have irony, loss, and sadness, and the book seems to question the very possibility of a genuine love plot. In other words, the romantic narrative that organized many earlier versions of the novel is blasted *prior* to the book's inception, due to Jake's famous war wound. Masculinity itself is cut to its core here as the very condition of the novel's discourse, and love becomes only a fantasy, a dream, something "pretty to think," in the marvelously horrible final sentence of *The Sun Also Rises.*

The Humanity They Carried in Vietnam

The stark difference between "pretty" thoughts and present reality, of course, haunts many war narratives. Henry's reorientation of himself as a body helps him escape the war, but without obvious alternative stories to follow, without possible life patterns not centered around war, many veterans simply rush headlong back into the fight when possible. The drastically circumscribed, hyperspecialized, and dehumanized selfhood produced by and for war, in other words, has its own powerful momentum and logic; once made into a soldier, a person often finds it difficult to be anything else. Or, abiding by the reductive life-or-death logic of war, the traumas of soldier subjectivity can lead to suicide, as a veteran reckons his or her own utter loss of familiar personal value. These circumscriptions and reductions of subjectivity, it should be said, are only more severe versions of what happens in laboring and capitalist subjectivity more generally, which, I argued in chapter 5, can be understood to be produced by slow violence. Examples of such fickle psychic uneasiness in and after war can be seen by reaching ahead in time to the Vietnam War.

Such questions about the soldier's relation to home are at the core of Tim O'Brien's celebrated short story "The Things They Carried," which is oriented around homesickness and its final excision from the protagonist.[51] This piece of traumatic literature, like Hemingway's war writing, broods on the transformation of important materiality into sheer dross, into weight that must be carried; hence O'Brien's title, also the title of the larger book. When Ted Lavender, one of the soldiers, is shot and killed in the story, his very body becomes waste, material that must be hauled. This tension between sheer, blank matter and important materiality is precisely at stake in much trauma literature more generally. In homesickness, one's own body is always at risk of becoming matter without legibility or importance—that is the condition of dislocation, of being a refugee. Similarly, as Vernon reports, Sam Hynes's term for what war does to the environment is "antilandscape," a place where everything is "grotesque, broken, useless rubbish—including human limbs."[52] War threatens to flatten everything, including people, into this same antilandscape, an utterly uncanny place.

O'Brien's story names and criticizes the kind of reduced selfhood that war requires. Everything is life or death. For the conscientious leader Lieutenant Jimmy Cross in "The Things They Carried," these life-or-death terms involve an impossibly heavy burden, an excessive responsibility. He tries to function as a perfect soldier, and he worries that his thoughts of home distract him from the conflict and lead to Ted Lavender's death. Yet Lieutenant Cross seems unfairly hard on himself. His daydreams of home, home represented and condensed in the personage of Martha, cannot really be faulted for Lavender's bad luck. And yet, if the commander is not responsible in some measure, who is? Lavender's death raises the broader question of individual agency in war, positioned as all agents are in a network that far outstrips the individual self. How far does one person's responsibility go in a war zone? That question too is terrifying. Perhaps it is better to feel the blame as Cross does than to feel utterly impotent, exposed to the whims of fate.

O'Brien narrates Lavender's death scene so that the character who really seems to be in danger is Lee Strunk, who unfortunately draws the unlucky number seventeen. He is thereby charged with exploring one of the enemy tunnels before that platoon uses explosives on them. O'Brien evokes the uncanny disorientation of being in the tunnel, feeling the "cobwebs and ghosts, whatever was down there—the tunnel walls squeezing in—how the flashlight seemed impossibly heavy in the hand and it was tunnel vision in the very strictest sense, compression in all ways, even time" (10). This is part of the estranging selfhood of soldiering.

But Strunk suffers no injury this time. Instead, even more shockingly, even less understandably, Lavender gets hit. He was ostensibly among the lucky staying out of the tunnels, at least this one time, and he is casually urinating, an utterly ordinary activity. Indeed, the irony of Lavender's death is heightened by the coincidence of Strunk's emergence from the tunnel, making "a funny ghost sound, a kind of moaning, yet very happy," a sound that can only be rendered phonically: "*Ahhooooo,* right then Ted Lavender was shot in the head on his way back from peeing" (12). Strunk's luck; Lavender's misfortune, so directly adjacent as to be dizzying. Life and death are too closely intertwined to separate them properly. Strunk's alinguistic sound, meant as a kind of grim joke—since he made it out!—ironically and even more horribly articulates the unspeakable surprise of Lavender being killed, despite all expectations. It resembles the "animal keening" discussed in chapter 5. The estranged identity of a soldier, then: there is the steady, deliberate creating and disciplining of a soldier's selfhood out of a civilian, and then there are these shocks in war that go well beyond, that are so much harder to absorb and understand, producing a long lag time of comprehension, a soldier's homesickness of self.

So in the posttraumatic language of the story, Lavender is "zapped while zipping," as Kiowa puts it with a grim playfulness, a gallows humor (17). It does not make any sense. Urinating is too ordinary an activity to bring death. It throws off everything we thought we knew about being a body, and the story registers this shock through the technique of estranged repetition, with Kiowa repeating what he cannot understand, the sight of Lavender simply dropping, "boom down" (6, 7, 17). The story is rife with other repetitions, which turn denotation into something else, something stuttering, something unnamable, something "Ahhooooo." As Kiowa continues riffing, joking in fact, trying to wrap his mind around this sudden, stunning death, his platoon-mate Norman Bowker says, "Why not shut the fuck *up*?" After a few more exchanges, Kiowa does just that, but then the silence is also too much to bear. Bowker comes back with this: "What the hell, he said. You want to talk, *talk.* Tell it to me" (18–19). Language proves both radically insufficient to represent the intense exigency of war and utterly necessary because the silence can be worse. This uneasy relationship to language in trauma is similarly crucial in Morrison's *Beloved,* treated in chapter 4, and in much of Hemingway's work. Morrison insists in her foreword to *Beloved,* for example, writing about the challenges of conveying trauma, that "to render enslavement as a personal experience, language must get out of the way."[53] Yet, it is clear, this is achieved in a novel through language.

O'Brien multiplies the perverse logic of war by driving the story toward its conclusion with Lieutenant Cross's decision to "dispense with love" (26). In this construction, "love" is one more thing that must be carried and that is, therefore, liable to be "dispensed with," like so much dross. The hypermobility of the story makes everything a person might carry into a weight that might bring them down to death, to ontological flatness, a point made relentlessly and formally with O'Brien's lists of the things soldiers carried. But the logic of these lists themselves also fractures, as they consistently move from literal objects toward intangible elements of subjectivity like "love." All these carried "things" are exposed to the hyperreality of war's life and death, and all of them, even love, become too much to bear. They expose soldiers to risk. "Love" and "subjectivity" become more crap to hump up and down the very real yet entirely dreamlike hills of Vietnam in this dizzying conflict that seemingly no one can understand.

These lists, then, upend representation itself, making the story a site where language fails, where narrative cannot be told, even as it must be. The hierarchies and distinctions that characterize systems of meaning are flattened in these horrible circumstances, and Cross finds himself dispensing with anything and everything, including love. What is left? For many veterans, only more war, as ordinary subjectivity must be stripped away in order to do justice to the exigencies and responsibilities of the fight. It is extraordinarily difficult for many veterans to put that humanity back after the conflict. In 2016 Tim O'Brien testified to the terrible power of these transformations to the veteran of war in a powerful keynote speech to the Hemingway Society in Hemingway's birthplace, Oak Park, Illinois, remarking on the difficulty connected to writing anything at all after war (among many other themes).[54]

War is akin to cosmopolitanism in that, in both, the self is exposed to radically other standards and norms of subjectivity. In war, and especially in the Vietnam War, identity, particularity, and place are evacuated in the slow violence of pure movement, as O'Brien shows with his treatment of "humping," of moving self and matériel from place to place, such that everything becomes a burden, subject to being jettisoned.[55] This logic of mobility and "creative destruction" not only serves capitalism in the Vietnam War and other wars; it also resembles capitalism's internal logic, as my wording signals: places become spaces for economic production and workers are deracinated from systems of meaning outside economics. War strips us down to pure soldiers; capitalism strips us down to mere economic entities.

As Wendy Brown argues in *Undoing the Demos,* neoliberalism works to make economic forms of understanding the only relevant ones, eliminating other forms of meaning in a violence akin to Cross's decision to dispense with love.[56]

O'Brien uses the dystopia, the nonplace of pure movement, or humping, to signify a criticism of such wars. While the circumstances of war heighten this emptying out of subjectivity, mobility itself is a parallel force that relativizes and undermines the cultural and emotional attributes many people stake their lives on. From one perspective, this is exactly what is meant by "postmodernism"; it is the exposure of even cosmopolitan truths about selfhood to a corrosive relativism.

But the willful self-destruction of creating a soldiering self is not complete in O'Brien's book. Even the apparently hard-boiled, hyperreal declaration by Cross that he will "dispense with love" proves faulty. We learn in the story "Love" that follows "The Things They Carried" that when Cross meets Martha again, years later at a college reunion, "nothing had changed. He still loved her."[57] At first, this feeling may seem welcome. But perversely, this declaration itself begins to seem like a betrayal, like the proper emotional response to Lavender's death is indeed to engage in that inner death-while-living that would be the end of love. Cross seems unable to enjoy what might have been the stoic, ascetic satisfaction of being entirely without sentiment, making him seem even less at home in any kind of functional self. One way to understand this twist in the story—Cross's abiding love for Martha—is that human emotion evades subjective control; it is a wild thing unto itself. No doubt it is the power of such passion that helps explain war itself, the classic endeavor that testifies to the failure of human reason.

Like Hemingway, O'Brien shows how the traumas of modern war reduce the self to a body and to bare life, in Hemingway's case a body whose survival depends precisely on the focus on hunger, embodiment, and fundamental animal joys. Recognizing these basic bodily facts strangely humanizes Hemingway's Henry and pulls him back from the maddening brink of absolute violence that is a military force killing its own members. O'Brien's narrative conceit turns human characters into humpers, into pack animals whose identities are revealed by what few things they *decide* to carry. These few items thus become tokens of identity, the thin shreds of the soldiers' former selfhood—a toothbrush, extra rations, tranquilizers, and foot powder. In the deindividualizing circumstances of war, personality can barely appear, by way of these small signs. Over the course of the narrative, the lieutenant dramatically dispenses even with many of those. He burns the photographs and letters of his love, Martha, as he also surrenders love itself.

The story's criticism of war derives force in large part from the success of this device—individuality signified as mere tokens, serving more to parody or perhaps simply expose selfhood in war than to celebrate it—and then even these tokens must be surrendered under the impossible pretense of perfect attention, caution, leadership, and the hyperagency of the ideal modern soldier. Global capitalism, with its commodity fetishism coupled with deracination, has a similar tendency to reduce individual identities to brand names and other reductive statements of selfhood. As Gary Cross shows in *Consumed Nostalgia,* even nostalgia is not what it used to be, as it is increasingly perceived and expressed via (mass-produced) consumer objects.[58]

While Martha functions in "The Things They Carried" as an index of home, a kind of register of Cross's own changes, she also seems to be a witness or a comrade in a larger sense. Martha is characterized throughout the story as somewhat distant, and this distance proves justified, as though her experience as a woman has taught her to keep a cool remove from others. In this regard, it is as though Cross, finally himself coming to terms with Lavender's death, catches up to Martha's emotional sophistication. At the end of the story, she is presented as a kind of fellow traveler in observing the emotional damage of men.

> Briefly, in the rain, Lieutenant Cross saw Martha's gray eyes gazing back at him.
>
> He understood.
>
> It was very sad, he thought. The things men carried inside. The things men did or felt they had to do.
>
> He almost nodded at her, but didn't. (24–25)

By this point, Cross has recognized that Martha does not love him, and he further sees that she is from "another world" (24), and yet her distant eyes somehow come to measure how much he had lost, how the death of Lavender would now be the thing Cross carried inside, instead of his ideal thoughts of Martha and of home. He has, in a sense, traveled so far from his native sense of self that he must dispense with it. It no longer serves. He has become sick of his ideas of home.

The estrangement of home, or homesickness, is rendered perhaps most dramatically by O'Brien's character Mary Anne in the story "Sweetheart of the Song Tra Bong" in *The Things They Carried.*[59] This "strange story" begins as an impossible kind of soldier's dream: a soldier brings his own girlfriend to him out in the thick of the theater of war in Vietnam. The girlfriend is presented as a kind of stereotypical, ideal vision of youthful beauty, a "cute blonde—just a kid, just barely out of high school—she shows up with a suitcase and one of those plastic cosmetic bags." Rat Kiley, telling the story, insists she wore "white culottes and this sexy pink sweater" (90). The vision emphasizes her appealing innocence and may at first seem to retrench the divide between men and women when it comes to war. This "friendly" girl "fresh out of Cleveland Heights Senior High" (93) spends some time in a kind of idyllic romance—right in the middle of a war zone—with her boyfriend, Mark Fossie. The extreme oddness of this romance accents the gulf of difference between the world of home and the reality of wartime Vietnam.

But this figure of feminine innocence, perhaps the clearest distillation of what many soldiers miss most about home, quickly begins to change. She feels increasingly curious about the war, wanting to learn more about it, and she begins asking around. She journeys out into the field, rather fearlessly, and she surrenders more and more of the signs of home, quitting her cosmetics and other hygiene (98), learning how to perform soldierly tasks like how to "disassemble an M-16" rifle, and changing in other fundamental ways. "There was a new confidence in her voice," O'Brien writes, and "Cleveland Heights now seemed very far away" (98). These changes in her begin to make her boyfriend uncomfortable, and his unease assumes a particular intensity when she disappears one night. It turns out she has begun going on nighttime ambushes with the Green Berets, and she returns the next morning changed nearly beyond recognition, wearing "a bush hat and filthy green fatigues; she carried the standard M-16 assault rifle; her face was black with charcoal" (102).

She and Mark try to repair their relationship, but Mary Anne has become a particularly focused and capable soldier, and she soon disappears on a three-week patrol with the Green Berets. When Mark and his compatriots next find her, she is in the Green Berets' quarters, a place of primal horror. The smell, we are told, "paralyzed your lungs. Thick and numbing, like an animal's den, a mix of blood and scorched hair and excrement and the sweet-sour odor of moldering flesh—the stink of the kill" (109–10). There are piles of bones, animal skins, and then Mary Anne: "For a moment she seemed to be the same pretty girl who had arrived a few weeks earlier. She was barefoot. She wore her pink sweater and a white blouse and a simple cotton shirt," but her eyes looked "utterly flat and indifferent," and she was adorned with "a necklace of human tongues" (110).

The scene is designed to be uncanny, to be *unheimlich,* to estrange a familiar image of a familiar woman who had been an idealized vision of the safe, ostensibly feminine home of the United States but who has become utterly changed. As Vernon asserts more generally, "One distinct aspect of war for twentieth-century Americans is that it has occurred entirely on foreign soil, that in every case it has been an *over there* experience that (with some notable exceptions) has excluded American women, so that women and love become associated in the male psyche with a very distant home."[60] For O'Brien, then, working changes on this idealized American woman means ringing changes on home itself.

In other words, Mary Anne evokes the fact that home itself has forever changed for the soldiers. The primal room of the Green Berets, like "an animal's den," is a more essential home for agrilogistic and wartime humanity in this account. It reveals what was inside Mary Anne's curiosity and desire, and she does not *want* to return to her innocent selfhood. She insists, furthermore, that these changes are "'not *bad*,'" that even though she feels "scared sometimes," she is more herself. She says, "'I feel close to myself. When I'm out there at night, I feel close to my own body, I can feel my blood moving, my skin and my fingernails, everything, it's like I'm full of electricity and I'm glowing in the dark—I'm on fire almost—I'm burning away into nothing—but it doesn't matter because I know exactly who I am'" (111).

Mary Anne has become self-consciously, even superconsciously, embodied, owning her—our—animality. The heightened stakes of her night patrols have intensified her awareness of what she can become. She also offers a familiar representation of immersion in observation—"I'm burning away into nothing"—that resembles Emerson's transparent eyeball experience and Ruth's surrender to the natural world, discussed in chapter 2. If when Mary Anne first appears she answers the men's feelings of homesickness and desire, those very feelings turn against them, turn profoundly strange, underscoring the fact that soldiers can never really come home again. And this implicitly means that "home" ceases to exist for the women who inhabit it too, even for the silent many who never leave the safe, North American shore, because they will be rejoined by radically changed veterans and because the women have had their own estranging experiences at home.

Mary Anne's innocent curiosity is akin to that of the newbie soldier, and even to that of the unknowing reader. She models me, author of this chapter. She journeys into a kind of animalistic, wartime self-knowledge that becomes the reader's, observing what can happen to an ordinary, innocent curiosity in the circumstances of war. She is an image of all the soldiers, whose innocence disappears in the traumatic events of the war: "What happened to her, Rat said, was what happened to all of them. You come over clean and you get dirty and then afterward it's never the same" (114). O'Brien has put this tale into the words of Rat Kiley, a character who "had a reputation for exaggeration and overstatement, a compulsion to rev up the facts" (89). Rat never stops insisting that the story is true, but the reader knows clearly by this point in the book that everything in it is suspect, that "it's difficult to separate what happened from what seemed to happen," that "a true war story cannot be believed," and that frequently "the crazy stuff is true and the normal stuff isn't" (71). One lesson from the story of Mary Anne, and from O'Brien's larger book, is that the horrors of war put everything into question. They are profoundly disorienting, so much so that a dubious tale, even an outright lie, is sometimes the best approximation of experience. While this account of the power of fiction to reveal the truth better than the truth itself is a convention dating back to Sir Philip Sidney's defense of poetry and earlier,[61] it turns on the *unheimlich,* on how going "home" to the self is an uncanny and sometimes terrifying journey. This is complex homesickness of the sort discussed in the opening of *Homesickness*'s chapter 1.

To clarify, though: I am not arguing that Mary Anne's primal engagement in war is the deep inner truth of human identity. I am saying it is one such truth, as Frans de Waal suggests. I noted above his argument in *The Age of Empathy,* where he criticizes the idea that aggression is "the hallmark of humanity."[62] He recognizes the existence of war but understands it merely as one possible outcome among many others. My larger point is simply that a search for the home of the self is inevitably bound to turn surprising and uncanny, including a surprising capacity for peace and beneficence.

In other words, war underscores a posthumanist reality. In the face of war's danger, O'Brien writes later in the book, a profoundly disorienting "terror" means that "you're not human anymore. You're a shadow. You slip out of your own skin, like molting, shedding your own history and your own future, leaving behind everything you ever were or wanted or believed in" (211). In this case, "all you can do is whimper and wait," like a prey animal without language, a purely vulnerable thing (211). Vernon echoes such ideas of selfhood in his discussion of modern war, beginning with World War I but also before, in which "soldiers were rendered passive by the new technology of machine guns, indirect fire artillery, and mustard gas. Soldiers rarely had the opportunity to fight the enemy, not in the classic sense in which one's own agency and skill might affect the outcome." Instead, Vernon notes, soldiers confronted their passive powerlessness.[63]

In this vulnerability, Jeremy Bentham's insistence, echoed and underscored by Derrida and discussed earlier in *Homesickness,* resonates: that the question about how to treat living beings is not about what those beings are capable of but the reverse, whether they can suffer.[64] Indeed, the capability measure of a being's value begins to look very strange indeed in the context of war literature, as soldiers inhabit supercharged moments of agency, only to later become as exposed and powerless as other whimpering animals. A capabilities model of ethics cannot serve well in such cases; as Martha C. Nussbaum notes in *Frontiers of Justice,* the conventional story has it that humans are owed rights because they are capable of economic production and reasoning (or language, or other attributes),[65] but war demonstrates that humans are uniquely capable of committing great and grave horrors as well. Does this mean humans are owed an equally horrible mistreatment?

O'Brien uses a conventional, humanist notion of animality to evoke the potential horrors of human behavior, putting Mary Anne into an animal's den smelling of blood. A posthumanist reading should pause here as well. We can reverse this reading using animal studies, for example, to emphasize that O'Brien's animal cave is reductive of both humans and animals, to assert that the category "animal" is in fact very complicated and must necessarily imply not just the potential for violence but the other passions of love, community, and the like. Coming home to the bloody animal cave need not be an end point to a narrative that, in fact, sounds very much like that of Joseph Conrad's Kurtz, uttering, finally, "the horror, the horror."[66] I suggest above that war literature like O'Brien's requires us to own these human horrors as possible but not inevitable. Humanism's excessive confidence in reason and human goodness fails to account for systematized violence like warfare, or biopolitics more generally. But rejecting humanism entirely, ignoring the very real alternatives to war and violence, is also reductive. Posthumanist approaches better permit us to engage both the horrors of war and the alternative possibilities, preventing us from having to tiredly reassert a patently false human exceptionalism based on reason or language or the like.

The story of Mary Anne and of Vietnam more generally also returns us to the theoretical discussion of mobility in this book's introduction. Although many proponents of mobility have underscored the cosmopolitan potentials of travel, I have noted, by contrast, Stephen Greenblatt's insistence that mobility also bears a bloody history.[67] Vietnam, a war nearly global in its causes and execution, reiterates the need for caution about mobility. Soldiers like Mary Anne—innocent, and dimly aware of the very complex political history of South East Asia—may too easily assume they are confronting core facts of human life, when in fact the horrors of that war were also largely manufactured. It was far from necessary that Mary Anne and the other young Americans be sent into a war zone to learn what some presume to be essential truths. Similarly, human animality is a biological fact, but what it means to be animal is as various as the animal kingdom itself. Difference, alterity, and otherness in the context of war are a threat, but in the context, say, of travel—or even merely shopping—those very same differences become interesting and desirable. In the cases of war and shopping, though, alterity is simplified, to either something killable or something consumable.

Homesickness resists such commodification and dehumanization, finding in the rich complexity of more-than-human place a key counter to the violent, homogenizing forces of war and global capitalism. Indeed, contrary to the simplifications of postmodernist mobility, place considered carefully proves unknowable. Morton makes this case compellingly in *Dark Ecology*, arguing against the idea, increasingly prevalent since the 1970s, that places have disappeared. On the contrary, he claims, "From the standpoint of the genuinely post-modern ecological era, what has collapsed is (the fantasy of empty, smooth) *space*." Instead, "*place* has emerged in its truly monstrous uncanny dimension, which is to say its nonhuman dimension." For Morton, the ecological era involves coming to terms with the utter specificity of material reality, of Earth and other such places. Thus "our sense of planet is not a cosmopolitan rush but rather the uncanny feeling that there are all kinds of places at all kinds of scale: dinner table, house, street, neighborhood, Earth, biosphere, ecosystem, city, bioregion, country, tectonic plate."[68] Each place is distinct, "fragile and contingent" but also evanescent, fluttering; places, like all other things, Morton insists, are not constantly present but are folded together with time: "Place doesn't stay still, but bends and twists." Thus place "isn't some organic village we find ourselves in, nor indeed a city-state surrounded by fields." Resisting these familiar clichés of place, Morton instead argues, "The local is far from the totally known or knowable."[69] Place, rife with the human and the nonhuman existing at all different scales and unfolding in and with time, becomes mysterious in this account, uncanny or homesick. Or it is a radically different version of home.

The Vietnam War Comes Home

So what is it like to inhabit an estranged home during and after a time of war happening elsewhere, happening *over there*? Bobbie Ann Mason's compelling posttraumatic novel *In Country* treats the repercussions of Vietnam on a teenage girl named Sam in the United States.[70] The novel applies the phrase "in country," commonly designating the war zone, to mean the United States, where the war is not happening. Sam and all of us are "in country" at home, as it were, in the 1960s, 1970s, and after, confronting the horrors of soldiers' experiences as they return home from what was then the United States' longest war, alongside the other significant social upheavals and changes of the period.[71]

This focus on the experiences outside the combat zone leads Mason to underscore another important dimension of contemporary homesickness: its inherence in a media world, in a virtual world. Questions of the virtual lead beyond what I have space to explore here. But for my purposes in this chapter, it is enough to note how Mason's Vietnam veteran Emmett feels homesickness for the virtual world of the hit television show *M*A*S*H*. In this virtual space, where he can make comparisons between its characters and his actual fellow soldiers in Vietnam (25), he can perform alliances with characters by dressing up like Klinger (27), he can reckon, to some extent, his inconsolable experiences in Vietnam. The word "homesickness" is important here because it underscores how unsettling and disorienting the war experience is. Largely by way of the safe reenactment of it—via a television show—Emmett can begin to confront his traumatic experiences. Of course, the *M*A*S*H* program itself, its success in the United States, was a cultural form of confronting Vietnam through a prism. The show dealt with the Korean War but unmistakably commented on Vietnam as well.

The interpretive structure of war, I have argued, depends essentially on ideas of home, a point the main character Sam emphasizes to her boyfriend,

Lonnie, while they wait for her veteran uncle Emmett to be checked by the doctor. In war tale after war tale, soldiers justify and endure their hardships by remembering the peace of home. Sam says to Lonnie, "My mom said not to worry about what happened to Emmett back then [in the Vietnam War], because the war had nothing to do with me. But the way I look at it, it had everything to do with me. My daddy went over there to fight for Mom's sake, and Emmett went over there for Mom's sake and my sake, to get revenge" (after her father was killed). Sam then says to Lonnie, "If you went to war, I bet you'd say it was for me" (71). This feeling of home, and the structure of homesickness involved in going away to war, is fundamental to soldiers' actions. Mason's novel is premised on this fact, as it views the war through the lens of a young woman who never went to Vietnam. The war comes home to her in many profound ways, as well as ordinary ones: she worries about her uncle constantly, refuses to move out of the house with him in order to care for him, and so on. Further, there is some suggestion that the itch to travel and escape, the drive to leave her home revealed in the book's first section, is spurred in part by her experiences connected to veterans of war. Mason writes, "She would like to move somewhere far away—Miami or San Francisco maybe" (7). War violence and trauma spread beyond those who experience them directly to those connected to them. Sam puts it this way: "The ones who don't get killed come back with their lives messed up, and then they make everybody miserable" (71).

Language as a medium reflects this intersubjective structure, as the war abroad impacted what words appeared how, and in what books, stateside in the United States. For example, *In Country* introduces the inexperienced Sam to new language. When she says at one point, "I want some ham and beans," her uncle Emmett replies, "In the Army we had ham and butter beans. We had so much of that we called them ham and mother-fuckers" (74). Reflecting Sam's steadily growing sense of what it was like to be at war, produced by her conversations with her uncle and his veteran friends, she adopts this usage the next night, as she watches Emmett playing a video game. She considers that "for the first time" she "had a picture of him with an M-16, in a tropical jungle, firing at hidden faces in the banana leaves. And then sitting down for a meal of ham and mother-fuckers" (89). Mason has prepared readers to understand this final word as potentially shocking, noting how Sam's grandmother would be upset by Sam's swearing in general (8). In this specific case, the phrasing reflects not just the hardened identity of veterans; it also reveals how nourishment is rendered into discomfort by the systematizing nature of warmaking, like other systems of modernity. In this way, this usage calls to mind the treatment of food, particularly fast food, in *What's Eating Gilbert Grape* as discussed in chapter 1, as well as Hemingway's sharp critique of elephant hunting discussed in chapter 3.

Thus this severe language, appearing in Mason's novel, is a concrete example of the war coming home. It is also a posthumanist event, in which some of the vaunted domains of humanist exceptionalism—language and art—are directly changed. War experience impinges on what counts as permissible language in polite discourse, such as the American novel and its criticism. Furthermore, learning about the war—ostensibly about others' experiences—proves in Sam's case to be learning about herself, about her own origins: uncanny homesickness. The appearance of this rough word "mother-fuckers" is coordinated, in fact, with this lesson for Sam. She recognizes that she is the product of a young relationship—her parents were only married a month when her father, Dwayne, left for the war—and she thinks "teen-age romances weren't very significant." Then, in this same sequence, she considers, "Making a baby had nothing to do with love, or anything mystical, or what they said in church. It was just fucking" (192).

In other words, the soldiers' very language has come home to young Sam, rendering her homesick in my argument's sense—alien from herself, from her very creation and existence, but also desiring a return to fundamental understandings and experiences. The earlier section underscores this reality, with Sam thinking, "She was feeling the delayed stress of the Vietnam War. It was her inheritance. It was her version of Dawn's trouble" (89). Dawn is Sam's friend who has gotten pregnant, so in this rich sentence Sam is pregnant with the trouble of Vietnam. This retrospective structure of understanding, homesickness, is not Sam's alone, which is part of why Mason's novel resonates. The Vietnam War, and other wars, fundamentally inform who U.S citizens are *as* citizens. Reading this novel, we too feel, or should feel, "the delayed stress of the Vietnam War." It is *our* inheritance.

Sam's growing knowledge of war divides her from her sense of home and sparks her desire to see *more* world. *In Country* is saturated with its teenage protagonist's desire for experience, for knowledge, and for travel, and it is the realization of that desire that frames the narrative. The novel opens and closes with an automobile trip from small-town Kentucky to the Vietnam Memorial on the National Mall in Washington, D.C. This trip reveals how desire like Sam's risks becoming injury, or traumatic marking. Sam's desire for travel is only too quickly answered by the awareness of loss, a kind of homesickness for innocence in Sam, when she comes to terms with the ghost of the father she never knew over the course of the novel by spending her time worrying for, and caring for, her uncle who was himself deeply scarred by his experiences in Vietnam. As noted above, in Mason's believable and tragic plotting, Uncle Emmett has gone to war precisely because his brother-in-law Dwayne, Sam's father, has been killed there.

Mason devotes much of the novel to the dawning homesickness afflicting Sam. In a key scene, Sam attends a veterans' dance in her hometown along with her uncle, and Sam has a great time with Tom, another of the veterans, who is much older than she. They dance together and finally go back to his place, only to confront the anticlimax of Tom's emotional damage, his functional impotence. Echoing other posttraumatic war texts, perhaps most notably Hemingway's *The Sun Also Rises* centered around Jake Barnes's infamous war injury to his penis (making the title a bawdy and mocking pun in this context),[72] Mason's scene shows how the war has alienated Tom from his very body, his sexual function. Sam asks him, "Did you get hurt down there too?" noting his other injuries in her question, and he answers, "No, It's just in my head. Like a brick wall. The Great Wall of China. I butt up against it" (127). Sam's desire for experience, her attraction to an older and sophisticated man, is answered by a redoubling of her awareness of trauma: sickness at home.

The remainder of that weekend, effectively described by Mason, shows the sickness of trauma seeping through the home that Sam shares with her uncle Emmett. Emmett does not return from the dance that night, or the next day, and Sam's worries deepen. Sitting at home alone, she smokes some of Emmett's marijuana and clicks on the television, tuning in to MTV. She channel surfs as Mason tracks her stream of consciousness, underscoring the restlessness of modern life, the machinery made to elaborate desire. What is channel surfing, after all, if not one of the clearest late twentieth-century expressions of desire, of paradoxical unease in the home, or of restless curiosity combined with utter ease and comfort—only to be supplemented by the even-more-elaborate surfing of the internet in the contemporary moment.

Sam looks for Bruce Springsteen on MTV, which puts her in mind again of Tom, her date the night before, and she considers, "Tom was the only exciting thing in Hopewell," her hometown. She then thinks, "The sadness of his affliction hit her then like a truck. She thought of all the lives wasted by the war. She wanted to cry, but then she wanted to yell and scream and kick. She could imagine fighting, but only against war. All the boys getting killed, on both sides. And boys getting mutilated. And then not being allowed to grow up" (140). In this scene, Sam's position closely resembles that of the veterans themselves, upended out of ordinary life, her desire for experience crossed against her awareness of how too much experience too quickly damages young people, soldiers not much older than she, and damages the families of soldiers back home. The war is still echoing through the culture in Sam, a kind of slow violence. Confronting all this, worrying about Emmett, and channel surfing, Sam finally names her estranged sense of home using a motif that recurs in literature about homesickness, as I have suggested throughout this book: inviting over her friend Dawn, Sam says she and her house are haunted: "It's so spooky here" (142).

When Uncle Emmett still does not return or call or make any sign the next day, and when she cannot convince Dawn to visit, Sam begins a gruesome search of the house's basement, worrying implicitly about suicide or some other horror (152). She does not find her uncle there, but the haunted feel of the damp and dark space represents Sam's fears. The basement is like the subconscious of the home, its underside, stacked as it is in this case with old newspapers and other material scraps of memory. Thankfully, Emmett is not there hanging from a beam (unlike the basement scene in *What's Eating Gilbert Grape* discussed in chapter 2), and it turns out Sam has exaggerated her fears, as Emmett returns from a lark of a trip several hours away to Lexington. He is brought back home by his sister, Sam's mother.

And yet this episode further underscores that Sam's position is well outside the conventional, domestic modes of being. Her mother pays only a quick visit before she returns to her new husband and newborn child, deserting Sam to her unusual life. Why? Sam's mother also embodies the desire to escape the confines of small-town America, and she turns the whole house into a metaphor for being caught in oppressive memory, encouraging Sam to get rid of the things lying around the house. "This house is going to fall apart from the weight of all the junk in it," she tells Sam, underscoring the metaphorics of home. Mason's larger point seems to be that, in many ways, Sam stands in for all Americans left behind in the United States during the war, a point underscored with a brief aside about Sam's name: "Sam wondered if her mother had named her after Uncle Sam" (167). In this scenario,

Sam's mother's forward-looking mobility, while understandable, seems to be a form of denial, one that dogs modern mobility more generally, haunting us with homesickness.

Sam's homesickness reaches beyond her uncle and other veterans, to evoke this larger unease in late twentieth-century American life (such as her mother's), and to some extent human life more generally.[73] *In Country* is one uncanny discovery after another. Sam's desire to know more about her past eventually leads her to her paternal grandparents' home, and she finds them "ignorant and country" (206): homesickness as sickness at home. Then, her grandparents present Sam with her father's diary from Vietnam, in which she learns of more horrors, both of her heritage and of the war: her father killed a Vietcong man, face to face, and wanted to kill more Vietcong (201–5). In the diary, she also sees the randomness of death, as when her father's comrade-at-arms Darrell gets killed while he was "in the bushes to take a shit" (204). To put this in the terms of O'Brien's story, Darrell was shot while shitting. These unnerving discoveries disgust her and drive her back home, only to find it under fumigation for fleas. The home space is violated as if it too is part of the war zone she is rediscovering.

Driven back out of her home much as many veterans feel they are, Sam turns then to her Girl Scout gear to take a trip to "the last place in western Kentucky where a person could really face the wild" (207–8). She considers that "if men went to war for women, and for unborn generations," as she had read in her father's journal, "then she was going to find out what they went through" (208). While her trip is to a local destination, Cawood's Pond, her experience there is fearful and estranging; she begins to realize how foreign her own home region is (208–18). In fact, she comes to feel she is herself *in country* even in the United States. Home becomes sick for her with war. Mason describes Sam's understandable nervousness, alone in a wild place, in terms of war and especially of Vietnam, referring to "her position," her need to practice "self defense," her effort "to face the terror of the jungle" (216–17). Then, she hears "footsteps" approaching and she considers, "This terror was what the soldiers had felt every minute" (217). The encroacher, however, is only Emmett, come to find her and bring her home.

In fact, however, they find more home out there in the wild. They discuss more of the fallout on Emmett's friends from Vietnam, and they articulate together a deep sense of anger and frustration about war. Then Emmett begins telling more about his traumatic experiences, spurred, it seems, by Sam's care for him and his comrades. The novel thus underscores how understanding war often requires this kind of sympathy or empathy from those at home, even if veterans often resist or resent it. But this strange place, Cawood's Pond, is also an agent here, seeming to enable these reconsiderations of the past, which finally drive Emmett to a powerful, "full-blown," wailing sorrow, "something monstrous and fantastic" (224), an expression not unlike O'Brien's "Ahhooooo." This mourning also seems to relate to the restored sense of agency that finally seizes Emmett after this episode. Going back to his Vietnam experiences while at Cawood's Pond helps resuscitate him. Thus Sam expects this experience will cause Emmett to "flip out . . . but to her surprise she was the one who went sort of crazy after" this visit to the pond (229).

Perhaps this is largely because Emmett is forced to worry more about Sam, to take steps to help her. Indeed, explaining his interest in birds while at the pond, Emmett tells Sam, "If you can think about something like birds, you can get outside yourself, and it doesn't hurt as much. That's the whole idea. That's the whole challenge for the human race" (226). This psychological approach is much akin to those used by Henry in Hemingway's *A Farewell to Arms,* discussed above, and to others enduring trauma.[74] Emmett's prescription is a compelling statement of posthumanist goals in the Anthropocene. At the very least, the nonhuman in general and Cawood's Pond in particular helped facilitate Emmett getting further outside himself. He acts on his concern for others after this episode, organizing a trip to the Vietnam Memorial in Washington, D.C., and helping Sam in other ways. Visiting the memorial reveals Emmett's resurgence of solidarity with other veterans, a microcosm of this novel's larger function for an American readership, bringing the war from *over there* back here.

Sam's sensibility is radically changed by her sympathetic, affective work and deepened by her embodied practices, such as camping at Cawood's Pond. Traveling to the memorial, Sam thinks, "America the beautiful. It is beautiful indeed. . . . The farms are pretty, the interstates are pleasant. Even the strip mines are hidden behind a ridge on the parkway. It is a good country. But she keeps getting flashes of it through the eyes of a just-returned Vietnam soldier." She feels increasingly estranged from her hometown and the nation more generally. Driving through the United States, she thinks,

"She didn't fit in that landscape. None of it pertained to her. They passed by the Burger Boy, McDonald's. She couldn't see herself working at the Burger Boy again. The soldiers must have felt like that, as though they belonged nowhere" (231).

This is much the same sentiment, expressed via a similar set of icons and semiotic elements (fast-food restaurants), as appears in *What's Eating Gilbert Grape*. The estrangement in both cases facilitates powerful insights, not unlike the experiences of Novalee Nation when she camps in Walmart (see chapter 5). Doing so, Novalee locates the home of the capitalist, neoliberal self in the heart of that vendor, Walmart, one both essential to and representative of capitalist modes of production commonly made *external* to domestic selfhood. Work and home get remixed. Similarly, wars overseas are commonly opposed to stateside selfhood, particularly for a young girl like Sam, but in Mason's novel, the war spurs Sam to revise radically her understanding of the United States, estranging her, making her homesick, both sick of home and longing for home.

At the novel's close, Sam finally has some of her cosmopolitan curiosity appeased, as she visits the Vietnam Memorial with her grandmother and uncle. There, in a final uncanny moment, she finds her own name written on the wall. She considers "how odd it feels, as though all the names in America have been used to decorate this wall" (245). Mason thus evokes that wars are fought in the name of the people back home, and we have seen how fundamentally soldiers rely on ideas of home to ferry them across the strangeness of war—the foreign places, the extreme and intensified dangers, and the trauma. But we should further recognize how the war also makes no sense, literally no sense, until it is brought home and measured in a context that has meaning for soldiers and their friends and family. It is by measurement against the known that the trauma of war appears, but Mason's story insists just as strongly that when these measures are taken, home becomes a foreign place. Indeed, in the case of her protagonist Sam, the home of her body and her name are both likewise estranged, made foreign in a subjectivity akin to the postcolonial forms of identity discussed in my introduction.

Further, for Emmett, the veteran who has survived, home never seems the same after the experience of war: this homesickness evinces what Jameson describes in passages quoted above—war's ability to transform the ordinary, familiar world into a place of terror and horror.[75] That fact leads to a perhaps surprising reality: the veterans in Mason's book, like many other veterans in many other texts, discuss being "homesick" for their memories of Vietnam (78–79). The powerful experiences mark them not only in negative ways but in positive ones too. Tom says on this point, "I wouldn't say I had a blast, exactly, but it's funny, how special it was, in a way, like nobody else could ever know what you went through except guys who have been there" (78). Critics have underscored this problem of knowledge connected to war experience, a problem signaled by Tom's word choice "funny," as well as his more explicit point that "no one else could ever know." This structure of feeling connects to the discussion in previous chapters of how the experience of homesickness unhomes the self in complex ways. Indeed, profound experiences of many sorts unhouse the self from itself, and these feelings often appear in the terms of home and homesickness, a powerful emotion, a feeling in the belly that is difficult to name. Such realities, I have argued, make a strong case against the possibility of a pure or entirely rational eco-cosmopolitanism. Eco-cosmopolitanism is stranger than we might first think.

In *Tribe,* Sebastian Junger underscores the same point: "So many soldiers find themselves missing the war after it's over. That troubling fact can be found in written accounts from war after war, country after country, century after century. As awkward as it is to say, part of the trauma of war seems to be giving it up."[76] Junger explains this by pointing to the close camaraderie in war, the "extreme brotherhood," the "deep emotions and understandings" that, for Junger, sharply contrast with contemporary capitalism's "individualized lifestyles that . . . seem to be deeply brutalizing to the human spirit."[77]

Junger's account may sound close to an apology for war, but it need not be read that way. War does offer profound experiences of life and death, camaraderie, and more, but such experiences are truly part and parcel of life, if we are not insulated from them by modern conveniences and contemporary social and economic structures. Serious engagement with food and its sources, shared experiences in wild or civil spaces, and the mutual production of music, dance, and other art—all offer entry into similar feelings. Junger notes that it is largely what happens to experience and to community during the "hard times" of war that makes those memories compelling.[78] That suggests how deliberate pursuit of difficulty might well be a crucial human good. We can do that outside war, and many do. In any event, all such powerful, robust experiences take shape for us retrospectively, in a homesick structure of subjectivity that both confirms our sense of self and, often, unhouses us from who we were.

Women Soldiers in Iraq: "Homesick for a Place You Hate"

War changes places and participants, and it has also been an endeavor that makes and reflects social changes, such as the steady though incomplete effort for greater gender parity. As more women have won the right to serve in the military, they have experienced their own distinctive forms of homesickness. Several books treat these experiences, both contemporary and more remotely historical, and Annie Proulx's third collection of Wyoming stories, *Fine Just the Way It Is,* offers a fitting, more recent fictional example.[79] In the story "Tits-Up in a Ditch," a young new mother from Wyoming named Dakotah enlists in the army to make a living. She has had a hardscrabble youth, having been abandoned by her mother, who was lured to Los Angeles, away from the Wyoming ranch she hated (179). Dakotah, something of an outcast, falls in with a young man named Sash Hicks and they marry during their senior year in high school. The marriage works in no way but one: reproduction. Thus Dakotah, pregnant but planning a divorce, and in need of money, joins the army as her undesired husband, Sash, had done. Proulx, amplifying the desperation of Dakotah's life, has her drop out of high school just prior to graduation, but as Beth Bailey's history makes clear, the failure to graduate would have made enlistment more difficult: "In 1992, only 2 percent of army recruits lacked a high school diploma."[80] Still, Dakotah's story is clearly possible.

Dakotah's grandparents take care of the child, doting on it, and Dakotah begins to hear the siren call of cosmopolitan mobility as her mother had before her. Once her plan to join the army is in place, she relishes "leaving behind the seedy two-story town, the dun-colored prairie flattened by wind, leaving the gumbo roads, the radio voices flailing through nets of static, the gossip and narrow opinions" (205). Proulx delights and excels in such descriptions of hopelessly remote Wyoming towns, but very quickly the new experiences drive Dakotah to a greater sense of self-consciousness. One way to know one's home is to leave it, but such knowledge is often uncomfortable. Dakotah develops homesickness not because of her view that "it was still a man's army and that women were decidedly inferior in all ways" (206). It was instead "the constant presence of too many people." Proulx writes,

"Someone who has grown up in silence and vast space, who was born to solitude, who feels different and shrinks from notice, suffers in the company of others. So homesickness took the shape of longing for wind, an empty landscape, for silence and privacy. She longed for the baby and came to believe she was homesick for the old ranch" (207).

This scenario captures many of the features of homesickness as discussed in this book. Her nostalgia for the past, for familiar places and things, is a feature of mortal life. Psychologist Clay Routledge argues that it is even healthy and valuable.[81] In this case even a past that had not been good to Dakotah looks nice in the receding distance, from the perspective of her new and worse circumstances. The past also clearly functions as a ballast to her uncertain subjectivity, tossed about on the uneasy seas of mobility.

Dakotah's move from the inhuman and wide-open landscape of Wyoming to the strict, orderly, and overwhelmingly human space of the army is not entirely new historically, of course, but such changes happen differently in contemporary times. In Dakotah's case, Wyoming begins to appear simply as a lesser of evils, better than the "heat and smells" of "too many people" (207). When Dakotah makes some friends in the army, the irony of her homesickness is made explicit: "'How can it be,' Dakotah asked them [her friends], 'that you feel homesick for a place you hate?'" (208–9). This structure of desire reveals the limitations of human life, how ordinary possibilities are deeply limited in the ways I have called "weak selfhood."

But this story, like other Proulx texts, is also a celebration of a kind of cosmopolitan desire. Dakotah tries sushi, learns a different set of restaurant manners, and meets people from far afield in her military training. She becomes very close to her friend Marnie, "closer than she had ever been to Sash. . . . Marnie said maybe they were in love," and they discuss "setting up house together with Baby Verl" as an established lesbian couple (212). In short, Dakotah develops what she decides her mother also had, a "curiosity and longing for the exotic" (210). Furthermore, as a military policewoman in Iraq, she learns to pity the Iraqis who seem to have it worse than she ever did. She considered one Iraqi woman she had to search, who was "unable even to buy and carry home a few eggplants without an American soldier groping at her" (213).

Like the many veterans discussed above, Dakotah does not escape her military commitment unscathed. Moments after searching the Iraqi woman, Dakotah loses her right arm to an IED—an improvised explosive device.

Worse, as she convalesces, a feeling of deeper loss dawns over her. The feeling is confirmed when her grandmother comes to visit and tells her that her child, Verl, had died, having fallen out of a pickup truck. Proulx piles on ironies and black humor when she exposes the masculinist gender codes as fault-worthy in this child's death: "The eighteen-month-old child had loved riding with his great-grandfather, but this day Verl put him with the dogs in the open truck bed. Big Verl was so proud to have a boy and wanted him to be tough. The dogs loved him" (214). But when the truck hit a bump, the baby flew out and was crushed under the wheels.

The sheer stupidity of this parenting approach is reinforced by Proulx's likening humans to other animals throughout the story. Not only is the child among the dogs when he is thrown to his demise, but the story's title, "Tits-Up in a Ditch" is an animal idiom. The phrase, which in the end stands for the altered condition in which Dakotah would have to live her life on her return home, is first uttered by her grandfather after he finds a cow that has fallen to its death in a ditch. In her dark sensibility, Proulx uses such pieces of local, idiomatic language to evoke our human narrowness and vulnerability, as I argued in chapter 2. A correlate of this weakness is the drive of economic need that presses Dakotah into the army in the first place.

Clearly, for many in at least some ways, the technological advances of modernity have made for better lives. By many statistical measures, we can see this is true: life expectancy, infant mortality, and so on. But in other, ordinary ways, for Proulx's Dakotah, the development of technology has made it easier for her to be knocked around the world, sent to Iraq to lose an arm, and brought back home because "there was nowhere else to go" (218). Her life is simply accelerated by technology, and it is that much easier for her to accept her role in the military as a professional soldier, someone who serves for the money. She comes back noticeably weakened, "disabled" because of her lost right arm. But the structure of Proulx's story implies that she was disabled when she left. Like the cow that Dakotah's grandfather finds "tits-up in a ditch" early in the story (182), like Dakotah's best friend, Marnie, who does not survive the explosion that takes Dakotah's arm, Dakotah is largely trapped by her circumstances. Her attempt to escape the place of her making ended more quickly than Mero's, discussed in chapter 1, but it comes to the same thing: an inability to escape the gravitational pull of her origin. All these characters end up mired, in Proulx's animal metaphor, "tits-up in a ditch."

From Football Star to Political Football: The Tragic Story of Pat Tillman in Afghanistan

If Proulx's account of cosmopolitan experiences in war tends toward dark irony, a prominent true story about a participant in the Iraq War begins with high idealism. Pat Tillman epitomizes vaunted inspirations for military service. As was widely reported in various media, after the attacks of 9/11, Tillman walked away from the NFL (National Football League)—in particular, from a $3.6 million contract extension offer with the Cardinals team in Arizona—to join the army. He felt a strong moral requirement to put himself on the line in defense of a country he saw as under attack in the events of September 11, 2001.[82] In other words, as Jon Krakauer's book *Where Men Win Glory: The Odyssey of Pat Tillman* explains, at the peak of his professional career, Tillman joined the Army Rangers, deciding against being an officer because he wanted "to be in the thick of the action, share the risk and hardship, and have a direct impact."[83] Pat's brother Kevin, also a professional athlete playing minor league baseball, joined with him.

This remarkable idealism makes subsequent events all the more galling: when Pat Tillman was killed by friendly fire, political and military powers covered up the circumstances and cynically used his sincere patriotism to support the increasingly unpopular wars. The Pat Tillman story, therefore, dramatically and tragically demonstrates the complications of soldiering selfhood and the long shadow of agency in the military. While many—probably most—members of the service are sincere, honest, and brave in their work, their ideals are always expressed via a structure—human, logistical, and technological—that largely determines their meaning. Invariably, those ideals are expressed via the pragmatic—in the Tillman narrative they are gruesomely calculated—logics that undergird the conduct of armed forces anywhere. Recognizing that much of the military's decision chains are practical, contextual, situated, even *realpolitikal,* or excessively abstract and theoretical, reiterates human weakness and provinciality, underscoring the practical problems with the cosmopolitan dream I have investigated throughout this book. These recognitions also underscore the point made at the opening of this chapter: that the extraordinary forms of agency enabled by military participation cast a long and dark shadow of disability and damage, two halves of that system of subjectivity.

Krakauer insists that Tillman's principled decision to join the military is part of his larger orientation in life, one of relentless self-improvement, industry, courage, and principle. Tillman embodied the desire to overcome one's physical and situational limitations, to become more able, more achieved, and more self. He was practically a superhero. Tillman had constantly faced doubts and detractors. When he decided to play high school football instead of baseball, an assistant coach discouraged him, saying he was not big enough.[84] As Krakauer points out, Tillman faced this same pattern as a young college player, and then again as an improbable professional player, and each time Tillman overcame the odds to become exceptional. When he walked away from his multimillion-dollar contract, he had already rejected an earlier five-year, $9.6 million offer from the St. Louis Rams on principle: he felt loyal to his Arizona team because they had drafted him and believed in him when he was not yet a sure thing. Tillman's agent, Frank Bauer, explained this decision, as reported by Krakauer: "In twenty-seven years . . . I've never had a player turn down that big of a package in the National Football League." Bauer continues, "You just don't see loyalty like that in sports today. Pat Tillman was special. He was a man of principle. He was a once-in-a-lifetime kid." From such stories, Krakauer concludes of Tillman, "He was one of those rare individuals who simply can't be bought at any price."[85]

Once Tillman was immersed in the military, he found his role frustratingly contracted and often expressed wariness about it. He thus expressed a soldier's familiar sense of homesickness, writing in his journal how much he missed his wife, Marie, going on to say, "I can't wait to start a family with Marie, absolutely can't wait."[86] Yet as Krakauer notes, Tillman nonetheless did not like being passed over on missions even as a newcomer to the service. Tillman wrote in his journal, "I'm not out for blood or in any hurry to kill people, however I did not throw my life to shit in order to fill sandbags and guard Hummers."[87] In this complex person, moreover, the lust for action weighed against awareness of what modern war actually does. As Baghdad came under attack, Tillman wrote in his journal, "My heart goes out to those who will suffer. Whatever your politics, whatever you believe is right or wrong, the fact is most of those who will feel the wrath of this ordeal want nothing more than to live peacefully."[88]

Tillman's wariness was compounded by his frustration at initially being deployed in Iraq, a war he wrote about as having "little or no justification other than our imperial whim." He felt he and his brother to be mere "pawns," since they had enlisted to pursue Osama bin Laden and al-Qaeda, not go to Iraq.[89] Such moments underscore the drastic changes in agency central to contemporary war. A soldier at one moment is afforded all the technology and organization to be extraordinarily powerful, flown from place to place with cutting-edge transportation technology, protected by sophisticated armor, and enabled even to break fundamental cultural taboos like the stricture against killing. At the next moment that same soldier is subject to the whims of a political system and a command structure that deny him or her basic personal freedoms, rendering the soldier a "pawn." Tillman's awareness of these complexities, and his articulate considerations of it presented in his journal, make him a compelling study in contemporary human agency and biopolitics.

Thus, such assemblages go two ways. An individual can only be a national hero if he or she does something that connects to a larger scenario and narrative, which depends on these links among individual units and larger strategic plans and timelines. But that larger structure can and regularly does turn individuals into pawns and into dead meat. These same paradoxes of human agency epitomize the Anthropocene, and for the same reasons, as human structures and technologies facilitate ever-more-miraculous forms of ability (airplanes, the internet, modern medicine, antibiotics, space travel), only to expose us and the planet to radically new forms of vulnerability. Cosmopolitanism, likewise, is fraught with these same paradoxes.

The resonances of Tillman's word "pawn" intensify in light of the political maneuvering that occurred after his death. President George W. Bush was mounting a reelection campaign and wanted to make use of the Tillman story. Krakauer writes, "When Tillman was killed, White House perception managers saw an opportunity not unlike the one provided by the Jessica Lynch debacle thirteen months earlier."[90] Krakauer amasses a strong case showing that the Bush administration used the Tillman story to rally support for wars that were not going particularly well, deliberately deceiving not just the American people to do so but also deceiving Pat Tillman's own family about the nature of Tillman's death, obscuring its cause in friendly fire. The Tillman family's outrage in response to this political posturing is made clear in Krakauer's book, in Pat Tillman's mother's book, *Boots on the Ground by Dusk: My Tribute to Pat Tillman,* and in the documentary film *The Tillman Story.*[91]

In warfare, the peaks of human heroism and agency drop vertiginously into canyons and abysses of utter unmeaning, blank space or sheer violence. Every single death in warfare represents profound human failures, failures to use reason, and failures to be cosmopolitan. Instead of recognizing the need to share the finite planet with many other forms of life, warfare exposes not only humans to damage, injury, and death but whole regimes of life, animals, and plants, the very landscapes that facilitate the existence of life. Viewed in this framework, the military presents a cautionary tale about cosmopolitan dreams, about planetary thinking. Soldiers' superagency and cosmopolitan knowledge crosses into destruction, underscoring human weakness, the dangers of mobility, and the human inability to be everywhere at once.

Despite the despicable manipulations of the Tillman story, Krakauer's conclusion about Tillman himself seems apt: that "the sad end he met in Afghanistan was . . . a function of his stubborn idealism—his insistence on trying to do the right thing." This insistence, Krakauer urges, "wasn't a tragic flaw" but rather a "tragic virtue."[92] This desire to do the right thing in service of the more-than-me world is central to the broader cosmopolitan dream, one that bears much transformative potential within it still, and all the more so when we can find and understand its weaknesses.

Conclusion

Dreams of Home

Literature and the Cultural Work of the Posthumanities

Don't just do something. Sit there.

—Silvia Boorstein, *Don't Just Do Something, Sit There*

The Power of Images, Memes, and Dreams

Flooded homes. Houses on fire. Ghosts of lost children. Murdered elephants. A half-skinned steer. A dead soldier, "boom down." A pregnant young woman labeled "MADE IN AMERICA." These images thrust themselves upon the reader's mind, which worries them and recirculates them, organizing itself around them like filings around a magnet. The images orient us here, in this book, and they haunt us. Or so one hopes at first, writing about them. But is it hope? Fear? This cluster of images evokes, in part, what it means to live in the Anthropocene, in which the ever-accelerating pace of modern life fuels the growing sense that human environmental control has gone too far, has undermined itself, making us homesick for the planet we thought we knew. Such anxieties invade our sleep, as noted in the preface. Indeed, climate change itself, materially, is keeping us up at night, as the warmer temperatures inhibit the human body's ability to descend into sleep, even if we have air-conditioning.[1]

In *Ecology without Culture: Aesthetics for a Toxic World*, Christine L. Marran calls images like half-skinned steers "biotropes," compellingly evoking the living materiality of these knots of meaning.[2] We can also understand climate change as a biotrope, and one of its denotations is "homesickness." Such biotropes evoke more-than-human powers in the world. In part, that is an old-fashioned humanist sentiment. Images, poems, and phrases matter. They have power. Indeed, in a general way I am echoing a long-standing debate, as displayed in Mark Edmundson's 1995 argument in *Literature against Philosophy, Plato to Derrida: A Defence of Poetry,* where, as the title signals, he defends the power of literature against sometimes overweening theory.[3]

While I am far from antitheory, there is much at stake in questions about the power of images, poetry, and literature. What and whence this power? Too often, humanists answer these questions by rushing to a set of dogmas about "the power of language," say, without scrutinizing where that power comes from, what it means. By contrast, posthumanism offers a radically different stance on this issue, one briefly summarized by Graham Harman in *New Literary History*: "The primary lesson of Bruno Latour for the humanities appears to be simple: the humanities are not just about humans. Though the ultimate picture is more complicated than this, it remains a useful guiding principle. . . . Such popular human-centered terms as 'language,' 'society,' 'power,' and even 'capitalism' are assigned by Latour to a derivative position."[4]

Similarly, in his book *The Practice of the Wild,* published in 1990, a year before Latour's breakout book *We Have Never Been Modern,* Gary Snyder radically redescribes language.[5] Applying a concept from thirteenth-century Zen Buddhist Dōgen Kigen to debates about language, Snyder writes, "When occidental logos-oriented philosophers uncritically advance language as a unique human gift which serves as the organizer of the chaotic universe—it is a delusion." To the contrary, this passage continues, "The subtle and many-layered cosms of the universe have found their own way into symbolic structures and have given us thousands of tawny human-language grammars."[6] This reversal of conventional views of language puts biotropes into a different light, revealing them to be typical of language and other semiotic systems. Snyder's reversal is also very much in keeping with the more recent work of Donna Haraway, Timothy Morton, Cary Wolfe, and others. Indeed, in *The Practice of the Wild* Snyder specifically aligns his claims with "a new breed of posthumanists" who were in the 1980s and '90s, he suggests, working to expand considerably our understanding of what it means to be human; Snyder may have been thinking of Haraway in particular, among others.

Emphasizing the power of images, those nonhuman entities, to fundamentally inform language and meaning entails recognizing a certain measure of subjective passivity. This status—passivity—I have emphasized in various ways in the preceding chapters, not least by repeated reference to philosopher Jeremy Bentham's radical reversal, amplified by Derrida and Wolfe.[7] Bentham insists that exposure to suffering, rather than some more positive form of ability, ought to be central in guiding our ethical judgments. Snyder's similar treatment of language and subjectivity, despite being published nearly thirty years ago, has not been fully digested even in ecocritical circles.

Homesickness in/for "First-Wave" Ecocriticism

As I have already begun to signal, this conclusion returns to two widely discussed and influential figures in "first-wave" ecocriticism, Snyder and Thoreau, under the premise that there are useful, latent ideas in their familiar texts. But not just "ideas." Key to the value of both of these figures are their personal practices, which model alternative modes of being a self. Returning to these much-studied figures, then, demonstrates a homesick reading practice in two senses: it involves interpretation as retrospection as well as prospection, reading out of linear order, a haunting by the past; and it is embodied, material, and worldly, involving practices with the physical, not just the intellectual. Bodies, houses, landscapes, texts.

In other words, homesickness calls for deliberate changes in the way we inhabit space and time, and for an acknowledgment that many tenets of humanist selfhood are mere fictions, showing that we never have inhabited the world quite as we tend to think we do. Deliberate changes, more passive acknowledgment: these modes are and ought to be interrelated, as we deliberately make room for more passive or receptive modes; and pensive, passive modes lead to better deliberate practices. Each mode is also its own reward. Consider sitting meditation as a good example: it requires making time and space for passivity and quiet; and, as a passive mode, it benefits subsequent active, deliberate undertakings. In short, meditation *works*, even according to familiar humanist notions of selfhood and value. This is a kind of paradox that is useful, open to engagement, if we recognize and engage these complex dynamics rather than simply naming it "paradox" and standing back from it. This more self-conscious, dynamic movement between active and passive modes is akin to the movement between and among scales that many posthumanist and anthropocenic thinkers are calling for; the dynamism and openness they require of subjects is like real-world ecologies, porous and changing systems that are strong precisely because of their "weak" openness, their incomplete or unbound character. That description also applies well to what I call homesickness in this book.

Snyder is well known for his intellectual interest in, and robust practice of, sitting meditation, and for his work on/in many other alternative subjective modes as sources of insight about the nature of self and world. For instance, his undergraduate honors thesis, published as a book, treats American Indian Haida myth, and myth more generally remains a focus throughout his career.[8] Myths are strangely in and out of time, like homesickness. Indeed, myths often aim to account for not just reality but also for time itself, prying themselves out of ordinary and linear temporalities to become circular, to circle around themselves, like miniature cosmoses, reiterating, reproducing the larger mysteries of interaction between matter and time, as investigated in relativity, for example.

One of the most passive forms of subjective experience, beyond even sitting meditation, is another useful guide: dreaming. It is *radical listening*, near kin to the forms of haunting repeatedly treated in this book. Dreaming also shares much with reading and even producing fiction and other texts. To put this point in an even more pragmatic register, the posthumanities ask us to sit and think for a moment rather than walk our lost selves in another circle on the burning mountainside of climate change. Thus, as Rita Felski argues in her introduction to the same issue of *New Literary History* mentioned above, focused on Bruno Latour and (post)humanism, it is not just the power of critique in the humanities that matters. She emphasizes "curating, conveying, criticizing, composing."[9] Similarly, I would underscore the humanities' methods of listening, recognizing multiplicities in meaning, acknowledging the power of the not-us that resides not only in the nonhuman but in what is often seen as the *human*—all these built and autopoietic, or self-built, structures that orient us practically all the time: houses, epistemologies, ontologies, languages, governments, and nostalgia. In suggesting *curating* as central to our work in the posthumanities, Felski explains that she means "guarding, protecting, conserving, caretaking, and looking after."[10] These are concepts and practices that the left needs to reclaim as part of reassessing the importance and even, I am arguing, the *inevitability* of nostalgia, which is too easily and reductively understood as conservative, as Jennifer K. Ladino argues.[11] Indeed, reclaiming nostalgia, in Ladino's phrase, may even help open lines of dialogue or escape between the firmly entrenched positions on right and left, especially since nostalgia is often seen as conservative. Recognizing nostalgia as an existential condition is a way to reiterate shared identity across political differences.

Curating and caring are specific and particular. That point brings me to another primary argument of this conclusion: literary discourse, or cultural studies, is oriented by the power of the particular: particular narratives in their own, immanent logics; particular images; and local, regional truths. Many of the texts addressed in this book double-down on these emphases, as in Proulx, when she insists that the power of places dwarfs individual human powers. While theories, philosophies, and other frameworks are essential to meaning, so are the particulars. Indeed, ultimately, even frameworks and theories (such as "cosmopolitanism") are particular and specific, though they may approach the status of hyperobjects in their expansiveness so that we experience them not as particular but as general. The larger disciplinary point here, then, is that the interpretation of cultural objects practiced in the humanities is actually not exceptional because its focus is excessively local (on specific texts); it is exemplary for that reason. Ultimately, all interpretation is local. However, practically, such an approach can make it too easy to hunker down in familiar local truths and narratives that fail to recognize their actual position or meaning in the larger reality. Thus the distinctions general/particular, planetary/local, and so on remain useful tools, especially when understood as tools rather than as absolutes. In other words, while philosophy can facilitate scrutiny of concepts and principles, and the sciences yield natural facts, we require particularity, the local truths of discourses like literature, film, and so on, to assess how all this matters to our lives. Practically, posthumanism and cultural studies need to continue to toggle between and among these forms of understanding from multiple disciplinary silos and contexts.

Keep at least some of the distinctions structuring language, but recognize them as artificial and even as local. This is a deconstructive point that appreciates the human need for tools and technologies, that appreciates human weakness and human homesickness better than some more corrosive versions of deconstruction. Local truths are limited, but we need them. That stance becomes more robust in light of posthumanism, object-oriented ontology, and related movements, reiterating the importance of the particular in innovative ways. As we more fully acknowledge the nonhuman, our conceptions of the local become even more robust. Thus, for example, a thin, anthropocentric account of the local dimensions of, say, Wyoming culture (thinking again of Proulx) would emphasize its historical crosscurrents, its history of immigration, imperialism, and warfare, and so on, focusing mostly on the human level. But posthumanism insists on a fuller account of human culture that includes nonhuman dimensions of ecology, landscape, weather, and much more.[12] Such particularized modes of interpretation are familiar from movements like New Historicism, for instance, which emphasizes the distinctness and complexity of objects even within their historical contexts or their dense multiplicity of meaning. However, *Homesickness* amplifies the temporal structure of interpretation as well. In this structure, it is not just that we cannot exclusively privilege context or text, or the global or the local, but that we cannot be overly presentist or futurist. I am arguing, instead, that our meanings are produced retrospectively, once some of the complex conditions that create meaning are already gone. Thus, attending to meaning itself is a kind of homesickness, necessarily. We cannot fully interpret events or texts at the moment of their occurrence or during their highest intensity. Their meaning only becomes clearer in retrospect, once we have lost many of the conditions of their creation, even as we are pulled forward in time.

It is this temporal structure of meaning in part that informs my notion of human weakness, drawn in large part from Derrida's animal writing, Morton's work in *Hyperobjects* and *Dark Ecology*, and Wolfe's accounts of posthumanism. In this structure, agency is displaced in time and space, and the provisionality common to much humanist interpretation appears as fundamental to all interpretation. This point is about both interpretive *practices* and *sensibility* more generally, helping restore the value of discourses like the literary, and of forms of experience such as dreams. The climate change nightmare with which this book begins, then, can be recognized now, in retrospect, as a form of meaning that should give us pause, as the saying has it, which is important in and of itself. That nightmare can and must also spur us to make a series of rational and pragmatic changes, ones that ripple through the social body and potentially reorient the ships of state, sailing on the acidifying, roiling, swelling seas. But without giving the pause its due, in practices and sensibility both, we are only more likely to rush to further harmful decisions. As Thom van Dooren and Deborah Bird

Rose note, writing about mourning, loss, and extinction, "Taking it seriously, not rushing to overcome it—may actually be the more important political and ethical work."[13]

Posthumanist modes dislocate us from familiar orientations, including from the powerful shorthand "home," used to name a cluster of entities generally including human culture, language, cuisine; nonhuman weather, geography, life; and assemblages like houses, transportation technologies, and more. A premise underlying this book is that our ideas of home are exceptionally rich and complex. A trace of this power appears in the use of the prefix "eco-" in such words as "ecology" and "economics." Eco-, tracing back through French to Latin and through Latin to Greek *oikos*, means "house" or "household." In our modern uses of the prefix, it has clearly taken on metaphorical meanings, as house is associated with systems of rules understood to govern both the natural world and the commercial one. But for my purposes, it is valuable to return to that root to clarify a meaning of "homesickness" that I have been suggesting throughout this book. If "home" and the *oikos* are places of familiarity and comfort, places that confer meaning, homesickness is a strange alienation from both, engendering a desire and an unrest. I have understood this scenario in a complex fashion, refusing either to surrender the value of concepts of home in favor of some naturalized mobility or to give ourselves over to some kind of simple nostalgia, some notion of desired absolute fixity in time and place.

Instead, I have suggested that complex homesickness is a figure for our subjectivity itself, and ought to perhaps even be cultivated as a way to tread a middle path between those positions of deterritorialization on the one hand and nostalgic fixity on the other. What might that involve? A fuller answer to that question appears throughout this book, but part of it involves how we imagine home. In short, we ought to dedomesticate home, to recognize it as radically inhuman in a range of ways. If certain versions of thinking about home—especially nostalgic ones—can seem entrapping and reductive, other versions so dislocate us as to make us seem lost. That same problem attends even to the way we think about the home as a building: especially in modernity, it is far too easy to get lost in the humanist echo chamber of television, electricity, and indoor life. The Anthropocene calls us to think about the outside much more in several senses. So one meaning of homesickness, sickness at home, is the feeling of cabin fever, of being cooped up too long. We need to get outside much more robustly.

I often make that argument programmatically and rationally in this book, but the preceding chapters also hinged on the more-than-rational power of images, dreams, and feelings to jar us out of the small cabins of our selfhood. While the power of images and of the past to haunt and inform us is not limited to the Anthropocene, it is a particularly anthropocenic feeling because this is an age when the whole globe is being haunted materially by human actions from the past, even as we seek a new way forward. Morton writes in *Dark Ecology,* as he names agriculture and agrilogistics as the deep source of the Anthropocene, that we nonetheless cannot conclude that we should simply go back to the time before agriculture appeared. That simplistic nostalgia is not only impossible practically; it is naïve theoretically. Morton exposes such thinking to satire,[14] which does not at all mean we should do nothing. There are steps we can take. But, as per my epigraph to this conclusion, we ought to learn to be much more circumspect about our agrilogistical bias toward action and movement. These impulses are so wired in the capitalist and agrilogistical mind that we take them as given. In his book *The Future and Its Enemies,* philosopher Daniel Innerarity labels this nearly automatic reliance on movement "false motion," or "false mobility." He underscores that too much of our thinking about the future "is simply forward motion that conceals an incapacity to confront needed reforms and to shape our collective future."[15]

Indeed, it is precisely because the impulse to move and act is so powerful—to scale this analysis back radically to much more local frames—that the humanities have come under such doubt in contemporary times. As higher education increasingly becomes understood as a training ground for professional occupations, subjected to cynical political pressures, the humanities seem not to have a point. Where do they take us? What are their outcomes? How can I make money from a poem, or from criticism of one? Or, as Felski puts it in *New Literary History,* "Thanks to an increasingly instrumental and market-driven view of knowledge, underwritten by ballooning bureaucracies that cast professors and students in the roles of managers and consumers, the concerns of the humanities are made to seem ever more peripheral."[16] But, sounding a note that harmonizes with Felski's argument there, I suggest that peripheral status may be precisely why we need the humanities more than ever. The Anthropocene has reiterated the question of purpose in a new and much more forceful way, since all our industry and activity is literally ruining the very entities we need to enjoy life—or even to live at all. The (post)humanities, understood to some extent as outside the dominant agrilogistical structures, can give us some perspective on them. Their seeming uselessness is what makes the (post)humanities useful.

For instance, the Anthropocene requires learning to resee the massive forms and regimes of technology that dominate our lives: Automobiles. Steel mills. The military industrial complex. These machines are completely entwined in our experiences, and recognizing that fact is a plank in the posthumanist platform. But recognizing it is not capitulating to it. While reliance on technology is older than, well, modern humans, technology is something that can be used in various ways. The Anthropocene is a dream or a nightmare of the machine age, and giving it a word and a set of images—memes, if you like, in Richard Dawkins's sense[17]—permits us to reconsider the function of these realities. If we can rethink their functions, we can revise their realities.

Homesickness as an Old Idea

This book begins with a consideration of global warming as a force of displacement. As the climate changes, places change and some places literally disappear from under our feet. Such cases dramatically render homesickness. They also point to deeper posthumanist questions about human relationships with the rest of Earth. As Jeremy Withers recently reiterated, a great deal of ecocritical discourse hinges on tacit notions of a stable and comfortable home.[18] In this book, I have argued that such ideas are both more important and less true than is sometimes recognized. More important, we tend not to recognize how much we rely on ideas of a stable home in the past to navigate the uncertain present; and less true, we also commonly fail to see how those conceptions of home are partly fantasies. My approach, then, is paradoxical. Studies of homesickness reveal the challenges of change in mortal human life. We cannot be at home in any final way on Earth, because we continually change and the world continually changes. Homesickness means we are mortal animals. Anthropogenic global warming and climate change reveal this truth all the more dramatically. Climate change dramatically shows the tenuous and fickle character of life for mortal creatures.

This is not a new reality. It is fundamental. We live in a very big universe and fitfully inhabit a very small part of it. Thoreau saw this in his famous moment of awe on Mount Katahdin, uttering, "*Contact! Contact! Who* are we? *Where* are we?"[19] Locales are inevitably affected by larger forces—not just climate change or global capitalism but the effects of a star we call the sun. However, such broad-brush sketches risk forgetting that our small, mortal lives matter immensely to us, and further that these lives impact many other forms of life and being that matter. We also have to attend to the finer details of the local to recognize the impacts of global warming and to grow cultures that might stem the global warming tide and mitigate more of its effects. But to avoid many of the historical hazards connected to certain, often exclusively narrow ideas of home, we must also bear in mind the sense that home has never been fixed and has never been perfect. Fond, nostalgic retrospection is selective. But selectivity is a principle of all conscious cognition. Here again we should dynamically engage this paradox.

An eco-cosmopolitan perspective—with emphasis on the root "cosmos"—can be understood to position us as small beings in a large universe. But our desire to make our smallness meaningful requires a person to "find your place where you are," as Dōgen puts it.[20] There is a compellingly odd circularity in this formulation; it is slightly unclear whether the phrase has us, as agents, doing the "finding," or whether it really involves a halt in trying to "find," a halt to our "agency." How can we "find" a place when we are already there? Further, it is our place ("your place"); why would we need to find it? The brief phrase turns what is "ours" inside out, rendering it uncanny, rendering us uncanny. Even though "we" are already "there," we must both "find" ourselves and find our place. "Find" is something like "recognize," and it is more passive, like "cosms of the universe" finding their way into us. But utter passivity will not do the trick either. That is precisely the active paradox that constitutes both self and place: a mixture of action and open passivity, a dynamism that is more than any single agent. Of course, the ambiguous phrase, lent more density by its selection and emphasis on Snyder's part, by his curation of it, holds both of these possibilities together for us, so we can access them at once, if we reread, muse, or circle about it. Indeed the phrase is, in precisely its movement, a guide, a demonstration, a kind of agent driving us, like software perhaps.

That kind of paradoxical density clarifies what it really means for this conclusion to argue that homesickness is a posthumanist feeling we should both acknowledge and practice. These are interbraided and related but distinct modes, acknowledgment and practice. I am advocating, retweeting perhaps, a practice of the wild, in Snyder's formulation, where "wild" signifies the nonhuman that we work hard to access; we then permit it to do its work on us, and on our practices. *The Practice of the Wild* rigorously engages many of the ideas argued in this book, as well as many ideas in Morton's justifiably celebrated work. Snyder's writing there is prescient in terms of new materialism, dark ecology, animal studies, posthumanism, politics, and much more.[21]

In Snyder, many of these ideas appear specifically in terms of home and place, but the full complexity of his accounts has often gone unregistered in subsequent criticism. For instance, in his essay "Blue Mountains Constantly Walking" in *The Practice of the Wild,* largely a meditation on Dōgen's "Mountains and Waters Sutra," Snyder discusses ninth-century Chinese poet Han-shan's understanding of the dynamics of home. Han-shan calls himself "homeless," which Snyder glosses in classically eco-cosmopolitan terms: "being at home in the whole universe."[22] This is the same kind of paradox I mean to evoke with the word "homesickness." In this definition, being at home is also being homeless or perhaps selfless, even coterminous with the universe. Snyder's discussion of home here presses further, into what might now be called a kind of new or vital materialism.

> And then the literal "house," when seen as just another piece of the world, is itself impermanent and composite, a poor "homeless" thing in its own right. Houses are made up, heaped together, of pine boards, clay tiles, cedar battens, river boulder piers, windows scrounged from wrecking yards, knobs from K-Mart, mats from Cost Plus, kitchen floor of sandstone from some mountain ridge, doormat from Longs—made up of the same world as you and me and mice.[23]

Snyder's list is itself significant. It is notably and purposely ordinary and long, a Whitmanian catalog of things that moves through capitalism, labor, and "nature" to "you and me and mice." Abruptly then—to powerful effect—after this passage Snyder immediately pivots from this mundane world of stuff back to Dōgen, whom Snyder quotes: "Blue mountains are neither sentient nor insentient. You are neither sentient nor insentient. At this moment, you cannot doubt the blue mountains constantly walking."[24] Here is a radical reinterpretation of the likenesses among human and nonhuman beings, akin to many arguments being made currently in posthumanist circles. Elsewhere in the chapter, Snyder reminds us that "blue mountains" is shorthand for the world, or physical reality, and it is in flux. The fact that *we* think and write and walk is proof, in this passage, of that flux. That is, studying things like mountains is a form of studying ourselves, and vice versa. So is studying houses. Houses are themselves, by their very materiality, homesick, like us.

Yet there is a further step, Snyder insists. The task is to recognize change, to see our homelessness, and then bring that wide, eco-cosmopolitan perspective back to the local and the routine, to the ordinary and the worldly. Snyder writes, again in *The Practice of the Wild,* "Some quote a Buddhist saying back at us: 'all is impermanent.' Indeed. All the more reason to move gently and cause less harm."[25] In other words, in the title of William E. Connolly's 2013 book: "the fragility of things."[26] This view returns Snyder to the local and particular, to the suggestion that we must defend "plants, bugs, and animals," to the idea that "weeds are precious, mice are precious."[27] He argues in *The Practice of the Wild* that "bioregional awareness teaches us in *specific* ways," but it is "not just a rural program; it is as much for the restoration of urban neighborhood life and the greening of the cities."[28] For Snyder, furthermore, "being inhabitory, being place-based, has never meant that one didn't travel from time to time."[29]

He further develops this deeply eco-cosmopolitan view in his essay "Kitkitdizze: A Node in the Net," published in *A Place in Space.*[30] The title does much work. "A Node in the Net" evokes Snyder's sense of home being one place in a much larger world. He writes, "I set up my library and wrote poems and essays by lantern light, then went out periodically, lecturing and teaching around the country. I thought of my home as a well-concealed base camp from which I raided university treasuries."[31] Robust cosmopolitanism, that is, has long been part of his bioregionalist program. But here again, he also resolutely attends to the local, signaled by the first word of the title. Snyder and his family adopted this word as the name of their house in the Sierras, and it signals their rich sense of community. It is a "low groundcover bush called *kitkitkdizze* in the language of the Wintun, a nearby valley people."[32] That is, a humble, hardy, local plant, named by Indian inhabitants, names Snyder's family's place of practice and inhabitation. Some might call this cultural or even ecological appropriation, but such an anticosmopolitanist critique fails to recognize both Snyder's politics and the larger realities of cultural and ecological hybridity, or sympoiesis.

Snyder's sensibility, an attention to the immediate and the local informed by wide, eco-cosmopolitan principles, also informs a crucially important issue for him, one he uses to conclude *The Practice of the Wild*: the "sacramental economy," or "the taking of life for food."[33] In the final pages, he writes,

> Eating is a sacrament. The grace we say clears our hearts and guides the children and welcomes the guest, all at the same time. We look at eggs, apples, stew. They are evidence of plenitude, excess, a great reproductive exuberance. Millions of grains of grass-seed that will become rice or flour, millions of codfish fry that will never, and *must* never, grow to maturity.[34]

And it is not just other forms of life: "We too will be offerings—we are all edible."[35] For Snyder, such insights should drive us into something like thankfulness in a gift economy/ecology; indeed these insights press us into an affective state that resists being named, in ways akin to the challenges of naming trauma discussed in many of my preceding chapters.[36] Beyond or just inside language, such insights lead to practice. They inspire a highly localized form of practice informed by the broadest, best information, by "High Quality Information," to borrow the title of one of Snyder's poems.[37] Snyder's approach aims to make community not only with human guests—as in the passage just quoted—but to recognize our deep kinship with all the rest of the material world in our shared physical selves, at a kind of slow banquet of intersubjectivity/interobjectivity.

Affective Homesickness

Snyder's sense of sacrament turns on the recognition of mortality, of weakness, a dark ecological truth that is also liberating. It is homesickness, or sickness at home. We feel homesickness because, despite the assurances of humanism, we are mortal, like the other animals, and our home cannot save us from that status. As Heather Houser argues in *Ecosickness in Contemporary U.S. Fiction: Environment and Affect,* data is not sufficient to adequately understand human illness and exposure to mortality.[38] We need to register affective states and, I emphasize, figures, images, tropes, narratives, and other elements central to the traditional humanities. I have insisted that such elements of meaning are better engaged in a posthumanities framework, which is not at all to say they are dismissed, as is sometimes supposed. Such a simplistic account of posthumanism misses its nuances, which aim not to surrender systems of meaning or human values but instead to reframe them in light of key premises such as species interdependence, human biology, the impacts of technology, and so on.

Houser also emphasizes that affective dispositions bear within them the power to shift social and ecological norms and behaviors, or, on the other hand, to suppress social changes. Her discussion of this point notes that negative affects like depression can themselves be useful, driving a course of action.[39] The argument in *Homesickness* often dwells on such negative emotions, and while I agree with Houser's point that we can find routes to action and change in those emotions, one of my persistent (posthumanist) claims is that these negative affects can teach us something else too: that, too often, more "action" is precisely the problem.

That is, one of the driving forces of the Anthropocene has been the long-standing bias toward change, activity, movement (mobility), and so on. Yet negative affects teach us about mortality, an inescapable condition, no matter how much we move, and it is mortality on a much larger scale—in terms of species and entire ecosystems—that the Anthropocene has instigated. We need to better recognize the reality of human weakness and more often heed the advice held together by the phrase that opened this chapter, this ahuman cosm: don't just do something, sit there.[40] It is a useful thing to have in one's pocket, so to speak. Morton's notion of *Dark Ecology* is also an effective way to name this attitude, which gathers to it ironic, gothic, humorous, depressive, and other less "positive" affective conditions, a kind of deep blues. Again, to recognize the larger ecocritical context, in *The Practice of the Wild,* Snyder emphasizes the importance of "the dark side of nature," devoting a section to discussion of it.[41]

To clarify, however: I am not arguing that we should *entirely* surrender to depression or stop getting up in the morning. I am sincerely arguing, with Thoreau, that we would *more often* be better served by sleeping in and by inhabiting affective states outside purposive labor. In "Walking," Thoreau writes, "Many a poor sore-eyed student that I have heard of would grow faster, both intellectually and physically, if, instead of sitting up so very late, he honestly slumbered a fool's allowance." The next paragraph continues, "There may be an excess even of informing light."[42] Dark ecology involves, among other things, sleeping.[43] Thoreau's resistance to the familiar Western tendencies toward action, progress, learning, and change relates to his wry declaration of faith in "Walking": "I believe in the forest, and in the meadow, and in the night in which the corn grows."[44] This credo completely reverses dominant conventions of labor, embodiment, and nonhuman nature more generally. Thoreau's trust in these nonhuman entities—forest, meadow, and night—is coupled with his skepticism about guiding Enlightenment humanist values. He shows our need to rethink how we inhabit space and time.

Thoreau makes a powerful case for what we might call *radical walking*, offering a funny and stinging case for the value of that undertaking. He claims in "Walking," contrary to Yankee industry and American norms of work, "No wealth can buy the requisite leisure, freedom, and independence" necessary to really walk.[45] On days when he fails to prioritize walking, Thoreau writes, he "felt as if I had committed some sin to be atoned for,—I confess that I am astonished at the power of endurance, to say nothing of the moral insensibility, of my neighbors who confine themselves to shops and offices the whole day for weeks and months, aye, and years almost together. I know not what manner of stuff they are of,—."[46] The interjection of these words between dashes produces grammatically what their content conveys—a sense of unnatural surprise, a sense of disruptive shock. The shock is intensified, of course, by Thoreau's inversions of concepts like "sin" and "moral insensibility," which he returns resoundingly to Earth, to embodied experience, to "stuff," severing them from abstract theological codes. Thoreau's reversals culminate later in the essay in his extravagant, hilarious, and powerful declaration that, faced with the choice between "the most beautiful garden that ever human art contrived" or "a Dismal Swamp, I should certainly decide for the swamp. How vain, then, have been all your labors, citizens, for me!"[47]

On the other hand, the key fact that guides so many ecocritics and others regarding questions of action is this: we are in a planetary ecological crisis, and the momentum is all on the side of the systems we have built over millennia that perpetuate and deepen this harm. To some extent, we must work to change and unravel these systems. True. Agreed. But if we can do more to live outside the forward-moving, ever-on-the-go mentalities and embrace resilience and other less, well, progressivist forms of thought, many of the systems that cause harm will wither on their own. In other words, we do not need to unwork all the harmful entities. In many cases, if enough of us decide to do so, we can, even must, simply walk away from them.

Some have worried that this sort of critique of action, agency, and movement is escapist, that it is an argument reflecting privilege. Can everyone implement my deliberately provocative suggestion, "don't just do something, sit there"? In short, yes, everyone can. In fact, everyone already does to some extent, since quiet reflection is a dimension of life, human and otherwise. I am simply insisting on its value. Further, to a significant extent, the bias toward movement and action is the privileged orientation. The default embrace of "progress" is often literally escapist. Thinking in a wider frame, as many scholars on the Anthropocene advocate, it becomes clear that much human injury—much racism, imperialism, colonialism; eugenics, ecological damage, war; and more—all derive from an assumption that change and "progress" must happen. Those progressivist modes are often materialized as mobility, movement, or even as cosmopolitanism. Many cultures were damaged and dislocated by this historical trajectory of modernity, writ large. My suggestion that we be more circumspect about mobility, action, agency, and progress has both cultural and personal dimensions that are intertwined. Undertakings such as sitting meditation or brooding about poems and novels, I am claiming, are forms of slow, recursive time and passive or receptive selfhood that markedly contrast with too-common assumptions about (often masculinist and ableist) action and agency.

Consider again another Henry, the figure of Frederic Henry in Hemingway's *A Farewell to Arms,* having deserted the war in utter desperation, narrowly escaping with his life and then being swept through the long curves of a river, holding for dear life onto a timber that happens to be floating near him.[48] He has escaped the subjectivity of war and begun to find another way to be, one that is outside those familiar forms of action. Although such an escape might be seen as apolitical, that would be too simple. Like Thoreau's long walks, Henry's is a political act, and all the more so if its importance, its justifications, and its nuances can be amplified by, say, putting the act in a resonant cultural text like a novel, or even, perhaps, in a work of cultural and literary criticism like this one. We should curate it as a past example. Then we posthumanists need to keep listening, musing on its significance, and conveying what we think, letting its implications haunt and direct us.

To a large degree, Henry gives himself over to the river. Trusting more to the world and less to our own teleologies is a powerful posthumanist gesture, one that can help us find ourselves more at home on planet Earth, a place that we hope will not change so radically or so quickly in the Anthropocene that we will cease to recognize it, or even cease to inhabit it at all.

Acknowledgments

Thanks to all whom I study and quote, and thanks to the many scholarly communities I am lucky to be (or to have been) part of—the Association for the Study of Literature and Environment; the Society for Literature, Science, and the Arts; Kent State University, including the University Research Council; La Salle University, the Program for Writing and Rhetoric at the University of Colorado, Boulder; the Hemingway Society, especially Susan Beegel, Kirk Curnutt, Suzanne del Gizzo, Hilary Justice, Verna Kale, Kevin Maier, Debra Moddelmog, Mark Ott, Robert Trogdon, and Alex Vernon; and the Western Literature Society. Thanks to many individuals who gave me good pointers: John Baky, La Salle Library director, for advice and research assistance; Kevin Harty, for much support and advice; La Salle Office of the Provost, Rich Nigro, for research support; Craig Franson; Dan Shea, for encouragement; Suzanne Clark, for much advice early in my thinking on these matters; Susan Wrynn; Sarah McFarland, for discussions of animals and agency; and special thanks to Jennifer Ladino for her scrupulous reading of the manuscript. Sheila McMahon improved the book with her suggestions. Thanks to Gabriel Levin and especially Douglas Armato at the University of Minnesota Press for supporting this work. Christopher Roman, Nicole Willey, Kevin Floyd, and, again, Robert Trogdon have been especially inspiriting colleagues at Kent State. Tammy Voelker and Thomas Warren helped at the Kent State library. At the University of Oregon, I would like to thank Molly Westling, whose scholarship and presence has continued to influence my thinking and work; John Gage; Jim Crosswhite; Linda Kintz; and Joseph Fraccia, for much good advice about early elements of this argument. Glen Love's ecocritical work and teaching continue to guide me. Mike Stamm and Marilyn Reid deserve thanks for their patient work, as does Karen Ford. At the University of Colorado English department years ago: thanks to Timothy Morton and John Graham. Thanks also to Gary Snyder, whom I don't know personally but whose work has been a guiding light for me and for many others. He taught me that we are all homesick.

David Adams and Vicki Millard helped me refine my arguments by listening to me talk about homesickness. My father, Dennis Hediger; my brother, Wes Hediger; my sister, Rebecca Hediger; and my extended family all supported me even as I disappeared into texts for much too long. Amanda Adams suggested texts, tested versions of arguments, and helped in innumerable other ways, too many to list. Our boys Samuel and Henry did not exactly let me work—which is right and good! To the many places I love (which means all of us), perched in your strange uniqueness in the world—thanks are owed you in politics and in gestures beyond this one.

Notes

Preface

1. Suzanne Goldenberg, "America's Climate Refugees," *The Guardian,* May 13, 2013.

2. *When the Levees Broke: A Requiem in Four Acts,* directed by Spike Lee (New York: HBO Documentary Films, 2006); *Treme,* created by Eric Ellis Overmyer and David Simon (Baltimore: Blown Deadlines Productions, 2010–13).

3. Timothy Morton, *Hyperobjects: Philosophy and Ecology after the End of the World* (Minneapolis: University of Minnesota Press, 2013), 123, 176.

Introduction

1. Peter T. Kilborn, *Next Stop, Reloville: Life inside America's New Rootless Professional Class* (New York: Times Books, 2009), 176.

2. Kilborn, 168–78.

3. Kilborn, 170.

4. Mobility has declined notably in the United States during the period 1980–2013, a reality that either helps cause or is caused by a "sluggish economy." Patricia Cohen, "A Dearth of Pioneers: Fewer Americans Strike Out for New Jobs, Crimping the Recovery," *New York Times,* May 25, 2016. Nonetheless, in a larger historical and geographical context, U.S. mobility remains high, especially for the educated and well-heeled classes.

5. My sense of the word "homesickness" here has much in common with the Welsh word "hiraeth," as described by Pamela Petro, "Dreaming in Welsh," *Paris Review,* September 18, 2012.

6. Leo Marx, *The Machine in the Garden: Technology and the Pastoral Ideal in America* (New York: Oxford University Press, 1964), 25.

7. Richard Grusin makes a case against "posthumanism" as a term, favoring instead "nonhuman." Grusin accuses the posthumanist movement of making "a claim

about teleology or progress in which we begin with the human and see a transformation from the human to the posthuman, after or beyond the human." Richard Grusin, introduction to *The Nonhuman Turn,* ed. Richard Grusin (Minneapolis: University of Minnesota Press, 2015), xi. While this may be an accurate account of some posthumanisms, it is not fair to all of them. In fact, Cary Wolfe explicitly distinguishes his meaning for the term from meanings centered on an after-humanity approach. Cary Wolfe, *What Is Posthumanism?* (Minneapolis: University of Minnesota Press, 2010), xv. Instead, Wolfe intends his term to mean after human*ism* (xiv), and this distinction is crucial. Although Grusin cites Wolfe's book, his critique fails to register this dimension of Wolfe's argument.

8. Clay Routledge, *Nostalgia: A Psychological Resource* (New York: Routledge, 2016), 83.

9. Ursula K. Heise, *Sense of Place and Sense of Planet: The Environmental Imagination of the Global* (Oxford: Oxford University Press, 2008), 4, 6.

10. David Harvey, *Cosmopolitanism and the Geographies of Freedom* (New York: Columbia University Press, 2009), 11.

11. See Heise, *Sense of Place and Sense of Planet,* 6, for a good summary of contemporary cosmopolitanism.

12. Lennard J. Davis, *Bending Over Backwards: Disability, Dismodernism, and Other Difficult Positions* (New York: New York University Press, 2002), 30.

13. Richard Shapcott summarizes anticosmopolitan criticisms, noting their worry about the "imposition of the culturally specific conception of justice upon others," contributing to "the dissolution of a desirable plurality of forms of human life." See Richard Shapcott, "Anti-cosmopolitanism, Pluralism, and the Cosmopolitan Harm Principle," *Review of International Studies* 34 (2008): 187. Often, asserts Chike Jeffords, this means eurocentrism. Chike Jeffords, "Appiah's Cosmopolitanism," *Southern Journal of Philosophy* 51, no. 4 (2013): 488–510. Shapcott answers to such concerns by emphasizing how the wariness of doing harm that characterizes much cosmopolitanism can correct against the risk of homogenizing universalism. Harvey's criticisms of cosmopolitanism, noted above, are also relevant here.

14. On dark ecology, see Timothy Morton, *Dark Ecology: For a Logic of Future Coexistence* (New York: Columbia University Press, 2016); Timothy Morton, *The Ecological Thought* (Cambridge, Mass.: Harvard University Press, 2010), chapter 2.

15. Jacques Derrida, *On Cosmopolitanism and Forgiveness,* trans. Mark Dooley and Michael Collins Hughes (London: Routledge, 2001), 21–22.

16. Derrida, 23.

17. In *What Is Posthumanism?* Cary Wolfe, drawing from Michel Foucault, points out that "humanism's 'anthropological universals' underwrite a dogma for which the Enlightenment, if we are true to its spirit, should have no patience" (xvi). Yet, as Wolfe recognizes, too often the Enlightenment fails to live up to its own ideals. So, depending on what form of Enlightenment thought we engage, posthumanism can be viewed as either in league with or opposed to the Enlightenment.

18. Christophe Bonneuil and Jean-Baptiste Fressoz, *The Shock of the Anthropocene: The Earth, History and Us*, trans. David Fernbach (London: Verso, 2015), 63–64.

19. Donna Haraway, *When Species Meet* (Minneapolis: University of Minnesota Press, 2008), 3–4.

20. Alison Abbott, "Scientists Bust Myth That Our Bodies Have More Bacteria than Human Cells," *Nature: International Weekly Journal of Science*, January 8, 2016, https://www.nature.com/news/scientists-bust-myth-that-our-bodies-have-more-bacteria-than-human-cells-1.19136.

21. Timothy Morton, *Hyperobjects: Philosophy and Ecology after the End of the World* (Minneapolis: University of Minnesota Press, 2013), 58.

22. Wolfe, *What Is Posthumanism?*, xv. Similarly, David Wills demonstrates the presence of technology in human thought, "a technology that was always there." David Wills, *Dorsality: Thinking Back through Technology and Politics* (Minneapolis: University of Minnesota Press, 2008), 3.

23. For a range of essays demonstrating human reliance on animals in war, see Ryan Hediger, ed., *Animals and War: Studies of Europe and North America* (Leiden: Brill, 2013). My introduction to *Animals and War* argues that this reliance is entangled with technology (6).

24. Morton, *Dark Ecology*, 45.

25. Morton, xvi–xvii.

26. Wolfe, *What Is Posthumanism?*, xv.

27. Wolfe, xv–xvi.

28. Heise, *Sense of Place and Sense of Planet*, 7.

29. Heise, 8.

30. Morton calls this interactive reality of selfhood a "fuzzy set" (*Dark Ecology*, 71), underscoring that the range and number of entities with which/whom the subject interacts are impossible to absolutely, discreetly determine.

31. Brian Massumi, *Politics of Affect* (Cambridge, UK: Polity, 2015), 93–94. This model of experience is closely parallel to the one Ralph Waldo Emerson describes in his canonical essay "The American Scholar." He notes that "recent actions" are too near, too much "a part of life" for us to fully register their significance. It is only later that "it detaches itself from the life like a ripe fruit, to become a thought of the mind." Ralph Waldo Emerson, "The American Scholar," in *The Portable Emerson*, ed. Carl Bode (New York: Penguin, 1981), 60. This retrospective movement of "the mind" is part of what I mean by homesickness, since this structure inaugurates a necessarily backward referencing system in the self.

32. This point is akin to Cary Wolfe's note that, in Martin Heidegger's argument, "Being is not 'present' (that Being is time)." Cary Wolfe, "Introduction: Cinders after Biopolitics," in *Cinders*, by Jacques Derrida, trans. Ned Lukacher (Minneapolis: University of Minnesota Press, 2014), xxv.

33. Morton, *Dark Ecology*, 25.

34. For instance, see Bonneuil and Fressoz, *The Shock of the Anthropocene*, in which the authors underscore Hannah Arendt's worry that the space age, announced

by the launch of the Soviet satellite Sputnik, represented "a modernist denial of the human condition." They quote Arendt's words, calling Sputnik "a rebellion against human existence as it has been given, a free gift from nowhere (secularly speaking), which he wishes to exchange, as it were, for something he has made himself" (61). See also Hannah Arendt, *The Human Condition* (Chicago: University of Chicago Press, 2013), 2–3.

35. David Wills puts that idea this way, as quoted by Cary Wolfe in *What Is Posthumanism?*: We are "'forever removed from ourselves' as the fundamental condition of what it means to be human" (36). See also David Wills, *Matchbook: Essays in Deconstruction* (Stanford, Calif.: Stanford University Press, 2005), 183–84.

36. Dylan Trigg argues that a sense of estrangement is also inherent to embodiment itself, since the body's general form transcends the individual. See Dylan Trigg, *The Memory of Place: A Phenomenology of the Uncanny* (Athens: Ohio University Press, 2012).

37. For instance, Greg Garrard notes wariness regarding the pastoral and its nostalgic function. Greg Garrard, *Ecocriticism*, 2nd ed. (London: Routledge, 2012), 37–65. Raymond Williams's proto-ecocritical book *The Country and the City* (New York: Oxford University Press, 1973) is a critique of the reactionary function of nostalgia. Similarly, Louise H. Westling criticizes what she understands as the "imperialist nostalgia" "at the heart of the American pastoral." Louise H. Westling, *The Green Breast of the New World: Landscape, Gender, and American Fiction* (Athens: University of Georgia Press, 1996), 52, 80–81.

38. Jennifer K. Ladino, *Reclaiming Nostalgia: Longing for Nature in American Literature* (Charlottesville: University of Virginia Press, 2012).

39. For instance, see Catherine L. Albanese, *Nature Religion in America: From the Algonkian Indians to the New Age* (Chicago: University of Chicago Press, 1991); Garrard, *Ecocriticism*, especially chapter 5, "Apocalypse."

40. Heise, *Sense of Place and Sense of Planet*, 62.

41. Morton, *The Ecological Thought*, 28.

42. Morton, *Hyperobjects*; Stacy Alaimo, *Bodily Natures: Science, Environment, and the Material Self* (Bloomington: Indiana University Press, 2010).

43. Rachel Carson, *Silent Spring* (New York: Houghton Mifflin, 1962).

44. Richard H. Grove, *Green Imperialism: Colonial Expansion, Tropical Island Edens and the Origins of Environmentalism, 1600–1860* (Cambridge: Cambridge University Press, 1996), 3.

45. Morton, *Dark Ecology*, 38. It is probably impossible to date a first "homesickness." On this point, I agree with Morton's insistence on a complex, nonlinear temporality. More specifically, he criticizes the search for "an origin point" of human realities (like homesickness), "exactly there, exactly then, constantly present in a definable archive." He suggests, "Such an assertion is recursively part of the very agrilogistic schema we are attempting to explain" (59).

46. Morton, 38–39.

47. Morton, *Hyperobjects*, 69–80.

48. Lance Newman and Laura Walls, "Cosmopolitics and the Radical Pastoral: A Conversation with Laurence Buell, Hsuan Hsu, Anthony Lioi, and Paul Outka," *Journal of Ecocriticism* 3, no. 2 (2011): 59.

49. Graham Harman, *Guerrilla Metaphysics: Phenomenology and the Carpentry of Things* (Chicago: Open Court, 2005), 76.

50. Morton, *Dark Ecology,* 10.

51. Morton, 9.

52. This case therefore builds upon but goes beyond the classic discussion of place by Heidegger in "Building Dwelling Thinking," when he insists that the very idea of space is contingent on the "locale," the particularized place. He writes, for instance, that building dwelling places for humans means making "locales that allow spaces." See Martin Heidegger, "Building Dwelling Thinking," in *Basic Writings,* trans. Albert Hofstadter, ed. David Farrell Krell (London: Harper, 1993), 347–63 (quote on 360). Space as an idea is not possible without place. But if "space" is the abstracted stranger of the familiar friend "place," then in homesickness, places revert to spaces to some extent. An uncanny place regains some of the attributes of space. The Anthropocene makes this clearer than ever, but at bottom, I am arguing that for mortal creatures like ourselves, places have always been stranger than we customarily admit.

53. Wolfe, *What Is Posthumanism?,* 3–29, especially 14.

54. Morton, *Hyperobjects,* 5.

55. Morton, 2.

56. For Jacques Lacan, the concept of "the Real" names reality itself, beyond language, beyond what can be captured by language and by other systems of meaning. The Real escapes representation and symbolization. More generally, for Lacan human understanding involves the interbraiding of three elements: the Real with the Symbolic (language, laws, rituals, and so on) and the Imaginary (consciousness and self-awareness). For a concise summary of Lacan's thought, see Adrian Johnson, "Jacques Lacan," in *Stanford Encyclopedia of Philosophy,* last modified July 10, 2018, https://plato.stanford.edu/entries/lacan/.

57. Morton, *Hyperobjects,* 36.

58. Morton, *Dark Ecology,* 5.

59. Morton, *Hyperobjects,* 4.

60. Morton, 5.

61. Morton, 4.

62. Morton, *Dark Ecology,* 14. For a similar critique of the logic of agriculture, see Gary Snyder, *The Practice of the Wild* (1990; repr., Berkeley: Counterpoint, 2010), 84. For a compelling account of the founding of agriculture, see James C. Scott, *Against the Grain: A Deep History of the Earliest States* (New Haven, Conn.: Yale University Press, 2017).

63. Cary Wolfe, *Before the Law: Humans and Other Animals in a Biopolitical Frame* (Chicago: University of Chicago Press, 2013).

64. Timothy Clark, *Ecocriticism on the Edge: The Anthropocene as a Threshold Concept* (London: Bloomsbury, 2015).

65. Bonneuil and Fressoz demonstrate in *The Shock of the Anthropocene* that the dismissal of nostalgia was a way of shoring up progressivist modernity (279). This point connects to the much-debated history of the pastoral. Terry Gifford reminds us of the pastoral's roots in Theocritus's *Idylls,* in which the Greek scholar remembered his youth in Sicily, writing from the temporally and geographically distant Alexandria. Terry Gifford, "Pastoral, Anti-Pastoral, and Post-Pastoral," in *The Cambridge Companion to Literature and the Environment,* ed. Louise Westling (New York: Cambridge University Press, 2014), 17–30, especially 18. This scenario can be reframed as a kind of homesickness—a desire to return to a known place and time. To the extent that Theocritus and other later pastoralist writers recognize both the desire to return and its impossibility, they write with precisely the kind of complex homesickness I treat in this book.

66. Gary Cross, *Consumed Nostalgia: Memory in the Age of Fast Capitalism* (New York: Columbia University Press, 2015).

67. Bashō, "Even in Kyoto—," trans. Robert Hass, in *The Essential Haiku: Versions of Bashō, Buson, and Issa,* ed. Robert Hass (New Jersey: Ecco, 1994). 11.

68. Albrecht qtd. in Daniel Smith, "Is There an Ecological Unconscious?," *New York Times,* January 31, 2010, Sunday Magazine, 36. See also Glenn Albrecht, "'Solastalgia': A New Concept in Health and Identity," *PAN: Philosophy Activism Nature,* no. 3 (2005): 41–55.

69. Rosemarie Garland Thomson, *Extraordinary Bodies: Figuring Physical Disability in American Culture and Literature* (New York: Columbia University Press, 1997), 137.

70. Jacques Derrida, *The Animal That Therefore I Am,* ed. Marie-Louise Mallet, trans. David Wills (New York: Fordham University Press, 2008), 146.

71. Homi K. Bhabha, *The Location of Culture* (London: Routledge, 1994), 9.

72. Sigmund Freud, "The Uncanny," in *Writings on Art and Literature,* trans. and ed. James Strachey (Stanford: Stanford University Press, 1997), 193n1.

73. Freud, 193.

74. Freud, 195.

75. Bhabha, *The Location of Culture,* 12.

76. Rob Nixon, *Slow Violence and the Environmentalism of the Poor* (Cambridge, Mass.: Harvard University Press, 2011), 233.

77. Bhabha, *The Location of Culture,* 6.

78. Bhabha, 9.

79. Robert Post, introduction to *Another Cosmopolitanism,* by Seyla Benhabib, ed. Robert Post (Oxford: Oxford University Press, 2006), 1.

80. Kilborn, *Next Stop, Reloville,* 7.

81. Stephen Greenblatt, "Cultural Mobility: An Introduction," in *Cultural Mobility: A Manifesto,* ed. Stephen Greenblatt (Cambridge: Cambridge University Press, 2010), 1–23.

82. Greenblatt, 6, 3.

83. Susan J. Matt, *Homesickness: An American History* (Oxford: Oxford University Press, 2011).

84. Matt, 3.

85. Matt, 75.

86. Matt, 4.

87. Matt, 4.

88. Jennifer Rae Greeson, "The Prehistory of Possessive Individualism," *PMLA: Publications of the Modern Language Association of America* 127, no. 4 (2012): 918. See also Toni Morrison for a related argument about Mark Twain's *The Adventures of Huckleberry Finn*: "freedom has no meaning to Huck or to the text without the specter of enslavement, the anodyne to individualism; the yardstick of absolute power over the life of another; the signed, marked, informing, and mutating presence of a black slave." Toni Morrison, *Playing in the Dark: Whiteness and the Literary Imagination* (New York: Vintage, 1992), 56.

89. Matt, *Homesickness*, 5.

90. Matt, 75.

91. Matt, 13.

92. Mark Tran, "Forced Migration in the 21st Century: Urbanised and Unending," *The Guardian*, October 16, 2012.

93. Bonneuil and Fressoz, *The Shock of the Anthropocene*, 25.

94. Matt, *Homesickness*, 15.

95. Matt, 16.

96. Matt, 23.

97. Matt, 19.

98. Matt, 25, emphasis mine.

99. Matt, 27.

100. Matt, 26.

101. Matt, 75.

102. Matt, 36.

103. Matt, 6.

104. Matt, 46.

105. Greenblatt, "Cultural Mobility," 14.

106. Greenblatt, 5.

107. Greenblatt, 4.

108. In a case parallel to Greenblatt's, Fredric Jameson addresses the Roman appropriation of Greek ideas and language. Jameson quotes Heidegger's idea that "*Roman thought appropriates the Greek words without the corresponding experience, equally original, of what they say, without the Greek word.* The groundlessness of Western thought begins with this translation." Fredric Jameson, *A Singular Modernity: Essay on the Ontology of the Present* (New York: Verso, 2002), 58.

109. Heise, *Sense of Place and Sense of Planet*, 47.

110. Bonneuil and Fressoz, *The Shock of the Anthropocene*, 271–79.

111. Harvey, *Cosmopolitanism and the Geographies of Freedom*, 14.

112. Gary Snyder, *Nobody Home: Writing, Buddhism, and Living in Places* (San Antonio: Trinity University Press, 2014), 162.

113. Heise, *Sense of Place and Sense of Planet*, 43–44.

114. Gary Snyder, "The Recovery of Turtle Island," in *A Place in Space: Ethics, Aesthetics, and Watersheds* (Washington, D.C.: Counterpoint, 1995), 247. Snyder's prominence and influence have too often made him an easy target for so-called second-wave and later ecocriticism, but his work is sometimes grossly simplified in such accounts. Indeed, many of the impulses of so-called first-wave ecocriticism remain instructive today, having been ignored in the stereotypes produced of them by later readers and critics.

115. Snyder, 237.

116. Gary Snyder, "Reinhabitation," in *A Place in Space: Ethics, Aesthetics, and Watersheds* (Washington, D.C.: Counterpoint, 1995), 191.

117. Harvey, *Cosmopolitanism and the Geographies of Freedom*, 8.

118. Harvey, 9.

119. Mary Louise Pratt, "Harm's Way: Language and the Contemporary Arts of War," in "War," special issue, *PMLA* 124, no. 5 (2009): 1515–31.

120. Routledge, *Nostalgia*, 4.

121. Harvey, *Cosmopolitanism and the Geographies of Freedom*, 11–12.

122. Elisabeth Rosenthal, "As More Eat Meat, a Bid to Cut Emissions," *New York Times*, December 3, 2008.

123. Elizabeth Kolbert, *The Sixth Extinction: An Unnatural History* (New York: Henry Holt, 2014), 17.

124. Clark, *Ecocriticism on the Edge*, 6–10.

125. Thomas L. Friedman, *The World Is Flat: A Brief History of the Twenty-First Century* (New York: Farrar, Straus and Giroux, 2005), 5.

126. Wolfe, *What Is Posthumanism?*, xx.

127. For a good discussion of the gap between a thing and its concept, see Jane Bennett, *Vibrant Matter: A Political Ecology of Things* (Durham, N.C.: Duke University Press, 2010), 14.

128. Maurice Merleau-Ponty, *Phenomenology of Perception*, trans. Donald Landes (New York: Routledge), 262. Louise H. Westling connects Merleau-Ponty with environmental thinking, animal studies, and biosemiotics in *The Logos of the Living World: Merleau-Ponty, Animals, and Language* (New York: Fordham University Press, 2014).

129. Bennett, *Vibrant Matter*, xii.

130. Harman, *Guerilla Metaphysics*, 65.

131. Harman, 66.

132. Harman, 67.

133. William Rasch, "Introduction: The Self-Positing Society," in *Theories of Distinction: Redescribing the Descriptions of Modernity*, by Niklas Luhmann, ed. William Rasch, trans. Joseph O'Neil, Elliott Schreiber, Kerstin Behnke, and William Whobrey (Stanford: Stanford University Press, 2002), 4.

134. Wolfe, *What Is Posthumanism?*, xxi.

135. Wolfe, 258. See also Levi R. Bryant, *The Democracy of Objects* (Ann Arbor, Mich.: Open Humanities Press, 2011), 20–21.

136. The framework of the local versus the global is geographical; many of these same points can be made within philosophical (or perhaps postphilosophical, rhetorical) discourse, as many of the scholars cited in this chapter note. This move toward a "rhetoric" is discussed by Newton Garver, who urges that Derrida's work is part of a larger turn that treats language rhetorically rather than logically. Newton Garver, preface to *Speech and Phenomena, and Other Essays on Husserl's Theory of Signs*, by Jacques Derrida, trans. David B. Allison (Evanston: Northwestern University Press, 1973), especially xii. This means the return of an interest in "the relation of language to the world" (x). Language does not offer absolute truths; it offers contingent, context-dependent statements.

137. Bill McKibben, *The End of Nature* (New York: Anchor, 1989).

138. It is awareness that "nature" is a deeply problematic term that partly inspires Timothy Morton's books *Ecology without Nature: Rethinking Environmental Aesthetics* (Cambridge, Mass.: Harvard University Press, 2007), *The Ecological Thought*, *Hyperobjects*, and *Dark Ecology*.

139. Jacques Derrida, "'Eating Well,' or the Calculation of the Subject: An Interview with Jacques Derrida," trans. Peter Connor and Avital Ronell, in *Who Comes after the Subject?*, ed. Eduardo Cadava, Peter Connor, and Jean-Luc Nancy (New York: Routledge, 1991), 106. See also Derrida, *The Animal That Therefore I Am*, 104.

140. Dipesh Chakrabarty makes a clear case for the need to stop thinking of humans and nature as separate in "The Climate of History: Four Theses," *Critical Inquiry* 35, no. 2 (Winter 2009): 201.

141. Greenblatt, "Cultural Mobility," 5.

142. "A Tern around the World," editorial, *New York Times*, January 21, 2010. See also David S. Wilcove, *No Way Home: The Decline of the World's Great Animal Migrations* (Washington, D.C.: Island, 2008), 2.

143. Kolbert, *The Sixth Extinction*, 17.

144. Kolbert, 18–19.

145. Homi K. Bhabha, "The World and the Home," in *Close Reading: The Reader* (Durham, N.C.: Duke University Press, 2003), 366.

1. Suffering in Our Animal Skins

1. Snyder writes, "Place is one kind of place. Another field is the work we do." Gary Snyder, *The Practice of the Wild* (1990; repr., Berkeley: Counterpoint, 2010), 154.

2. Donna Haraway, *When Species Meet* (Minneapolis: University of Minnesota Press, 2008). In "Crittercam: Compounding Eyes in Naturecultures," chapter 9 of *When Species Meet*, Haraway shows how humans, other animals, and tools become interwoven into one ensemble of natureculture (249–63). See also Cary Wolfe, *What Is Posthumanism?* (Minneapolis: University of Minnesota Press, 2010), xxv.

3. For a key account of the relationship between body image and the physical body, see Elizabeth Grosz, *Volatile Bodies: Toward a Corporeal Feminism* (Bloomington: Indiana University Press, 1994).

4. David Harvey exposes the practical hazards of cosmopolitanism's universalizing gestures, which often tend to reiterate existing power structures, racism, sexism, and so on. David Harvey, *Cosmopolitanism and the Geographies of Freedom* (New York: Columbia University Press, 2009). More specifically, Linda F. Selzer explores how opponents of President Barack Obama resisted him as a figure of cosmopolitanism by reading his "raced body" as "subversively un-American." Linda F. Selzer, "Barack Obama, the 2008 Presidential Election, and the New Cosmopolitanism: Figuring the Black Body," *Melus* 35, no. 4 (2010): 16, 17. Similarly, De-Jung Cheng criticizes the deployment of cosmopolitan logic in the subculture of "couchsurfing," obscuring dangers to women couchsurfers and exemplifying how cosmopolitanism can tacitly reiterate a "disembodied, universalized, masculinist, and middle-class-centric perspective." De-Jung Cheng, "Gendered Couchsurfing: Women from Western Europe and East-Asia Contesting De-sexualised Cosmopolitanism," *Gender, Place & Culture* 24, no. 8 (2017): 1091.

5. On the importance of embodiment and its particularity, see Stacy Alaimo, *Bodily Natures: Science, Environment, and the Material Self* (Bloomington: Indiana University Press, 2010); Grosz, *Volatile Bodies.*

6. Haraway, *When Species Meet,* 4.

7. Annie Proulx, "The Half-Skinned Steer," in *Close Range: Wyoming Stories* (1999; repr., New York: Scribner, 2000), 31. Further citations to this work are given parenthetically in text.

8. Martha C. Nussbaum makes this point about disability, that every human endures times of relative disability, both in youth and in old age. Martha C. Nussbaum, *Frontiers of Justice: Disability, Nationality, Species Membership* (Cambridge, Mass.: Belknap Press of Harvard University Press, 2006), 101.

9. Cathy Caruth, introduction to *Trauma: Explorations in Memory,* ed. Cathy Caruth (Baltimore: Johns Hopkins University Press, 1995), 3–12.

10. The word "rendered" here is meant to conjure Nicole Shukin's discussion of rendering animal bodies in the process of transforming them from living creatures into commodities. See Nicole Shukin, *Animal Capital: Rendering Life in Biopolitical Times* (Minneapolis: University of Minnesota Press, 2009). Intellectual activity understood as a "rendering" restores the fact of embodiment to our thinking, making it material again; this approach also resonates with accounts of materiality in object-oriented ontology, such as Ian Bogost's notion of "carpentry" in *Alien Phenomenology, or What It's Like to Be a Thing* (Minneapolis: University of Minnesota Press, 2012), 85–111.

11. Timothy Clark, "Nature, Post Nature," in *The Cambridge Companion to Literature and the Environment,* ed. Loiuse Westling (Cambridge: Cambridge University Press, 2014), 75–89.

12. Clark, 86–87.

13. Timothy Morton, *Hyperobjects: Philosophy and Ecology after the End of the World* (Minneapolis: University of Minnesota Press, 2013); Clark, 82.

14. See Cora Diamond, "The Difficulty of Reality and the Difficulty of Philosophy," in *Philosophy and Animal Life* (New York: Columbia University Press, 2008), 43–89; and Wolfe, *What Is Posthumanism?,* for more on, in Wolfe's words, "the limits of our own thinking in confronting" difficult realities (69–70).

15. Annie Proulx, *The Shipping News* (New York: Scribner, 1999). Further citations to this work are given parenthetically in text.

16. Annie Proulx, *Close Range*; Annie Proulx, *Bad Dirt: Wyoming Stories 2* (New York: Scribner, 2004); Annie Proulx, *Fine Just the Way It Is: Wyoming Stories 3* (New York: Scribner, 2008).

17. Alex Hunt, ed., *The Geographical Imagination of Annie Proulx: Rethinking Regionalism* (Lanham, Md.: Lexington Books, 2009).

18. Alex Hunt, "Introduction: The Insistence of Geography in the Writing of Annie Proulx," in *The Geographical Imagination of Annie Proulx: Rethinking Regionalism,* ed. Alex Hunt (Lanham, Md.: Lexington Books, 2009), 1.

19. Annie Proulx, *Barkskins* (New York: Scribner, 2016). In *Barkskins* Proulx treats a vast span of time, 1693–2013, and this wide temporal focus, according to reviewer Kevin Grauke, prevents her from exploring character with the nuance we might expect from a novelist, especially one of her caliber. Kevin Grauke, "'Barkskins': Sweeping, Not Always Captivating Tale of Ecological Tragedy," *Philadelphia Inquirer,* June 26, 2016. However, that tendency to downplay human character is exactly consistent with my reading of her oeuvre in this chapter.

20. J. Baird Callicot and Michael P. Nelson, eds., *The Great New Wilderness Debate* (Athens: University of Georgia Press, 1998); Michael P. Nelson and J. Baird Callicot, eds., *The Wilderness Debate Rages On: Continuing the Great New Wilderness Debate* (Athens: University of Georgia Press, 2008).

21. William Cronon, "The Trouble with Wilderness; Or, Getting Back to the Wrong Nature," reprinted in *The Great New Wilderness Debate,* ed. J. Baird Callicot and Michael P. Nelson (Athens: University of Georgia Press, 1998), 471–99; Annette Kolodny, *The Lay of the Land: Metaphor as Experience and History in American Life and Letters* (Chapel Hill: University of North Carolina Press, 1975); Stephanie Rutherford, *Governing the Wild: Ecotours of Power* (Minneapolis: University of Minnesota Press, 2011).

22. Timothy Morton, *The Ecological Thought* (Cambridge, Mass.: Harvard University Press, 2010), 14–15.

23. Frederick Turner, "Cultivating the American Garden," in *The Ecocriticism Reader: Landmarks in Literary Ecology,* ed. Cheryll Glotfelty and Harold Fromm (Athens: University of Georgia Press, 1996), 40–51. Cronon, "The Trouble with Wilderness," also engages the notion of nature as a garden (494). I find the garden metaphor insufficient, given the clear differences between what we normally understand as a garden and the kind of biotic regimes that flourish in places with far less human intervention.

24. See Roderick Frazier Nash, *Wilderness and the American Mind,* now in its fifth edition, for a history of ideas of wilderness (1967; repr., New Haven, Conn.: Yale University Press, 2014).

25. Cronon, "The Trouble with Wilderness," 495.

26. See Timothy Morton, "Queer Ecology," *PMLA* 125, no. 2 (2010): 273–82, for thinking in this direction—though Morton does not try to recuperate the notion of "wilderness" as I do here.

27. Morton, *The Ecological Thought,* 5–6.

28. Morton, 7.

29. Lawrence Buell, *Writing for an Endangered World: Literature, Culture, and Environment in the U.S. and Beyond* (Cambridge, Mass.: Belknap Press of Harvard University Press, 2001), 6.

30. Haraway, *When Species Meet,* 3.

31. See Haraway, 330n33, for her explanation of this word choice.

32. Haraway, 4.

33. Jane Bennett, *Vibrant Matter: A Political Ecology of Things* (Durham, N.C.: Duke University Press, 2010), 1.

34. Bennett, 1.

35. Bennett, 2–3.

36. Snyder, *Practice of the Wild,* 15.

37. Snyder, 17–19.

38. Timothy Morton, *Ecology without Nature: Rethinking Environmental Aesthetics* (Cambridge, Mass.: Harvard University Press, 2007); Timothy Morton, *Realist Magic: Objects, Ontology, Causality* (Ann Arbor, Mich.: Open Humanities Press, 2013); Timothy Morton, *Dark Ecology: For a Logic of Future Coexistence* (New York: Columbia University Press, 2016).

39. Wolfe, *What Is Posthumanism?*; Wolfe, *Critical Environments: Postmodern Theory and the Pragmatics of the "Outside"* (Minneapolis: University of Minnesota Press, 1998). See also Morton, *The Ecological Thought,* 4.

40. William Rasch makes this point in "Introduction: The Self-Positing Society," in *Theories of Distinction: Redescribing the Descriptions of Modernity,* by Niklas Luhmann, trans. Joseph O'Neil, Elliott Schreiber, Kerstin Behnke, and William Whobrey (Stanford: Stanford University Press, 2002).

41. See chapter 4 of Luhmann, *Theories of Distinction.*

42. Rob Nixon, *Slow Violence and the Environmentalism of the Poor* (Cambridge, Mass.: Harvard University Press, 2011), 90.

43. For example, see Emmanuel Levinas, *Otherwise than Being, or Beyond Essence,* trans. Alphonso Lingis (Pittsburgh: Duquesne University Press, 1998), 156.

44. See Haraway's discussion of Vitruvian Man and its stakes in posthumanism, in *When Species Meet,* 7–8.

45. Haraway, 3–4.

46. Alison Abbott, "Scientists Bust Myth That Our Bodies Have More Bacteria than Human Cells," *Nature: International Weekly Journal of Science,* January 8, 2016,

https://www.nature.com/news/scientists-bust-myth-that-our-bodies-have-more-bacteria-than-human-cells-1.19136.

47. Fiona Polack, "Taking the Waters: Abjection and Homecoming in *The Shipping News* and *Death of a River Guide*," *Journal of Commonwealth Literature* 41, no. 1 (2006): 93–109.

48. Hunt, introduction to Hunt, *The Geographical Imagination of Annie Proulx*, 7. See also Jennifer Denise Ryan, "Landed Bodies: Geography and Disability in *The Shipping News*," in *The Geographical Imagination of Annie Proulx: Rethinking Regionalism*, ed. Alex Hunt (Lanham, Md.: Lexington Books, 2009), 127–40.

49. Hunt, *The Geographical Imagination of Annie Proulx*, 4 (on fate), 6 (on determinism and possibilism).

50. Jacques Derrida, *The Animal That Therefore I Am*, ed. Marie-Louise Mallet, trans. David Wills (New York: Fordham University Press, 2008), 27.

51. Derrida, 27.

52. David Harvey, *Cosmopolitanism and the Geographies of Freedom* (New York: Columbia University Press, 2009), 6–14, 73.

53. Ursula K. Heise, *Sense of Place and Sense of Planet: The Environmental Imagination of the Global* (Oxford: Oxford University Press, 2008), 30–33.

54. Heise, 119–59; Ulrich Beck, *World Risk Society* (Cambridge, UK: Polity Press, 1999).

55. Ryan, "Landed Bodies," 129. To clarify and be fair: I recognize that every interpretation is subject to the norms and protocols of its interpretive framework. So even though I am disputing some of Ryan's argument, I find it valuable. In fact, it is precisely its difference that helps me formulate my case, demonstrating the perspectives posthumanism helps make possible. In making this point, I am writing in the spirit articulated by Rita Felski, discussing Bruno Latour, when she insists that the model of critique in which we aim to expose the naïveté of earlier critics and writers is misguided. See Rita Felski, "Introduction," *New Literary History* 47, no. 2 (2016): 221. It is more precise to understand writers as differently positioned.

56. I draw this conception of selfhood in part from Emmanuel Levinas, especially his *Otherwise than Being, or Beyond Essence*.

57. Wolfe, *What Is Poshumanism?*, 262.

58. Ryan, "Landed Bodies," 132.

59. Ryan, 132.

60. Alex Hunt, "The Ecology of Narrative: Annie Proulx's *That Old Ace in the Hole* as Critical Regionalist Fiction," in *The Geographical Imagination of Annie Proulx: Rethinking Regionalism*, ed. Alex Hunt (Lanham, Md.: Lexington Books, 2009), 185.

61. Annie Proulx, *Bird Cloud: A Memoir of Place* (New York: Scribner, 2011).

62. Ryan, "Landed Bodies," 133.

63. Ryan, 134.

64. Ryan, 135.

65. Morton, *Dark Ecology*, 9.

66. See Rob Wilson, "The Postmodern Sublime: Local Definitions, Global Deformations of the US National Imaginary," *American Studies* 43, no. 3 (1998): 517–27.

67. Ryan, "Landed Bodies," 136.

68. See Sarah Jaquette Ray, *The Ecological Other: Environmental Exclusion in American Culture* (Tucson: University of Arizona Press, 2013), especially 35–82, for a critique of ableism in the context of environment.

69. Ryan, "Landed Bodies," 134.

70. Rosemarie Garland Thomson, *Extraordinary Bodies: Figuring Physical Disability in American Culture and Literature* (New York: Columbia University Press, 1997); Lennard J. Davis, *Bending Over Backwards: Disability, Dismodernism, and Other Difficult Positions* (New York: New York University Press, 2002).

71. See Davis, *Bending Over Backwards,* for a discussion of the idea that "the contemporary body can only be completed by means of consumption" (27).

72. Tracy Whalen, "'Camping' with Annie Proulx: *The Shipping News* and Tourist Desire," *Essays on Canadian Writing* 82 (2004): 51–70, qtd. in Ryan, "Landed Bodies," 140n83.

73. Proulx, "Brokeback Mountain," in *Close Range: Wyoming Stories* (1999; repr., New York: Scribner, 2000), 253–85. Further citations to this work are given parenthetically in text.

74. Wolfe, *What Is Posthumanism?,* 83–84.

75. Wolfe, 84.

76. Metonymy often tends to emphasize *continuity* between the two elements in a figure of speech, whereas metaphor emphasizes the *distance* between them. See Greg Garrard, *Ecocriticism,* 2nd ed. (London: Routledge, 2012), 153.

2. Burning Down the House

1. Linklater makes this point about the Wampanoag, for instance, before going on to show that land use was distinct from ownership "under Judaic law" and in Islam under "sharia law." In those cases, "mortals, as mere 'strangers and sojourners,' were unable to own it [land]." Andro Linklater, *Owning the Earth: The Transforming History of Land Ownership* (London: Bloomsbury, 2013), 26. Such regimes more fully acknowledge the homesickness of the self; that sort of concept of human relationship to land—not oriented by ownership—is possible in a more secular frame too.

2. Robert P. Marzec, *Militarizing the Environment: Climate Change and the Security State* (Minneapolis: University of Minnesota Press, 2015), 19.

3. Timothy Morton, *Dark Ecology: For a Logic of Future Coexistence* (New York: Columbia University Press, 2016), 44.

4. Marilynne Robinson, *Housekeeping* (New York: Noonday, 1980); Peter Hedges, *What's Eating Gilbert Grape* (New York: Simon and Schuster, 1991). Further citations to these works are given parenthetically in text.

5. Martin Heidegger, "Building Dwelling Thinking," in *Basic Writings,* ed. David Farrell Krell, trans. Albert Hofstadter (London: Harper, 1993), especially 352–53.

6. Stephen J. Pyne, *Fire: A Brief History* (Seattle: University of Washington Press, 2001), 24.

7. Richard Wrangham, *Catching Fire: How Cooking Made Us Human* (New York: Basic Books, 2009), 14.

8. Alfred W. Crosby, *Throwing Fire: Projectile Technology through History* (Cambridge: Cambridge University Press, 2002).

9. Timothy Clark, *Ecocriticism on the Edge: The Anthropocene as a Threshold Concept* (London: Bloomsbury, 2015), 60–61.

10. Charlotte Brontë, *Jane Eyre* (1847; repr., New York: Norton, 2001); Sandra M. Gilbert and Susan Gubar, *The Madwoman in the Attic: The Woman Writer and the Nineteenth-Century Literary Imagination* (New Haven, Conn.: Yale University Press, 1979).

11. Jean Rhys, *Wide Sargasso Sea* (New York: Norton, 1966).

12. Jane Blocker, "Woman-House: Architecture, Gender and Hybridity in *What's Eating Gilbert Grape?*," *Camera Obscura: A Journal of Feminism, Culture, and Media Studies* 39 (1996): 127.

13. Susan J. Matt, *Homesickness: An American History* (Oxford: Oxford University Press, 2011).

14. Emmanuel Levinas, *Difficult Freedom: Essays on Judaism*, trans. Seán Hand (Baltimore: Johns Hopkins University Press, 1990).

15. Marilynne Robinson, *Home* (New York: Farrar, Straus and Giroux, 2008).

16. Marilynne Robinson, "Wilderness," in *The Death of Adam: Essays on Modern Thought* (New York: Picador, 1998), 246.

17. Marilynne Robinson, *Gilead* (New York: Picador, 2004).

18. Robinson, "Wilderness," 246.

19. Cary Wolfe, *What Is Posthumanism?* (Minneapolis: University of Minnesota Press, 2010), 262.

20. Ralph Waldo Emerson, *Nature/Walking* (1836; repr., Boston: Beacon, 1991), 8; also qtd. in Wolfe, *What Is Posthumanism?*, 250.

21. Wolfe, *What Is Posthumanism?*, 258. See also Levi R. Bryant, *The Democracy of Objects* (Ann Arbor: Open Humanities Press, 2011), 20–21.

22. Robinson, *Gilead*; Robinson, *Home*; Marilynne Robinson, *Lila* (New York: Farrar, Straus and Giroux, 2014).

23. Marcia Aldrich, "The Poetics of Transience: Marilynne Robinson's *Housekeeping*," *Essays in Literature* 16, no. 1 (1989): 127–40.

24. Herman Melville, *Moby-Dick; or, The Whale* (1851; repr., New York: Penguin, 1992).

25. Kristin King, "Resurfacings of the Deeps: Semiotic Balance in Marilynne Robinson's *Housekeeping*," *Studies in the Novel* 28, no. 4 (1996): 572.

26. For a related use of the characterization "weak," see Timothy Morton, *Hyperobjects: Philosophy and Ecology after the End of the World* (Minneapolis: University of Minnesota Press, 2013), 2.

27. Herman Melville, "Bartleby, the Scrivener," in *Tales, Poems, and Other Writings,* ed. John Bryant (1853; repr., New York: Modern Library, 2001), 65–98.

28. Posthumanist thought can be articulated with strains of the wilderness tradition in these terms, as I further suggested in chapter 1.

29. King, "Resurfacings of the Deeps," 565.

30. King, 569–70.

31. King, 565.

32. For example, see Julia Kristeva, *Powers of Horror: An Essay on Abjection,* trans. Leon S. Roudiez (New York: Columbia University Press, 1984). An article by Jacqui Smith emphasizes the importance of transience, or homelessness, reframing gender inquiries in light of human weakness and homelessness. Jacqui Smith, "Sheltered Vagrancy in Marilynne Robinson's *Housekeeping,*" *Critique: Studies in Contemporary Fiction* 40, no. 3 (1999): 281–91.

33. Christine Caver, "Nothing Left to Lose: *Housekeeping*'s Strange Freedoms," *American Literature* 61, no. 8 (1996): 111–37; Cathy Caruth, ed., *Trauma: Explorations in Memory* (Baltimore: Johns Hopkins University Press, 1995).

34. Marilynne Robinson, "Marilynne Robinson: At 'Home' in the Heartland," interview by Lynn Neary, *National Public Radio,* September 20, 2008, http://www.npr.org/templates/transcript/transcript.php?storyId=94799720.

35. For example, see Graham Harman, *Guerrilla Metaphysics: Phenomenology and the Carpentry of Things* (Chicago: Open Court, 2005), 76. See also Levy R. Bryant, *The Democracy of Objects,* 26.

36. *What's Eating Gilbert Grape,* directed by Lasse Hallström (Hollywood, Calif.: Paramount Pictures, 1993).

37. Martha C. Nussbaum, *Frontiers of Justice: Disability, Nationality, Species Membership* (Cambridge, Mass.: Harvard University Press, 2006), 101.

38. Blocker, "Woman-House," 142.

39. Nussbaum argues that disability is a condition everyone faces sometimes, as in old age (*Frontiers of Justice,* 101). Cary Wolfe extends and deepens her case in his chapter "Flesh and Finitude," in *What Is Posthumanism?* (49–98), emphasizing human frailty and treating thinking itself as a form of suffering (71). Wolfe focuses on death particularly on pages 83–84.

40. On the animalization of human labor and its connection to Taylorism, see Nicole Shukin, *Animal Capital: Rendering Life in Biopolitical Times* (Minneapolis: University of Minnesota Press, 2009), 73.

41. Eric Schlosser, *Fast Food Nation: The Dark Side of the All-American Meal* (Boston: Houghton Mifflin, 2001), 20.

42. Michael Pollan, *In Defense of Food: An Eater's Manifesto* (New York: Penguin, 2008), 196.

43. Hiroko Tabuchi, "Walmart Raising Wage to at Least $9," *New York Times,* February 19, 2015.

44. Blocker, "Woman-House," 140.

45. Blocker, 145.

46. Blocker, 150n12.

47. Blocker, 144.

48. Blocker, 149.

49. Jacques Derrida, *The Animal That Therefore I Am*, ed. Marie-Louise Mallet, trans. David Wills (New York: Fordham University Press, 2008), 27.

50. Morton, *Hyperobjects*, 2.

51. Alan Blinder, "Trooper Listens to, and Connects with, a Ferguson Torn by Violent Unrest," *New York Times*, August 15, 2014.

52. Morton refigures time this way, arguing that "it might be best to see history as a nested series of catastrophes that are still playing out rather than as a sequence of events based on a conception of time as a succession of atomic instants" (*Dark Ecology*, 69).

53. Tanzina Vega and John Eligon, "Around St. Louis, a Circle of Rage," *New York Times*, August 16, 2014.

54. Janet L. Abu-Lughod, *Race, Space, and Riots in Chicago, New York, and Los Angeles* (New York: Oxford University Press, 2007), 18.

55. Abu-Lughod, 15.

3. The Elephant in the Writing Room

1. Kevin Maier, "'A Trick Men Learn in Paris': Hemingway, *Esquire*, and Mass Tourism," *Hemingway Review* 31, no. 2 (2012): 65.

2. Susan J. Matt, *Homesickness: An American History* (Oxford: Oxford University Press, 2011), 141–42.

3. Thomas L. Friedman, *The World Is Flat: A Brief History of the Twenty-First Century* (New York: Farrar, Straus and Giroux, 2005).

4. Carlos Baker, *Ernest Hemingway: A Life Story* (New York: Scribner, 1969), 44–45.

5. Ernest Hemingway, "Soldier's Home," in *The Complete Short Stories of Ernest Hemingway: The Finca Vigía Edition* (New York: Scribner, 1998), 111–16.

6. Paul Hendrickson reports this in passing in "The Old Man and the Boat," *New York Times*, August 7, 2005.

7. This is not to say that Hemingway's roots in the United States do not matter, of course. It is to say that we should acknowledge not only origins but also later destinations. The tendency to prioritize the importance of birthplace runs contrary to eco-cosmopolitan thinking in all sorts of theoretical and practical ways, including in debates about immigration.

8. Loiuse H. Westling, *The Green Breast of the New World: Landscape, Gender, and American Fiction* (Athens: University of Georgia Press, 1996), 52.

9. For more on this account of ethics, see Ryan Hediger, "Hunting, Fishing, and the Cramp of Ethics in *The Old Man and the Sea, Green Hills of Africa,* and *Under Kilimanjaro,*" *Hemingway Review* 27, no. 2 (Spring 2008): 35–59.

10. Ernest Hemingway, *Death in the Afternoon* (New York: Scribner, 1932), 4. It might be tempting to dismiss Hemingway's characteristically succinct definition as

hedonistic, but that would misconstrue—along common, predictable lines—his thinking about and practice of pleasure in his life. Rather than condemning that inquiry, we need to reopen it much more rigorously.

11. Miriam B. Mandel, introduction to *Hemingway and Africa,* ed. Miriam B. Mandel (Rochester, N.Y.: Camden House, 2011), 18.

12. William Wordsworth and Samuel T. Coleridge, *Lyrical Ballads,* 2nd ed., ed. W. J. B. Owen (New York: Oxford University Press, 1969), 157.

13. Philip Young, *Ernest Hemingway: A Reconsideration* (University Park: Pennsylvania State University Press, 1966).

14. Baker, *Ernest Hemingway,* 499.

15. Baker, 54.

16. Ernest Hemingway, *A Farewell to Arms* (New York: Scribner, 1929), 249; see also 153 and 309. These moments involve temporary living quarters understood and discussed explicitly as "home." Further citations to this work are given parenthetically in text.

17. Baker, *Ernest Hemingway,* 194, 197.

18. Ernest Hemingway, *Selected Letters, 1917–1961,* ed. Carlos Baker (London: Granada, 1981), 359.

19. Ernest Hemingway, *A Moveable Feast: The Restored Edition* (1964; repr., New York: Scribner, 2010).

20. Ernest Hemingway, *Under Kilimanjaro,* ed. Robert W. Lewis and Robert E. Fleming (Kent, Ohio: Kent State University Press, 2005); Ernest Hemingway, *True at First Light,* ed. Patrick Hemingway (New York: Scribner, 1999). For clarification of the completion of *A Moveable Feast,* see Robert W. Trogdon, "*A Moveable Feast: The Restored Edition*: A Review and a Collation of Differences," *Hemingway Review* 29, no. 1 (2009): 24–45. Further citations to *Under Kilimanjaro* and *True at First Light* are given parenthetically in text.

21. Ernest Hemingway, *Green Hills of Africa* (New York: Scribner, 1935); Hemingway, *Death in the Afternoon.* Further citations to *Green Hills of Africa* are given parenthetically in text.

22. Toni Morrison, *Playing in the Dark: Whiteness and the Literary Imagination* (New York: Vintage, 1992), 88–89. Cary Wolfe quotes Morrison's phrase in "Fathers, Lovers, and Friend Killers: Rearticulating Gender and Race via Species in Hemingway," *Boundary 2: An International Journal of Literature and Culture* 29, no. 1 (2002): 253.

23. Morrison, *Playing in the Dark,* 84.

24. Morrison, 88–89.

25. Ernest Hemingway, "The Snows of Kilimanjaro," in *The Complete Short Stories of Ernest Hemingway: The Finca Vigía Edition* (New York: Scribner, 1998), 39–58.

26. Robert W. Lewis and Robert E. Fleming, introduction to Ernest Hemingway, *Under Kilimanjaro,* ed. Robert W. Lewis and Robert E. Fleming (Kent, Ohio: Kent State University Press, 2005), xii.

27. Jeremiah M. Kitunda, "'Love Is a Dunghill. . . . And I'm the Cock That Gets on It to Crow': Hemingway's Farcical Adoration of Africa," in *Hemingway and Africa,* ed. Miriam B. Mandel (Rochester, N.Y.: Camden House, 2011), 141.

28. Kitunda, 140.

29. Mandel, introduction, 26.

30. Njabulo S. Ndebele, "Game Lodges and Leisure Colonialists," in *Blank: Architecture after Apartheid,* ed. Hilton Judin and Ivan Vladislavic (Cape Town: David Phillips, 1998).

31. Achille Mbembe, *On the Postcolony* (Berkeley: University of California Press, 2001), 1.

32. Mbembe, 7.

33. See Patrick Murphy, *A Place for Wayfaring: The Poetry and Prose of Gary Snyder* (Corvallis: Oregon State University Press, 2000).

34. Maier, "'A Trick Men Learn in Paris,'" 66.

35. Timothy Morton, *Dark Ecology: For a Logic of Future Coexistence* (New York: Columbia University Press, 2016), 146.

36. Suzanne Clark, *Cold Warriors: Manliness on Trial in the Rhetoric of the West* (Carbondale: Southern Illinois University Press, 2000), 69.

37. Clark, 70.

38. Clark, 59.

39. Clark, 64.

40. Clark, 65.

41. Donna Haraway, *Primate Visions: Gender, Race, and Nature in the World of Modern Science* (London: Routledge, 1989), 31.

42. Haraway, 31.

43. Haraway, 31.

44. Haraway, 27.

45. Haraway, 31.

46. Haraway, 28–29.

47. Haraway, 26.

48. Haraway, 26.

49. Donna Haraway, *When Species Meet* (Minneapolis: University of Minnesota Press, 2008).

50. Morton, *Dark Ecology,* 38.

51. Morton, 59; see also 58, 54.

52. Morton, 43.

53. Morton, 114, 143.

54. Morton, 5.

55. Ernest Hemingway, *The Garden of Eden* (New York: Scribner, 1986). Further citations to this work are given parenthetically in text.

56. See Ryan Hediger, "Animals," in *Hemingway in Context,* ed. Suzanne Del Gizzo and Debra A. Moddelmog (Cambridge: Cambridge University Press, 2013), 217–26;

Ryan Hediger, "Becoming with Animals: Sympoiesis and the Ecology of Meaning in London and Hemingway," *Studies in American Naturalism* 11, no. 1 (2016): 5–22.

57. Mandel, introduction, 27.

58. Robert E. Fleming, "The Endings of Hemingway's *Garden of Eden*," *American Literature* 61, no. 2 (1989): 261–70.

59. Carl Eby, *Hemingway's Fetishism: Psychoanalysis and the Mirror of Manhood* (Albany: State University of New York Press, 1999), 5.

60. Harold Bloom, ed., *Ernest Hemingway's The Old Man and the Sea* (Philadelphia: Chelsea House, 1999).

61. Christophe Bonneuil and Jean-Baptiste Fressoz, *The Shock of the Anthropocene: The Earth, History and Us,* trans. David Fernbach (London: Verso, 2015), 220.

62. The published text was cut under the direction of editor Tom Jenks from the extensive, unfinished manuscripts Hemingway left at his death. The present chapter works primarily with that published novel nonetheless. For one justification of doing so, see Robin Silbergleid, "Into Africa: Narrative and Authority in Hemingway's *The Garden of Eden*," *Hemingway Review* 27, no. 2 (2008): 96–117; for accounts of the posthumous texts, see also Rose Marie Burwell, *Hemingway: The Postwar Years and the Posthumous Novels* (Cambridge: Cambridge University Press, 1996); and Hilary K. Justice, *The Bones of the Others: The Hemingway Text from the Lost Manuscripts to the Posthumous Novels* (Kent, Ohio: Kent State University Press, 2006). The remainder of this chapter was published in slightly different form in the *Hemingway Review* 31, no. 1, copyright 2011, Ernest Hemingway Foundation, all rights reserved. It is reprinted here with permission.

63. Justice, *The Bones of the Others,* 57.

64. Justice, 55.

65. James Nagel, "The Hunting Story in *The Garden of Eden*," in *Hemingway's Neglected Short Fiction: New Perspectives,* ed. Susan F. Beegel (Ann Arbor: University of Michigan Research Press, 1989), 329–38.

66. Justice, *The Bones of the Others,* 56.

67. Justice, 60. See also Burwell, *Hemingway*; and Silbergleid, "Into Africa."

68. Justice, *The Bones of the Others,* 71.

69. Justice, 71–72.

70. See, for instance, Suzanne del Gizzo, "Going Home: Hemingway, Primitivism, and Identity," *Modern Fiction Studies* 49, no. 3 (2003): 496–523. She claims that Hemingway in Africa is, in part, trying to escape the culture of the archive. She argues that Hemingway's primitivism in *True at First Light* shows his frustration with his identity as author, leading him to seek "to become a member of a culture without writers—a place where he would have the opportunity to explore himself and redefine his identity on other terms" (518).

71. Cary Wolfe, *What Is Posthumanism?* (Minneapolis: University of Minnesota Press, 2010).

72. Jacques Derrida, *The Animal That Therefore I Am,* ed. Marie-Louise Mallet, trans. David Wills (New York: Fordham University Press, 2008), 27. As noted in the

introduction, Martha C. Nussbaum argues for a "capability approach" that works to aid many kinds of flourishing in the world, including that of nonhumans. See Martha C. Nussbaum, *Frontiers of Justice: Disability, Nationality, Species Membership* (Cambridge, Mass.: Belknap Press of Harvard University Press, 2006).

73. Morton, *Dark Ecology,* 16.

74. Morton, 5.

75. For more on Catherine's actions as response to and criticism of David, see Kathy Willingham, "Hemingway's *The Garden of Eden*: Writing with the Body," in *Ernest Hemingway: Seven Decades of Criticism,* ed. Linda Wagner-Martin (East Lansing: Michigan State University Press, 1998), 293–310. See also Burwell, *Hemingway,* 95–128.

76. Burwell, *Hemingway,* 100.

77. Nagel, "The Hunting Story," 337. For a similar perspective, see Frank Scaffela, "Clippings from *The Garden of Eden,*" *Hemingway Review* 7, no. 1 (1987): 20–29.

78. Julie Bosman, "To Use and Use Not," *New York Times,* July 4, 2012.

79. Burwell, *Hemingway,* 113.

80. Burwell, 110, 113.

81. Burwell, 107.

82. Burwell, 111.

83. See Cynthia Moss, *Elephant Memories: Thirteen Years in the Life of an Elephant Family* (Chicago: University of Chicago Press, 2000), 73. See also Marc Bekoff and Jessica Pierce, *Wild Justice: The Moral Lives of Animals* (Chicago: University of Chicago Press, 2009). The tradition of dismissing such analyses as "anthropomorphic" has been increasingly criticized in a growing scientific recognition that social animals have emotions that resemble human emotions in important ways. See Frans de Waal, *Primates and Philosophers: How Morality Evolved* (Princeton, N.J.: Princeton University Press, 2006).

84. See Morton, *Dark Ecology,* for a reading of Genesis in line with the Anthropocene (38).

85. Morton, 9.

86. Burwell, *Hemingway,* 125, 105.

87. Philip Armstrong, *What Animals Mean in the Fiction of Modernity* (London: Routledge, 2008).

88. "Askari" is the plural of the Swahili word for "soldier" (*Under Kilimanjaro,* 448); Hemingway adds "friend" in the text, having first suggested "askari."

89. Wolfe, "Fathers, Lovers, and Friend Killers," 249.

90. Hemingway describes the *querencia* as the "part of the ring that the bull prefers to be in; where he feels at home" (*Death in the Afternoon,* 439).

91. Burwell, *Hemingway,* 122.

92. Burwell, 100. See also Silbergleid, "Into Africa," 101.

93. Michael Reynolds, *Hemingway: The Final Years* (New York: Norton, 1999), 23.

94. Wolfe, "Fathers, Lovers, and Friend Killers," 251–52.

95. To be clear, my approach here is largely consonant with Wolfe's writing on ethics; I am quibbling with his reading of this specific episode and underscoring consequences as they apply to questions of hunting.

96. Cary Wolfe, *Animal Rites: American Culture, the Discourse of Species, and Posthumanist Theory* (Chicago: University of Chicago Press, 2003), 194.

97. For discussions of Hemingway's shifting attitude toward animals, see Glen Love, "Hemingway's Indian Virtues: An Ecological Reconsideration," *Western American Literature* 22, no. 3 (1987): 201–13; Charlene M. Murphy, "Hemingway's Gentle Hunters: Contradiction or Duality?" in *Hemingway and the Natural World,* ed. Robert E. Fleming (Moscow: University of Idaho Press, 1999); and Carey Voeller, "'He Only Looked Sad the Same Way I Felt': The Textual Confessions of Hemingway's Hunters," *Hemingway Review* 25, no. 1 (2005): 63–76.

98. Morrison, *Playing in the Dark,* 88–89. As noted above, Wolfe quotes Morrison's phrase: "Fathers, Lovers, and Friend Killers," 253.

99. Wolfe, "Fathers, Lovers, and Friend Killers," 225, 254.

100. Wolfe, 250.

101. I am working with Wolfe's terminology here; he uses "mimetic" (248–49).

102. See Scaffela, "Clippings." See also Nagel, "The Hunting Story"; and Burwell, *Hemingway.*

103. Justice, *The Bones of the Others,* 143n14.

4. "124 Was Spiteful"

1. Susan J. Matt, *Homesickness: An American History* (Oxford: Oxford University Press, 2011), 13.

2. The Great Migration is a compelling example of limited human agency. Migrants "chose" to leave the South, but generally, in large measure, because racism and violence drove them out. Their destinations, similarly, tended to be largely determined by the train lines and by the places where friends and contacts had already settled. Eco-cosmopolitanism should register both these *constraints* on freedom and the real value of having some choice. Isabel Wilkerson, *The Warmth of Other Suns: The Epic Story of America's Great Migration* (New York: Vintage, 2010), 178.

3. Wilkerson, 9.

4. Wilkerson, 10.

5. Mark Tran, "Forced Migration in the 21st Century: Urbanised and Unending," *The Guardian,* October 16, 2012.

6. Christophe Bonneuil and Jean-Baptiste Fressoz, *The Shock of the Anthropocene: The Earth, History and Us,* trans. David Fernbach (London: Verso, 2015), 25.

7. Alana Semuels, "The Role of Highways in American Poverty," *The Atlantic,* March 18, 2016. For more on Haussmann's transformation of Paris, including the destruction of poorer districts, see Stephane Kirkland, *Paris Reborn: Napoléon III, Baron Haussmann, and the Quest to Build a Modern City* (New York: St. Martin's, 2013).

8. Toni Morrison, *Beloved* (1987; repr., New York: Vintage, 2004), 3. Further citations to this work are given parenthetically in text.

9. Morrison modeled *Beloved* after the real-world case of Margaret Garner. Garner's response to slavery, to attempt to kill her children, was not uncommon. For a sophisticated engagement in the representation and politics of infanticide, see Sarah N. Roth, "'The Blade Was in My Own Breast': Slave Infanticide in 1850s Fiction," *American Nineteenth Century History* 8, no. 2 (June 2007): 169–85; for a discussion of a case parallel to Margaret Garner's, see Jessica Murray, "When 'Good' Mothers Kill: A Representation of Infanticide," *Agenda: Empowering Women for Gender Equity,* no. 76 (2008): 32–41. See also Pamela Scully, "Narratives of Infanticide in the Aftermath of Slave Emancipation in the Nineteenth-Century Cape Colony, South Africa," *Canadian Journal of African Studies* 30, no. 1 (1996): 88–105.

10. William Faulkner, *Requiem for a Nun* (1950; repr., New York: Vintage, 2011), 69.

11. For a related argument about the novel, see Homi K. Bhabha, "The World and the Home," in *Close Reading: The Reader* (Durham, N.C.: Duke University Press, 2003), especially 372.

12. See Cendrine Bursztein Lipsicas, Itzhak Levav, and Stephen Z. Levine, "Holocaust Exposure and Subsequent Suicide Risk: A Population-Based Study," *Social Psychiatry and Psychiatric Epidemiology* 52, no. 3 (March 2017): 311–17; Bryann B. DeBeer et al., "Preventing Suicide Risk in Trauma Exposed Veterans: The Role of Health Promoting Behaviors," *PLOS One* 11, no. 12 (December 21, 2016): 1–11.

13. Jacques Derrida, *Specters of Marx,* trans. Peggy Kamuf (New York: Routledge, 1994), xvii.

14. Derrida, xvii.

15. Derrida, xviii.

16. Halle is Sethe's husband, driven mad by the assaults on Sethe at Sweet Home. We might worry about the internal contradiction here: is Sethe her own person, "with iron eyes and backbone to match," or is she "Halle's girl"? One way out of this problem is simply to read the description "Halle's girl" as colloquial, as Paul D's expression of a romantic boundary between him and Sethe in deference to her relationship with Halle.

17. Toni Morrison, *Playing in the Dark: Whiteness and the Literary Imagination* (New York: Vintage, 1992), 56; Jennifer Rae Greeson, "The Prehistory of Possessive Individualism," *PMLA: Publications of the Modern Language Association of America* 127, no. 4 (2012): 918–24.

18. Nancy Jesser, "Violence, Home, and Community in Toni Morrison's *Beloved,*" *African American Review* 33, no. 2 (1999): 329.

19. On trauma, see Abdennebi Ben Beya, "The Question of Reading Traumatic Testimony: Jones's *Corregidora* and Morrison's *Beloved,*" *Alif: Journal of Comparative Poetics,* no. 30 (2010): 85–108. See also many of the other articles cited in this chapter.

20. For a discussion of how remembering changes memories, see Donna J. Bridge and Ken A. Palier, "Neural Correlates of Reactivation and Retrieval-Induced Distortion," *Journal of Neuroscience* 32, no. 35 (2012): 12144–51.

21. For a related argument about how literature can be understood as a force unto itself, one not entirely controlled by humans, see Timothy Morton, *Dark Ecology: For a Logic of Future Coexistence* (New York: Columbia University Press, 2016), 174–75.

22. Morton, 45.

23. For a trenchant critique of the idea of Nature, see Timothy Morton, *Ecology without Nature: Rethinking Environmental Aesthetics* (Cambridge, Mass.: Harvard University Press, 2007).

24. Emmanuel Levinas makes this philosophical case with special force in *Otherwise than Being, or Beyond Essence,* trans. Alphonso Lingis (Pittsburgh: Duquesne University Press, 1998).

25. Jesser emphasizes Morrison's effort to show history as "an unfinished process and a working through of traumatic events and daily, repeated violences." Jesser, "Violence, Home, and Community," 327.

26. It is perhaps an only half-appreciated sense of this dimension of the novel that leads D. G. Myers to condemn it, arguing that it "is almost never read to be enjoyed," as if reading powerful literature is exclusively or even primarily about "enjoyment." Why would one expect to "enjoy" a novel about the violence of slavery? He further contends, "Family breakdown is the tragedy facing blacks today, not white racism in the form of evil Dr. Mengele's experimenting on unsuspecting black women." This sentence usefully exposes how, his protestations to the contrary, Myers's rejection of Morrison stems from his refusal to recognize persistence of racism and its effects, which is precisely the point of *Beloved.* D. G. Myers, "Beloved by Whom? Toni Morrison, Master at Seeming the Master," *Commentary* 133, no. 5 (2012): 71, 73.

27. Semiramis Yağcioğlu engages Gaston Bachelard to make a similar point about *Beloved,* noting, "Like any space, homes are also loci, which create ontological horizons or lifeworlds of subjectivity by setting boundaries between what can be done and what cannot be done." Semiramis Yağcioğlu, "Re-membering Dismembered Identities at 'Sweet Home': Reading Space in Toni Morrison's *Beloved,*" *Interactions* 17, no. 2 (2008): 125–26.

28. Jesser notes that Sethe is not the only mother who commits infanticide in the novel: "The woman who cares for Sethe when she is a child tells her that her mother killed all the babies conceived on the slave ship, as well as those of white men, and that Sethe was not killed because she was a child of love." Jesser, "Violence, Home, and Community," 341. See also Morrison, *Beloved,* 74.

29. Ben Beya, "The Question of Reading Traumatic Testimony," 88.

30. Jean Wyatt, "Giving Body to the Word: The Maternal Symbolic in Toni Morrison's *Beloved,*" *PMLA* 108, no. 3 (1993): 474.

31. We can fairly say that these women in *Beloved,* and Sethe and Ella in particular, are coming to terms with life by learning from death, as Jacques Derrida contends we must do in his *Specters of Marx* (xvii), a text organized by a metaphorics of haunting, as noted previously.

32. Jesser, "Violence, Home, and Community," 325.

33. Morton makes a related argument regarding locality in *Hyperobjects*: "There is indeed something like a *genius loci*." Timothy Morton, *Hyperobjects: Philosophy and Ecology after the End of the World* (Minneapolis: University of Minnesota Press, 2013), 174.

34. Jennifer C. James, "Ecomelancholia: Slavery, War, and Black Ecological Imaginings," in *Environmental Criticism for the Twenty-First Century*, ed. Stephanie LeMenager, Teresa Shewry, and Ken Hiltner (New York: Routledge, 2011), 163.

35. James, 164.

36. Jesser, "Violence, Home, and Community," 329.

37. Wilkerson, *The Warmth of Other Suns*, 210.

38. For an argument along these lines, see Timothy Morton, *Realist Magic: Objects, Ontology, Causality* (Ann Arbor, Mich.: Open Humanities Press, 2013).

39. Jesser, "Violence, Home, and Community," 331.

40. Ta-Nehisi Coates, *Between the World and Me* (New York: Spiegel and Grau, 2015).

41. Coates, 101.

42. Coates, 15.

43. Coates, 114.

44. In *Between the World and Me*, for example, Ta-Nehisi Coates writes about the violence of the segregated streets where he grew up, about the African American "crews" who "walked the blocks of the neighborhood, loud and rude, because it was only through their loud rudeness that they might feel any sense of security and power. They would break your jaw, stomp your face, and shoot you down to feel that power, to revel in the might of their own bodies" (22).

45. Morton, *Dark Ecology*, 51.

46. Jesser, "Violence, Home, and Community," 338.

47. On implicit bias, see Anthony G. Greenwald and Linda Hamilton Krieger, "Implicit Bias: Scientific Foundations," *California Law Review* 94, no. 4 (2006): 945–67.

48. Greenwald and Krieger, 946.

49. Jacques Derrida, "'Eating Well,' or the Calculation of the Subject: An Interview with Jacques Derrida," trans. Peter Connor and Avital Ronell, in *Who Comes after the Subject?*, ed. Eduardo Cadava, Peter Connor, and Jean-Luc Nancy (New York: Routledge, 1991), 116–17.

50. Morton, *Hyperobjects*, 4.

51. Graham Harman, *Guerilla Metaphysics: Phenomenology and the Carpentry of Things* (Chicago: Open Court, 2005), 247.

52. Wyatt, "Giving Body to the Word," 482n1.

53. Wyatt, 475, bracketed addition in original.

54. Wyatt, 476.

55. Wyatt, 476.

56. Wyatt, 476.

57. Wyatt, 476.

58. Wyatt, 485n4.
59. Wyatt, 485n5.
60. Wyatt, 485n4.
61. Wyatt, 477.
62. Wyatt, 477.
63. Wyatt, 477.
64. Wyatt, 484.
65. Wyatt, 482.
66. Wyatt, 484.

5. Shopping as Suffering

1. Ellen Ruppel Shell, *Cheap: The High Cost of Discount Culture* (New York: Penguin, 2009), 232.

2. Ruppel Shell, 231.

3. Anne Norton, *Republic of Signs: Liberal Theory and American Popular Culture* (Chicago: University of Chicago Press, 1993), 74.

4. Norton, 75.

5. Ruppel Shell, *Cheap*, 70.

6. Daniel Kahneman, *Thinking, Fast and Slow* (New York: Farrar, Straus and Giroux, 2011).

7. This business now spells its name "Walmart," but the novel and much of scholarship I treat in this chapter use the older spelling, "Wal-Mart." I use the current spelling, "Walmart," unless I am quoting scholarship that presents the older spelling.

8. Cary Wolfe, *What Is Posthumanism?* (Minneapolis: University of Minnesota Press, 2010), xv.

9. Cary Wolfe, *Before the Law: Humans and Other Animals in a Biopolitical Frame* (Chicago: University of Chicago Press, 2013), 2–23; Wolfe, *What Is Posthumanism?*, 49–98.

10. Wolfe, *What Is Posthumanism?*, 65.

11. Wolfe, *Before the Law*, 22–23.

12. Billie Letts, *Where the Heart Is*, Oprah's Book Club Edition (New York: Warner, 1995). Further citations to this work are given parenthetically in text.

13. Wolfe, *Before the Law*, 23. Wolfe's comment is not aimed at this novel.

14. See an exploration of this problem in Alphonso Lingis's book *Dangerous Emotions* (Berkeley: University of California Press, 2000).

15. For more on postpolitics and its implications for the security state and the military, see Robert P. Marzec, *Militarizing the Environment: Climate Change and the Security State* (Minneapolis: University of Minnesota Press, 2015), 235.

16. Tara McPherson, "On Wal-Mart and Southern Studies," *American Literature* 78, no. 4 (2006): 695–98.

17. Jameson qtd. in Cary Wolfe, *Animal Rites: American Culture, the Discourse of Species, and Posthumanist Theory* (Chicago: University of Chicago Press, 2003), 98.

18. *Where the Heart Is,* directed by Matt Williams (Los Angeles: 20th Century Fox, 2000).

19. See Natalie Portman, "Jonathan Safran Foer's *Eating Animals* Turned Me Vegan," *The Blog: Huffington Post,* March 18, 2010.

20. McPherson, "On Wal-Mart and Southern Studies," 695.

21. John Dicker, *The United States of Wal-Mart* (New York: Penguin, 2005), 33–53.

22. Susan Strasser, "Woolworth to Wal-Mart: Mass Merchandising and the Changing Culture of Consumption," in *Wal-Mart: The Face of Twenty-First-Century Capitalism,* ed. Nelson Lichtenstein (New York: New Press, 2006), 33.

23. Dicker, *The United States of Wal-Mart,* 62.

24. Dicker, 79–89; Nelson Lichtenstein, "Wal-Mart: A Template for Twenty-First-Century Capitalism," in *Wal-Mart: The Face of Twenty-First Century-Capitalism,* ed. Nelson Lichtenstein (New York: New Press, 2006), 3–30.

25. Dicker, *The United States of Wal-Mart,* 148; Lichtenstein, "Wal-Mart," 3, 21; Bethany Moreton, *To Serve God and Wal-Mart: The Making of Christian Free Enterprise* (Cambridge, Mass.: Harvard University Press, 2009), 51.

26. Lichtenstein, "Wal-Mart," 17.

27. Dicker, *The United States of Wal-Mart,* 96.

28. Lichtenstein, "Wal-Mart," 6–7.

29. Moreton, *To Serve God and Wal-Mart.*

30. Lichtenstein, "Wal-Mart," 24.

31. Moreton, *To Serve God and Wal-Mart,* for example, also shows the anxiety about gender roles connected to this shift in labor regimes away from farming and toward clerical work in the South (49–66).

32. Richard Vedder and Wendell Cox, *The Wal-Mart Revolution: How Big-Box Stores Benefit Consumers, Workers, and the Economy* (Washington, D.C.: AEI Press, 2006), 98.

33. Ruppel Shell, *Cheap,* 50.

34. David Karjanen, "The Wal-Mart Effect and the New Face of Capitalism: Labor Market and Community Impacts of the Megaretailer," in *Wal-Mart: The Face of Twenty-First-Century Capitalism,* ed. Nelson Lichtenstein (New York: New Press, 2006), 152–53.

35. Karjanen, 154.

36. Ruppel Shell, *Cheap,* 48–49.

37. Lichtenstein, "Wal-Mart"; Dicker, *The United States of Wal-Mart,* 4–5; Karjanen, "The Wal-Mart Effect," 146.

38. Dicker, *The United States of Wal-Mart,* 29.

39. Lichtenstein, "Wal-Mart," 14.

40. Lichtenstein, 14–15.

41. McPherson, "On Wal-Mart and Southern Studies," 696.

42. McPherson, 696. See also Dicker, *The United States of Wal-Mart,* 54; and Lichtenstein, "Wal-Mart," 14–15.

43. Dicker, *The United States of Wal-Mart,* 2.

44. Lichtenstein, "Wal-Mart," 9.

45. Misha Petrovic and Gary G. Hamilton, "Making Global Markets: Wal-Mart and Its Suppliers," in *Wal-Mart: The Face of Twenty-First-Century Capitalism,* ed. Nelson Lichtenstein (New York: New Press, 2006), 122–23.

46. McPherson, "On Wal-Mart and Southern Studies," especially 695–96.

47. McPherson, 696.

48. Peter T. Kilborn, *Next Stop, Reloville: Life inside America's New Rootless Professional Class* (New York: Times Books, 2009).

49. Timothy Morton, *Dark Ecology: For a Logic of Future Coexistence* (New York: Columbia University Press, 2016), 4; see also 42.

50. Morton, 42.

51. Lawrence Buell, *Writing for an Endangered World: Literature, Culture, and Environment in the U.S. and Beyond* (Cambridge, Mass.: Belknap Press of Harvard University Press, 2001), 129.

52. Dicker, *The United States of Wal-Mart,* 134.

53. Dicker, 185.

54. Karjanen, "The Wal-Mart Effect," 153.

55. Karjanen, 161; Vedder and Cox, *The Wal-Mart Revolution,* 117–25.

56. Karjanen, "The Wal-Mart Effect," 161.

57. Dicker, *The United States of Wal-Mart,* 123.

58. Dicker, 163.

59. John Updike, "A&P," in *The Norton Introduction to Literature,* portable 12th ed., ed. Kelly J. Mays (New York: Norton, 2017), 163–67.

60. Strasser, "Woolworth to Wal-Mart," 49–52. See also Dicker, *The United States of Wal-Mart,* 162.

61. Dicker, *The United States of Wal-Mart,* 58–60.

62. Dicker, 60.

63. Moreton, *To Serve God and Wal-Mart,* 51.

64. Moreton, 54.

65. Dicker, *The United States of Wal-Mart,* 118.

66. Hiroko Tabuchi, "Walmart's Imports from China Displaced 400,000 Workers, Study Says," *New York Times,* December 9, 2015, A28.

67. Dicker, *The United States of Wal-Mart,* 118.

68. Stephen Greenblatt, ed., *Cultural Mobility: A Manifesto* (Cambridge: Cambridge University Press, 2010).

69. Scott qtd. in Dicker, *The United States of Wal-Mart,* 122.

70. Dicker, 109.

71. Dicker, 108.

72. *South Park,* season 8, episode 9, "Something Wall-Mart This Way Comes," written and directed by Trey Parker, aired November 3, 2004, on Comedy Central, http://southpark.cc.com.

73. Dicker, *The United States of Wal-Mart,* 160–205.

74. Lichtenstein, "Wal-Mart," 16.

75. I allude here to Adam Smith's much-quoted notion of "an invisible hand" that creates broader social good out of narrow pursuit of self-interest. For example, see Adam Smith, *The Theory of Moral Sentiments*, ed. Knud Haakonssen (1759; repr., Cambridge: Cambridge University Press, 2002), 215. This faith that considerations of justice or social good are unnecessary—let capitalism, or an "invisible hand" sort it out—is a dogma of much neoliberal and modern conservative thought.

76. Wendy Brown, *Undoing the Demos: Neoliberalism's Stealth Revolution* (New York: Zone, 2015), 38.

77. Dicker, *The United States of Wal-Mart*, 109–11, 101.

78. Petrovic and Hamilton, "Making Global Markets," 128, 120, 140 (on international store growth); Dicker, *The United States of Wal-Mart*, 118–20 (on international sources).

79. Naomi Klein, *This Changes Everything: Capitalism versus the Climate* (New York: Simon and Schuster, 2014).

80. See Brown, *Undoing the Demos*, for more on neoliberalism's work in these ways.

81. Ruppel Shell, *Cheap*, 7–11.

82. Strasser, "Woolworth to Wal-Mart," 40–43; Dicker, *The United States of Wal-Mart*, 165; Ruppel Shell, *Cheap*, 17.

83. Dicker, *The United States of Wal-Mart*, 67; Ruppel Shell, *Cheap*, 46.

84. Dicker, *The United States of Wal-Mart*, 73–77.

85. Ruppel Shell, *Cheap*, 39.

86. Norton, *Republic of Signs*, 47–86. See also Pierre Bourdieu, *Distinction: A Social Critique of the Judgment of Taste*, trans. Richard Nice (Cambridge, Mass.: Harvard University Press, 1984); and Juliet B. Schor, *The Overspent American: Why We Want What We Don't Need* (New York: Harper, 1998). Schor refers to many other relevant texts.

87. Gary Cross, *Consumed Nostalgia: Memory in the Age of Fast Capitalism* (New York: Columbia University Press, 2015).

88. Strasser, "Woolworth to Wal-Mart," 47–49.

89. Dicker, *The United States of Wal-Mart*, 52.

90. Gilles Deleuze and Félix Guattari, *A Thousand Plateaus: Capitalism and Schizophrenia*, trans. Brian Massumi (Minneapolis: University of Minnesota Press, 1987).

91. Lichtenstein, "Wal-Mart," 17–18.

92. Ruppel Shell, *Cheap*, 49.

93. Norton, *Republic of Signs*, 74.

94. Karjanen, "The Wal-Mart Effect," 148. See also Ruppel Shell, *Cheap*, 48.

95. On new materialism and object-oriented ontology, see Graham Harman, *Guerrilla Metaphysics: Phenomenology and the Carpentry of Things* (Chicago: Open Court, 2005); Jane Bennett, *Vibrant Matter: A Political Ecology of Things* (Durham, N.C.: Duke University Press, 2010); Levi R. Bryant, *The Democracy of Objects* (Ann Arbor, Mich.: Open Humanities Press, 2011); Ian Bogost, *Alien Phenomenology; Or, What It's Like to Be a Thing* (Minneapolis: University of Minnesota Press, 2012);

and Katherine Behar, ed., *Object-Oriented Feminism* (Minneapolis: University of Minnesota Press, 2016).

96. The Animal Studies Group, *Killing Animals* (Urbana: University of Illinois Press, 2006), 1.

97. See National Chicken Council, "Broiler Chicken Industry Key Facts 2018," accessed January 21, 2019, http://www.nationalchickencouncil.org/about-the-industry/statistics/broiler-chicken-industry-key-facts/.

98. Nicole Shukin, *Animal Capital: Rendering Life in Biopolitical Times* (Minneapolis: University of Minnesota Press, 2009), 226.

99. Herman Melville, *Moby-Dick; or, The Whale* (1851; repr., New York: Penguin, 1992); Nathaniel Philbrick, *In the Heart of the Sea: The Tragedy of the Whaleship Essex* (New York: Penguin, 2000); *In the Heart of the Sea,* directed by Ron Howard (Burbank, Calif.: Warner Bros., 2015).

100. *Alive,* directed by Frank Marshall (Burbank, Calif. Buena Vista, 1993); Yann Martell, *Life of Pi* (Toronto: Knopf, 2001); *Life of Pi,* directed by Ang Lee (Los Angeles: Fox 2000 Pictures, 2012).

101. Wolfe, *Animal Rites,* 99, 100.

102. Wolfe, 120.

103. Wolfe, 120–21.

104. Frans de Waal, *Primates and Philosophers: How Morality Evolved* (Princeton, N.J.: Princeton University Press, 2006); Marc Bekoff and Jessica Pierce, *Wild Justice: The Moral Lives of Animals* (Chicago: University of Chicago Press, 2009).

105. Deleuze and Guattari, *A Thousand Plateaus,* 240.

106. Deleuze and Guattari, 240.

107. Donna Haraway, *When Species Meet* (Minneapolis: University of Minnesota Press, 2008), 27.

108. See the opening of chapter 2 for more on this view of homes.

109. Philip Armstrong, *What Animals Mean in the Fiction of Modernity* (London: Routledge, 2008), 28.

110. Brian Massumi, "Translator's Foreword: Pleasures of Philosophy," in *A Thousand Plateaus: Capitalism and Schizophrenia,* by Gilles Deleuze and Félix Guattari (Minneapolis: University of Minnesota Press, 1987), xv.

111. Jane Tompkins, *Sensational Designs: The Cultural Work of American Fiction, 1790–1860* (New York: Oxford University Press, 1985), xi.

112. For example, see Alisa Smith and J. B. Mackinnon, *The 100-Mile Diet: A Year of Local Eating* (Toronto: Random House Canada, 2007).

113. Susan J. Matt, *Homesickness: An American History* (Oxford: Oxford University Press, 2011), 4.

114. Wolfe, *What Is Posthumanism?,* 65.

115. Leonard Lawlor, *This Is Not Sufficient: An Essay on Animality and Human Nature in Derrida* (New York: Columbia University Press, 2007), 101.

116. Donna Haraway makes a case for sympoiesis—mutual self-making—in *Staying with the Trouble* (Durham, N.C.: Duke University Press, 2016).

6. Killing Words in War

1. See Rob Nixon, *Slow Violence and the Environmentalism of the Poor* (Cambridge, Mass.: Harvard University Press, 2011).

2. Clay Routledge, *Nostalgia: A Psychological Resource* (New York: Routledge, 2016), 4. See also Susan J. Matt, *Homesickness: An American History* (Oxford: Oxford University Press, 2011), 26.

3. Robert P. Marzec, *Militarizing the Environment: Climate Change and the Security State* (Minneapolis: University of Minnesota Press, 2015), 21.

4. Fredric Jameson, "War and Representation," in "War," special issue, *PMLA* 124, no. 5 (2009): 1538.

5. Jameson, 1547, 1543.

6. Matt, *Homesickness,* 100. An especially clear example of the unworlding of human sensibility in war is the catastrophe of child soldiers. Their challenges of reintegrating into peaceful culture are described in Jeffrey Gettleman, "We Witnessed South Sudan's Anguish," *New York Times,* April 5, 2017.

7. Glenn Albrecht, "'Solastalgia': A New Concept in Health and Identity," *PAN: Philosophy Activism Nature,* no. 3 (2005): 41–55.

8. Sebastian Junger, *Tribe: On Homecoming and Belonging* (New York: Twelve, 2016).

9. For this version of the history of war and agriculture, see Frans de Waal, *The Age of Empathy: Nature's Lessons for a Kinder Society* (New York: Harmony, 2000), 22–25.

10. De Waal, *The Age of Empathy,* 22.

11. De Waal, 24.

12. Alfred W. Crosby, *Throwing Fire: Projectile Technology through History* (Cambridge: Cambridge University Press, 2010), 25.

13. Steven Pinker, *The Better Angels of Our Nature: Why Violence Has Declined* (New York: Viking, 2011), xxi.

14. Srivinas Aravamudan, "Introduction: Perpetual War," in "War," special issue, *PMLA* 124, no. 5 (2009): 1508.

15. Alisa W. Coffin, "From Roadkill to Road Ecology: A Review of the Ecological Effects of Roads," *Journal of Transport Geography* 15, no. 5 (2007): 396–406. On the environmental impacts of transportation, see also Jeremy Withers, "Introduction: The Ecologies of Mobility," *ISLE: Interdisciplinary Studies in Literature and Environment* 24, no.1 (2017): 66–67.

16. This image is also discussed in Christophe Bonneuil and Jean-Baptiste Fressoz, *The Shock of the Anthropocene: The Earth, History and Us,* trans. David Fernbach (London: Verso, 2015), 161–67.

17. Junger, *Tribe,* 107.

18. Brian Massumi, *Politics of Affect* (Cambridge, UK: Polity, 2015), 96.

19. Junger, *Tribe,* 107.

20. Junger, 107–8.

21. Mary Louise Pratt, "Harm's Way: Language and the Contemporary Arts of War," in "War," special issue, *PMLA* 124, no. 5 (2009): 1515–31.

22. Pratt, 1526.

23. Pratt, 1525.

24. Pratt, 1526.

25. Pratt, 1527.

26. Pratt, 1517.

27. Pratt, 1519.

28. Pratt, 1518.

29. Gilles Deleuze and Félix Guattari, *A Thousand Plateaus: Capitalism and Schizophrenia,* trans. Brian Massumi (Minneapolis: University of Minnesota Press, 1987), 130.

30. Timothy Morton, *Dark Ecology: For a Logic of Future Coexistence* (New York: Columbia University Press, 2016), 42.

31. Morton, 6.

32. Ernest Hemingway, *A Farewell to Arms* (New York: Scribner, 1929). Further citations to this work are given parenthetically in text.

33. Philip Young, *Ernest Hemingway: A Reconsideration* (University Park: Pennsylvania State University Press, 1966), 6, 79–80.

34. Rosemarie Garland Thomson, *Extraordinary Bodies: Figuring Physical Disability in American Culture and Literature* (New York: Columbia University Press, 1997), 8–9.

35. Alex Vernon, *Soldiers Once and Still: Ernest Hemingway, James Salter, and Tim O'Brien* (Iowa City: University of Iowa Press, 2004), 74.

36. Giorgio Agamben, *Homo Sacer: Sovereign Power and Bare Life,* trans. Daniel Heller-Roazen (Stanford: Stanford University Press, 1998).

37. Jameson, "War and Representation," 1538.

38. See chapter 3 for more on this idea.

39. Cary Wolfe, *What Is Posthumanism?* (Minneapolis: University of Minnesota Press, 2010), xv, 31–47.

40. Donna Haraway, *Staying with the Trouble* (Durham, N.C.: Duke University Press, 2016), 58–98; for a related argument about the more-than-human self, see Jane Bennett, *Vibrant Matter: A Political Ecology of Things* (Durham, N.C.: Duke University Press, 2010).

41. Vernon, *Soldiers Once and Still,* 72.

42. Ernest Hemingway, *For Whom the Bell Tolls* (New York: Scribner, 1940), 340. Further citations to this work are given parenthetically in text.

43. Elizabeth Grosz explores the difference between the physical body and our body image, our mental perception of our body, in *Volatile Bodies: Toward a Corporeal Feminism* (Bloomington: Indiana University Press, 1994).

44. Ernest Hemingway, *The Old Man and the Sea* (New York: Scribner, 1952).

45. Mary A. Favret, "Still Winter Falls," in "War," special issue, *PMLA* 124, no. 5 (2009): 1552.

46. Self-trickery as a form of mental discipline is a theme in other Hemingway texts. For example, in *The Old Man and the Sea,* Santiago uses "tricks" to mobilize and goad his sense of agency (14, 23, 50, 99). Agency as a kind of trick: here is an apt posthumanist shorthand.

47. Carlos Baker, *Ernest Hemingway: A Life Story* (New York: Scribner, 1969), 300.

48. Baker, 299.

49. Baker, 275.

50. Baker, 408.

51. Tim O'Brien, "The Things They Carried," in *The Things They Carried* (1990; repr., Boston: Mariner, 2009), 1–26. Further citations to this work are given parenthetically in text.

52. Vernon, *Soldiers Once and Still,* 42.

53. Toni Morrison, *Beloved* (1987; repr., New York: Vintage, 2004), xix.

54. Tim O'Brien, "An Evening with Tim O'Brien" (keynote address, At Home in Hemingway's World: The 17th Biennial International Hemingway Society Conference, Dominican University, Oak Park, Ill., July 19, 2016).

55. On slow violence and war, see Nixon, *Slow Violence.*

56. Wendy Brown, *Undoing the Demos: Neoliberalism's Stealth Revolution* (New York: Zone, 2015).

57. Tim O'Brien, "Love," in *The Things They Carried* (1990; repr., Boston: Mariner, 2009), 28. The ambiguous genre of O'Brien's book connects to his larger arguments about how disorienting war experience is. It defies familiar forms of understanding, such as genres.

58. Gary Cross, *Consumed Nostalgia: Memory in the Age of Fast Capitalism* (New York: Columbia University Press, 2015).

59. Tim O'Brien, "Sweetheart of the Song Tra Bong," in *The Things They Carried* (1990; repr., Boston: Mariner, 2009), 89–116. Further citations to this work are given parenthetically in text.

60. Vernon, *Soldiers Once and Still,* 74.

61. Sir Philip Sidney, "The Defense of Poesy," 1595, https://www.poetryfoundation.org/articles/69375/the-defence-of-poesy.

62. De Waal, *The Age of Empathy,* 22.

63. Vernon, *Soldiers Once and Still,* 74.

64. Jacques Derrida, *The Animal That Therefore I Am,* ed. Marie-Louise Mallet, trans. David Wills (New York: Fordham University Press, 2008), 27.

65. Martha C. Nussbaum, *Frontiers of Justice: Disability, Nationality, Species Membership* (Cambridge, Mass.: Belknap Press of Harvard University Press, 2006), 14–22. Terminology can be a bit confusing here because Nussbaum advocates what she calls a "capabilities approach" to justice in this book (155–223), but she explicitly derives her approach more from vulnerability than conventional ability.

66. Joseph Conrad, *Heart of Darkness* (1899; repr., Claremont, Calif.: Coyote Canyon Press, 2007).

67. Stephen Greenblatt, "Cultural Mobility: An Introduction," in *Cultural Mobility: A Manifesto,* ed. Stephen Greenblatt (Cambridge: Cambridge University Press, 2010), 14.

68. Morton, *Dark Ecology,* 10.

69. Morton, 11.

70. Bobbie Ann Mason, *In Country* (New York: Harper, 1985). Further citations to this work are given parenthetically in text.

71. The war in Afghanistan, from 2001 to the present of my writing this book, is often now called the longest U.S. war, though some historians grant that title to the U.S. Indian Wars. For an example of the former view, see Council on Foreign Relations, "The U.S. War in Afghanistan, 1999–2018," accessed January 22, 2019, https://www.cfr.org/timeline/us-war-afghanistan.

72. Michael Reynolds specifies the exact nature of Jake's injury, which is not made entirely clear in the text of the novel: "Jake's problem was different: his testicles were intact, his penis was missing." Michael Reynolds, *Hemingway: The Paris Years* (New York: Norton, 1989), 308.

73. In *Dark Ecology,* for example, Morton makes this case, arguing that some measure of anxiety is a baseline condition of being human.

74. Laurence Gonzales narrates many nonfictional accounts of the psychology of those who survive dangerous conditions or events. See Laurence Gonzales, *Deep Survival: Who Lives, Who Dies, and Why; True Stories of Miraculous Endurance and Sudden Death* (New York: Norton, 2005).

75. Jameson, "War and Representation," 1538.

76. Junger, *Tribe,* 91.

77. Junger, 93.

78. Junger, 92.

79. Annie Proulx, "Tits-Up in a Ditch," in *Fine Just the Way It Is: Wyoming Stories 3* (New York: Scribner, 2008), 177–221. Further citations to this work are given parenthetically in text. Gayle Tzemach Lemmon describes the development of a distinctive special ops role for women soldiers, which involves a significant sense of social isolation for them, or, in the terms of this study, homesickness as sickness at the home of the self. See Gayle Tzemach Lemmon, *Ashley's War: The Untold Story of a Team of Women Soldiers on the Special Ops Battlefield* (New York: Harper, 2015). See also Helen Thorpe, *Soldier Girls: The Battles of Three Women at Home and at War* (New York: Scribner, 2014), which emphasizes homesickness; and DeAnne Blanton and Lauren M. Cook, *They Fought Like Demons: Women Soldiers in the Civil War* (Baton Rouge: Louisiana State University Press, 2002). There are many other books in this robust literature of women's roles in war.

80. Beth Bailey, *America's Army: Making the All-Volunteer Force* (Cambridge, Mass.: Belknap Press of Harvard University Press, 2009), 197.

81. Routledge, *Nostalgia.*

82. Tillman's searching admiration for military personnel in the wake of the attacks can be seen in an interview posted online. TGriffinProductions, "Remembering Pat

Tillman," YouTube, February 14, 2008, http://www.youtube.com/watch?v=kBM2hiXRZAo.

83. Jon Krakauer, *Where Men Win Glory: The Odyssey of Pat Tillman* (New York: Doubleday, 2009), 140.

84. Krakauer, 4.

85. Krakauer, 113.

86. Krakauer, 169.

87. Krakauer, 172.

88. Krakauer, 171.

89. Krakauer, 166–67.

90. Krakauer, 295.

91. Mary Tillman and Narda Zacchino, *Boots on the Ground by Dusk: My Tribute to Pat Tillman* (New York: Modern Times, 2008); *The Tillman Story*, directed by Amir Bar-Lev, written by Amir Bar-Lev and Mark Monroe (Los Angeles: Diamond Docs, 2010).

92. Krakauer, *Where Men Win Glory*, 344.

Conclusion

1. Eric Roston, "Climate Change Is Making It Harder to Sleep," *Bloomberg*, May 26, 2017.

2. Christine L. Marran, *Ecology without Culture: Aesthetics for a Toxic World* (Minneapolis: University of Minnesota Press, 2017). Similarly, Donna Haraway uses the figure of "knot" to evoke the materiality of clusters of meaning. Donna Haraway, *When Species Meet* (Minneapolis: University of Minnesota Press, 2008), 4.

3. Mark Edmundson, *Literature against Philosophy, Plato to Derrida: A Defence of Poetry* (Cambridge: Cambridge University Press, 1995).

4. Graham Harman, "Demodernizing the Humanities with Latour," *New Literary History* 47, no. 2 (2016): 249.

5. Gary Snyder, *The Practice of the Wild* (1990; repr., Berkeley: Counterpoint, 2010); Bruno Latour, *We Have Never Been Modern*, trans. Catherine Porter (1991; repr., Cambridge: Harvard University Press, 1993).

6. Snyder, *The Practice of the Wild*, 83.

7. Jacques Derrida, *The Animal That Therefore I Am*, ed. Marie-Louise Mallet, trans. David Wills (New York: Fordham University Press, 2008), 27.

8. Gary Snyder, *He Who Hunted Birds in His Father's Village: The Dimensions of a Haida Myth* (1951; repr., Berkeley: Counterpoint, 2007). The title of Snyder's early book of poetry, *Myths and Texts* (1960; repr., New York: New Directions, 1978), signals his interest in myth, as does his work in essay collections like *The Practice of the Wild*, which includes a retelling of a story or myth about human relationships with bears.

9. Rita Felski, introduction to *New Literary History* 47, no. 2 (2016): 216.

10. Felski, 217.

11. Jennifer K. Ladino, *Reclaiming Nostalgia: Longing for Nature in American Literature* (Charlottesville: University of Virginia Press, 2012).

12. This argument borrows from and resonates with Jane Bennett when she insists, "I will emphasize, even overemphasize, the agentic contributions of nonhuman forces (operating in nature, in the human body, and in human artifacts) in an attempt to counter the narcissistic reflex of human language and thought." Jane Bennett, *Vibrant Matter: A Political Ecology of Things* (Durham, N.C.: Duke University Press, 2010), xvi.

13. Thom van Dooren and Deborah Bird Rose, "Keeping Faith with the Dead: Mourning and De-extinction," *Australian Zoologist* 38, no. 3 (2017): 376.

14. Morton, *Dark Ecology*, 66.

15. Daniel Innerarity, *The Future and Its Enemies: In Defense of Political Hope*, trans. Sandra Kingery (Stanford: Stanford University Press, 2012), 5.

16. Felski, introduction, 216.

17. Dawkins coined the term "meme" in *The Selfish Gene*, 2nd ed. (1976; repr., Oxford: Oxford University Press, 1989). It has become a widely used concept. But brief aside: While Dawkins's analysis takes the materiality and power of genes very seriously, the concept of "selfish" is notoriously problematic in his argument. From a perspective like Morton's, however, we can see a measure of truth in this idea of "selfish" insofar as it recognizes the measure of agency and independence held by all material entities. In this sense, borrowing Morton's discussion in *Dark Ecology*, we could call genes narcissistic but not selfish exactly. They are narcissistic in their ability to hold together as entities and to have a function in the world. However, that is true of all objects, and that does not exactly make them "selfish." Such a label is terribly reductive, since genes, by definition, are also entities that are involved with many things that are not themselves, as are we all. Timothy Morton, *Dark Ecology: For a Logic of Future Coexistence* (New York: Columbia University Press, 2016), 104–5.

18. Jeremy Withers, "Introduction: The Ecologies of Mobility," *ISLE: Interdisciplinary Studies in Literature and Environment* 24, no. 1 (2017): 66–74.

19. Henry David Thoreau, *Three Complete Books: The Maine Woods, Walden, Cape Cod* (1864; repr., New York: Gramercy Books, 1993), 46.

20. Dōgen qtd. in Snyder, *The Practice of the Wild*, 27.

21. Snyder, 83, 118, 18, 73.

22. Snyder, 112.

23. Snyder, 112–13.

24. Snyder, 113.

25. Snyder, 188.

26. William E. Connolly, *The Fragility of Things: Self-Organizing Processes, Neoliberal Fantasies and Democratic Activism* (Durham, N.C.: Duke University Press, 2013).

27. Snyder, *The Practice of the Wild*, 188; Gary Snyder, *The Real Work: Interviews and Talks, 1964–1979* (New York: New Directions, 1980), 21.

28. Snyder, *The Practice of the Wild*, 42, 47.

29. Snyder, 27–28.

30. Gary Snyder, "Kitkitdizze: A Node in the Net," in *A Place in Space: Ethics, Aesthetics, and Watersheds* (Washington, D.C.: Counterpoint, 1995), 252–63.

31. Snyder, 255.
32. Snyder, 254.
33. Snyder, 197.
34. Snyder, 197.
35. Snyder, 197.
36. For an example of Snyder's thoughts on the challenges of using language to describe affective states, see *The Real Work,* 21–22. See also Snyder, *The Practice of the Wild,* 76–77.
37. Gary Snyder, "High Quality Information," in *No Nature* (New York: Pantheon Books, 1992), 346.
38. Heather Houser, *Ecosickness in Contemporary U.S. Fiction: Environment and Affect* (New York: Columbia University Press, 2014).
39. Houser, 221.
40. "Don't just do something, sit there," a twist on a familiar phrase, is the title of a book on meditation by Sylvia Boorstein, *Don't Just Do Something, Sit There: A Mindfulness Retreat with Sylvia Boorstein* (New York: HarperCollins, 1996). In *Vibrant Matter,* Bennett notes that the "ethical and aesthetic turn," involving Foucault's "care of the self," "helped put 'desire' and bodily practices such as physical exercise, meditation, sexuality, and eating back on the ethical radar screen" (xi). My case is consonant with that movement.
41. Snyder, *The Practice of the Wild,* 118–21. One theme of this conclusion is the broad point about retrospective interpretation, how ideas from the past invariably inform the present, often in unacknowledged ways; but I am also making a more specific, genealogical argument that seeks to credit Snyder's work with continuing to inform contemporary ecocritical and posthumanist writing, giving him credit when he often goes unacknowledged or even rejected. The impulse to kill the father or mother in the function of criticism seems deeply engrained and symptomatic of the larger ideology of progress and forward movement. Homesickness, by contrast, would value a more sympathetic relationship to the past, when possible.
42. Henry David Thoreau, "Walking," in *Nature/Walking* (Boston: Beacon, 1991), 110–11.
43. On teenagers' need for sleep, for example, see Perri Klass, "The Science of Adolescent Sleep," *New York Times,* May 22, 2017.
44. Thoreau, "Walking," 95.
45. Thoreau, 73.
46. Thoreau, 75.
47. Thoreau, 99.
48. Ernest Hemingway, *A Farewell to Arms* (New York: Scribner, 1929), 226.

Index